COMMENTARY ON LUTHER'S CATECHISMS

CREED

COMMENTARY ON LUTHER'S CATECHISMS

CREED

ALBRECHT PETERS

CHARLES P. SCHAUM,
GENERAL EDITOR, ENGLISH EDITION

TRANSLATED BY THOMAS H. TRAPP

FOREWORD BY GOTTFRIED SEEBASS

CONCORDIA PUBLISHING HOUSE · SAINT LOUIS

English translation © 2011 Concordia Publishing House
3558 S. Jefferson Ave., St. Louis, MO 63118-3968
1-800-325-3040 • cph.org

Creed translated from *Der Glaube*, © Vandenhoeck & Ruprecht, Albrecht Peters: *Kommentar zu Luthers Katechismen*, 5 volumes, edited by Gottfried Seebaß, Göttingen 1990-94.

Unless otherwise noted, all quotations from Scripture, the Confessions, and other authors in this work are translated from *Der Glaube*, volume 2 of Albrecht Peters *Kommentar zu Luthers Katechismen*, edited by Gottfried Seebaß (Göttingen: Vandenhoeck & Ruprecht, 1991).

Manufactured in the United States of America

Library of Congress Cataloging-in-Publication Data

Peters, Albrecht, 1924-87
[Kommentar zu Luthers Katechismen English]
Commentary on Luther's catechisms / Albrecht Peters ; Charles P. Schaum, general editor, English edition ; translated by Thomas H. Trapp ; foreward by Gottfried Seebass.
p. cm.
Includes bibliographical references.
ISBN: 978-0-7586-1149-9
1. Luther, Martin, 1483—1546. Kleine Katechismus. 2. Luther, Martin, 1483—1546. Grosse Katechismus. 3. Lutheran Church—Catechisms—History and criticism. 4. Schaum, Charles P. II. Title.

BX8070.L8P3713 2011
238'.41—dc22 2008050520

5 6 7 8 9 10 11 12 13 14 31 30 29 28 27 26 25 24 23 22

Contents

Abbreviations

AC	Augsburg Confession
AE	*Luther's Works*. American Edition. 55 vols. General editors Jaroslav Pelikan and Helmut Lehmann. St. Louis: Concordia; Philadelphia: Fortress, 1955–86.
Ap	Apology of the Augsburg Confession
BSLK	*Die Bekenntnisschriften der evangelisch-lutherischen Kirche*. Edited by Deutscher Evangangelischer Kirchenausschuß. 9th ed. Göttingen: Vandenhoeck & Ruprecht, 1982.
CCSL	Corpus Christianorum: Series latina. Turnhout, 1953–.
CR	Corpus reformatorum
Ep	Epitome of the Formula of Concord
FC	Formula of Concord
GCS	Die griechische christliche Schriftsteller der ersten [drei] Jahrhunderte
LC	Large Catechism
LCMS	The Lutheran Church—Missouri Synod
LTK	*Lexikon für Theologie und Kirche*. Edited by Josef Höfer and Karl Rahner. 14 vols. 2d ed. Herder-Verlag: Freiburg, 1957–1968.
MGP	*Monumenta Germaniae Paedagogica*. Vols. 20–22. Edited by K. Kehrbach.
NR	Neuner, Joseph, and Heinrich Roos. *Der Glaube der Kirche in den Urkunden der Lehrverkündigung*. 5th ed. Edited by K. Rahner. Regensburg, 1958.
PG	*Patrologia Graeca*. Edited by J.-P. Migne. 161 vols. Paris, 1857–66.
PL	*Patrologia Latina*. Edited by J.-P. Migne. 217 vols. Paris, 1844–64.

RGG	*Religion in Geschichte und Gegenwart*. Edited by Kurt Galling. 7 vols. 3d ed. Tübingen, 1957–65.
SA	Smalcald Articles
SC	Small Catechism
SD	Solid Declaration of the Formula of Concord
TWNT	*Theologische Wörterbuch zum Neuen Testament*. Edited by G. Kittel and G. Friedrich. Stuttgart, 1932–79.
WA	*D. Martin Luthers Werke: Kritische Gesamtausgabe*. Weimar: Herman Böhlau, 1883–.
WABr	*D. Martin Luthers Werke: Kritische Gesamtausgabe. Briefwechsel*. Weimar: Herman Böhlau, 1930ff.
WATR	*D. Martin Luthers Werke: Kritische Gesamtausgabe. Tischreden*. Weimar: Herman Böhlau, 1912ff.

Publisher's Preface to the English Edition

Concordia Publishing House is pleased to present this important scholarly work that interprets Martin Luther's Small and Large Catechisms, together with the sermons and other documents by Luther that make up their context. This series originally was undertaken by the late Professor Dr. Albrecht Peters, longtime member of the theological faculty of the Ruprecht-Karls-Universität in Heidelberg, Germany. His material was gathered and edited by Gottfried Seebaß, his junior colleague, and published by Vandenhoeck & Ruprecht as the five-volume *Kommentar zu Luthers Katechismen*. Most recent scholarship regarding Luther's catechisms refers to this work in some fashion. CPH extends its thanks to the Reverend Paul Strawn for his efforts in organizing the initial work on this series, especially regarding this volume. We thank the Commission on Doctrinal Review of The Lutheran Church—Missouri Synod for their approval to publish these volumes as resources for study purposes.

Format of the Translation

The body text of this volume retains titles in the original language for all works except those of Luther. The first occurrence of titles of Luther's works in the body text generally includes both the title in the original language and a translation; generally the translated form is used in subsequent references. This convention is observed because in many cases these works do not exist in the American Edition of Luther's Works, thus translating all titles into English might create the false impression that the represented works themselves had been translated into English. In the footnotes, all titles are given in their original language. The reader is encouraged to consult Heinrich J. Vogel's *Cross-Reference and Index to the Contents of Luther's Works* and Kurt Aland's *Hilfsbuch zum Lutherstudium*. To aid the reader in this effort, cross-references to extant works in the American Edition have been included, but only to the selected works as respective page ranges, not to exact corresponding page numbers. As the process of translating and publishing later volumes affords, more exact references to the American Edition should appear. References to the *Bekenntnisschriften* are not mapped to an English version of the Lutheran Confessions in order to avoid adding layers of editorial choices onto the extant translation.

Quotations in the body text have been translated into English unless doing so would adversely affect the places where Peters refers specifically to the features and content of the material in its original language. The bulk of the notes, though translated, refer generally to non-English research. The translation intends to remain faithful to the original text. We have also given attention to the consistent use and translation of technical terms. Titles in the notes and of the suggested reading material at the end of each chapter are not translated because many of these resources do not exist in English. This also helps the student or theologian who wishes to look deeper into the Weimar Edition.

Historical-Critical Methods

The reader will notice that historical-critical exegetical methods are used throughout the series, but the use remains less extreme than that of some formerly within the LCMS.[1] Peters does look for a Lutheran middle way when he speaks of a Lutheran orthodox "confessionalist hardening" on the right and a humanist tradition on the left, with Luther in the center. He does not embrace the same view of confessional theology long held by the LCMS. There will be points in this volume where the reader that rejects historical-critical methods will come into sharp disagreement with the author on issues such as the JEDP documentary hypothesis, the assertions regarding source and form criticism, and related issues involving philosophical presuppositions. The Lutheran Church—Missouri Synod rejects the errors of the higher-critical study of Scripture, as explained most pointedly in *A Statement of Scriptural and Confessional Principles*.[2]

Although Peters criticizes the radical rejection of the third use of the Law based on the philosophy and influence of Albrecht Ritschl,

[1] See Paul A. Zimmermann, *A Seminary in Crisis: The Inside Story of the Preus Fact Finding Committee* (St. Louis: Concordia, 2007).
[2] Zimmermann, 430–36.

nevertheless he has some points of conflict with the third use of the Law. The Lutheran Church—Missouri Synod affirms the Lutheran Confessions' teaching that there is a third use of the Law.[3]

Renewed Interest in the Catechisms

In recent years, scholarly interest in Luther's catechisms has been rekindled in the LCMS by the original German edition of this work. For example, consider the recent work of Charles Arand, such as his book on the setting, content, and purpose of Luther's catechisms, *That I May Be His Own* (St. Louis: Concordia, 2000). One sees an opportunity to examine again the catechisms of Luther that have only started to realize a scholarly awakening after a hiatus in the LCMS for the better part of a century.

This work by Albrecht Peters sheds needed light on Luther's catechisms. At the same time it brings a different set of presuppositions to the table. It allows one in the LCMS to examine how people outside the LCMS may view, study, and use Luther's catechisms. It will doubtlessly create points of friction with readers that reject higher-critical approaches. Nevertheless, it remains a translation that seeks to uphold the responsibility to be faithful to the author's texts and viewpoints, yet also provide material usable by a faithful Church. We pray that it succeeds to that end.

---

[3] A helpful resource in this area is Scott R. Murray, *Law, Life, and the Living God: The Third Use of the Law in Modern American Lutheranism* (St. Louis: Concordia, 2002).

FOREWORD AND INTRODUCTION

I must begin by thanking my assistant, Herr Jürgen Kaiser, for all the work that he did. He made it possible for me to present this second volume of the massive commentary on Luther's catechisms, which was left by Albrecht Peters, in such short order after the first volume appeared. Corresponding to the Chief Parts of the catechism, this volume offers commentary on the confession of the faith.

Whatever needs to be said by way of introduction to explain the way this scholarly effort took shape and how it is to be characterized can be found by the reader in the introduction to Volume 1. This volume follows the same basic framework that was set forth there, on pp. 13–16.

One's attention needs to be drawn to the fact that the footnotes in the German text that have no further reference point refer to the *Bekenntnisschriften der evangelisch-lutherischen Kirche*, which was published in 1930, the anniversary year that celebrated the presentation of the Augsburg Confession (4th corrected edition, with further subsequent printings, Göttingen, 1959). [Tr.: The English edition adds *BSLK*.] References to writings of Luther are always given with a short title to which page information is related. References to the Church fathers were partly retained, partly replaced by newer editions. Sources and secondary works are listed in the bibliography. Other references, such as those for documents in the Book of Concord and Migne's Greek and Latin series, are included in a table of abbreviations. Any remaining references that are not found in the bibliography or on the abbreviations table correspond to those of Siegfried Schwertner, *Theologische Realenzyklopädie, Abkürzungsverzeichnis* (Berlin: de Gruyter, 1976).

Since I have thanked Herr Kaiser already, it remains only to offer thanks to Frau Gisela Peters and Frau Andrea Chudaska. Both were constant and conscientious at reading the proof pages. Thanks are also in order at this point to the publisher for the way this edition has been presented, which is pleasingly laid out for the readers and users. The publication was made possible once again because of the financial support of the Evangelical Lutheran Church in Bavaria and the

Selbstständige Evangelisch-lutherischen Kirche (SELK). As was the desire of Albrecht Peters, it is my since hope as well, that this volume will result in a better understanding of the faith of our fathers when it is used in both scholarly pursuits and in the catechesis of the Church and that it will guide us in the proper way that we carry out our own work.

Heidelberg, in March 1991
G. Seebaß

TRANSLATOR'S PREFACE

I appreciate the opportunity to offer a few comments and observations as well. As a Fulbright doctoral student studying Old Testament in Heidelberg in the early 1970s, I often heard friends talking about "Peters." I am sorry I never had the opportunity to meet him. In the 1990s, I heard mention of this massive commentary on the catechisms and was intrigued by the concept itself. As a translator of this wonderful volume on the Faith, the Apostles' Creed, I count it an honor to be involved in building a bridge so that the arduous work of this scholar can benefit an English-speaking audience.

Each discipline has its own secret codes and understandings. I thank theology faculty friends at Concordia-St. Paul, especially David Lumpp, and Joshua Miller, a doctoral student at Luther Seminary and member of the congregation that called me as pastor, for help and discussion and insights. The translation is richer for their help. I also thank Adam Morton, a student at Luther Seminary, who helped with the Latin when it was determined that it should be translated as well. Finally, I thank Laura Mews, a student at Concordia-St. Paul, who coaxed the translation bit by bit into the template and inserted all the footnotes appropriately.

People often ask why I do not just use one of those "programs" when translating! The slightest nuance of meaning in word selection can explicate or twist a passage. I have tried to be very literal, sometimes more than I would like to be, when technical matters of the faith are being discussed. But I find so many translations cumbersome and awkward. They make the authors look as if they do not know how to speak smoothly and intelligently. Sentence structure is different in different languages and I seek to make the author easy for the reader to understand. My methodology: Translate a rough draft, arranging sentences as best I can in English word order. Then check it carefully for substance and clarify what seemed odd. Then rework, rearrange, and simplify sentences, again and again, checking for every last detail to make sure all is correct and accurate. I found typos in the German and some will survive my best efforts here too. I thank

Concordia Publishing House for asking me and for the assistance they have provided.

My wife Kathy continues to look for that time when we can relax some more together. I appreciate her continued love as I seek to use the opportunities the Lord opens for me in the ministry of His Church. Benefit comes not only in my own life but for my students at Concordia-St. Paul and for members and visitors at Emmaus Lutheran Church of St. Paul. I pray wider circles will benefit as well, for the good of the Lord's Church on earth.

Thomas H. Trapp

CREED: THE *APOSTOLICUM*

Luther's Understanding of the Apostles' Creed within the Context of the Creedal-Tradition of Western Christendom

Luther's Position on the Apostles' Creed[1]

1. Introduction and Summary of the Interpretation in the Large Catechism[2]

As is the case for the conclusion, the introduction to Luther's exposition of the Creed in the Large Catechism deals with two major issues. The reformer identifies the reason why he positions the Creed between the Decalogue and the Lord's Prayer[3] and then he highlights the aspects that make the Apostles' Creed [the *Apostolicum*] unique. The one God reveals Himself to us according to His three persons through the three activities of creation, redemption, and sanctification.[4] Luther develops the external and internal relationships with respect to both context and content. He develops simultaneously both an outer ring (the relationship of the Creed to the Decalogue and the Lord's Prayer) and an inner ring (the relationship among the three articles of the faith) as he interprets the three articles. We have already analyzed that outer ring[5] in the section that discussed the arrangement of the three Chief Parts.[6] The inner ring is divided as follows:

---

[1] For literature here, see p. 56.
[2] *BSLK*, 646.2–647.21, 660.18–662.4.
[3] *BSLK*, 646.3–22, 661.21–662.4.
[4] *BSLK*, 646.22–647.21, 660.18–661.18.
[5] *BSLK*, 646.3–22, 661.21–662.4.
[6] See Volume 1, pp. 40–51.

(a) At the outset, Luther writes:

(1) The "faith" (the Apostles' Creed) is to be explained for the common people in a way that can stand alone.[7]

(2) Explicated in this way, the Apostles' Creed is no longer divided according to the legendary tradition of the early Church into twelve articles; its teachings are set forth according to the way it was discussed in the visitation instructions,[8] in the format of the three "chief articles" that correspond to the three persons of the Godhead.[9]

(3) To the Father, the work of creation is appropriated; to the Son, redemption; to the Spirit, sanctification.[10]

(4) The one faith in the one God is thus explicated in the three articles on the basis of the three persons.[11]

(b) At the conclusion, the reformer underscores the mystery of how God reveals Himself and places that revelation within the framework of the tension between Law and Gospel, judgment and grace.

(1) According to the way God's activity is described in the Apostles' Creed, God has revealed both His innermost nature and His unconditional will to save. But no human being is inherently capable of recognizing either of these aspects.[12]

(2) With respect to the creation, as well as redemption and sanctification, God thus reveals Himself to us as the gracious Father only through the Son, Jesus Christ, by means of the Holy Spirit, and is thereby able to appear as a benevolent creator as well.[13]

(3) As is demonstrated in the three articles, the twofold way in which the triune God reveals Himself separates true Christians from all other human beings. Even though, as

---

[7] *BSLK*, 646.22–26.

[8] Melanchthon, *Studienausgabe*, 1:259, 7–10.

[9] *BSLK*, 646.35–647.9.

[10] *BSLK*, 647.9–17.

[11] *BSLK*, 647.18–21.

[12] *BSLK*, 660.18–32.

[13] *BSLK*, 660.32–47.

> creatures, the latter may yearn for a relationship with the one creator God, they remain under the holy God's judgment of wrath for as long a time as God's free grace in Jesus Christ has not yet been opened to them through the Spirit.[14]

As set forth by Luther in the form of theses, these insights are to be explicated in this section. We include his observations about the Apostles' Creed.

2. Name and Origin of the Apostles' Creed

In the catechisms, Luther never departs from the common designation that the people used, calling it "the faith." The word "*fides*" begins to be used to designate a fixed Symbol already at the time of Tertullian and Cyprian. But the term is first used as a shorthand code word for the community's confession of faith at the time of Hilary and Jerome.[15] Augustine was already familiar with it as a unique term of reference; he distinguishes the Church's confession from the teachings of the heretics by using the term "*fides catholica.*"[16] The Greek ἡ πίστις would have furnished the conceptual term that is replicated with the Latin rendering "*fides.*"[17]

The early High German ditty "*gelaupa, gelauba, gelouba*"[18] continued in use as well, remaining on the lips of the common people even at the time of Luther, so he made use of it.[19] He used the word "*credo*" as well, as when he says: "I have a little book here, which is called the Credo."[20] His understanding of the word is formulated in "The three Symbols or Creeds of the Christian Faith," 1538: "The

---

[14] *BSLK*, 661.5–18.

[15] Hilary, *De Trinitate* 7.7, 10.65 (PL 10:205B; 394B); Jerome, *Commentariorum in Ev. Matth. 28:20* (PL 26:218C); cf., on this, Eichenseer, *Das Symbolum Apostolicum beim hl. Augustinus* [= *Apostolicum*], 46, contra Kattenbusch, *Symbol*, 2:67.

[16] On the citations from Augustine, see Eichenseer, *Apostolicum*, 47, note.

[17] One encounters this terminology most especially in the fifth catechetical lecture of Cyril of Jerusalem.

[18] On this point, cf. von Raumer, *Einwirkung des Christentums auf die altdeutsche Sprache*, 388f.; Meyer, *Historischer Kommentar*, 258f.

[19] "Von den guten Werken, 1520," WA 6:204.1: "until the time that . . . I can make the faith completely transparent in a German commentary" (AE 44:15–144); cf. "Eine kurze Form, 1520," WA 7:214.24, 215.23; "Eine einfältige Weise zu beten, 1535," WA 38:373.12 (AE 43:187–211); "Die drei Symbola, 1538," WA 50:262.2 (AE 34:197).

[20] "Von Jesu Christo eine Predigt, Torgau, 16./17.4.1533," WA 37:55.12.

first confession or Symbol is the common confession of the apostles; the foundation of the Christian faith is set forth therein."[21]

In addition, as this summary demonstrates, the reformer makes use of additional specific terminology that had come down to him: *confessio/professio*,[22] whereby he reflects on his own Confession of 1528, in which he uses such terminology to position the act of ὁμολογία in the center,[23] but most especially by using the word "Symbol,"[24] even though it seems to be for him a technical term that is hardly understood and that does not express much. In his Latin expositions, this term dominates. Along with Ambrose, Rufinus, Cassian, Faustus of Riez, and later authors,[25] Luther seems to have explained the meaning of Symbol by referring to the Greek term συμβολή as a *collatio* that is drawn from the entire Scriptures.[26] He does not understand it, as we do, in the sense of the sign of the covenant that God offers to us in baptism; the way the early Church linked the *credo* (I believe) with baptism was much less significant for him.[27] For Luther, the root meaning of the word *symbolum* was hidden in the shadows and its meaning was elusive.[28] Despite that, the saving acts of God that are set forth in the Creed brought him to a new point of access to what the early Church understood. The starting point was not God's command, calling for performance by the human being, but rather the Gospel of God and the grace that comes first. As a sign of the covenant, the Symbol is not primarily a form of

---

[21] WA 50:263:18 (AE 34:197–229).

[22] Concerning these terms, see Eichenseer, *Apostolicum*, 42–45.

[23] "Vom Abendmahl Christi, 1528," WA 50:262.2–10 (AE 34:197–229); cf. WA 26:499–509 (AE 37:151–372).

[24] WA 50:262.6: "the three Symbols (as they are so designated)."

[25] See the texts in Eichenseer, *Apostolicum*, 31–33.

[26] "Pred. über den 1. Art. vom 4.3.1523," WA 11:48.25: "The whole Gospel is in this Symbol, in that anyone is able quickly to grasp the whole Gospel in it. Many may certainly pray it, but they do not understand what the Symbol is; it is, one might say, a little letter, in which is the whole Gospel."

[27] Luther uses key phrases from the early Church in what he writes against Ambrosius Catharinus in 1521, but at the same time still uses them with reference to the sacramental '*notae ecclesiae*,' WA 7:720.34–36: "The sign is necessary, so we certainly have baptism, bread, and above all the Gospel: these three are the Symbols of Christians, tokens and markers"; cf., as well, WA 7:721.9–14. Luther is cognizant of the paraphrases of the Symbols from the Middle Ages that included the renunciations that accompanied baptism when he makes reference to the renunciation of Satan in "Eine kurze Form, 1520," on the First Article (WA 7:215.26–216.3).

[28] Concerning the various nuances of the word σύμβολον, see the overview in Kelly, *Creeds*, 52–61 and Eichenseer, *Apostolicum*, 9–41.

confession that is imposed upon the human being as a confession that one was duty-bound to articulate; as "*verbum abbreviatum et consummatum*,"[29] it is the summation of the Gospel; when it is confessed, the triune God Himself places the description of His saving acts in one's mouth, so that we can confess faith in Him thereby and can find refuge for our faith in those words when it is under attack; "*virtus virtutum est symbolum seu fides* (the Symbol or faith is most excellent of all)."[30] "The Symbol provides a way to express the forgiveness of sins; it is God's saving covenant word. At the moment when baptism takes place, the human being is placed into the history of salvation, about which testimony is provided in the Symbol."[31]

This understanding of the "Symbol of the apostles"[32] gives shape, as well, to Luther's comments about its supposed apostolic origin, which Lorenzo Valla had questioned already.[33] Luther knew of Valla's critical observations, at the latest, when he read Erasmus' "Explanatio Symboli, quod dicitur apostolorum," written in 1533, which he read in 1534.[34] But these critical observations did not sway him all that much.[35] Although he had remained silent about the question of the apostolic origin in his own expositions,[36] he did offer an opinion on the issue in a Trinity Sunday sermon in 1535 and in a Table Talk in 1539. For him, "this Symbol is assembled . . . by using

[29] "Pred. über Joh. 1:1 vom 25.12.1514," WA 1:24.13: The way the early Church used plays on words from Isa. 10:22 and Rom. 9:28 has been gathered together by Eichenseer, *Apostolicum*, 3f., n. 13.

[30] *Bibel- u. Bucheinzeichnungen Luthers*, edited by von Aurifaber and Rörer, 1547, WA 48:281.3; the parallels from the Table Talk are mentioned as well in WA 48:282f.

[31] Skydsgaard, *Glaubensbekenntnis*, 58.

[32] "Die drei Symbola, 1538," WA 50:262.17 (AE 34:197).

[33] On Laurentius Valla, see Kattenbusch, *Symbol*, 1:1–5; on Luther's opinion, see also Meyer, *Apostolikum*, 35ff.

[34] Cf. Luther's letter to Amsdorf, written in March, 1534, in WABr 7:27–40, esp. 31.105ff.

[35] The critical observations of Erasmus are in *Explanatio Symboli*, esp. cols. 1140D–1142F. Besides raising questions about his methodologically errant procedures, Luther especially accuses Erasmus of using the great number of historical observations to lead students astray, so that they could come to doubt the teachings about the faith. Bornkamm provides a detailed comparison of the catechisms of Luther and Erasmus, in *Das Verständnis christlicher Unterweisung in den Katechismen von Erasmus und Luther*.

[36] Cf. "Kat.-Pred. vom 15.12.1528," WA 30.1:109.5ff. (AE 51:182–188).

the beloved prophets and the books of the apostles."[37] The apostles themselves would have assembled it from their own writings "like a bee gathers honey from a goodly number of beautiful, colorful, little blooms."[38]

With such observations, Luther refers to legends that go back to Rufinus and that circulated widely in the Western world. According to these, before they took the Gospel out into the whole world, the apostles succinctly articulated the teaching norm for the proclamation. Later versions reported that each apostle was said to have contributed one of the twelve statements of faith.[39] Such ancient legends would have expanded on the earlier attribution of both the "Didache" and the *Regula fidei* (Rule of Faith) to the apostles, so that it was now expanded to include the Creed as well. Such legends gave strong support to the confidence expressed throughout the early Church that the Creed was rooted in the proclamation of the apostles.[40] Such certainty is intimated in the writings of Augustine.[41]

Luther takes no pains to go beyond such brief observations. But he emphasizes more strongly at this point that the Apostles' Creed is drawn from the Holy Scriptures. The confidence about the apostolic source of the Creed is encompassed by, and carried forth by, the insight that such unpretentious, childlike words, in the deepest sense, were drawn together by God the Holy Spirit Himself to describe the

---

[37] "Pred. von den hl. Dreifaltigkeit vom 23.5.1535," WA 41:275.27.

[38] Ibid., WA 41:275.29ff.: "We neither constructed nor thought to construct the prayer or Creed, nor did the earlier fathers. Instead, as a bee gathers together the honey from many different beautiful, attractive little flowers, in the same way this Symbol was assembled by making use of the beloved books of the prophets and apostles, which means, from the entire Holy Scripture, pieced together in a wonderfully short form for the children and simple Christians." WATR 4:230.6 (no. 4434; Anton Lauterbach): "The words of the Symbol, from the apostles, are set together to constitute a Creed, which, when assembled together, have made this fine Symbol both short and comforting."

[39] Rufinus, *Expositio symboli* 2:1–18 (CCSL 20:134). On the legends, see Kattenbusch, *Symbol*, 2:3–24 and Eichenseer, *Apostolicum*, 48–53.

[40] Trillhaas, *Das Apostolische Glaubensbekenntnis*, 9: "The content of the Creed (is) an authentic replication of that which the earliest Church accepted as the teaching of the apostles."

[41] Augustine, *Sermo* 52.2.2 (PL 38:355): "For our faith, that is, true faith, right faith, catholic faith, not presumed as opinion, but the testimony of collected readings, not doubtful heresies by accident, but founded on apostolic truth, insinuates this; this we have learned, this we believe."

divine work of creation and redemption.[42] In this way, the reformer was just as little concerned as the fathers in the fourth and fifth centuries to be tied slavishly to the exact wording, since this had not yet achieved a completely fixed form in the early Church; but, in the ultimate sense, what was stated in the Apostles' Creed, as a pregnant summary of the Scriptures, placed Luther under its teaching in the same way as did the Scriptures themselves.[43] Even though not every individual point of teaching is articulated word for word[44] in the Apostles' Creed, and even though one must take into account that the more extensive Nicene Creed and the Athanasian Creed are "protecting Symbols"[45] that surround this childlike faith statement, the Apostles' Creed is still invested with complete dignity and with highest authority in its catechetical relationship with the Decalogue, the Lord's Prayer, baptism and the Lord's Supper. The most compact formulation of the self-revelation of God the Father through His Son

---

[42] WATR 4:230.8 (nos. 4334, 1539). "And it is the work of the Holy Spirit to write out such a great thing in such brief, very powerful and emphatic words. I, Doctor Martin, am not able to wonder enough at the constitution of that Symbol. Those words must therefore be examined." Cf., as well, "Die drei Symbola, 1538," WA 50:262.17ff. (AE 34:197).

[43] One needs to be reminded of Luther's basic principle of interpretation at this point: One ought to depart from the literal wording of Scripture only at those places where such is called for by other clear statements of Scripture or by a clearer article of faith; "Vom Anbeten des Sakraments des hl. Leichnams Christi, 1523," WA 11:436.21f. (AE 36:269–305); "Wider die himmlischen Propheten, 1525," WA 18:147.23–27; 180.17–20 (AE 40:73–223); "Daß diese Worte Christi noch fest stehen, 1527," WA 23:93.25–28 (AE 37:3–150); "Vom Abendmahl Christi, 1528," WA 26:403.27ff. (AE 37:151–372), and often elsewhere.

[44] "Kat.-Pred. vom 15.12.1528," WA 30.1:109.6 (AE 51:182): "And yet there is nothing in the Symbol about the sacraments, nothing about temporal power, about the office of bishops, etc." In the seventeenth century, this was the case for the orthodox Lutherans against what Georg Calixt was attempting, when he tried to reconcile the disputed confessions on the basis of the councils of the first five centuries and especially on the basis of the Apostles' Creed: Many articles that are necessary for salvation are not contained in the Symbol, for example the teachings about original sin, about God's universal grace, about Christ's merits, about justification, confession, and the new birth; from a different angle, Christ's descent into the realm of the dead, as well as His miraculous conception and Mary's virginity, were not doctrines necessary for salvation (according to Hoffman, *Die altlutherische Orthodoxie*). Such limitations with respect to the Apostles' Creed were pointed out already by commentators during the Middle Ages; cf. Alexander, *Summa* III, no. 699; Thomas Aquinas, *In Sententiarum* III, dist. 25, q. 1, a. 2; Bonaventure, *In Sententiarum* III, dist. 25, a. 1, q. 1; Duns Scotus, *Opus Oxoniense* III, dist. 25, q. 1, n. 4f.

[45] "Die drei Symbola, 1538," WA 50:263.6 (AE 34:197–229).

by means of the Holy Spirit is articulated therein, encompassing what life really is for all human beings.

The apostolic source of the Symbol is thus itself enveloped within the divine origin of the faith; this holds true both with reference to its salvation-historical content as well as with respect to how God's actions take hold of us, thus both with respect to the "*fides, quae creditur*" as well as the "*fides, qua creditur*." (1) With reference to the "*fides, quae creditur*," Luther says: In the Creed, God has "revealed Himself and opened up His fatherly heart to a most unfathomable depth and in His truly inexpressible love in all three articles."[46] "Symbolum, the confession of our holy, Christian faith, is *historia historiarum*, a history above all histories, which is the highest history, in which the immeasurably miraculous work of the divine majesty is set forth for us from the beginning and on into eternity."[47] On the deepest level, the Creed sets forth the teaching about the creative and redeeming work of God Himself in what is set forth therein. (2) With reference to the "*fides, qua creditur*," the same is true, by analogy: The unanimity about what is confessed in the Creed is not something we are capable of acquiring by our own efforts; it is and remains exclusively and solely the gift of the Spirit of God. "The Ten Commandments are also written elsewhere on the hearts of all human beings. But the faith cannot be comprehended by any human wisdom and must be taught solely by the Holy Spirit."[48]

THE APOSTLES' CREED AND ITS DEVELOPMENT IN THE EARLY CHURCH AND IN THE MIDDLE AGES[49]

The basic form of the Apostles' Creed took shape when the threefold baptismal confession that expressed belief in God the Father, the Son, and the Holy Spirit was linked with an expansive Christological passage. This still had the form of a rather loose structure in the writings of Irenaeus, but it is set forth with utter clarity by Hippolytus. It has been assumed that it arrived at its present complete form toward the end of the second century, or by the middle of the third century, in Rome, and thus the basic original form of the

[46] *BSLK*, 660.29–32 (LC).
[47] WATR 5:581.36 (no. 6288).
[48] *BSLK*, 661.25–29 (LC).
[49] For sources and literature used here, see p 56f.

Apostles' Creed is the early Roman Baptismal Symbol, the Roman Creed [the *Romanum*]. But the actual wording of that Creed is accessible to us for the first time in an apology of Marcellus of Ancyra (Cappadocia) that was written to Pope Julius I (about 340),[50] and in the writings of Rufinus (about 404),[51] which are preserved in two ancient handwritten copies.[52] According to these codicies, the *Symbolum Romanum* reads as follows:

Credo in Deum Patrem omnipotentem;
et in Christum Iesum filium eius unicum, dominum nostrum,
qui natus est de Spiritu sancto et Maria virgine,
qui sub Pontio Pilato crucifixus est et sepultus,
tertia die resurrexit a mortuis,
ascendit in caelos
sedet ad dexteram Patris,
unde venturus est iudicare vivos et mortuos;
et in Spiritum sanctum,
sanctam ecclesiam,
remissionem peccatorum,
carnis resurrectionem.

This Symbol can be found in a similar form in the sees of other bishops in the Western lands. Among many similar forms, one is the so-called *Textus receptus*, which is mentioned for the first time in the *Scarapsus* of Pirminius[53] and is encountered, as well, in the sacramentaries of the early Gallican Rite.[54] Due to its similarity with the confessions of faith in Spain and Gaul,[55] it might be a widely used version of the Roman Creed that was common in southwestern France during the sixth to eighth centuries.[56] Since Charlemagne pressed for a uniform liturgical formulary, it gradually became the official

[50] Hahn, *Bibliothek*, § 17; Denzinger, 11; *BSLK*, 21.
[51] Hahn, *Bibliothek*, § 19; Denzinger, 12.
[52] Kelly, *Creeds*, 102; Denzinger, 12.
[53] Hahn, *Bibliothek*, § 92; Denzinger, 28.
[54] Hahn, *Bibliothek*, § 66; Denzinger, 27 and also, ibid., 30.
[55] Especially close to this is what comes from Caesarius of Arles (Hahn, *Bibliothek*, § 62; Denzinger, 27).
[56] This is the viewpoint of Kelly, *Creeds*, 398–420; cf. also the summary in Kelly's article in *LTK* 1:761f., as well as Kattenbusch, *Symbol*, 2:759–874.

baptismal confession of the empire and even found acceptance in the ninth century in Rome itself.[57]

Because of the alliteration in this *Textus receptus*, "*creatorem coeli et terrae*" was preferred to other similar formulations that were appended to *Deus Pater omnipotens*.[58] The exact phraseology "conceptus *de Spirito sancto, natus* ex *Maria virgine*" is not reflected as yet in Augustine;[59] it makes the involvement of both the divine and human elements in the conception and birth of Jesus more precise, accenting the sovereign activity of the Spirit of God.[60] Jesus' descent into Hades, the "*descendit ad inferna*," with its many variant forms, was supposedly inserted by the Syrian Marcus of Arethusa at the Synod of Sirmium in 359, having as its source the Creed of Aquileia.[61] The phrases "*sanctam ecclesiam* catholicam, "*sanctorum communionem*" and "*vitam aeternam*" are found in Niceta from Remesiana (about 400), and likely forged their way into the West from the more expansive Eastern confessions.[62]

The use of this basic statement as a confession of faith at the baptism of Christians in a congregational setting, which was becoming ever more standardized, and which was developing during the third century in several variations in Western and Eastern centers, does not as yet have a solemn Christology, to say nothing of a teaching about the Trinity. Using the style of a "*narratio*,"[63] this praise-filled retelling of God's great deeds of salvation most particularly directs our gaze, in the more developed form of the *Textus receptus*, to those places where God's activity reaches into the earthbound setting, into our world, telling about that which we can see and comprehend. The Symbol praises God the Father as the

---

[57] According to Kelly, *Creeds*, 420–34.

[58] Cf. Kattenbusch, *Symbol*, 2:875–78; Kelly, *Creeds*, 372ff. In Augustine, *Sermo* 215.2 one reads: "*universorum creatorem regem saeculorum, immortalem et invisibilem* (Creator of the universe, king over the world, immortal and invisible)."

[59] See Eichenseer, *Apostolicum*, 236–39.

[60] Cf. Kattenbusch, *Symbol*, 2:879–87; 616–25.

[61] Hahn, *Bibliothek*, § 163; cf. *BSLK*, 23; Kattenbusch, *Symbol*, 2:895–915; Kelly, *Creeds*, 378–83.

[62] Hahn, *Bibliothek*, § 40; Denzinger, 19, *BSLK*, 24f. See, as well, the overviews in Kattenbusch, *Symbol*, 2:917–56, and Kelly, *Creeds*, 388–97, 383–88. Small alterations include the rearrangement of the archaic "Christus Jesus" to "Jesus Christus" and the insertion of "suffered" ("*passus*") and "died" ("*mortuus*"), as well as the "Father almighty" ("*Patris omnipotentis*"), in the Second Article (on this, see Kattenbusch, *Symbol*, 2:887–94 and Kelly, *Creeds*, 374ff.

[63] Augustine, *De catechizandis rudibus* (passim).

creator of heaven and earth; for the Son it underscores the behind-the-scenes activity of the Spirit of God in the virgin birth and inserts the scene that details Christ's invasion into the realm of Hades and its power; accent is placed in the Third Article on the mystical Body of Christ, an entity so comprehensive as to include the living and the dead, human beings as well as angels. This article goes on to turn one's gaze toward the eternal consummation [of the world].

According to the legend passed down by Rufinus, which began to take shape in Syria from the time of the third century and onward, the original kernel of this confession originates with the apostles.[64] Before each of them scattered abroad to where they would proclaim the Gospel, they assembled one last time in Jerusalem, on which occasion they formulated this common Creed.[65] It was later still that a particular, distinct phrase in the Creed was attributed to each of the apostles.[66] After a variety of other groupings were proposed, twelve as the number of articles was established: 1 + 1+6 + 1+3 = 12; this holy number is reflected in the [twelve-sided] construction of [some] baptisteries.[67]

Both bishops and clerics expand the very brief congregational confession, resulting in more comprehensive teaching formulas. As this takes place, one can observe two different directions of activity that take place concurrently:

(1) The early Church-Eastern Church's "Protectionist Symbol" poses the question about the *Arché*, about the original nature of God and of Christ, which precedes all historical revelation, and this Symbol shows its strength in this aspect. Such formulas thus set forth the teaching about the two natures and about the Trinity. This is demonstrated most especially in the Niceno-Constantinopolitan Creed

---

[64] In this way a statement that was originally used for the *Regula fidei* is transferred for use with the baptismal Symbol; cf. Irenaeus, *Adversus haereses* 1.2; Tertullian, *Apologeticus* 47.10; Niceta, *Explanatio symboli* 8.

[65] *Didaskalia* 6.12.1: "When therefore the whole Church was in peril of falling into heresy, all we the twelve Apostles came together to Jerusalem and took thought what should be done. And it seemed good to us, being all of one accord, to write this Catholic Didascalia for the confirming of you all. And we have established and set down therein that you worship God Almighty and Jesus Christ and the Holy Spirit [Connolly, ad loc.]" (Funk translation, *Didascalia* 1:326.4ff.).

[66] See the texts in Hahn, *Bibliothek*, §§ 42f.

[67] Concerning the alterations in the artistic form of the Symbol, as well as the numerical symbolism that is connected therewith, see Eichenseer, *Apostolicum*, 124–133.

(325/381),[68] in the Chalcedonian Creed,[69] and in the Athanasian Creed as well.[70] Such a doxological and dogmatic overview draws together the results of the early Church's battles concerning Christology and the Trinity and provides an overlay over the baptismal confession of the laity that accentuates salvation history.

(2) By contrast, the confessions from the Middle Ages, employed as a means of giving instruction, deal with the Church as the mysterious means that God uses to bring about salvation, in which and through which alone we come to faith. In this way, these confessions expand on the Egyptian "*Credo* in *sanct*a *ecclesi*a," (I believe *in* a holy Church) or the North African "*Credo* per *sanctam ecclesiam*" (I believe *through* a holy Church).[71] At the same time, they concentrate one's attention on the sacraments as God's most impressive instruments to deliver salvation. The creed of the Fourth Lateran Council of 1215 thus mentions the necessity of the Church itself for salvation, along with the Lord's Supper that includes teaching about the transubstantiation of the earthly elements into the body of Christ and the blood of the covenant that was offered, effected by the full power of the ordained priest, along with baptism, confession of sins, and marriage.[72] The creed that was delivered to the emissaries of the Eastern Roman emperor at Lyon in 1274 fixes, even more specifically, the current differences in teaching between the East and the West; in addition to the *filioque*, it mentions the practice of private confession, purgatory, seven as the number of the sacraments; it speaks, as well, about transubstantiation in connection with the Eucharist, stating that only unleavened bread was to be used, that only one marriage was to be permitted and, finally, includes the teaching about the power and primacy of the pope.[73] At this point, the means by which the divine actions to bring about salvation, the description

---

[68] Cf. *BSLK*, XIIIf.

[69] Cf., on this, Grillmeier/Bacht, *Das Konzil von Chalkedon*.

[70] Cf. *BSLK*, XIV.

[71] The texts can be consulted in Eichenseer, *Apostolicum*, 361–65.

[72] Denzinger, 800ff. Thomas Aquinas follows this arrangement in *De articulis fidei et ecclesiae sacramentis*.

[73] Denzinger, 851ff. The Tridentine confession of faith (1564) deserves mention here as well; at the end of the Nicene Creed it simply inserts an explicit "No" to the Reformation; it follows the path of accepting the apostolic tradition and also church practice; one places oneself under the authority of the Church's interpretation of the Scriptures and carries this "Yes" further to include Church traditions of the Middle Ages, including indulgences and the primacy of the pope (Denzinger, 1862ff.).

of which had taken a fixed form over time during the history of the Church, are incorporated into the confession. In addition to the doxological praise of God, a new genus of confession appears on the scene at the same time; the *Media salutis* (means by which salvation is delivered) are circumscribed both with respect to sacrament and ceremony and are fixed juridically at the same time.

Analyzed schematically, the development of the confession from its most ancient creedal form unfolded in three distinct directions: (1) The Apostles' Creed presents a lively narrative of God's saving acts and thereby makes use of the mythologizing statements that are positioned at the edge of the New Testament. (2) The instruction-filled confessions of the bishops from the early Church seek to articulate the nature of this God who reveals Himself in these saving acts. (3) The confessions from the Middle Ages identify the means of grace, through which those who are making their confession are able to participate in these saving acts that are offered by God.

The way this developed in three different directions can be seen even in the way the Apostles' Creed was explicated in the early Church and in the Middle Ages. In the discussions about the Symbols in the fourth and fifth centuries,[74] the battle against the heretics stands at the center. Thus Augustine sought a way to make the fruits of the Christological and trinitarian battles accessible to the ordinary members of the community. When he uses the key phrase "*Filius eius unigenitus*," he sketches out how the Logos is eternally being begotten from the being of the Father and then, after mentioning the Spirit, he draws together the teaching about the Trinity.[75] Since Augustine was probing for an explanation about the nature of the *una essentia Dei* (single essence of God), a fissure threatened to develop between how to articulate the inner-trinitarian nature of God and how

[74] An overview is provided by Wiegand, *Symbol und Katechumenat*, § 3, 60–83.

[75] The supporting materials are in Eichenseer, *Apostolicum*, 223–32 and 347–56. In addition, Rufinus, *Expositio symboli* 33, Niceta of Remesiana, *Explanatio symboli* 8f., and Peter Chrysologus, *Sermo* 57, 58, 59, 61 (PL 52:360A; 362B; 364C; 371A) expand on the mention of the Spirit to articulate the teaching about the Trinity; Rufinus, *Expositio symboli* 33 (CCSL 20:169): "We complete the mystery of the Trinity with our mention of the Holy Spirit [ACW 20:71]." *Sermones* (232–51) that have been transmitted under the name of Augustine, (PL 39:2173–2210) pass these Christological and trinitarian expansions on into the Middle Ages. Even more clearly, the three "Sermone de Symbolo ad catechumenos" (PL 40:637–68) show Augustinian influence; they constitute "a memorial of the African Church under Vandal overlordship" (Wiegand, *Symbol und Katechumenat*, 53).

to characterize His turning toward the world, which the church fathers were able to negotiate only with much difficulty. Even though the eternal Word of God is revealed in the creation and in the fact that humans came into existence, in the final analysis the full reality remains undetectable and unalterable within the Father.[76] Even though the Father and the Son turn toward the world through the gift of the Spirit, the Spirit essentially remains the internally divine band of love between the two.[77]

The explications of the Symbols that were taken up in the Frankish scrutiny rites,[78] the master patterns for catechesis during the Carolingian reform,[79] and the paraphrases of the Symbols from the early Middle Ages that are based on these documents,[80] do not make use of the highly speculative work of Augustine; instead, they use the bare formulations of the teaching about the Trinity and about the two natures. The explications that come from the high and late Middle Ages follow them in this regard: most generally, one counts at present fourteen articles of faith, seven "*articuli divinitatis*" and seven "*articuli humanitatis*."[81]

---

[76] Augustine, *Sermo* 212.1 (PL 38:1059): "In fact, the Word of God is invisible by nature because He was in the beginning and He was God. In this same nature He is also completely immortal, that is, He remains immutable in every respect [Muldowney translation, 118]."

[77] On this, see Schmaus, *Die Spannung von Metaphysik und Heilsgeschichte in der Trinitäts-lehre Augustins*, and Schindler, *Wort und Analogie in Augustins Trinitätslehre*.

[78] On this, see Wiegand, *Symbol und Katechumenat*, § 14, 248–60.

[79] This is promulgated essentially by Augustine, Maximus of Turin, and Isidore of Seville; cf. the summary provided by Wiegand, *Symbol und Katechumenat*, § 18, 331–51.

[80] Hahn, *Bibliothek*, §§ 100–17; on this, see the critical observations by Kattenbusch, *Symbol*, 2:864ff.

[81] Thomas Aquinas, *De articulis fidei*, §§ 598, 605f., 611; idem, *Summa theologiae* II/II, q. 1, a. 8; Bonaventure, *Commentaria in quatuor libros sententiarum*, III, dist. 25, a. 1; Richard of Middleton, *Quaestio in mag. sent. lib.* III, dist. 25, a. 1, q. 2; Duns Scotus, *In Sententiarum* III, dist. 25, q. 1, a. 4. Further exemplars are found in Ritschl, *Fides implicita*, 15ff.; Weidenhiller, *Untersuchungen*, 17, 138f. But the articles are placed together in a completely new way. The seven articles "About Faith in the Godhead" are 1. The Unity of the Divine Essence in Three Persons – 2. God the Father – 3. The Son – 4. The Holy Spirit – 5. Creation – 6. Church and forgiveness – 7. Resurrection and eternal life. The seven articles "On the Humanity of Christ" are 1. Becoming human – 2. Birth – 3. Crucifixion and death – 4. Descent into hell – 5. Resurrection – 6. Redemption – 7. Coming again. But even this numbering system varies widely.

The paraphrases of the Symbols thereby seek to retain the sequence of events in the history of salvation, as contained in the Apostles' Creed, in that—in a way that is similar to Luther at a later time in his Confession of 1528[82]—they place the Trinity at the beginning. They describe the distinctiveness of the Spirit and distinguish Him thereby from being merely linked with the Church, inserting Him after the confession about the Son; these statements lump together the numbering of the three names, in that they give witness to the oneness of God: "*Credo in deum patrem omnipotentem, creatorem caeli et terrae et totius creaturae. Et credo in ejus unigenitum filium, dominum nostrum, Jesum Christum. Et credo in Spiritum sanctum, Credo quod istae tres personae, pater et filius et spiritus sanctus, una vera deitas est, quae semper fuit sine initio et semper erit sine fine*" (I believe in God the Father almighty, creator of heaven and earth and all creatures. And I believe in His only-begotten Son, our Lord, Jesus Christ. And I believe in the Holy Spirit. I believe that these three persons, Father and Son and Holy Spirit, are one true God, which always was, without beginning, and will always be, without end).[83] The confession about God as triune is thus articulated clearly; the threefold arrangement of the Symbol is distorted, however. The creation remains attributed uniquely to the Father, the Spirit is split off from the Church; after one has mentioned the Trinity, one must go back to concentrate primarily on the Son.[84]

A second important issue is shaped by those paraphrases that are based on early Church commentaries that deal with the Christ event. At this point, the results of the Christological conflicts are taken up; terminology from the Chalcedonian Creed,[85] "*Consubstantialis Patri secundum divinitatem et consubstantialis nobis secundum humanitatem*" (of common substance with the Father according to His divinity and of common substance with us according to His

---

[82] "Vom Abendmahl Christi, 1528," WA 26:500.27–32 (AE 37:151–372).

[83] Hahn, *Bibliothek*, § 107; cf. §§ 100, 102, 104–06, 109–12, 114–17; Kattenbusch, *Symbol*, 2:871. This is similar to what was stated already by Peter Chrysologus, *Sermo* 60 (PL 52:366B).

[84] The congregational Symbol according to Honorius Augustodunensis goes on to say (Hahn, *Bibliothek*, § 107): "I believe, as well, that the Son of God was conceived of the Holy Spirit and was born of Saint Mary, perpetual virgin."

[85] Denzinger, 301; cf. also Pseudo-augustine, *Sermo* 245–47 (PL 39:2198–2204).

humanity) is inserted into the reference to the incarnation and the virgin birth.[86]

Despite this, such confessions clearly place the emphasis on the God-Logos in His humanity. In this way, they strengthen an element that is visible already in the Apostles' Creed itself. The *Textus receptus* had inserted into the Christological section the two terms "*Passus*" and "*Mortuus*" (suffered and died). The preceding "*passus sub Pontio Pilato*" (suffered under Pontius Pilate) functions "as a sort of caption or qualitative summary" for the words that follow: "'Suffered under Pontius Pilate,' which means concretely: 'crucified, died, and was buried'."[87] The paraphrases of the Symbols underscore this; in Jesus, God has taken part in our human existence, which holds us as prisoners on earth, in our hunger and thirst, weariness and work, torment and suffering, neediness and death.[88]

The elements in the "*fides dogmatica*" that are thus highlighted (Trinity, Christology), as well as in the "*fides historica*" (that Jesus became completely human), intersect with those who are making their confession in the third expansion of the original Symbol. At this point, the concern during the Middle Ages about how the *Applicatio salutis* (application of salvation) is articulated. The addresses to the catechumens in the early Church era already commenced generally with the thought: the Symbol is the covenantal sign of the heavenly agreement between God and the human being, and they conclude with the forceful admonition: "*Retinete semper pactum, quod fecistis Domino, id est hoc symbolum, quod coram angelis et hominibus confitemini*" (Preserve always this covenant, which you made with the Lord; it is this Symbol that you confess before angels and

---

[86] Hahn, *Bibliothek*, § 106: "*Unde gloub daz diu sin gotelicha natura geinsamot wart der menisclichun in der magidlichun wamba, und daz die zvo nature an imo sint an einandera unzisaminevirmiscta*" (And I believe that His divine nature was one with the human nature in the womb of the virgin, and that the two natures are together in one another without being mixed); a congregational confession according to a handwritten copy from Bamberg from the eleventh century).

[87] Kattenbusch, *Symbol*, 2:891; cf. ibid., 887–94. Pseudo-augustine, *Sermo* 238.4 (PL 39:2186): "who *suffered* all things on our behalf: hunger, thirst, weariness, weeping, anguish, at the last, even death."

[88] Hahn, *Bibliothek*, § 106: "I believe that the eternal Christ lived on this earth like any other human being, that He drank, slept, was hungry, was thirsty, moved about, cried, and worked like anyone else, and that He never sinned"; cf., ibid., §§ 105, 108, 110.

humans).[89] The paraphrases of the Middle Ages insert this upward glance toward the Lord of the covenant into the confessions themselves; in this way, they reflect at the same time on the position where one takes a stance when confessing, when uttering the Creed. They do so, most interestingly, in a way that is more radically existential than is the case in the Symbols designed by the clergy at the Fourth Lateran Council and at the Second Council of Lyon.[90] The confessions from those communities remain silent about the additional sacraments, bringing only confession front and center. They mention nothing about the power of the pope; even the Church itself receives only brief mention.[91] The application of the *Fides dogmatica et historica* takes place in that one looks up to the one who, as the future judge of the living and the dead, is enthroned as ruler at the right hand of the heavenly Father.[92] Since the Spirit had been mentioned already, the Church receives only brief mention and, due to the connection with the forgiveness of sins, the eternal goal toward which the one who confesses rushes forward with remorse and contrition is depicted.[93] At this point, where pressing forward to come

---

[89] Niceta, *Explanatio symboli* 13 (PL 52:873A): this thought is developed particularly intensively by Peter Chrysologus, In his writings a whole collection of terms are given for the covenant sign, all the way to the phrase "The symbol of our interaction with heaven" [Fathers of the Church, 109:232] (Peter Chrysologus, *Sermo* 60 PL 52:366A).

[90] But along with the Athanasian Creed (38f.) and the Creed of the Council of Toledo, XI, of 675 (Denzinger, 540), the confession of the Fourth Lateran Council (Denzinger, 801) under-scores that all who bear the visage of humanity must appear before the exalted judge who sits at the right hand of the Father; the Council of Lyons responds in this way to the necessity that becomes apparent at this point, as indicated by the references in the Pseudo-augustine *Sermone* to the final judgment (*Sermone* 249–51, PL 39:2206–10), to the penance that accompanies confession, being explicated at this time with respect to the teaching about purgatory and through the implementation of frequent confessions (Denzinger, 856ff.).

[91] In his late writing *Expositio in Symbolum Apostolorum*, Thomas Aquinas includes a reference to the papacy (§§ 985f.) when dealing with the subject of the Church and refers to the seven sacraments (§§ 989–96) when discussing the forgiveness of sins.

[92] Pseudo-augustine, *Sermo* 238.6 (PL 39:2187): "For the one who came in weakness to redeem will come in power to judge."

[93] Hahn, *Bibliothek*, § 107: "I believe that He will still come thence to judge the living and the dead, each one according to his works and according to His own mercy. I believe in the holy Church (catholic and apostolic). I believe in the communion of the saints. I believe in the forgiveness of all sins for which I (have done penance and) made confession and have not repeated further. I believe that eventually I must die in the body in which I appear today. I must rise again; I must give an accounting to God of everything that I have done, either good or bad, and

before God's countenance is discussed, the believer himself is on the scene in the "*Fides, quae creditur*"; the saving acts of God that are described in the Creed reach out to him and draw him in a physical way into the scene. At this point, for the Christian in the Middle Ages, baptism is no longer most important; since baptism takes place for an infant, that event occurred in the distant past; now the "torturous baptism" connected with the institution of confession was front and center.[94] "*Credo remissionem omnium* meorum *peccatorum post veram paenitentiam*" (I believe in the remission of all of *my* sins after true repentance).[95]

In this way, we have sketched out the alterations to the Apostles' Creed that were carried out in the paraphrases of the Symbol during the Middle Ages. Such adjustments can be seen, as well, in the admittedly sparse commentaries of the high and late Middle Ages:[96] (1) The confession of the triune God is drawn forward to the beginning point of the Symbol, though that is merely juxtaposed to the original beginning that identifies God the Father as the creator of everything. Augustine's insistence on emphasizing the "*unitas*" in the "*trinitas*"[97] goes beyond any grounding in the New Testament and beyond the viewpoint of the early Church, according to which, instead of taking the role of "*una essentia divina*," ὁ θεός is God-Father, creator of the world and lord of the covenant.[98] The Christ

---

then accept punishment according to this, since at last I shall have been found out. And I also believe in eternal life. Amen." For a still more detailed treatment, see ibid., §§ 105, 106, 109; Kattenbusch, *Symbol*, 2:871. Niceta, *Explanatio symboli* 10 (PL 52:871D): "For we believe everything because we believe in our resurrection." *Explanatio symboli ad initiandos* (Caspari, *Alte und neue Quellen*, 219): "For what was the work for which Christ should take on flesh? What was the work for which Christ should ascend the cross? What was the work for which Christ should taste death and receive burial and rise again, unless for the sake of your resurrection? This whole sacrament is for your resurrection (If Christ has not been raised, our faith is in vain; but because He has been raised, therefore our faith is firm)."

[94] Pseudo-augustine, *Sermo* "De iudicio extremo" (*Sermones* 249–51, PL 39:2206–2210) extends an invitation to this "gate of repentance" (*Sermo* 249.5), using all the means available in ancient rhetoric. Cf. also Augustine, *Sermo de symbolo* (PL 40:649ff.).

[95] Hahn, *Bibliothek*, § 108; cf. also §§ 100, 110, 111, 114, 115, 117.

[96] An overview of the documents that are largely unedited can be found in Wiegand, *Symbol und Katechumenat*, and Weidenhiller, *Untersuchungen*.

[97] For a critical evaluation on this point, Scheffczyk, *Lehramtliche Formulierungen und Dogmengeschichte der Trinität*, 202ff. and Rahner, *Der dreifaltige Gott*, 323ff., 344ff.

[98] Cf. Rahner, *Theos im Neuen Testament*, esp. 152f.

event is interpreted within the framework of the "*vere Deus—vere homo*." The early Church's Christological and trinitarian formulas are used in this way. But the theologians of the Middle Ages distinguished now explicitly between the underdeveloped confession of an everyday member of a community and the "*fides explicita*" of the clerics. According to Thomas Aquinas, the common Christian would be expected to know about the mystery of the Trinity and the incarnation; but they could be spared from having to deal with the "*subtiles considerationes*" of the Scholastic theologians.[99] Leaders in the Middle Ages were thus reticent as well, with respect to the laity, about going beyond the short formulas offered by Augustine in their interpretation of the Apostles' Creed; by contrast, the clerics were counseled to gain basic knowledge about the heresies dealt with by the early Church; in his exposition,[100] even Thomas Aquinas described the authors and formulas of the early Church's Symbols, providing a basic sketch so that such heresies could be countered.

(2) God's saving actions through His Son are depicted with robust colors, which would underscore His role as "*verus homo*."

(3) The third main point developed from the conclusion to the Second and Third Articles, which were treated together. At the point when Christ's return for judgment is mentioned, the beam of light is directed toward the one who is confessing, with respect to his contrition, his repentance, and his good works, toward the forgiveness of guilt that is promised to him: "*Credo remissionem omnium meorum peccatorum post veram poenitentiam*!"

How Luther Reflects on the Way Faith Statements Developed in his Creedal Expositions

Luther himself is cognizant of the purpose and thrust in the paraphrases of the Symbol that took shape during the Middle Ages, which intensified the connectedness with those who were making

---

[99] Thomas Aquinas, *Summa theologiae* II/II, q. 2, a. 7 and 6; Peter Lombard, *Sententiarum* III, dist. 25, a. 2f.

[100] On Christology, see Thomas Aquinas, *Expositio in Symbolum Apostolorum*, §§ 888–90, 898–904; concerning the teaching about the Holy Spirit, ibid., §§ 959–65; the catalog of heretics in *De articulis fidei*, addressed to the archbishop of Palermo, is much more extensive. Albrecht Ritschl pursued the topic of the Scholastic way to differentiate between the *Fides explicita* of the clerics and the *Fides implicita* of the laity, in *Fides implicita*, 1–41.

their confession; at the same time, he polemicizes against placing trust in our own actions before God. The reformer engages the tradition thereby with respect to three different aspects.

(1) No matter how they differed, one from the other, the paraphrases from the Middle Ages all reiterated that "*Credo*" (I believe) was being uttered as the confession of the individual who was present for baptism.[101] In his first commentary, the Short Form of 1520, Luther makes use of this term; he repeatedly reiterates the "I believe."[102] The majority of these creedal paraphrases, which were spoken aloud in conjunction with the public confession and absolution that followed the sermon, begin with a rejection of Satan and his works and "luxuries" (*opera et pompa*).[103] As in the baptismal act itself, the two elements are thus linked together in this harkening back to one's baptism: renunciation of the powers of destruction and the confession of faith in the triune God.[104] This practice is still reflected in Luther's Short Form of 1520, since he begins, as well, with the renunciation: "I renounce the evil spirit, all idolatry, and all magical activity and false belief."[105]

(2) The creedal paraphrases direct the attention of the one who makes confession to one's own self, most especially at the point where the focus is on the forgiveness of sins and one's own standing with God at the final judgment. In the late Middle Ages, the activities that immediately followed the sermon were linked with the Decalogue and with other catechetical reflections that provided a way to reflect on one's sins, those that had risen to the level of public offense. After he had spoken the Creed in the place of and in the name of every individual believer, the priest thereby confessed: "I, a guilty, sinful human being, confess to the Almighty God and to His beloved mother Mary and to all of God's saints, and to you, O priest, who stands in the place of God, all the sin about which God knows me to be guilty . . . I admit that I am guilty, that I have sinned against

---

[101] Roughly also in the form of an encouragement in Pseudo-augustine, *Sermo* 234.1 (PL 39:2194f.); it is also found in the form of a confession in the *Christenspiegel des Dietrich Kolde*, 51ff.

[102] WA 7:214–20.

[103] Hahn, *Bibliothek*, §§ 109, 114, 115; despite this, most of these formulas begin with the abrenuntiation, which is not apparent in Hahn.

[104] On this, see Kirsten, *Die Taufabsage*, 39–51.

[105] WA 7:215.27. Concerning the placement of the prayers after the sermon in the worship service in the late Middle Ages, cf. Meyer, *Luther und die Messe*, 117–21.

the twelve elements of the Christian faith, that I have not upheld them completely, which I rightly ought to have done, whether I have doubted them by word or deed; I suffer thereby and am sorry with my whole heart."[106] At this point, the Creed is used to concentrate on the confession of guilt, which is answered by the statement of forgiveness. Our vacillating between trust and doubt comes thereby front and center.

In his sermon of December 19, 1528, on John 18:15–18,[107] Luther reflects on this concentrated effort to look at sin and seeks to make it understandable from the Scriptures. At this point, he refers to Peter's denial and explains: All the evangelists, who describe the entire passion of Christ with as few words as possible, get wordy at this point, bordering practically on the verbose. "No passage in the entire Passion narrative is described with so many words as is the fall of Peter."[108] Why this strange attention to detail? Peter is to serve for us as "an *examplum remissionis peccatorum*" (an example of the forgiveness of sins)[109] and portrays thereby the complete but hidden direction and goal of the entire passion of Christ. "The fruitfulness and usefulness of the suffering of Christ is to be this: that we obtain thereby the forgiveness of sins."[110] Discerned in the late Middle Ages and providing the center of the piety of that era, this insight into Jesus' passion is expanded by Luther in all the articles of the Creed. The other articles, considered in and of themselves, could leave us distant, even though God appears in each as one who exists in Himself from eternity to eternity, who has called into existence out of nothing the world that will never cease to be, who traversed the earth hundreds of years beforehand in the person of Jesus of Nazareth, and who would establish His reign in some shadowy future as something for all eyes to see. The highpoint of this creative and redemptive activity, which applies to each of us in the present and in our own life setting, takes hold of us in the statement about the *Remissio*

---

[106] "Verkündigung am Sonntag," according to the Regensburg Missal of 1485 (cited according to Meyer, *Luther und die Messe*, 117, n. 7).

[107] WA 28:271.3–276.6. The basic thoughts from this sermon are used by Emil Brunner as the leading concept for his *Dogmatik*; cf., on this, 1:71; 2:285f.; 3:241ff.

[108] WA 28:273.25.

[109] WA 28:273.6, 273.10: "The fruit of the Passion and its benefit is this, that in it we may have the forgiveness of sins"; ibid., 274.2: "Therefore the fulfillment of the passion, so that one thinks: the forgiveness of sins is valid."

[110] Ibid., 273.30.

peccatorum (remission of sins). The personal dimension of the faith breaks forth at this point. "The other articles take hold of someone else and do not touch us in our own life experiences. If they are to take hold of us and touch us personally, they have to take hold of and touch us through this statement, that all of us, I for myself, you for yourself, each person for himself or herself, can believe in the forgiveness of sins."[111] This is, therefore, "the most significant statement that one must believe."[112] Only at this point do the other statements in the Creed arrive at the unavoidable decision between faith or unbelief, acceptance or rejection. At this point, one can no longer circumvent the *Pro me* aspect of what it means when I say: "I believe."

(3) A third point of access to the tradition developed out of the differentiation between "*Credere in*" with the dative or accusative and the simple "*Credere*," once again with the dative or accusative. The scholarly Rufinus was the first one to come out against the phrase "*credo* in *sanctam ecclesiam*" in his "Expositio Symboli"; he taught that "*Credo* in" can be directed only and exclusively to the three persons of the Trinity, to the Father, to the Son, to the Holy Spirit. And yet, this little preposition does serve to set off the creator from the created, the divine from the human.[113] Faustus of Reji (Riez) goes so far as to call for rejecting faith "[up]on" (German: *an*) the Church as blasphemous human idolatry.[114]

In a strikingly similar way, Augustine distinguished between *Credere Deum, credere Deo*, and *credere in Deum.*[115] "For him *credere Deum (Christum)* (to believe [Tr.: about] God [Christ]) is the act of faith as an assertion of the plain fact that God exists; *credere*

---

[111] Ibid., 278.28.

[112] Ibid., 272.32: "But the article, 'I believe [in] the forgiveness of sins' applies to us and accompanies us in experience and makes it possible for the other articles to apply to us as well, so that they also accompany us in experience. That is why this is the hardest article to believe."

[113] Rufinus, *Expositio symboli* 34.15 (CCSL 20:170): "*Hac itaque praepositionis syllaba creator a creaturis secernitur et divina separantur ab humanis.*"

[114] Faustus of Reji [Riez], *De Spiritu Sancto* 1.2 (CSEL 21:104): "Whoever believes in the Church believes in a Man . . . therefore, retreat from this conviction of blasphemy, that to a degree, to believe a human being you must esteem a creature." Pseudo-augustine *Sermo* 242.4 (PL 39:2193): "It is understood that to believe the Church, we must not, however, believe in the Church; for the Church is not God, but it is the house of God." Further examples are in Eichenseer, *Apostolicum*, 359ff.

[115] Augustine, *Sermo* 144 (PL 38:788); In "Ioh. tract," 29.6 (PL 35:1631); cf., on this, Mohrmann, *Etudes sur le latin des chrétiens*.

Deo (Christo) (to believe by [Tr.: the power of] God [Christ]) is the acknowledgment of divine authority as the source of truth; *credere in Deum (Christum)* (to believe in God [Christ]) is the *fides formata* in its fully Christian form. This takes place in the movement of love, which binds and unites us most closely with Christ, thus in a manner that moves one to reliance on Christ.[116] As we move in this way, turning our back on the numerous elements of this earthly world that are passing away and turning instead with burning desire toward the God who will never go away, faith leads to acts of love because of hope. Peter Lombard[117] and Thomas Aquinas[118] reiterate the tradition about this distinction. Erasmus of Rotterdam attributes such distinctive ways of believing to different groups; most people believe that God exists, even the philosophers; the demons themselves believe in God's authoritative truth; the complete trust associated with a faith that holds back nothing is unique to the pious alone.[119]

Although Luther mentions the threefold distinction articulated by Augustine in his lectures on Romans,[120] he distinguishes more simply between faith "about" and faith "in" God in the Short Form of 1520:[121]

(a) The first type remains within the context of considering something to be true, "when I believe that what one says about God is

---

[116] Eichenseer, *Apostolicum*, 160.

[117] Peter Lombard, *Sententiarum* III, dist. 23.4 (PL 192:805): "It is one thing to acknowledge God, another to believe God, another to believe in God. To acknowledge God is to acknowledge that what He says is true, as the wicked do, as we acknowledge a man, but do not trust in a man. To believe in God is to believe that God Himself exists, as the wicked do as well. To trust in God is to trust to follow Him, believing by trusting in Him and being incorporated with His members. Through this faith the sinful man is justified; faith itself may begin to work through love." See Ivo of Chartres, *Sermo* 23 (PL 162:604D–605A); Jocelin of Soisson, *Expositio symboli et orationis dominicae* 4 (PL 186:1481D–1482A); Hugo of Rouen, *De fide catholica et oratione dominica* (PL 192:1323C).

[118] Thomas Aquinas, *Summa theologiae* II/II, q. 2, a. 2; cf. Bonaventure, *In Sententiarum* III, dist. 23, dub. 3.

[119] Erasmus, *Explanatio Symboli*, cols. 1144f.: "Numerous philosophers also believe *that* God exists; demons also *believe God*, for they know that he cannot lie. But only the devout believe *in God*—it makes no difference whether the accusative phrase *in Deum* or the ablative phrase *in Deo* is used for 'in God'—for they have fixed all their trust and all their hope in him" [Perraud, 1974].

[120] WA 56:252.3ff. (AE 25:1–524), with a reference to Peter Lombard, *Sententiarum* III, dist. 23.4.

[121] WA 7:215.1–22; cf. "Pred. über den 1. Art. vom 4.3.1523," WA 11:49.5–13.

true."[122] Luther would rather call this way to look at faith "intellectual activity or observation" (*cognitio, notitio*). Dogmatic teachings about the Trinity and Christology, as well as the historical description about Jesus' life and suffering, death and resurrection, would be set within this context. For this reason, Melanchthon discusses both together in the Apology as "*notitia historiae seu dogmatum*" (observations of history or about dogma),[123] and Johann Dietenberger writes in his catechism: "Saint Augustine calls this faith the faith of a Christian confession, by means of which we learn and confess the twelve articles of the holy Christian faith."[124] Such an historical and dogmatic knowledge or opinion about the faith could be articulated by both the godless and the demons; it does not save because God is not really given honor thereby.

(b) By contrast, faith *in* God ventures to take hold of the unseen hand that is described in the statements, by means of which God the creator, redeemer, and fulfiller reaches out to us. As a "*fides specialis*,"[125] this faith places its "trust" in God.[126]

Based on the tradition that was inaugurated by Rufinus,[127] the reformer uses the insight that this "faith *in*" ought to be and should be directed toward the triune God alone, but that it still stands under the applicable standard of the First Commandment.[128] In this sense, God

---

[122] WA 7:215.2.

[123] Ap IV (*BSLK*, 232.14).

[124] Dietenberger, *Katechismus* (Moufang, *Katholische Katechismen*, 8).

[125] Ap IV (*BSLK*, 168.54). Luther explicates the "*fides specialis*" in a precise manner in the "Acta Augustana, 1518," (WA 2:13–16; AE 31:253–292). He carefully works through the encounters with Christ in the Gospels at this point and uses them to show the difference between *fides generalis* and *fides specialis*. "And if you look through the entire gospel you will find many other examples, all of which refer not to a general but to a particular faith and which pertain to achieving some immediate result" (AE 31:273); cf. ibid., 14.15f., 25; 15.23 and Peters, *Reformatorische Rechtfertigungsbotschaft*, 81–86.

[126] "Eine kurze Form, 1520," WA 7:215.6.

[127] Cf. p. 24, n. 113f.

[128] The First Commandment is mentioned in the "Sermon von den guten Werken, 1520," WA 6:209.24–210.9 (AE 44:15–114), and in "Eine kurze Form, 1520," WA 7:215.14; 216.13; cf. also 205:12–18, and the "Sermon und Eingang in das 1. Buch Mose vom 22.3.1523," WA 12:439.16–26, as well as the commentary on the First Commandment, Volume 1, 114–41. The connection between the faith and the First Commandment was comprehended fully already in the commentaries from the late Middle Ages, in the sense that the offenses against the Creed were included on the widely circulated sheets that listed sins against the First Commandment; cf. Geffcken, *Bildercatechismus*, 53–58; Weidenhiller, *Untersuchungen*, 17.

the Father, Son, and Spirit separate themselves from everything else that is confessed as our faith in the Symbol. Only with respect to the three persons can one make use of the statement "*Credere in*"; "one is to direct one's faith to God alone; the divinity of Jesus Christ and the Holy Spirit is properly confessed in this way alone, that we believe in each one in the same way that we believe in the Father. And just as the same faith is in all three persons, in the same way the three persons are also one God."[129]

Whereas the reformer makes use of tradition in this threefold sense, he alters it as well, at the same time, and develops it further beyond what it had articulated. This can be shown with reference to each of those three points.

(1) We start with the third point, with "*Credo in Deum*," with "I believe in God."[130] In the Short Form of 1520, Luther formulates it: "I believe . . . *in* God the Father, *in* Jesus Christ, *in* the Holy Spirit."[131] In his sermon from March 4, 1523, he replaces the "in," based on his edition of the New Testament, with the German "*an*," "[Tr.: I set my faith up]*on*," since this sounds more appropriate in the German mother tongue.[132] With that adjustment he returns, naturally unbeknownst to him, to the common rendering that had been in use for more than 900 years, until it was set aside at the beginning of the fifteenth century, to be replaced by "I believe in."

Although Luther initially made this alteration on purely linguistic grounds, a change in the understanding of the faith lurks in the background. Due to his grounding in a Neoplatonic and mystical yearning for God, Augustine understood *Credere in Deum (Christum)* to mean "a movement of the will toward God (or Christ) . . . , in order to bring about a stirring of love in Him, guided by hope, in order to become completely one with Him."[133] "*Quid est ergo credere in eum? Credendo amare, credendo diligere, credendo in eum ire, et eius membris incorporari*" (What is it then to believe in Him?: By believing, to love; by believing, to be diligent, by believing, to come

[129] "Eine kurze Form, 1520," WA 7:215.18; cf. "Pred. über den 1. Art. vom 4.3.1523," WA 11:49.1–3.

[130] On what follows, see Meyer, "'In Gott' und 'an Gott' glauben . . . ," and idem, *Historischer Kommentar*, 92f.

[131] WA 7:215.17.

[132] WA 11:49.3: "*an melius esset, die Mutter Teusch*"; cf. "Taufbüchlein, 1523," WA 12:45.24, 27 (AE 53:95–103).

[133] Eichenseer, *Apostolicum*, 160; cf. Söhngen, *Die Einheit in der Theologie*, 101–06.

into Him, and to be incorporated as one of His members).[134] The Augustinian mysticism that was still at work in the waning Middle Ages purposely chooses "I believe *in* God," in order to emphasize that the one who believes is able to penetrate with faith and hope into the sphere of the divine, which almost transitions into a material and spatial sense. "I believe in God; that is as much as if to say, I have and confess such a faith that God incorporates me into Himself, which leads and brings me into the knowledge of His mystery and ultimately to God Himself. This faith is what Saint Augustine calls the faith of Christian grace."[135] The German turn of phrase, with the preposition "I believe [up]*on*," by contrast, would seem concurrently to show awareness of distance; it does not seem to give voice to such humble pressing on toward God and to a loving contemplation of His gracious presence.[136] In Luther, as well, one notices the spatial component with respect to our relationship to Christ; "*credere enim in Christum est eum induere, unum cum eo fieri.*"[137]

But as the relationship between promise and faith (*promissio—fides*) becomes clearer to the reformer, it is that much clearer that God is the one who is acting. The human being does not actually strive to draw close to God, who is in repose; instead, God the Father takes possession of us through Christ in the Holy Spirit and draws us up to Himself.[138] The "*Fides caritate formata*" (faith formed by love) deepens thereby to the level of "*Fiducia promissionis*" (faith in the promise), which is effected by God. The nature of the human being as person is thus grounded, in the deepest sense, when faith reaches such a complete form. Luther draws to the fore the comprehensive and simultaneously complete understanding of faith, as it is intimated

[134] Augustine, "In Iohannis evang. tractatus," 29.6 (PL 35:1631; CCSL 36:287); cf. idem, *Sermo* 144.2.2 (PL 38:788).

[135] Dietenberger, *Katechismus* (Moufang, *Katholische Katechismen*, 8f.).

[136] "Auslegung des Glaubens," about 1500 (Meyer, "'In Gott' und 'an Gott' glauben . . . ," 274): "*Ed is underscheyd an god to gelovende und in god. wente de bösen geiste gelöwen ok an god* (There is a difference between believing *an* [Tr.: having one's trust reliant (up)on] God and believing *in* God. The evil demons could only wish to be reliant upon God)."

[137] "Gal.-Komm., 1519," WA 2:535.24 (AE 27:151–410); "Röm.-Vorl., 1515–16," WA 56:252.5 ("Schol. zu Röm. 3:20, 22") (AE 25:238): "For to believe in Christ is to reach out to Him with one's whole heart and to order all things in accord with Him"; cf. "Von den guten Werken, 1520," WA 6:210.4ff. (AE 44:15–114).

[138] On faith terminology used by Luther early on, see Schwarz, *Fides, spes und caritas . . .*, 241–59; Metzger, *Gelebter Glaube*, 121–36; 171–95.

most clearly in the Old Testament in Isaiah and as it is accentuated in the New Testament by Paul and John.[139] Faith is the only possible form of existence for the human being before God; it takes into account the entirety of one's inner and external life. "Faith is and also ought to be a stable aspect of the heart, which does not waver, wobble, shudder, wriggle, or doubt, but which stands fast instead and is confident in its essential elements."[140] The ground of faith can thus be nothing but "the mere, invisible, imperceptible, one God."[141] Our own certainty is at the same time grounded in faith's certainty about God, both in its relationship with God as a certainty about salvation and also in its relationship with the world as certainty about the world.[142] Faith [up]*on* God is established in the most pointed way possible. "I consider and place my trust in nothing else than the mere, invisible, imperceptible, one God, who created heaven and earth and who alone is over all creatures."[143]

(2) Since the faith, hidden as it is according to this understanding in God, hovers over "everything that is and is not, over what is sinful and virtuous,"[144] Luther does not direct his attention outwardly only, to speak against trusting in the other opposing forces, as was done in the paraphrases of the Symbol from the Middle Ages. Faith such as this is directed inwardly at the same time, against one's own self, which is intimated in the confessions from the late Middle Ages;[145] it takes into account the doubts that lurk within one's own heart. Luther calls attention to this inner battle of faith. Wherever the Christian is aware of the self as existing before God, in addition to our external needs and pressures, one's own self-confidence appears as well, along with our enslavement to sin; these are the external and even more importantly the internal realities against which the confidence of faith

---

[139] Cf. Weiser, πιστεύω, 189.5–191.22; 195.8–197.32; Wildberger, *Glauben im Alten Testament*, as well as Bultmann, πιστεύω, 217.20–218.13.

[140] "Von den letzten Worten Davids, 1543," WA 54:32.22 (AE 15:265–352).

[141] "Eine kurze Form, 1520," WA 7:216.1.

[142] At this point, see Ebeling, *Gewißheit und Zweifel*; Peters, "'Ich glaube an Gott!'."

[143] "Eine kurze Form, 1520," WA 7:216.1; "Sermon von Gewalt S. Peters [Mt. 16:13-19] vom 29.6.1522," WA 10.3:214.26: "The faith is an almighty thing, as is God Himself."

[144] "Eine kurze Form, 1520," WA 7:216.11.

[145] See passages such as the formulas for public offense in Surgant, *Manuale curatorum*, 2:6; the prayer of confession in Beck, *Kirchliche Studien und Quellen*, 277ff.; the "Kurze Gebet, wie man Gott soll bitten um einen starken Glauben," in the *Christenspiegel des Dietrich Kolde*, 58ff.

must press forward. Faith will be aware of its constant companion and its most irritating enemy, our own vacillating back and forth between a hybrid confidence in the self and in disconcerting doubt.[146]

Whereas Luther, in his Treatise on Good Works and in the Short Form of 1520,[147] distinctly envisions that there is an inner battle concerning trust in God, he lets this aspect fade into the background in the catechisms. But the polemic against trusting in oneself,[148] as well as that which speaks against salvation by works,[149] is not ignored completely; the reformer exhorts us at the same time that we are to accept the pure gifts of faith with a spirit of praise.[150] And yet, he postpones discussion of that inner struggle for certainty until he offers his commentary on the Lord's Prayer.[151] But this is the second characteristic of Luther's creedal explanations; he accentuates that inner front for the battle of faith and identifies unbelief as the real enemy that militates against our being certain about our faith, in both its forms. A naïve or subtle trust in oneself and in the world stands on the one side; the sinister anxiety about the world and insidious doubts about oneself stand on the other side.

(3) The third characteristic grows out of Luther's observation that urges faith forward beyond "*notitia historiae seu dogmatum*"[152] to make it "*Fides specialis*,"[153] the *Fiducia promissionum Dei* (faith in the promises of God). The *Pro nobis* (for us) is accentuated in this way. This third aspect provides the culminating point for the other two characteristic observations that Luther contributes. The reformer proceeds by posing a question: What does it mean that I place my trust directly [up]on God the Father, Son, and Spirit when I confess everything that is stated in the Creed to be an act of God?[154] In this

---

[146] See the commentary on the First Commandment, Volume 1: 134–41, and on the Sixth Petition of the Lord's Prayer in Volume 3.

[147] WA 6:207.15–210.35 (AE 44:15–114) and WA 7:216.1–17; cf. also Erasmus, *Explanatio Symboli*, cols. 1147E–1150A.

[148] *BSLK*, 649.18–41 (LC).

[149] *BSLK*, 658.35–42.

[150] *BSLK*, 660.18–47.

[151] See the commentary on the Sixth Petition of the Lord's Prayer in Volume 3.

[152] See the commentary on the Sixth Petition of the Lord's Prayer in Volume 3.

[153] Ap IV (*BSLK*, 168.54).

[154] "Pred. über den 3. Art. vom 6.3.1523," WA 11:54.7: "Where those external signs are, do not doubt that most certainly Father, Son, and Holy Spirit are at hand, along with the forgiveness of sins." A plethora of further examples has been assembled by Meyer, *Apostolikum*, 11ff., as well as in idem, *Historischer Kommentar*, 269ff. In addition, see also Luther's own comprehensive comments in the "Habbakuk-Ausl.

way, the works of creation and acts of redemption become at the same time signs and larvae, in, with, and under which the triune God draws near to us, is recognized by us in faith, and seeks to be apprehended by us in trust.

God the Father, Son, and Spirit are thus drawn into the central position; they are therefore in each case the material subject for the explanations of the individual articles. As this happens, the trinitarian references that are explicated at the time of the early Church and during the Middle Ages fade into the background; the foundational Christological dogma is dealt with only appositionally in the Small Catechism; it is touched upon only lightly in the Large Catechism.[155] In contrast to the way it was articulated in great detail during the era of the early Church and during the Middle Ages, Luther does not discuss the Trinity and the teaching about the two natures as independent topics. Instead, he explicates the narrative about the activity of God as it impacts those who are confessing. The *applicatio*, which crystallized from that narrative to become its own separate topic during the Middle Ages, does in fact receive his attention. But the reformer stresses the importance of the *Pro me* first, after he has had the Christians recite the Apostles' Creed in a complete form that comes beforehand and that lays a foundation. But the explication that probes deeper into the 'for us' and expands on the 'for us' remains in service to and is placed within the wider context of the common praise that is called forth by the evidence of God's creative and redeeming activity.

This can be demonstrated with reference to the various dimensions of faith, which we can thus coordinate, one with the other, in what follows schematically:

(a) Christian faith is primarily and foundationally "*Faith* [up]*on God*" (*credo in Deum*), a personal grounding of oneself (*fiducia*) upon the triune God Himself, who incorporates the human being and gives

---

vom 1525," WA 19:390.3–23 (AE 19:149–237) and in the "Gen.-Vorl., 1535–45," WA 42:9.15–13.10 (AE 1:1–359); 293.39–395.17 (AE 2:1–399). In the "Trinitatispred. vom 23.5.1535," WA 41:270.13–23, the reformer differentiates between this dogmatic festival and all the other festivals connected with salvation throughout the church year: all the others "describe the involvement of our Lord God in His works and wonders, which He has performed. . . . But this festival today is about who He is in Himself, unencumbered by any clothing or works, solely about His divine nature."

[155] *BSLK*, 511.23–26 (SC); 651.32 (LC): "true Son of God."

Himself to the human being by means of His saving actions, as well as in the promise of salvation that is inextricably bound to Him.[156] This "faith [*up*]*on*" ought to be and should be directed toward God alone; such faith stands under the standard of the First Commandment. This "faith [up]*on*" is concurrently the demand and gift of God; within the framework of all the tensions with our human powers, it is always experienced and witnessed only and exclusively as a free gift of God.

(b) The Christian faith is secondarily, and at the same time, fully bound, as "faith *about God* (*credo Deum*), an experience, understanding, and apprehension of what is attested as God's revelation of both salvation and creation according to the implications of what took place in the historical realm and according to the implications rooted in the content and dogma; as "I believe that . . . ," it is also *cognitio* or *notitia historiae seu dogmatum* (knowledge or awareness of history or dogma).

(c) Within the Christian faith, the primary dimension of one's personal trust and the secondary dimension of knowledge about the events are bound together in the very same action of God—belief—gift (*credere Deo*) as the trusting and risk-taking acknowledgement (*assensus*) which, under the cover of worldly indicators, itself gives witness to the Lord who is above the world.

These three accents are merely various dimensions to which one can call attention; the entire nature of the faith is as one unity. For this reason, the content of the faith (*fides, quae creditur*) that is confessed and described cannot be demarcated in the Creed so as to separate that aspect from the Creed as an active and personal commitment (*fides, qua creditur*).[157]

---

[156] Both Herrmann, *Der Verkehr des Christen mit Gott*, and Ritschl, *Fides implicita*, tirelessly keep referring back to this. But one errs if one follows Ritschl and says: "In this discovery of Luther, that faith or the religious way of knowing involves a direct evaluation of worth, one arrives at the proper opposite sense over against knowledge or evaluation of worth in all its many ramifications (Ritschl, *Fides implicita*, 68).

[157] Some, such as Thieme, *Zur Trinitätsfrage*, and Meyer, *Historischer Kommentar*, 263–71, have stated this over against Ritschl, *Fides implicita*, 59–68; Hoffmann, *Die Lehre von der fides implicita*, 35, 52f.; Hardeland, *Katechismusgedanken*, 187f., 209.

The Creative and Redeeming Actions of the One God in the Three Articles that Describe Creation, Redemption, and Sanctification

Already in the Short Form of 1520, the reformer concentrates all the specific statements of the Creed on the relationship of the one who is making confession to God the Father, Son, Spirit.[158] At this point, two aspects enter upon the scene, which bring with them a certain tension for Luther's interpretation of the Creeds: Primarily and foundationally, the wide-ranging work of God the Father's creative and redeeming actions through the Son and with the Holy Spirit are set forth in a structure that remains; secondarily, and because of the need to set this forth in catechetical form, Luther arranges each of the three activities of God, at each stage, by assigning each of the three to one of the persons of the Trinity.[159] Appropriating such activities to various articles makes less clear the enduring insight that the one indivisible God turns toward us, in the creation as well as in the act of redemption.

This tension between theological statement and catechetical form needs to be analyzed further at this point. We begin with Luther's reflections about the catechism. Although the tradition generally counted twelve articles, Luther arranges these already in the Short Form of 1520 "into three chief parts, according to which the three persons of the holy, divine Trinity (*Dreifaltigkeit* [Threefoldedness]) will be described therein."[160] Already in 1523, based on their content, he also referred to each one of those chief sections[161] as articles.[162] In connection with his comments that introduce Melanchthon's visitation instructions (1528),[163] he standardized this new division into

---

[158] See esp. WA 7:216.21f.; 217.11ff.; 218.25ff.; 220.2ff.

[159] "Pred. über die Trinität vom 23.5.1535," WA 41.277.4: "One attributes creation to the Father, redemption to the Son, and to the Spirit the power that He forgives sins, makes one happy, strengthens, and finally will bring one from death into an eternal life. At the same time, these are different garments, so that one does not wrap up the persons in the same way"; cf. ibid., 276.39–277.16; 279.31, 34.

[160] "Eine kurze Form, 1520," WA 7:214.25.

[161] "Pred. über das Symbolum vom 5. u. 6.3.1523," WA 11:51.4; 53.6; cf. "Eine kurze Form, 1520," WA 7:215.23; 216.30; 218.20.

[162] "Pred. über den 2. und 3. Art. vom 5.3.1523," WA 11:49.4, 26; 50.27; 51.2; 52.7.

[163] Melanchthon, *Studienausgabe*, 1:259.7: "Therefore one should preach the three articles of the faith and diligently show the people these three chief articles that are explicated in the faith: creation, redemption, and sanctification."

three parts, both in a sermon he preached on December 10, 1528,[164] and in the Large Catechism.[165] But it is most important to note, at the same time, that he additionally gave the three articles fixed titles after the time that the visitation instructions were crafted: On Creation, On Redemption, On Sanctification.[166] For the First and Second Articles, the key terms creation and redemption were easy to assign. With respect to the Third Article, Luther struggled long and hard to find a simple catechetical term for what is confessed therein about the Holy Spirit. It is first in the visitation articles that the key word "sanctification" is used. Luther takes a cue from the way the Second Article is divided and treats the Third Article the same way in his sermon on December 10, 1528.[167] As each of the individual "statements" should demonstrate for us "the way in which" Christ became our Lord and what "was involved" for Him to effect our salvation,[168] the Spirit also makes us holy by means of the following elements of the Creed.[169] In this way, the tightly worded catechetical arrangement was established: "I believe [up]on God the Father, who made me; I believe [up]on God the Son, who redeemed me; I believe [up]on the Holy Spirit, who makes me holy."[170]

Since the reformer attributes what is said in the individual articles, in each case, to one of the persons of the Trinity, for a time he is forced to do away with the interconnections that link the

---

[164] WA 30.1:86.8: "In former times you heard preaching on the twelve articles of the Creed. If anybody wants to divide it up, he could find even more. You, however, should divide the Creed into the main parts indicated by the fact that there are three persons"; ibid., 88.16 (AE 51:162): "the uneducated and the children"; cf. ibid., 86.15f.

[165] *BSLK*, 647.3–7.

[166] Melanchthon, *Studienausgabe*, 1:259.8–25; WA 30.1:87.1f.; 88:17f.; 94.10ff. (AE 51:162–169).

[167] In the first set of Catechetical Sermons of 1528, Luther still places together the following on May 23 (WA 30.1:11.1): "To create, to redeem, to give eternal life"; and in WA 29:363.14 he reiterates it in a sermon on John 14:23ff., once again, on May 17, 1529: "The work of the Holy Spirit is to make the Christian Church, the forgiveness of sins, to revive the flesh from death, and to give eternal life."

[168] "Kat.-Pred. zum 2. Art. vom 10.12.1528," WA 30.1:90.1f., 16f. (AE 51:162–169).

[169] "Kat.-Pred. zum 3. Art. vom 10.12.1528," WA 30.1:91.8 (AE 51:162–169): "*Spiritus Sanctus sanctificat* per *sequentia membra*"; cf. ibid., 91.18; 93.15; 94:1, 8, 17f.

[170] *BSLK*, 647.14–17; cf. ibid., 647.5–12. This pattern is adopted, among other places, in the Nuremberg Catechetical Sermons (Reu, *Quellen*, 1.1:507, 40–48), in Dietenberger, *Katechismus* (Moufang, *Katholische Katechismen*, 11), and in Tetelbach's *Güldenes Kleinod* (Reu, *Quellen*, 1.1:684.25ff.).

activities of the Trinity as described in the paraphrases of the Symbol that were commonly used in the Middle Ages and which functioned as a resumé of the battles in the early Church that had been articulated in the Apostles' Creed. Not a single comment is thus made in the Small Catechism to describe the unity of God; except for brief references,[171] there is but one sentence in the Large Catechism that addresses this mystery: "One God and faith, but three persons."[172]

Some have accused Luther of falling prey to a certain type of Modalism;[173] one could certainly be more justified, with respect to the catechisms, to conclude that he articulates in them a "naïve Tritheism."[174] But the reformer was most definitely aware that he had abbreviated the testimony of the Scriptures and the confession of the Church at this point, in order to articulate the faith for those who had a simple faith. Not only his exegetical and dogmatic writings but also his sermons about the Trinity clarify and unfold what is admittedly only hinted at, what is more or less assumed in the catechisms. Luther was a little more direct in articulating his teaching about the Trinity in his early commentaries on the Creed.[175] It is certainly problematic that this teaching is not set forth in greater detail in the Large Catechism either, since that was intended not merely for the common people in the congregation but was intended additionally as a way to offer pastors a primer for preaching about the catechism.[176]

Luther seems to have wanted to rectify this dearth of comments in his later writings and disputations, as well as in his sermons about the Trinity,[177] but despite this he could write in his Treatise on the Last

---

[171] *BSLK*, 651.10f., on the Son: "Here we become acquainted with the Second Person of the deity"; 653.42f., on the Spirit: "But God's Spirit alone is called a Holy Spirit"; cf. also the summary on 660.18–47; 661.35–42.

[172] *BSLK*, 647.18. This is similar to what is found already in "Eine kurze Form, 1520," WA 7:215.21: "And as it is the same faith in all three persons, so the three persons are also one God."

[173] Von Harnack, *Dogmengeschichte* 3:874; Holl, *Was verstand Luther unter Religion*, 71f. (note). For the opposite view, see Schlink, *Theologie der lutherischen Bekenntnisschriften*, 99, n. 22, and Prenter, *Spiritus Creator*, 183ff., 356f.

[174] This is the way it is handled by Thieme, *Die Augsburgische Konfession und Luthers Katechismen*, 169; cf. ibid., 165, 174.

[175] "Pred. über den 2. und 3. Art. vom 5.3.1523," WA 11:51.10: "regarding the majesty of the Trinity, how the Father and the Son and the Holy Spirit are one God": cf. "Kat.-Pred. zum Symbolum vom 21.9.1528," WA 30.1:44.28f.

[176] Luther delivers to the preachers his own sermons to his congregation, without explicating for the pastors the necessary transitions in thought and knowledge.

[177] For texts and literature on Luther's views on the Trinity, see pp. 57–58.

Words of David (1543): "Thus it is useful and proper that there be some, both among the laity and the educated, particularly pastors, preachers and schoolmasters, who think it important to learn about such centrally important articles of our faith and to speak of them in German." But he adds the comment at the same time: "But for the one for whom this is too difficult, that person should stay with the children by using the catechism and should pray against the devil and his nonsense."[178] The problem that surfaced already in the sermons on the Symbols during the fourth and fifth centuries, and which could not be silenced in the commentaries from the late Middle Ages, is framed by the question: "How much of the teaching about the Trinity and the two natures of Christ needs to be known by ordinary Christians?" and Luther needs to provide an answer at this point as well. In this regard, he also cannot avoid the necessity of differentiating between a *Fides implicita* and a *Fides explicita*.[179]

Those who have written commentaries about Luther's catechisms have discovered the gap that the two documents leave open here, when one compares them with the tradition that took shape under Augustine; they compensate for that by noting that young people who are growing up are receiving instruction about the trinitarian formulas. Thus Osiander has the pastor who is addressing the young people in the Nuremberg Children's Sermons say: If you, "little children," cannot yet understand "at this time" the mystery of the Trinity, "at the proper time you will hear and learn more about it; at this point, simply note that the one, true, eternal God is Father, Son, and Holy Spirit and that is what we call the Holy Trinity, which means that the three, Father, Son, and Holy Spirit, are one, divine being."[180]

---

[178] WA 54:59.2 (AE 15:265–352); see also WA 63.14–28 and "Gen.-Vorl., 1535–45," WA 42:276.39–277.16 (AE 2:1–399). In contrast to Luther, Calvin developed the teaching about the Trinity in his dogmatic writings and in the *Genfer Kat.* (Geneva Catechism), quest. 19f., but he left such ideas in the background in the sermons that were based on texts; cf. Koopmans, *Das altkirchliche Dogma in der Reformation*, 132–42.

[179] This is observed correctly by Ritschl, *Fides implicita*, 56ff., though it is interpreted incorrectly.

[180] Reu, *Quellen*, 1.1:506.40; cf. the entire text, ibid., 506.29–507.18; similarly, Dietenberger, *Katechismus* (Moufang, *Katholische Katechismen*, 10) and Tetelbach, *Güldenes Kleinod* (Reu, *Quellen*, 1.1:684.22ff.). Among the efforts that preceded Luther to develop a catechism during the Reformation, Agricola provided great detail in his questions for children about the Trinity, basing these on Hilary and Augustine,

But what is foundational for Luther's explanation about the Creed is not that he assumes that each catechetical reference in the articles is attributed exclusively and individually to just one person of the Trinity, but that he takes up the Augustinian and Scholastic speculations about the Trinity and renews the effort to explain them on the basis of the biblical record. In this regard, he does not start out with the immanent movement of the three persons within the one divine being, but concentrates instead strictly on how God the Father turns toward the world through the Son, Jesus Christ, by means of the Holy Spirit.[181] Wherever the living God reveals Himself, in His actions to effect salvation but also in His creative activity, at that point the Scriptures bear witness to that mysterious activity with one another and in one another. Luther expressed this in a classic way, in the summary in the Large Catechism:[182] We find God's gracious, fatherly heart only through the Son; only the Holy Spirit leads us to the Son. This comprehensive point of view that is used by the reformer is not stated with such clarity and simplicity in the sermons on the Creed that are preached in 1528. But such statements use almost the same exact words in the Confession of 1528.[183] Already in the "*Diktata super Psalterium*" this foundational thought is stated in the classic phraseology: "*Filius per spiritum patris sui uniat me sibi*" (The Son through the Spirit of His Father unites me to Himself),[184] which "rightly understood, encapsulates Luther's entire teaching about the Trinity."[185] This viewpoint is the guiding thought in the Short Form of 1520 and in the Sermons on the Symbol from 1523.[186] Whatever we confess in the Creed, particularly the eschatological fulfillment, is what has been given us as a gift by "the Father, through

---

and he makes reference to the effects of the sun with respect to its light, energy and heat (*lumen – radii – calor*) (MGP 21:66.8–70.31). Capito mentions these in his "Kinderbericht" (ibid., 147, quest. 67), and Gräter does the same in his *Catechesis* (ibid., 344f., quest. 91–96). Expansive reflections about the Trinity are found in Erasmus as well, *Explanatio Symboli*, cols. 1150F–1151D; 1166E–1169E.

[181] In the churches of the Reformation, to an extent that is hard to fathom, traditions from catechisms, prayers, confessions, and academic instruction are overlaid with the nature of the Trinity; on this, see Peters, *Trinitätslehre*.

[182] *BSLK*, 660.18–661.18.

[183] "Vom Abendmahl Christi, 1528," WA 26:505.38–506.9 (AE 37:151–372).

[184] WA 3:553.28 (AE 11:1–553).

[185] Vogelsang, *Die Anfänge von Luthers Christologie*, 171, n. 1.

[186] See esp. "Eine kurze Form, 1520," WA 7:217.6–15; 218.25–32; 220.1–4; "Pred. zum Credo vom 4. u. 5.3.1523," WA 11:49.4f.; 51.10–15.

the Son, Jesus Christ, our Lord, with and by means of the Holy Spirit."[187]

The reformer purposely concentrates his observations on the revelation of the triune God as it pertains to the economy of salvation; in that way, at the same time, he reached farther back than the time of Thomas Aquinas and Augustine to the early Church's view about the Trinity, as it had been developed up to the time of the Cappadocians,[188] and he anticipates, at the same time, a central thesis of modern theology: "When a particular teaching about the Trinity is not apprehensive about discussing the economy of salvation, then it is even more directed toward saying what is essential when describing the immanent Trinity and when bringing out what is really important to articulate a theoretical and existential understanding of the faith."[189] God discloses His nature to us here on earth in His revelatory activity only as in a mirror, through a word that is at the same time a hidden one; only in the *eschaton* will we be able to see Him in His uncovered nature, as He really is. Here we find "the complete divine being," who provides for us salvation, only and exclusively in this "will and action" of His revelation in creation and redemption;[190] we recognize both elements, what God is and what He has in mind for us,[191] with one another and within ourselves, only from this revelation of Himself that He offers.

This mirror-like relationship, between the economy of salvation discussion of the Trinity and the discussion of the immanent Trinity, is presented for us in a comprehensive description offered by Luther in his treatise on the Three Symbols or Creeds of the Christian Faith (1538): "It is enough that we would establish a certain level of differentiation of persons when confessing the faith, namely, that the Father is from no one, that the Son is from the Father, but begotten, that the Holy Spirit is from Father and Son, but proceeding . . . In the same way, the differentiation of the same names is necessary for the Son and the Holy Spirit, since each reveals Himself to us outside the divine being, within creatures; for the Son was born physically from His mother and is also at this point called son and is born, and yet He is still the same Son of God in both births. And the Holy Spirit goes

[187] "Eine kurze Form, 1520," WA 7:220.1.
[188] Cf. Peters, *Trinitätslehre*, cols. 566ff.
[189] Rahner, *Der dreifaltige Gott*, 341; cf. 323ff., 336ff., 344ff., 382ff.
[190] *BSLK*, 660.18f.
[191] *BSLK*, 660.25f.

forth physically in the form of the dove, in fiery tongues, in a strong wind, etc., and is called, here as well, one who proceeds forth or one who is sent, and yet He is still the same Holy Spirit in both ways of proceeding and is neither the Father nor the Son."

"For this reason, it matches that the middle person was born physically and became Son, who beforehand was born in eternity and is Son, and that neither the Father nor the Holy Spirit were born physically or became Son; in the same way, it matches up very nicely that the Holy Spirit goes forth physically, He who proceeded earlier, in eternity, and who is neither born nor Son. Thus the Father remains Himself, so that the persons of all three are in the majesty, and yet that the Son has the deity from the Father through His eternally indwelling birth, not the other way around, and that the Holy Spirit has deity from the Father and the Son through His eternally indwelling proceeding. The Son thus shows His eternal birth through His physical birth and the Holy Spirit shows His eternal proceeding when He proceeds physically; each one has for their internal nature an external comparison or depiction."[192]

Without being weakened in any way, the Father, Son, and Holy Spirit are one, true God and, as the Lord of Life stands over against all the creatures who have fallen under the pall of death, they stand in terms of majesty; in this respect, there is no ranking within the Trinity. The nature of being God, for all three personal hypostases, proceeds from eternal existence before time and remains in all eternity after time comes to an end. But the one God points our gaze far enough into the hidden "depths of His fatherly heart"[193] when, within time and history, He gives forth His Son, as also when He sends the Spirit, and permits us in that fashion to become somewhat aware of the inner workings of life within the Trinity; and yet God still reveals Himself to us within time as the one who existed in Himself before all time and before the world came to be. As is true of the inner workings within the Trinity Himself, revelation thus proceeds, as well, from God, the Father; it reaches us through the Son, the *Logos*, who became human by means of the Spirit, the *Pneuma* that was sent. Jesus Christ functions for us as the mirror that shows the fatherly heart of God, and the Spirit leads us to the Son.

---

[192] WA 50:275.1–26 (AE 34:197–229); cf. also "Von den letzten Worten Davids, 1543," WA 54:58.15–33; 63.29–64.7 (AE 15:265–352).
[193] *BSLK*, 660.30 (LC).

The Son reveals Himself to us only in the Spirit; the Father, only through the Son.[194]

All three articles of faith are incorporated into this self-revelation of God in His nature as Trinity, which depicts the economy of salvation.[195] God created us, so that "He might redeem us and make us holy."[196] The reformer sets forth this self-revelation of God by means of creation, redemption, and sanctification in the Confession of 1528,[197] and in the Large Catechism,[198] as a comprehensive overview of the three articles. In creation, the Father gifts us "with heaven and earth, and all creatures, so that they serve us and are to be useful for us."[199] We have forfeited and lost this self-giving nature of God as our good creator because of the original fall of Adam. For this reason, the Son gives Himself to us in the work of redemption, freely providing us the gift of all His "works, suffering, wisdom, and righteousness"; He reconciles us with the Father, "so that we can once again be alive and righteous, so that we can recognize and have a relationship with the Father and all His gifts."[200] But the deliverance from tyranny under the destructive powers, along with the reconciliation with God the Father through the offering of His Son, must still be appropriated

---

[194] *BSLK*, 660.38–47. Along with the Western tradition, the reformer adopts the *filioque* wording, or, said another way, that the Spirit proceeds "*ab, ex, de utroque*" (Augustine, *De Trinitate* 15:26.47); among other passages, see *BSLK*, 414.17 (SA); "Pred. über Joh. 1:1 vom 25.12.1514," WA 1:28.17; "Op. in Ps., 1518–21," WA 5:185.26; "Gen.-Vorl., 1535–45," WA 42:273.2; 275.15 (AE 2:1–399); "Pred. über Röm. 11:33ff. vom 27.5.1537," WA 45:90.15; "Die drei Symbola, 1538," WA 50:274.13; 275.3 (AE 34:197–229). And yet he never polemicizes specifically against the Eastern Church's decision, set forth by John of Damascus (*De fide orthodoxa* 1.8), that the Spirit is not from the Son, even though He is called the Spirit of the Son. The reformer seizes on John of Damascus's concern to preserve the primacy of place to the Father, when he says: "The Father is the origin or source (which is what one ought to say, as do the fathers) of the deity, from whom the Son has deity, and the Holy Spirit from Son and Father in eternity" ("Von den letzten Worten Davids, 1543," WA 54:64.4 [AE 15:265–352]; cf. "Promotionsdisp. von Georg Major vom 12.12.1544," WA 39.2:293.3ff.). These words remind one of precise formulas of the Decretal for the Jacobites, 1442 (Denzinger, 1331), or for the Greeks, 1439 (Denzinger, 1300); see also Peter Lombard, *Sententiarum* I, dist. 11f. Cf. Ullmann, *Das filioque als Problem ökumenischer Theologie*.

[195] *BSLK*, 660.27–38.

[196] *BSLK*, 660.33.

[197] "Vom Abendmahl Christi, 1528," WA 26:506.38–507.12 (AE 37:151–372).

[198] *BSLK*, 660.27–47.

[199] "Vom Abendmahl Christi, 1528," WA 26:505.40 (AE 37:151–372).

[200] Ibid., 505.42.

to us in the sanctifying activity that comes through the Spirit; "thus the Holy Spirit comes and gives Himself to us absolutely completely";[201] He brings us to the Son and through Him to the fatherly heart of God "inwardly through the faith and other spiritual gifts, but externally through the Gospel, through baptism and the Sacrament of the Altar. Through these, as through three means or ways, He comes to us and works the suffering of Christ in us, and for [our] benefit He brings us salvation."[202] "These are the three persons and the one God, who absolutely completely gave Himself to us with everything that He is and has."[203] The Father gives Himself to us as a gift in the First Article, along with all creatures; the Son does the same in the Second Article, with His work of redemption; and the Spirit does likewise in the Third Article with all His gifts.[204]

But Luther does not differentiate the self-revelation of God as the Father in the Son through the Spirit in this resumé of the Creed in sufficient detail to avoid the appearance of a "naïve Tritheism" or even that the trinitarian persons arrive on the scene one after the other in the economy of salvation. Since the reformer seems to assign the works of creation, redemption, and sanctification each to only one person of the Trinity, the appropriation of unique activities of each person to each person is thereby solidified.[205] The basic Augustinian statement, "*Opera trinitatis ad extra sunt indivisa*" (the actions of the Trinity are externally indivisible), which Luther often cites approvingly,[206] seems to undergo damage. Since these unique activities are assigned at each point to just one person as a sign and point of recognition, God the Father, Son, and Holy Spirit each present themselves within history, but each at a different point. Just as within human history the Father appears at the beginning when the genders are created, the Son effects redemption under Pontius Pilate

[201] Ibid., 506.4.
[202] Ibid., 506.8.
[203] Ibid., 505.38.
[204] *BSLK*, 660.35–42 (LC).
[205] The Nuremberg Catechetical Sermons formulate this specifically, on the basis of the teaching about the Trinity that had been explicated: "But now God the Lord has three kinds of work, which He works out on our behalf and continues to practice, until He gives us bliss and brings us to eternal life, just as He is also threefold, namely, Father, Son, and Holy Ghost" (Reu, *Quellen*, 1.1:507.28).
[206] The Scholastic tradition inherited this from Augustine, *De Trinitate* 5:5ff.; 6:11ff.; cf. passages such as in "Von den letzten Worten Davids, 1543," WA 54:57.31–58.14; 60.31–61.6 (AE 15:265–352).

in Palestine, and the Spirit carries out His work of sanctification among us from Pentecost until the consummation of the world;[207] thus it seems, as well, in the life of the individual believer, that the creative work of God the Father, the redemptive work of God the Son, and the sanctifying work of the Spirit[208] come in succession, one after another.

This impression is left by the fact that the reformer introduces the second and third persons of the Trinity, in both the Small Catechism and the Large Catechism, in each case only according to the work that is attributed to each and thus of necessity can intimate a trinitarian connection only at that point. Once again, we encounter the unique connection to what has preceded, which provided links already, between the three main sections.[209] Thus, with respect to both the Small and Large Catechisms, Luther mentions neither the Son nor the Spirit in the First Article,[210] and the Spirit is likewise never mentioned in the Second Article. By contrast, Luther does refer back to the Father in the Second Article,[211] and, more than elsewhere, the name of the Son dominates the Third Article in the Small Catechism,[212] since the office and work of the Spirit, the "Holy One," is "nothing other than to bring one to the LORD Christ."[213]

This provides us with a point of reference for rightly assessing the arrangement of the three articles in the catechisms: From one vantage point, the Second and Third Articles, dealing with redemption and sanctification, are deeply interwoven, since the office of the Spirit is to apply the work of Christ without interruption. By contrast, the creative activity of the Father is uniquely isolated. In this way, Luther arranges two activities of God in relation to each other in his interpretation of the Creed, God's work of creation in the temporal realm and God's work of redemption in His spiritual realm. The reformer turns our attention in the First Article especially to the "daily blessings"[214] "of this body and life";[215] only in the Second and Third

---

[207] *BSLK*, 659.44–660.3 (LC).

[208] Ibid., 647.12–19.

[209] Cf. Volume 1, pp. 46–51.

[210] The exception is *BSLK*, 650.27–33 (LC); anticipating the Second and Third Articles only underscores this observation.

[211] Ibid., 651.43; 652.8.

[212] It is mentioned three times, in *BSLK*, 511.47; 512.7, 12.

[213] *BSLK*, 654.39f. (LC).

[214] *BSLK*, 651.12.

[215] *BSLK*, 510.40 (SC); 650.29 (LC).

Articles does he raise our sights to direct our attention to our eschatological deliverance.

Because of this, what is set forth in the First Article brings us into murky waters; neither our standing under God's wrath nor our renewed access to the goodness of the Father's creative gifts in the offering of Christ, and in the sending of the Spirit, can be explicated completely. It is rather intimated indirectly and is made explicit only in the summarizing section at the end of the Large Catechism.[216]

Luther characterizes our sinful lost condition only in the Second Article, in the thick colors of imprisonment by the powers of death and the forces of Satan,[217] from which Christ extracts us. Since the First Article comes before the explicit reference to the fall of humanity, a shimmering wisp of the glory of Paradise still hovers over the scene. In neither the Small Catechism nor the Large Catechism does Luther mention that the fatherly provisions of the good things, which are part of our everyday existence, are not all that surrounds us; the punishing judgment of His curse surrounds us as well,[218] that countenance of the "wrathful and terrorizing judge,"[219] to which reference is made in the threat that comes at the conclusion of the interpretation of the Decalogue.[220] Such a reference is appended only in the conclusion to the commentary on the Symbol. Within the interpretation of the First Article itself, the "*vestigia irae Dei . . . in corpore nostro . . . in terra et in omnibus creaturis*" (the vestiges of the wrath of God . . . in our body . . . , on earth and within all creatures) are dulled[221] by the radiant glow of the *all*-encompassing care provided by God.[222]

From a different vantage point, Luther also intimates only indirectly that the offering of God's Son is present already, in a hidden way, within His fatherly provisions of the good things of creation, in that he allows us to confess: The unseen God turns toward us daily with His "fatherly, divine goodness and mercy" and holds onto us "all without" our "merit or worthiness."[223] The later

---

[216] *BSLK*, 660.18–661.18.
[217] *BSLK*, 511.23–30 (SC); 651.42–653.3 (LC).
[218] *BSLK*, 661.14.
[219] *BSLK*, 660.43f.
[220] *BSLK*, 510.15–18 (SC); on this, see Volume 1, pp. 128–141.
[221] "Gen.-Vorl., 1535–45," WA 42:155.36 (AE 1:1–359).
[222] In the Small Catechism, the little word "all" is used ten times.
[223] *BSLK*, 511.4f. (SC); cf. *BSLK*, 648.42–649.2; 650.21–33; 651.10–22 (LC).

catechisms found a gap at this point as well. By using the explications[224] from the early Church, they inserted once again the Christological and trinitarian references into this imagery of creation and preservation.[225] In addition, at the conclusion to the Large Catechism, Luther merely intimates that we arrive at our proper relationship with the creation only through the redemption in Christ and the work of the Spirit; but even here he does not state that the creation itself has arrived at its proper relationship already by the action of God, the Father, through the Son, the *Logos*, by means of the Breath, the *Pneuma*.

At this point, we need to expand upon and correct the catechisms by using Luther's words about the activity of the Trinity in the creation.[226] Since the reformer stays close to the sequence of events that are described in the Apostles' Creed, Luther cannot fully integrate the biblical insights offered in the confessions from the Eastern Church, as well as in the *Regula fidei*,[227] that God, the Father already creates and preserves the creatures in the Son, the *Logos* through the Breath, the *Pneuma*. His early interpretations of the Symbol include terminology that is used in the Nicene Creed, but such references are to a great extent removed here.[228]

---

[224] See passages such as in Rufinus, *Expositio symboli* 5 (CCSL 20:139–41); Peter Chrysologus, *Sermo* 60 (PL 52:366B); Pseudo-augustine, *Sermo* 237 (PL 39:2183f.).

[225] Dietenberger, *Katechismus* (Moufang, *Katholische Katechismen*, 14f.); *Genfer Kat.*, quest. 22; *Heidelberger Kat.* (Heidelberg Catechism), quest. 26; Erasmus, *Explanatio Symboli*, col. 1147A: "The Father created all things through the Son with the cooperation of the Holy Spirit."

[226] At this point, in addition to the texts cited on pp. 57–58, "Pred. über Joh. 1:1 vom 25.12.1514," WA 1:20–29; "Pred. zum Eingang in das 1. Buch Mose vom 22.3.1523," WA 12:447.22–451.24 = WA 14:100.7–101.20; "Pred. über Gen. 1, 1527," WA 24:28–32; "Gen.-Vorl., 1535–45," WA 42:8.15–29; 10.17–35; 13.11–17.32; 37.25–38.14(AE 1:1–359); "Pred. über Joh. 1:3–5 vom 14.7.1537," WA 46.558–64 (AE 22:1–530); "Von den letzten Worten Davids, 1543," WA 54:55.1–58.33 (AE 15:265–352).

[227] On this, see esp. Hägglund, *Die Bedeutung der "regula fidei."*

[228] Already in the Short Form of 1520, Luther merely mentions the Father as our creator and lord, without offering any reflection on the eternal Son-Logos, in whom we are created and brought into sonship, even though he placed "Ihesus" as the title over the entire interpretation of the Creed. He takes up the "through whom all things were made" (Denzinger, 150) of the Niceno-Constantinopolitan Creed only at the point of the Second Article and as an addendum designates the Son as the mediator of creation, having to do with the First Article in this sense: "I believe . . . that Jesus Christ . . . is placed over me and all things as a Lord according to His human nature, which He created with the Father according to His divine nature" (WA 7:217.6; cf.

That observation, that the reformer appropriates but does not exclusively attribute the creative activities to God the Father, finds support in his two solemn confessions, the Confession of 1528 and the Smalcald Articles, which honor the triune God as the creator.[229] He formulates this in a precise way in a disputation thesis: "*Indisputabilis veritas est, unum esse Deum et trinum, omnium rerum extra se creatorem unicum*" (It is indisputably true that God is one and three; the only creator of all things outside Himself).[230] In his Genesis commentaries, the Son, the *Logos*, is the creative Word and the Breath, the *Pneuma*, is the blessing of God the Father that brings pleasure onto His creatures. The Son is the "*ratio, imago et sapientia*" (reason, image, and wisdom)[231] of the Father who, in His "neverending birth"[232] before all time and before the world, is the *Logos*, being eternally begotten of the Father.[233] For His part, as the "great plow" of our Lord God, He calls creatures forth, from not existing into life, He "who is called: *DIXIT*."[234] The Spirit, the "*bonitas et charitas*" (goodness and grace),[235] proceeds eternally from the Father and the Son and yet "remains in this never-ending proceeding"[236] within Him in an ongoing fashion as the bond of love

---

"Weihnachtspost. über Hebr. 1:1–12, 1522," WA 10.1.1:152.16–153.9. The Spirit, as the "*Spiritus vivificans* (the life-giving Spirit)" (WA 11:53.30), is specifically designated as involved in God's work of creation only in the "Symbolpred. vom 6.3.1523": "The Father created heaven and earth with the Holy Spirit" (idem). In that the reformer increasingly de-emphasizes especially the Christological aspect of our createdness, but also the pneumatological aspect of that createdness, he allows himself to be guided by the decision that is already at the basis of the *Textus receptus* of the Apostles' Creed (cf. Scheffczyk, *Schöpfung und Vorsehung*, 25f.).

[229] "Vom Abendmahl Christi, 1528," WA 26:500.27–32 (AE 37:151–372); *BSLK*, 414.12–15 (SA).

[230] "Zirkulardisp. de veste nuptiali vom 15.6.1537," WA 39.1:287, Thesis 5.

[231] WA 42:15.3 (AE 1:1–359); "Pred. über Joh. 1:1 vom 25.12.1514," WA 1:24.7: "The Word is the counsel, wisdom, truth, judgment, and thought of God, whence Christ is called the wisdom and truth of God"; cf. "Promotionsdisp. von Petrus Hegemon vom 3.7.1545," WA 39.2:339, Thesis 8.

[232] "Die drei Symbola, 1538," WA 50:274.31 (AE 34:197–229).

[233] "Gen.-Vorl., 1535–45," WA 42:17.24 (AE 1:22): "The created word is brought into being by the uncreated Word. What else is the entire creation than the Word of God uttered by God, or extended to the outside? But the uncreated Word is a divine thought, an inner command which abides in God, the same as God and yet a distinct person"; cf. "Pred. über Joh. 1:1f. vom 7.7.1537," WA 46:543.23–33; 544.3–10; 546.23–30 (AE 22:1–530).

[234] "Gen.-Vorl., 1535–45," WA 42:27.3 (AE 1:1–359).

[235] "Op. in Ps., 1518–21," WA 5:198.31.

[236] "Die drei Symbola, 1538," WA 50:274.24 (AE 34:197–229).

"in" Him. He is God's creative bringer of pleasure and in that sense is the divine "band . . . that preserves all creatures and gives them all their tasks and work";[237] He is the *Spiritus creator et vivificator*.[238]

Luther thus uses the terminology from Paul's speech at the Areopagus in his 1519 Galatians commentary: "In Him we live and move and are" (Acts 17:28), which is extracted from popularized Greek philosophy, supposedly referring to the relationship that human beings have with God,[239] and he uses it to refer to our life in relationship with the triune God: "*Sumus propter patrem, qui substantia divinitatis est, movemur imagine filii, qui ex patre nascitur divino et aeterno velut motu motus, vivimus secundum spiritum, in quo pater et filius quiescunt et velut vivunt*" (We have our being because of the Father, who is the substance of the Godhead. We are moved by the image of the Son, who, moved by a divine and eternal motion, so to speak, is born of the Father. We live according to the Spirit, in whom the Father and Son rest and live, as it were [AE 27, on Gal. 5:6, 1519]).[240] The inner-trinitarian movement of love within God is reflected not only in His activities to bring about salvation; in light of His activity to bring salvation, the believer recognizes in the Scriptures that structure that is seen within the Godhead, as well, in God's work of creation; thus, Luther can craft the formula: "Now the Scriptures contain the manner, since they say: the world is created through Christ and is created by the Father and by means of the Holy Spirit, all of which has its reason . . . so that it is shown that the Father does not have existence from the Son, but that the Son has His divine

---

[237] "Pred. über Gen. 1, 1527," WA 24:30.26; cf. ibid., 30.1f.; "Weihnachtspost. über Joh. 1:1–14, 1522," WA 10.1.1:186.1f. (AE 52:41–88); "Gen.-Vorl., 1535–45," WA 42:38.7–14 (AE 1:1–359).

[238] "Promotionsdisp. von Petrus Hegemon vom 3.7.1545," WA 39.2:339.24; "Gen.-Vorl., 1535–45," WA 42:8.28 (AE 1:1–359). Luther's Pentecost hymns (see *EKG* 97–99 [*LSB* 498/499, 497, 768]) show that he is deeply grounded at this point in the concepts of the early Church and the early Middle Ages. But according to Church teaching, even these words deal only with applications of an indivisible power, strength, wisdom, goodness, and life-giving ability from God with respect to the three persons; cf. "Promotionsdisp. von Petrus Hegemon vom 3.7.1545," WA 39.2:339, Theses 7–10.

[239] According to Haenchen, *Die Apostelgeschichte*, 462.

[240] WA 2:536.28 (AE 27:151–410). This statement of Luther is quite unique, sounding much like the Augustinian-mystical interpretations of the *Vestigia trinitatis*, which Luther set forth in his Christmas sermon of 1514 (WA 1:20–29).

nature from the Father and that the Father is the first original person in the Godhead."[241]

For the reformer, as for the Christian Church in general at the time of the early Church and during the Middle Ages, the creation is thus the work of the entire Trinity; "it is a single one that makes it, and a single work, which all three persons create."[242] In a certain contrast to the Augustinian and Thomistic-Scholastic tradition, however, Luther turns toward the beginning point of the Scriptures, where the Father is God, pure and simple, and thus brings back to life the view of the fathers up to the point of the Cappadocians. That God turns toward the world, and also the inner-trinitarian life of God, is characterized by the prepositions: ἐκ—διά—ἐν (εἰς) (*ex—per—in*).[243] Even God's work of creation thus appears within the clearly recognizable structure in which God reveals His nature in His saving activity. In creation, redemption, and sanctification, God the Father reveals and gifts Himself to us through the Son by means of the Holy Spirit and thus makes it possible for us to participate in the divine life that is within Him.

Different Emphases in the Assessment and Arrangement of the Three Articles

The insight that the reformer continues to reiterate, that God is always giving Himself through the Son by means of the Spirit, clarifies the reason why he does not treat each of the individual articles in exactly the same way. For this reason, interesting shifts in emphasis can be observed in the way this plays out.

Those who engage in catechetical studies, as well as those who are engaged in scholarly research about Luther, proceed from what is a *communis opinio*: "The actual center of the Small Catechism"—and this applies to the Large Catechism as well—is "the Second Chief

---

241 "Weihnachtspost. über Hebr. 1:1–12, 1522," WA 10.1.1:152.16; similarly, "Pred. über den 2. und 3. Art. vom 5.3.1523," WA 11:51.15f.; "Op. in Ps., 1518–21," WA 5:185.4ff.; "Crucigers Sommerpost. über Röm. 11:33–36 auf Trinitatis, 1544," WA 21:521.31–34; "Pred. über Joh. 1:3 vom 14.7.1537," WA 46:558.15–32 (AE 22:1–530).

242 "Von den letzten Worten Davids, 1543," WA 54:57.20 (AE 15:265–352).

243 One can allow oneself to be guided at this point by the ancient form of the doxology: "Glory be to the Father through the Son in the Holy Spirit!" Cf., on this, Dörries, *De Spiritu sancto*, esp. 44–51, and Kretschmar, *Studien zur frühchristlichen Trinitätstheologie*, 134–96.

Part, with the three articles that deal with the Creed"; within that chief part, to carry the discussion further, "the most central part that cuts to the heart of the matter is the Second Article"; consequently, this has to be considered to be the unstated central point "not only of the Second Chief Part but also of the entire Small Catechism."[244] But Luther's unique way of going back and forth between statements that accentuate widely different aspects shows us that we ought not to isolate the Second Article so absolutely as one might tend to do because of the impetus of its strongly Christocentric formulation in the Small Catechism. Luther does not proceed from an understanding of the Second Article, in terms of its central focus, to concentrate unilaterally on Christ becoming lord over our life; in everything that he describes, the reformer looks much rather, in all aspects, to the way God gifts Himself to us as our gracious Father through the Son by means of the Spirit and thus, at the same time, on how we are being brought by the Spirit, through the Son, to the Father.

This emphasis is articulated more clearly in the Large Catechism. It is here that Luther says: The "entire *Evangelion*" can be summarized in this article "on which our entire salvation and blessed future depends":[245] Christ, as our lord and redeemer, has brought us forth "from the devil to God, from death to life, from sin to righteousness," and preserves us in that same relationship.[246] In the conclusion, Luther demonstrates that it is only in this article that we are set apart from all other human beings, as those who believe in Christ.[247] Even if such as are outside that relationship still yearn to remain connected to God as their creator and preserver, His fatherly heart is still hidden from them beneath the punishing judgment of His wrath. Without trust in the mercy of Christ, they persist in being under the curse of the Law. For this reason, the reformer maintains that this article is and remains central, as it states "that the office and work of Jesus Christ, [what affects] our salvation,"[248] is the root and fruit of our faith; "everything that we teach and live in opposition to the pope, the devil, and the world is in this article."[249] But this

---

[244] Hoffmann, *Der Kleine Katechismus als Abriß der Theologie Martin Luthers*, 57. On this section, cf. Meyer, *Apostolikum*, 17–29.
[245] *BSLK*, 653.13f.
[246] *BSLK*, 652.28f.
[247] *BSLK*, 661.5–18.
[248] *BSLK*, 415.4f. (SA).
[249] *BSLK*, 416.3f. (SA).

reformational "*articulus stantis et cadentis ecclesiae*" (article on which the Church stands or falls)[250] encompasses much more than the isolated teaching about redemption or even justification; it circumscribes the way that God reveals Himself as our gracious Father as He gives forth His Son and as He sends forth the Spirit, which we can receive only by means of the word of promise in the Gospel.

In Luther's diverse statements, which accentuate various emphases, he articulates at the same time many dimensions of what it means that God turns toward us.

In the Short Form of 1520, he speaks of confession of the Trinity as the "highest article" of the faith, "on which all the other articles depend";[251] in the Confession of 1528 and in the Smalcald Articles he speaks of "the highest article[s] of divine majesty."[252] When we praise the Holy Trinity and Undivided Unity, we press forward "high above all angels and all heavens"[253] into the unfathomable mystery of God Himself, about which we can have little more than a vague awareness by faith while here on earth and can make confession merely with stuttering voices. Despite this, we are certain that God, in the innermost depth of His being, is none other than the one who reveals Himself in redemption and creation. The exalted nature of these mysteries of the Trinity, as well as their all-encompassing breadth, receives expression when Luther brings it all together with the formulaic phrase: "*Est supremus articulus fidei.*"[254]

In the Creedal Commentary of 1523, as well as in his early sermons on Genesis, Luther set the First Article into the foreground. He tirelessly restated the point: trust firmly in the fact that God is our good creator and gracious father; for us poor, miserable sinners this is the most important and hardest point, in our creaturely condition, for which reason one must call the First Article "The most important part:

---

250 Cf. Loofs, *Der articulus stantis et cadentis ecclesiae*.

251 WA 7:214.27.

252 "Vom Abendmahl Christi, 1528," WA 26:500.23 (AE 37:151–372); *BSLK*, 414.10 (SA). "Pred. über Joh. 3:1ff. vom 31.5.1523," WA 11:122.6: "*Est supremus articulus fidei*"; "Pred. über Joh. 1:1 vom 27.12.1532" WA 36:411.13: "That is the highest article, which Christians have"; similarly, "Pred. über Röm. 11:33ff. vom 27.5.1537," WA 21:508.13 = WA 45:89.18; "Pred. über die Trinität vom 23.5.1535," WA 41:270.9f.; "Pred. über die Trinität vom 16.6.1538," WA 46:436.5f.; "Pred. über Joh. 1:1f. vom 7.7.1537," WA 46:541.4–11 (AE 22:1–530).

253 "Pred. über die Trinität vom 23.5.1535," WA 41:270.20.

254 "Pred. über Joh. 10:1ff. vom 26.5.1523," WA 11:122.6.

I believe [upon] the Father, the Creator! This article is the highest; Christ leads [us] to Him through the Spirit."[255] Only a very few human beings can dare to risk trusting on such a level that they consider God, as their creator, to be the one who guarantees their entire existence, to the extent that He holds onto them every second to protect them from the abyss of nothingness;[256] "such a person must be dead to all things, good and evil, death and life, hell and heaven."[257] This insight reverberates in the Large Catechism, where Luther warns and opines: How few recognize God in concrete, everyday existence as their lord and creator; we all stand under the judgment of this article.[258]

In Sermons on the Symbol that date to March 4 & 5, 1523, Luther inserts reference to Christ already here in the relationship of trust with the fatherly creator, at which point he distinguishes between "*confessio*" and "*instructio*."[259] According to the "order of the topics to be considered," the Symbol begins with the First Article, without any further ado, with the eternal and invisible God, with the "*Deus nudus in majestate sua*"; but according to the "sequence of what is known," which is at the root of the topic, he maintains that one must, at that point already, be drawn up concurrently onto another path as well, to the highly exalted God via the means of the God who was "wrapped up within"[260] the humanity of Christ.[261] This is the proper

---

[255] "Pred. über den 1. Art. vom 4.3.1523," WA 11:49.4; ibid., 50.27: "The First Article, that I believe God is my Father, is the highest article"; cf. "Sermon u. Eingang in das 1. Buch Mose vom 15.3.1523," WA 12:439.16–26; "Pred. über Gen. 1 vom 22.3.1523," WA 14:98.17–23; "Vorrede auf die Gen.-Predigten von 1527," WA 24:18.8–14, 24–33; 21.6–23.8 or else 21.27–23.32. On this section, see also Meyer, *Doppelgestalt*.

[256] "Sermon u. Eingang in das 1. Buch Mose vom 22.3.1523," WA 14:97.15: "But few are able to confess that God does everything, because if one does this, he confesses that he can do nothing himself."

[257] "Sermon u. Eingang in das 1. Buch Mose vom 22.3.1523," WA 12:439.20; cf. "Pred. über den 1. Art. vom 4.3.1523," WA 11:50.4f.

[258] *BSLK*, 649.15–41.

[259] WA 11:51.29: "When confessing, it is fitting that you begin from what is the highest, when instructing, from the human nature of Christ."

[260] WA 11:52.7.

[261] Karl Barth makes use of the way this is differentiated when he states in his explication of the Creed: The Apostles' Creed "apparently [seeks to] describe the order of events, the path God takes as He comes down," rather than to "organize the knowledge"; the Second Article is certainly the beginning point for that stage (Barth, *Credo*, 38f.). Barth accentuates the Second Article; for him, "it is the source of light,

arrangement of the Scriptures, which leads us to the Father only through the Son and to the creator via the redeemer.[262]

We stand once again at the central thesis offered by the concluding summary in the Large Catechism: The fatherly heart of the creator reveals itself to us only in the Son and redeemer.[263] When Luther plumbs the depths of true faith in Christ in the First Article, already in the Short Form of 1520 and in the Sermons on the Symbol from 1523,[264] he does so by having Christ and the Spirit, and thus the Second and Third Articles, present here already, since true faith is nothing other than "complete reliance [up]on God"[265] in our concrete existence; this complete trust in God comes according to the Good News about Christ as the gracious work of the Spirit of God.

And yet, since one cannot reverse the direction of the eschatological movement—from our being created to the point of salvation in Christ—it must be said that God "actually created us in order that He might redeem and sanctify us."[266] As is stated in Luther's Creedal Commentary of 1523, this forces one to articulate this "twofold starting point."[267] Our existence as human beings precedes our being Christian, both temporally and materially; even the human being who remains enslaved under his guilt and has not yet been reached by the Gospel exists within the context of the good things that are all around, as well as under the anonymous demands of his creator. For this reason, the First Article can also be explicated without one thereby starting, *expressis verbis*, with the redemption in Christ. This is the path that Luther traverses in the sermons of 1528 and in the catechisms. At this point, he accentuates more intensively the word "creator" and lets the word "father" stay in the background. Despite this, as we have shown,[268] Luther's statements concerning the

---

by means of which the other two are illuminated"; from a historical point of view, it is also the source for the entire Creed (Barth, *Dogmatik im Grundriß*, § 10, 69).

[262] WA 11:52.5: "through the one wrapped in flesh we come to the Father."

[263] *BSLK*, 660.28–47.

[264] WA 7:215f. and WA 11:49.1–50.36.

[265] Ebeling, *Das Wesen des christlichen Glaubens*, 88ff.

[266] *BSLK*, 660.32f.

[267] In the present theological debates, Gustav Wingren has made a valid point over against Barth's Christocentric starting point; in this way he accentuates the need for a "twofold starting point" (Wingren, *Schöpfung und Gesetz*, 187f.; idem, *Evangelium und Kirche*, 93, 109).

[268] Cf. pp. 42–44.

First Article in the catechisms are made, as well, in light of deliverance in Christ.

With this "twofold starting point" Luther accentuates God's fatherly nature in his earlier explications of the Creed and emphasizes the full sense of faith in Jesus Christ in the First Article; in this way, "belief in God the Father" can and must appear as the "crown" of the entire Christian Church.[269]

In the catechisms, by contrast, the reformer reduces his treatment of the First Article to what is involved in the temporal realm of the creator and His earthly gifts that bring blessings, so that this article functions more as a possible point of entry to the full Gospel about our salvation in Christ, even for those who are not Christian.[270] Despite this, Luther has the act of redemption in mind from the very beginning. Thus one must say: The reformer starts out neither with the one-sided treatment of Karl Barth, who goes right to the Christ event, sketching the arch backward to the point of God's creation of humans, nor does he travel the road with the Norwegian Lutherans by starting simply with the concept of being human and then becoming Christian;[271] instead, he unfolds the interplay in its lively connectedness, though it cannot be reconstructed rationally, in which he continues to introduce new aspects, ever and again, into one and the same picture of our existence as Christian human beings.

But since Luther does limit the First Article in his Catechetical Sermons of 1528, and in the catechisms themselves, to an articulation of the gifts of blessing that are provided by the creator, the Second Article takes on greater weight; it draws us into the center of the discussion. It is thus only after 1528/29 that Luther designates, in a unique way, how the article about our redemption in Christ is the "*verus Christianus articulus*" (really Christian article),[272] and that it is

---

[269] Meyer, *Apostolikum*, 19; cf. idem, *Doppelgestalt*, 539 and, in addition, Ritschl, *Unterricht*, §§ 12ff., 51.

[270] *BSLK*, 661.5–18.

[271] The order: first human, then Christ is articulated particularly by Grundtvig: "Human being first, and Christ afterward, that is a major point; we receive the Christian faith for no reason, it is pure good fortune, but it is the kind of good fortune that only encounters one who is already basically God's friend, from the honorable family tree of truth!" (cited from Prenter, *Schöpfung und Erlösung*, 1:264, n. 94).

[272] "Kat.-Pred. zum 2. Art. vom 10.12.1528," WA 30.1:90.20 (AE 51:162–169); "Osterpred. vom 28.3.1529," WA 29:266.4: "Whoever understands this article is a Christian."

the "chief article" of our Christian existence.[273] In the comments made in 1523, where this insight was still being inserted into the discussion about trusting in God as the heavenly father, this thought is anticipated already, when Luther says: "*Totum Euangelium est in symbol . . . Euangelium enim nihil aliud docet quam Jesum Christum*" (The entire Gospel is in the Symbol . . . the Gospel certainly teaches nothing but Jesus Christ).[274]

Luther had hardly finished placing the accent on the Second Article in the Catechetical Sermons of 1528 when he pressed on still further, especially in the Large Catechism, beyond this article to give special accent to the Third Article. In this way, he deals with the inner workings of the Scriptures, which press on from creation, and then through redemption, to arrive at the new creation. In one respect, the Third Article is without question an "assisting article" that provides support for the Second Article, being articulated with respect to it and in service to it.[275] But, in another regard, especially in the Large Catechism, Luther unfolds the office and work of the Spirit more extensively and in a more penetrating way than when he describes the office and work of Christ. The decision about whether redemption and creation, which leads to salvation, is carried out for us is attributed, in the end, to the activity of the Spirit, so that we do not in fact end up in eternal damnation. Thus, for the catechisms, it is certainly proper to state the following thesis: the accent is placed on the Third Article, even though one can cite no comparable parallel evidence where Luther designates this as the most important or chief article. But one can garner a significant number of indirect statements as evidence.

In the opening summary in the Large Catechism, Luther uses the present tense only when describing the work of the Spirit: "I believe [up]on God the Father, who *has* created me; I believe [up]on God the Son, who *has* redeemed me, I believe [up]on the Holy Spirit, who *makes* me holy."[276] That this goes deep, to the heart of the matter for

---

[273] Cf. "Pred. über Joh. 8:46ff. vom 14.3.1529," WA 29:131.12; "Osterpred. vom 28.3.1529," WA 29:276.10; "Pred. über Joh. 6:52f. vom 4.3.1531," WA 33:193.10; 197.24; 200.9 (AE 23:1–197); "Die drei Symbola, 1538," WA 50:266.33 (AE 34:197–229); further examples are in Meyer, *Historischer Kommentar*, 281.
[274] "Pred. über den 1. Art. vom 4.3.1523," WA 11:48.23.
[275] Cf. Meyer, *Apostolikum*, 43; idem, *Historischer Kommentar*, 374; this is accepted by Thieme, *Die Augsburgische Konfession und Luthers Katechismen*, 169f.
[276] *BSLK*, 647.14–17.

Luther, is seen when he makes the point at the conclusion of the Third Article: creation and redemption lie in what is in the past for us; only the work of the Spirit leads us on into God's eschatological future.[277] Already in the here and now the Spirit is bringing about our eschatological renewal, in that He richly forgives all our sins every day. Everything that takes place in the Christian life is oriented on the basis of this ongoing forgiveness of sins;[278] this is what serves the Gospel; on its account the sacraments are instituted in the same way as are the offices of the Church.[279] Forgiveness of sins, life, and salvation all appear once again to provide orientation and they serve as the central terms in baptism, the Lord's Supper, and confession. We are reminded of the words from the sermon of December 19, 1528: All the articles of the Creed first take on concrete form for us in forgiveness. "If these are . . . to come to us by experience and are to confront us, thus it is in this article they are to come to us by experience and must apply to us, so that all of us, I for myself, you for yourself, each person for his own self, believes in the forgiveness of sins."[280] Thus, in the sense Luther intends it, one could certainly say: Because the *Applicatio salutis* (application of salvation) and, therewith, "the great, high article *de remissione peccatorum*" (of the remission of sins)[281] is given its proper home in the Third Article,[282] the most important element of what is articulated in the Creed, as far as we are concerned, is the office and work of the Holy Spirit. But this statement of Luther would abbreviate too radically the overall witness of the Creed as a whole.

By way of summary we need to say: the center of the catechisms for Luther is not the Second Article of the Creed, in a narrowly focused and isolated sense, though one might assume that to be the case merely by looking at the wording in the Small Catechism; instead, the center is in the entirety of the way God turns toward us as our Father through the Son by means of the Holy Spirit. This revelation of self and this gifting of self on the part of the triune God

---

[277] *BSLK*, 659.44–660.3.

[278] *BSLK*, 658.25–35.

[279] *BSLK*, 658.10–25.

[280] WA 28:272.29.

[281] "Pred. über Mt. 9:1ff. vom 5.10.1529," WA 29:564.7.

[282] That would still result in the difficulty that Luther understands the article about justification concurrently and primarily as an article about Christ; cf. Meyer, *Apostolikum*, 24f.

must always be envisioned as one whole activity, from the point of view of the way He turns toward us. Thus, in his first commentary on the Creed, Luther places the accent on our confidence in God the Father, who rules over the whole world, to whom the Son and the Spirit lead us; in the later commentaries, central importance is directed rather to the Second and Third Articles. This overall description of the revelation of God can be set forth schematically in the following statements:

(1) In the gracious way He turned toward the world, the triune God reveals to us the mystery of the internal workings of His divine nature and, in this way also, we are presented with the "high article of divine majesty."

(2) God reveals Himself to us as the gracious Father, however, only in the offering that led to death and in the resurrection of Jesus of Nazareth; for this reason, our salvation is dependent upon the Second Article as the "chief article," which deals with "the office and work of Jesus Christ, with our redemption."[283]

(3) In Jesus of Nazareth the eternal God reaches down to us in a fatherly way; for this reason, we do not need to know Him merely with trembling, as the sinister power on high, who forced us into being, who threatens us with death, and who causes terror in our conscience. We are to call out to Him in the light of the Christ event as a benevolent father and creator, as one whose unseen hand of grace enwraps us to keep us safe from all external threats and from agonizing internal struggles. To this extent, the concrete "faith in God the Father" in the First Article appears in Luther's early commentaries on the Creed as the "crown of the Christian Church."

(4) But God is not merely giving us a way to mark time in this earthly life, which ends up with the downhill journey into death; by means of Word and Sacrament He prepares us to encounter His eschatological future; by means of the forgiveness of our guilt, He sanctifies us day by day and prepares us for His eternal lordship. Along with our existence

---

[283] *BSLK*, 415.4f. (SA).

as created beings, the Christ event is situated in what happened in the past; only the work of the Spirit, which provides an opening for us already now, affords us a future that will be present beyond our earthly death. What is thus articulated for the believer in the Creed in the Third Article, as a witness to the office and work of the Spirit, is the "high article of the forgiveness of sins."

The confusing way Luther alternates among terms that praise the articles as "high," "highest," and "the high article" unfolds aspects of one and the same activity of God, who turns in our direction as our Father[284] through the Son, Jesus Christ, in and with the Holy Spirit, thereby presenting various aspects of that one overall activity. Despite the various nuances and perspectives from which such knowledge is established and viewed, the insight provided in the sermon of March 5, 1523, still stands: "*Scriptur hunc habet morem, ut per Christum ad patrem nobis iter demonstret, et hoc facit* zum dritten *per spiritum sanctum, hoc est quod venio ad patrem auxilio Christi et opere spiritus sancti*" (Scripture works in this way, that it shows us the way through Christ to the Father; the third point is that this is done through the Holy Spirit; this is because I come to the Father with the help of Christ and by the action of the Holy Spirit).[285]

Literature on Luther's Views on the Apostles' Creed

Kattenbusch, *Luther's Stellung zu den ökumenischen Symbolen*

Kinder, *Der Gebrauch des Begriffs "ökumenisch" im alten Luthertum*

Köhler, *Luther und die Kirchengeschichte*, chs. 5, 6, 9

Koopmans, *Das altkirchliche Dogma in der Reformation*

Meyer, *Luther und das Apostolikum*

Prenter, *Spiritus Creator*, 177–87, 238–45

O. Ritschl, *Dogmengeschichte des Protestantismus*, 1:268–75

Steck, *Undogmatisches Christentum?*

Wolf, *Asterisci und Obelisci zum Thema: Luther und Athanasius*

---

[284] Girgensohn, *Katechismus-Auslegung*, 1:110: "God's name as Father is actually the gift by means of which He communicates to us all of His love, and this is the gift that is set forth in detail in the Gospel presented in the three articles of faith."

[285] WA 11:51.12.

Sources and Literature Dealing with the Development of the Apostles' Creed in the Early Church and in the Middle Ages

Sources

Hahn, *Bibliothek*

Lietzmann, *Symbole*

Denzinger, 1–76

Literature

Adam, *Lehrbuch der Dogmengeschichte*, 1:194–200

Adam/Hoffmann, art. "Apostolikum"

Crehan, *Early Christian Baptism and the Creed*

Cullmann, *Die ersten christlichen Glaubensbekenntnisse*

Dörries, *Das Bekenntnis in der Geschichte der Kirche*

Eichenseer, *Apostolicum*

Ghellinck, *Patristique et moyenage* (Literature!)

Kattenbusch, *Symbol*

Kelly, Art. "Apostolisches Glaubensbekenntnis"

_____. *Creeds*

Lietzmann, *Symbolstudien*

Trillhaas, *Das Apostolische Glaubensbekenntnis*

For the Middle Ages

Wiegand, *Symbol und Katechumenat*. Part 1

_____. *Das apostolische Symbol im Mittelalter*

Weidenhiller, *Untersuchungen*, esp. 17f., 228f.

Cf. also *BSLK*, XIVf.

Texts and Literature on Luther's Views on the Trinity

WA 5:184.4–188.9; 197.36–199.16: Operationes in Ps., 1518–21 (on the Tetragrammaton and on the Gloria Patri)*

WA 10.1.1:147–80: Weihnachtspost. 1522 on Hebr. 1:1–12

WA 10.1.1:180–88: Weihnachtspost. 1522 on Joh. 1:1–14 (AE 52:41–88)

WA 11:450.27–451.20: Vom Anbeten d. Sakraments d. hl. Leichnams Christi, 1523 (AE 36:269–305)

WA 12:585–91: Trinitätspred. from 15.6.1522

WA 21:508–22 = WA 45:89–93: Crucigers Sommerpost., Pred. über Röm. 11:33–36 from 27.5.1537

WA 36:407–11: Pred. über Joh. 1:1–14 from 27.12.1532

WA 39.2:287f.: Promotionsthesen 1–26 für Georg Major from 12.12.1544

WA 39.2:339f.: Promotionsthesen 1–17 für Petrus Hegemon from 3.7.1545

WA 41:270–79: Trinitatispred. from 23.5.1535

WA 43:11.18–14.17: Gen.-Vorl. on Gen. 18, 1535–45* (AE 3:1–365)

WA 45:89–93: Trinitatispred. from 27.5.1537*

WA 49:233–54: Pred. über Joh. 1:1, 14 from 25.12.1541

WA 50:273.22–282.29: "Die drei Symbola," 1538* (AE 34:197–229)

WA 54:34–92: Von den letzten Worten Davids, 1543* (AE 15:265–352)

LITERATURE

Jansen, *Studien zu Luthers Trinitätslehre*

Knolle, *Hebräische Heilsnamen in Luthers Liedern*

Koopmans, *Die altkirchliche Dogma in der Reformation*

Von Loewenich, *Die Eigenart in Luthers Auslegung des Johannes-Prologs*

Peters, *Trinitätslehre*

Prenter, *Spiritus Creator*

Schwarzwäller, *Theologia crucis*

Thieme, *Tritheismus 1529 und 1929*

_____. *Zur Trinitätsfrage*

Wobbermin, *Die Frage nach Gott in Luthers Großem Katechismus*

_____. *Luthers trinitarischer Monotheismus*

*Peters additionally included excerpts from these texts and from the texts noted on page 44, note 226, in the manuscript (note from the editor).

The First Article about God as Our Creator

Luther's Efforts concerning the Correct Catechetical Form of Interpretation for the First Article[1]

Luther presents the First Article as it had been rendered in the tradition of the Middle Ages: "I believe [up]on God, the Father almighty, maker of the heavens and the earth."[2] It has been mentioned already[3] that he reverts to the earlier rendering "I believe [up]*on*," instead of "I believe *in* (*credo in*), which had come into common use since the fifteenth century. The attribute "almighty" was applied during the Middle Ages exclusively to the Father; at this point, the Old German "*fater almahtigon*"[4] shows its influence. At the time of the Reformation, the adjective began to be connected with the word creator.[5] Since Luther emphasizes this word in his later interpretations, the attribute itself becomes especially important for him on its own merits.[6]

The understanding of the First Article was solidified in such a way that the presentation followed the same pattern in both catechisms; Luther sought to articulate this catechetical framework in his sermon on December 15, 1528.[7]

---

[1] Literature: Meyer, *Doppelgestalt*; idem, *Historischer Kommentar*, 273–95 (older literature, ibid., 257, note); Hardeland, *Katechismusgedanken*, 188–204.

[2] *BSLK*, 510.29–31 (SC); 647.24–26 (LC).

[3] Cf. pp. 24–27.

[4] Cf. *BSLK*, 555f., n. 5.

[5] As, for example, Gräter, MGP 21:333.20; Sam, MGP 22:96.24.

[6] Cf. pp. 77–79.

[7] WA 30.1:78.4–89.5 (AE 51:155–169); cf. also "Pred. über den 1. Art. vom 11.7.1529 in Kemberg," WA 29:471–73.

In the Short Form of 1520 and in his sermon on March 4, 1523,[8] he focused on faith as a venture or risk,[9] explicating it almost by means of an existential interpretation. But, at the same time, he limited what faith meant, to guard, on the one hand, against a self-confident construct that relied on one's own creaturely power, as well as against the demand, on the other hand, for some form of assurance. Such a treatment called attention, as well, to the contradictory nature of what one is to trust, that is, the "simple, invisible, incomprehensible, one God,"[10] who is creator and lord of all things. At the same time, it was assumed that God had created us together with all creatures and preserves us daily; the accent was placed on the fact that we are to know that we are completely hidden within His almighty hand. Every creature is under Him; He allows them all to serve us;[11] He protects us against the onslaughts of the powers of destruction;[12] finally, He sets at naught the accusations of one's own conscience.[13] What stands in the center is not the word creator, but rather the tension between the exalted ruler over everything and the goodly Father:[14] "*Quandoquidem est omnipotens, potest me iuvare, pater est: igitur faciet*" (Since He is almighty, He is able to save me; He is Father: therefore He will do it).[15]

In his catechetical sermon on May 23, 1528,[16] Luther connects our relationship with God more explicitly to the creation and summarizes what comes of this in the pithy dictum: "*Tuus deus est*

---

[8] WA 7:215f. and WA 11:48.17–50.36; in connection with the sermon "Von den guten Werken, 1520," WA 6:204–16 (AE 44:15–114).

[9] Cf. pp. 21–32.

[10] "Eine kurze Form, 1520," WA 7:216.1.

[11] "Pred. über den 1. Art. vom 4.3.1523," WA 11:49.23: "If God is omnipotent, then it is nothing that everything is a creature"; "Eine kurze Form, 1520," WA 7:216.18: "so then He is almighty, so what is able to destroy me?"

[12] "Pred. über den 1. Art. vom 4.3.1523," WA 11:49.30: "Whoever believes this does not fear the devil and hell"; cf. "Eine kurze Form, 1520," WA 7:216.4f.; "Kat.-Pred. zum Symbolum vom 23.5.1528," WA 30.1.1:10.24f. .

[13] "Pred. über den 1. Art. vom 4.3.1523," WA 11:50.2: "Do not believe that the greater lord is conscience": cf. "Eine kurze Form, 1520," WA 7:216.10. This threefold application follows the way the First Commandment is treated in "Von den guten Werken, 1520," WA 6:206.33–210.9 (AE 44:15–114).

[14] As is true in the application of the individual creedal assertions in "Eine kurze Form, 1520," WA 7:216.18–29, an arch is formed between the words "almighty" and "father."

[15] "Pred. über den 1. Art. vom 4.3.1523," WA 11:20.5.

[16] WA 30.1:10.17–26.

creator caeli et terrae, ergo omnia sunt tua" (Your God is creator of heavens and earth; therefore, all things are yours).[17] The catechetical sermon of September 21, 1528[18] explicates just this one idea, that God the Father offers Himself to us in the entire creation; His creatures are both the masks and signs in which we comprehend His fatherly blessing by faith: "The Father poured Himself out freely, with all the creatures that He created."[19] The things of daily life are described in their relationship with God. One can be certain that the sermons on Genesis would have given the reformer certain points to emphasize. The experiences with the visitations would have demonstrated that it "was necessary that one must teach about the creation, so that the people know that God still creates, provides sustenance for our daily needs, lets us grow, and so forth."[20]

The catechetical sermon on December 10, 1528[21] goes into more detail concerning the main concepts and typical points that are made in the catechisms.

(1) The reformer is "insistent" on highlighting the word "creator"[22] and relates it to the one who is confessing the faith; within the framework of the First Article, each one is to understand himself to be a "creature of God."[23] The other two words, "father" and "almighty," fade into the background.[24] (2) The believer declares thereby: my physical and spiritual existence, the world that is provided for me, and the human beings who are given to me as a gift, have not come to me on the basis of my own choice or by absolute power; moreover, I cannot guarantee that I can keep them from being destroyed, since I receive it all from God's hand.[25] (3) For this reason, I must forego praising myself and seeking to have confidence in my

---

[17] WA 30.1:10.18.

[18] WA 30.1:44.28–36.

[19] WA 30.1:44.36. These phrases are used in the Large Catechism, *BSLK*, 650.27–30; 651.13f.; 660.34ff.; 661.40f.

[20] Melanchthon, "Unterricht der Visitatoren," *Studienausgabe*, 1:259.10.

[21] WA 30.1:87.4–89.5 (AE 51:162–169).

[22] WA 30.1:89.1: "I have emphasized the word 'creator' "; cf. ibid., 87.9f.; 88.4.

[23] Ibid., 87.6.

[24] Ibid., 87.14 (AE 51:163): "the Father almighty has still more in store."

[25] Ibid., 87.13: "Do not let us think that we have created ourselves, as the proud princes do": ibid., 88.10 (AE 51:163): "all that I possess. These things I have not of myself, that I may not become proud. I cannot either give them to myself or keep them by myself."

own power; instead, I bow down subserviently under the unseen creator, trusting in God, praising God, and serving God.[26]

These seminal thoughts characterize the catechisms as well. Even so, particularly in the Large Catechism,[27] since Luther brings to the fore the insight that God holds tightly to His sinning creatures, even though He is under no obligation, the words "Father Almighty" are not ignored completely[28] Four or possibly five elements are thus emphasized.

(a) The scope of the article is framed with a view toward God: The Christian person, who is called into existence under the First Commandment, gives an account of his faith[29] and confesses: "My God and father, the creator of the heavens and the earth, has made me;[30] "I believe that God has created me together with all creatures."[31] At this point in the Large Catechism, Luther hearkens back to his sermon of May 23, 1528, in which the question was posed concerning the Creed as a whole: "What kind of God do you have?"[32] Christians can be distinguished from the Gentiles, Turks, and Jews only when reference is made to the Son; Luther appends this observation in the Large Catechism at the conclusion of his explication of the Creed.[33] At the same time, in his sermon on December 10, the reformer places particular emphasis[34] on the word "creator," for the sake of the "young students,"

[26] Cf. ibid., 87.17–88.3; 88.6–8; 89.4; the visitation instructions call for the petition on the basis of the faith, Melanchthon, *Studienausgabe*, 1:259.12–15.

[27] *BSLK*, 648.42–649.2.

[28] *BSLK*, 649.2.

[29] The characteristic that calls for giving an account is accentuated on the basis of models from the early Church—as for example Niceta, *Explanatio symboli* 13 (PL 52:873A)—as well as in the commentaries of the late Middle Ages. In his Mirror of Conscience, Martin of Amberg speaks about the statutes for Christians, that one must know and keep (33.13–34.33); cf. Weidenhiller, *Untersuchungen*, 17f., 149, 157, 164.

[30] *BSLK*, 647.27–648.8 (LC).

[31] *BSLK*, 510.33f. (SC).

[32] WA 30.1:9.18: "What kind of God do you have? What do you look for from Him?"; ibid., 10.1: "The Symbol is thus nothing other than a response to this question: What kind of God is yours, who brings to you the Ten Commandments?"

[33] *BSLK*, 661.5–18. 647.35f. shows that Luther has the entire *Credo* in view at this point already.

[34] *BSLK*, 648.4–8.

writing that word in "capital letters"[35] and thus, as is the case with the visitation instructions,[36] entitles the First Article "On Creation."[37]

(b) At this point, Luther directs his attention to the "I," to the one who confesses himself to be God's creature, discussing this individual's creaturely nature within the context of all creatures that exist: God creates and preserves for me bodily life, in that He provides for me the other creatures that He has made and has them serve me.[38] In the Small Catechism, the second set of observations extends from the words "He has given and still preserves . . . for me body and soul" as far as "He richly and daily provides [me] with all necessities and nourishment for *this* body and life."[39]

To be sure, Luther directs these words to "the young students"[40] and to the "household servants,"[41] but they are formulated as a direct address to the "father of the household." In both the Small and Large Catechisms, the confession is put into the mouth of the "head of the household who works the land in the small village," the father in the family.[42] The reformer addresses such a person, with reference to "this life," with respect to four areas in the Large Catechism (three in the Small Catechism); he starts out by dealing with our bodily existence according to its external and internal aspects, moving on then to matters of life in their widest created context and matters of one's home setting; he goes into greater detail in the first two areas, emphasizing particularly those things that deal with what is closest to us, that which deals with our body, our most immediate world. For the third and fourth areas, he starts with what is farthest away and moves to what is closest, the expanse of the cosmos and life on this earth as well as the gifts of life in organized communities.

---

35 Cf. *BSLK*, 647.25 (LC) and 510.30 (SC); see p. 61, n. 22.

36 Melanchthon, *Studienausgabe*, 1:259.9.

37 *BSLK*, 510.28 (SC).

38 *BSLK*, 648.9–32 (LC).

39 *BSLK*, 510.34–511.1.

40 *BSLK*, 648.4f. (LC).

41 *BSLK*, 510.26f. (SC).

42 Albrecht, *Luthers Katechismen*, 186; cf. Bornhäuser, *Der Ursinn des KK D. M. Luthers*, 1–26.

(1) Luther begins the discussion in both catechisms with that which is closest to us, our physical and spiritual existence. He starts out by speaking of the person as a whole according to what each one deals with externally and internally, starting with the general category of "body, soul, and life,"[43] and moves then to what is external, what of the body one can see and touch, singling out "eyes, ears, and all members,"[44] or "bodily parts, small and large";[45] this is followed by that which is within, the cognitive and spiritual aspects of a person: "reason and all senses";[46] "all senses, reason, and understanding."[47] The words "and so forth" demonstrate that what is selected for mention is typical and, at the same time, that there are limitations to what can be said here.

(2) The second area of focus deals with what is provided by the creation in general, as well as matters of the specific communal setting in which one lives.[48] Luther starts by mentioning "foodstuffs and coverings,"[49] clothing and nutriments,[50] and then what is connected with operating a household. In the Small Catechism, Luther conceptualizes "house and home" as a general, overarching term, then mentions individual persons, and finally concludes with the

---

[43] *BSLK*, 648.14f. (LC). Luther otherwise commonly places only "body and soul" together, as in 510.34 (SC); 649.36 (LC); "Kat.-Pred. vom 10.12.1528," WA 30.1:87.6, 17; 88.5; 89.3 (AE 51:162–169); but from time to time he also refers to "body and life," in 565.29f. (LC); "Kat.-Pred. vom 10.12.1528," WA 30.1:88.10.
[44] *BSLK*, 510.35 (SC).
[45] *BSLK*, 648.15 (LC); "Kat.-Pred. vom 10.12.1528," WA 30.1:87.7; "healthy eyes"; ibid., 87.17: "all the members of the body"; ibid., 89.3: "all the members"; "Pred. über das Symbolum vom 11.7.1529," WA 29:473.1: "two eyes, two hands, and all members."
[46] *BSLK*, 510.35f. (SC).
[47] *BSLK*, 648.15f. (LC); "Kat.-Pred. vom 10.12.1528," WA 30.1:87.7; 88.10: "*rationem* (reason)"; ibid., 87.15: "and five senses, reason"; ibid., 88.5: "the five senses."
[48] On this, see Volume 3 on the Lord's Prayer.
[49] BSLK, 679.39 (Large Catechism on the Fourth Petition of the Lord's Prayer).
[50] BSLK, 565.30 (Large Catechism on the First Commandment): "eating, drinking, nourishment, health"; "Kat.-Pred. vom 10.12.1528," WA 30.1:88.5: clothing, nourishment, housing"; "Pred. über das Symbolum vom 11.7.1529," WA 29:473.2: "clothing and all goods."

land and cattle that are part of the scene.[51] In the Large Catechism, he mentions the persons who are placed under the father of the house and then takes brief note of the house as an overarching term for what is owned, without going into further detail;[52] this approach results in a line of sight that proceeds from the wife and on down to the level of the farm.[53]

(3) According to the Large Catechism, the third area of importance is the cosmos in its great expanse and the earth that is teeming with life: the starry host, day and night, the elements as well as the earth, with everything that moves about on it and grows on it.[54] In a lively manner, Luther makes his way from what is the most distant to the closest. In his mind, all such powers appear in such a way that they demonstrate their usefulness for the human being.

(4) Almost as an addendum, introduced by *item* (likewise),[55] the essential goods of the political or communal setting in life, the temporal realm, are listed, which God has installed as a protecting wall around the community of the household, with respect to life and commerce.[56] By mentioning "good government, peace, security,"[57] Luther underscores with

---

[51] "Kat.-Pred. vom 10.12.1528," WA 30.1:88.5 (AE 51:162–169): "House, wife, child, cattle, farmland"; cf. ibid., 87.7 and "Pred. über das Symbolum vom 11.7.1529," WA 29:473.3.

[52] Cf. the "etc." in BSLK, 648.18 (LC).

[53] This corresponds to the progressively more important lines in the hymn "A Mighty Fortress": "Goods, fame, child and wife," WA 35:457.9 (AE 53:283–385).

[54] "Kat.-Pred. vom 10.12.1528," WA 30.1:87.8 (AE 51:162–169); this is mentioned with reference to the four elements; but cf. even earlier "Kat.-Pred. vom 21.9.1528," WA 30.1:44.34: "These creatures are to serve me, the sun has to shine; water has to wash, etc."; cf. also "Eine einfältige Weise zu beten, 1535," WA 38:374.1f. (AE 43:187–211).

[55] *BSLK*, 648.24 (LC).

[56] These gifts are merely mentioned in the discussion of the Fourth Commandment (*BSLK*, 594.32–44) and it is taken up once again and given more expansive treatment in the Fourth Petition of the Lord's Prayer (*BSLK*, 679.33–681.23). The full array is provided in the chain of gifts mentioned by Luther with respect to the First Commandment: "body, life, food, drink, nourishment, health, protection, peace and all of what is required in time and eternity" (*BSLK*, 565.29–32). Melanchthon uses this in the *Catechismus puerilis*, 1532 (Reu, Quellen, 1.2.2:10.23–30).

[57] *BSLK*, 648.25f. (LC).

greater intensity the authoritative dimension of that area of importance, rather than the neighborly dimension.

(a) These two aspects, both of which reach beyond daily home life, are summarized in the Small Catechism with the phrase: "richly and daily provides [me] with all necessities and nourishment for this body and life,"[58] which is very close to the introductory phrase in the Large Catechism: "in addition, allows all creatures to serve for the needs and necessities of life."[59] These words provide the concluding point at the end of the second area for discussion, in which the earthly life of the person making the confession is related to God; it thus includes everything "that belongs to one's entire life in the world."[60]

(b) Luther had set the stage for the first two of these four areas, which describe how all the creatures of God surround the person making the confession, the areas of bodily life and the larger setting of creation as a whole, in the sermon he preached on December 10, 1528. He particularly characterized how Adam is provided with the broad realm of the creation in his sermons on Genesis. He depicts the "neighborly or community existence and realm"[61] when he comes to the Fourth Petition.[62]

(c) Luther identifies a third circle of thought: God has not only called us into existence and provided for us the creatures that surround us; He preserves us day by day as well, in this our world.[63] Luther effects the transition to speak of God's protective hold on His sinful creature with the words "and

---

[58] *BSLK*, 510.39–511.1.

[59] *BSLK*, 648.19f.

[60] *BSLK*, 679.34–36 (Large Catechism, on the Fourth Petition of the Lord's Prayer).

[61] *BSLK*, 679.44–46 (ibid.).

[62] On this, cf. Volume 3 on the Lord's Prayer; "Das schöne Confitemini, 1530," WA 31.1:78.27 (AE 14:41–106): "Futile war, unrest, famine, bloodshed, uproar, murder and wretchedness are not a permanent state of affairs in countries, cities, villages and all sorts of handiwork, commerce, and various activities that provide nourishment survive; that is as great a miracle and power worked by God as that He made the world out of nothing and daily preserves it still."

[63] "Pred. über das Symbolum vom 11.7.1529," WA 29:473.11: "In the second place, you know that you are not only created, but also preserved by God."

still preserves,"[64] as well as "richly and daily provides."[65] This is the first time that the fatherly nature of God appears, which had been secretly in the background from the outset;[66] now it is front and center.[67] Despite our guilt and unworthiness, as the faithful father, God holds tightly onto His children. At this juncture in the Large Catechism, though only in passing, Luther refers to what "*omnipotens pater*" (father almighty) means.[68] The Small Catechism has a reference that corresponds to this, when Luther transitions from God's caring provisions to the aspect that He shelters from all danger, which is the first time that the goodness of the Father and the mercy of the Lord come fully into the light. Despite this, certainly in the Small Catechism, but also in the Large Catechism,[69] the reference to the pure grace of the Father points back to "everything" that has been mentioned until now, thus to God's entire activity. This third grouping of observations receives only brief mention in the sermon on December 10, 1528;[70] in the Large Catechism, it seems to function more as an inserted element that did not quite fit;[71] in the Small Catechism, it serves as a crowning element that summarizes everything that had been stated to that point.[72]

(d) The fourth circle articulates the duty of those who are created, and specifically with reference to the children of God, to thank and to obey. In the Small Catechism, this follows immediately from the comprehensive description of all the gifts of love proffered by the Father.[73] For the Large Catechism, such responses are arranged on the basis of the Decalogue[74] and are described in concrete fashion by the way

---

64 *BSLK*, 510.36 (SC).

65 *BSLK*, 510.40–511.1 (SC).

66 *BSLK*, 647.28f. (LC): "God the Father's name, will, action and work"; cf. ibid., 647.4; 648.10.

67 *BSLK*, 648.49 (LC): "as a pleasant father"; cf. ibid., 650.16f.

68 *BSLK*, 648.42–649.2.

69 *BSLK*, 647.28; 648.42–44; 650.14–17.

70 WA 30.1:87.14 (AE 51:163): "The Father almighty has still more in store."

71 *BSLK*, 648.42–649.2.

72 *BSLK*, 511.3: "and all that."

73 *BSLK*, 511.6: "all that."

74 *BSLK*, 649.14f.: "as He has called for and commanded in the Ten Commandments."

they contrast with human self-confidence. This section[75] thus summons the child of God to the duty to offer thanks and rejects the self-declared importance of the child of the world who would steal from God.[76] Such points are intoned in passing here and there in Luther's earlier writings;[77] they are unfolded in this specific form first in the sermon on December 10, 1528.[78]

(e) The Small Catechism's closing Amen, and "that is certainly true,"[79] receive expanded treatment by Luther in the Large Catechism, recapitulated by means of the key word about practicing this daily.[80] Luther gives concrete expression to the way the children are to offer daily thanks by means of several illustrations mentioned in a sermon on July 11, 1529.[81] At the same time, this recapitulation demonstrates how Luther himself was able to draw these four or five sections together by means of the two key words: gift and work (*Gabe und Aufgabe*); one notes that the first three circles describe "what we have and receive from God,[82] whereas the fourth circle identifies "our responsibilities."[83] This summary and transition shows at the same time that God acts as our gracious father, and gifts us with Himself, when He provides the gifts of the creation.[84] "With heaven and earth and all creatures, the Father gives us Himself, so that these can serve and can be useful."[85] How comprehensively—the one syllable word "all" is used ten times in the Small Catechism—Luther

---

[75] *BSLK*, 649.7–41.

[76] Cf. also "Das schöne Confitemini, 1530," WA 31.1:68–182 (AE 14:41–106).

[77] See passages such as "Pred. über den 1. Art. vom 4.3.1523," WA 11:50.10–17.

[78] WA 30.1:87.13 (AE 51:163): "Do not let us think that we have created ourselves, as the proud princes do"; cf. ibid., 87.17–88.4; 86.6f., 11f.

[79] *BSLK*, 511.8.

[80] *BSLK*, 650.10–33.

[81] WA 29:473.1–10; cf., from even earlier, "Kat.-Pred. vom 10.12.1528," WA 30.1:87.11ff., and the examples from the Scripture and experience in "Das schöne Confitemini, 1530," WA 31.1:110.24–114.33 (AE 51:182–188).

[82] *BSLK*, 647.27–649.2.

[83] *BSLK*, 649.7–41 (Citation: 650.25).

[84] *BSLK*, 650.27–30; cf. 651.10–15; 661.41 and "Kat.-Pred. vom 21.9.1528," WA 30.1:44.36: "The Father has given all that He can, along with all creatures that He has created."

[85] "Vom Abendmahl Christi, 1528," WA 26:505.39 (AE 37:151–372).

depicts God's fatherly care as well! Such provisions remain specifically restricted to the realm of the "First Article," focusing on the "bodily and temporal goods"[86] of this body and life, lived out under the pall of death.[87]

How "Pro Me" Affects the Way the Statements of the Apostles' Creed Are Used

We turn our glance first of all toward observations about "God the Father's nature, will, activity, and work"[88] and analyze the use Luther makes of the confessional statements of the early Church. The reformer linked the entire Creed to the Decalogue and treated particularly the First Article as the response that the person making confession offers to the summons of the First Commandment.[89] Because of His holy jealousy, God established the First Commandment over everything that carries the imprint of humans and summons each one: "Let me alone be your God and seek no other."[90] God's divine nature is clearly shown in the *Creatio ex nihilo* (creation from nothing). This action stands at the beginning of the cosmos, before which nothing can be comprehended as existing. But it also impacts the here and now, with respect to my own existence, in the world that has been provided for me, moment by moment, calling me forth from the abyss of nothingness that entangles everything.[91] To believe [up]on God thus means "to take with utter seriousness that God, He alone and no other, is the lord of my life and of the entire world in which I live."[92]

In this way, the reformer brings the discussion of the *Pro nobis* (for us) already into the First Article. The believer does more than just

---

[86] *BSLK*, 648.24f.; 651.12 (LC).

[87] *BSLK*, 510.40 (SC); 650.28–30 (LC).

[88] *BSLK*, 647.28f. (LC).

[89] *BSLK*, 647.35–38 (LC); "Eine kurze Form, 1520," WA 7:215.13: "That is a living faith, and such is commanded in the First Commandment, as it states there: 'I am God; you shall not have any other gods',"; cf. "Von den guten Werken, 1520," WA 6:209.24ff. (AE 44:15–114).

[90] *BSLK*, 560.35f. (Large Catechism on the First Commandment); on this, see Volume 1 on the First Commandment, 115–21.

[91] *BSLK*, 648.26–32 (LC); "Kat.-Pred. vom 10.12.1528," WA 30.1:87.8 (AE 51:163): "Thus this article teaches that you do not have life of yourself, not even a hair. . . . Everything that exists is comprehended in that little word "creator."

[92] Doerne, *Praktischer Schöpfungsglaube nach Luther*, 26.

confess that an eternal, invisible God created the world out of nothing, more than that He has additionally caused the one who confesses to come into existence. In, with, and under the visible world that surrounds him, the believer comprehends the hand of the invisible father who provides blessings, in that he addresses that tremendous, awesome power as his God and father. Two points are established thereby: (1) From one vantage point, the creatures that surround us are masks that conceal and yet reveal God giving Himself to us and are tools by means of which He preserves us. "In this way I comprehend the Father, namely, by means of the external activities, that He created heaven and earth."[93] The creatures are "simply the hand, conduits, and means, through which God gives everything."[94] (2) But viewed another way, we venture to consider our own selves to be in the center of all that has been created. In seemingly naïve fashion, Luther has us confess in the Small Catechism: "I believe that God has created me together with all creatures."[95] Furthermore, in the Large Catechism, he does not describe household organization minimally as a circumscribed community where one lives out each day and where economic activity occurs; he surrounds the "young learner" with the larger context of the socio-political order within society and state, expanding this ultimately to place each one within the entire cosmos.

And yet, the human being does not comprehend the hand of the invisible divine being intrinsically and independently, forcing God's power somehow to help the individual to be front and center in the cosmos and to affirm one's uniqueness thereby. Instead, he recognizes at this point that he is placed here by the one who alone is the "eternal wellspring"[96] and who remains the exalted center of life. This Lord established an ordered framework for all creatures, just as He commanded human beings to love one another; the creatures become thereby the masks through which He provides His care and mercy.

---

[93] "Kat.-Pred. vom 21.9.1528," WA 30.1:44.32.

[94] *BSLK*, 566.21f. (Large Catechism on the First Commandment); "Vorrede zu Joh. Lichtenbergers Weissagung, 1527," WA 23:8.36: "How wonderfully He Himself accomplishes it through us and we are simply His masks, underneath which He hides Himself and works all in all, as we Christians certainly know." Cf. Volume 1 on the First Commandment, pp. 121–27.

[95] *BSLK*, 510.33f.

[96] *BSLK*, 565.41 (Large Catechism on the First Commandment).

God is not the creator and preserver solely for our daily life in this world. He protects us, at the same time, from the destructive power of what can bring to naught. Such sinister opposition that is identified at this point in the First Article is not connected with God's judgment that punishes our sins, nor does it relate to the personal traits of the old, evil foe, in fear of which we flee in prayer to God.[97] Luther concentrates his observations on our life that is lived in relation to the world; for this reason, he employs concepts that are thus both vague and yet expansive, such as danger and accidents,[98] evil and misfortune,[99] needs and distresses.[100] Such were there already in the First Commandment[101] and appear in the daily prayers as well.[102]

No matter how expansive the dangers, the nature of God's help is just as extensive. More than anywhere else, the descriptions in the catechisms[103] confront us again and again with the way the reformer never holds back when helping us to attest that God provides His benevolent protection and shelter, day in and day out. No mention is made about the precious gift of suffering, which threatens to separate me from God's fatherly gifts and behind which He is hidden; "and yet, He watches out for me and never forsakes me. For He is at hand and stands ready to help by grace, and He permits Himself to be

---

[97] The trio of terms, sin-death-the devil (Small Catechism: *BSLK*, 511.29f.) surfaces for the first time in the Second Article; these are the tyrants from whose prison Christ frees us (Large Catechism, *BSLK*, 652.2). In the Third and Sixth Petitions of the Lord's Prayer (Small Catechism, *BSLK*, 513.28; 514.34) and in the Admonition concerning Holy Communion (Large Catechism: *BSLK*, 722.8–724.41), the opponents show up as the trio of flesh-world-devil. An original explanation of the Symbol that was copied frequently in the second half of the fifteenth century in southern Germany designates the entire Symbol as a means of protection against the three enemies that would rob us of Christ's salvation, against the devil, world, and one's own flesh (Nürnberger Stadtbibliothek, Cent. 6.59; Munich, Cgm. 564 (a. 1455); 543 (a. 1469); 1141 (a. 1479); 638 and 1121 (saec. 15), according to Wiegand, *Das apostolische Symbol im Mittelalter*, 43ff.

[98] *BSLK*, 648.46f. (LC); cf. ibid., 650.13f.: "from needs or dangers."

[99] *BSLK*, 648.45f. (LC).

[100] *BSLK*, 648.50 (LC): "suffering."

[101] In the discussion of the First Commandment in the Large Catechism, *BSLK*, 560.39: "misfortune and need"; ibid., 565.33, 36: "misfortune"; ibid., 567.1: "in times of need and scarcity."

[102] In the discussion about the Morning Blessing in the Small Catechism, *BSLK*, 521.27f., 30: "trouble and danger," as well as "sins and evil."

[103] See the overview in Meyer, *Historischer Kommentar*, 292f.

detected through the window of darkish faith."[104] At this point, the reformer seems to have given up on using the *Theologia crucis* that was so central to him at first and seems to have forgotten his "beloved, holy cross,"[105] which was given its own section, "On Troubles,"[106] in the visitation instructions. Luther takes up these issues only later, when he comes to the Second and Third Articles of the Creed and when he discusses the Lord's Prayer. The cross is discussed when he speaks of the attack of the devil and the world against the Word of God.[107] Such a placement of the "beloved, holy cross" is determined by the coordinated system that the reformer explicates in his first Invocavit sermon of 1522 and in the Preface to the German Mass in 1526: Faith comes forth from Law and Gospel—love in service to the neighbor and in obedience when suffering.[108]

In this way, we have come to see the threefold uniqueness of the application of the First Article. (1) Luther concentrates its cosmological breadth on the anthropological center of the one who is confessing, without thereby giving up on the aspect that the alignment goes in the direction of all creatures toward the creator. (2) Luther condenses discussion about the good things that God created so as to focus on what impacts our earthly existence, ending as it will with our

---

[104] "Von den guten Werken, 1520," WA 6:208.15 (AE 44:15–114); cf. ibid., 208.6–33 and "Magnificat, 1521," WA 7:585.13–587.22 (AE 21:295–355).

[105] *BSLK*, 677.21 (Large Catechism on the Third Petition of the Lord's Prayer).

[106] Melanchthon, *Studienausgabe*, 1:235.10–236.15; Luther unfolds this most impressively in "Das schöne Confitemini, 1530," WA 31.1:92–98 (AE 51:162–169): "Trouble and cross are only half as necessary for us as is life itself and much more necessary and useful than all worldly goods and honor" (ibid., 95.33).

[107] *BSLK*, 677.14–678.48 (Large Catechism on the Third Petition of the Lord's Prayer).

[108] WA 10.3:1–6 (AE 51:70–75) and WA 19:77.11–78.24 (AE 53:51–90). In his little book of sayings, Melanchthon discusses these citations from Scripture within this framework (MGP 21:243–53). When one speaks of suffering in the creaturely realm fading away, one is reminded of Luther's comments in *Das schöne Confitemini*, that we who are "weaklings" and "weak martyrs" (WA 31.1:73.24 [AE 51:150–155]) seek so quickly to forget God's all-encompassing gifts of creation because of some little problem. By contrast, God seeks to awaken us from the unthankfulness in which we slumber by means of that little problem and to remind us of His acts of kindness, which we take for granted. "Thus we ought to look at all our misfortune as nothing else but the way that God turns on the light, so that we can see his goodness and gracious acts in other aspects that are beyond number and that we might recognize them as such, so that we can let ourselves think: That was such a minor misfortune that it was hardly a little drop of water in a great fire or a little ember falling into a large body of water" (WA 31.1:71.29ff. [AE 51:145–150]).

death. But he depicts God's assistance as comprehensively as possible and allows us to see ourselves in the grasp of the almighty Father's gracious hand. (3) Luther is content simply to make reference to that which is in opposition, from which God protects us, to be in the realm of the needs of this bodily life. The description does not go into the dimension of what is satanic. This means such existence cannot be restricted to punishment from God because of our guilt nor qualified by the cross that is laid upon us as Christians.

Insofar as the reformer brackets out such more significant issues at this point, he keeps himself within the framework of traditional interpretation. But such an interpretation points, as well, to deep tensions, which grow out of the arrangement of the key terms: God—Father—Almighty—Creator.

The relationship between the key terms God and Father itself brings out deep tensions. The word θεός is often juxtaposed with the word πατήρ in the New Testament, without the article, as if an epithet.[109] The accent is thus placed not upon God but on Father. The two terms are likely connected in the Apostles' Creed because of the command to baptize and because of the reference in the Lord's Prayer to our Father.[110] The eternal, supernal God makes us into His children in baptism; we are enabled to address Him in prayer as our father. The only-begotten Son, who is the subject of the Second Article, through whose cross and resurrection we become children of God, is thus secretly present in the word father in the First Article, as can be demonstrated in interpretations from the early Church[111] and in some of the modern paraphrases of the Creed as well.[112]

Since the results of the trinitarian battles are reflected to some extent in the Apostles' Creed, one can assume a trinitarian reference is behind the word "*Deus*." Two emphases are thus at play when the word "God" is used. This word is the personal name for the Father in biblical and early Church tradition. At the same time, it is a code

---

[109] Cf. Gal. 1:3; Phil. 2:11; 1 Thess. 1:1; in addition, Wis. 2:16.

[110] Thus Eichenseer, *Apostolicum*, 172–75; Kelly, *Creeds*, 134f.; Lietzmann, *Symbolstudien*, 242f.

[111] Rufinus, *Expositio Symboli* 4.21 (CCSL 20:138): "Thus the very title by which God is called 'Father' proves that a Son coexists side by side with the Father"; cf. Niceta, *Explanatio symboli* 2 (PL 52:867B); Peter Chrysologus, *Sermo* 57 (PL 52:358A, B); *Sermo* 58 (ibid., 361C); *Sermo* 59 (ibid., 363A, B); *Sermo* 60 (ibid., 366B–367A); *Sermo* 61 (ibid., 370A, B); *Sermo* 62 (ibid., 373A–C).

[112] Cf. *Werkbuch Gottesdienst*, Bekenntnisse nos. 2, 3, 4, 9.

word for the unity of the divine being in three persons, as explicated in the Augustinian and dogmatic tradition. Luther initially stays with the original word usage from the Apostles' Creed in his catechisms.[113] For him, God the Father is the creator. The concluding sentence of the Large Catechism reads: "One God and faith, but three persons,"[114] along with the statement that it takes all three articles to provide an answer to the question: "What then is God as human being?"[115] This comes closer to that second emphasis, as is evident most especially in the confessional statements from the Reformation: The term God functions here primarily as a code word for the "*una essentia divina*" (one divine essence)[116] in three persons. In his Confession of 1528, Luther does not discuss creation primarily with respect to God the Father, but refers to the Father, Son, and Holy Spirit as the "correct, singular, natural, true God," with His three distinguishable persons.[117]

Early Church confessions about the Trinity[118] and doctrinal decisions from the Middle Ages[119] described the nature and unique qualities of this "*Unitas*" in the "*Trinitas*," without referring thereby to God's revelatory actions. These formulas made their way into the catechisms as well. They are in the Nuremberg Children's Sermons, according to which the children are to "note, first of all, that God the Lord is a spirit and not a physical object, so that someone could comprehend or see Him."[120] At this point, however, such comments

---

[113] *BSLK*, 647.14, 28; 648.42f. (LC); cf. also passages such as "Pred. über Joh. 15:26ff. vom 28.5.1525," WA 17.1:263.30ff.

[114] *BSLK*, 647.18; cf. also 660.23–27; 661.38–42.

[115] *BSLK*, 647.32f.

[116] *BSLK*, 50.7f. (AC I).

[117] "Vom Abendmahl Christi, 1528," WA 26:500.28 (AE 37:151–372); cf. 36–47 and 48ff.

[118] Augustine, *De Trinitate* 7:6.12 (PL 42:945): "Let him believe in the Father, Son, and Holy Spirit, one God, alone, great, omnipotent, good, just, merciful, creator of all things visible and invisible" [Nicene & Post Nicene Fathers, First Series, 3:113]; Rufinus, *Expositio symboli* 4.12 (CCSL 20:137): "When 'God' is uttered, you are to understand a substance without beginning or end, simple, uncompounded, invisible, incorporeal, ineffable, incomprehensible: a substance in which there is nothing accidental, nothing creaturely"; Niceta, *Explanatio symboli* 2 (PL 52:867A, B); Peter Chrysologus, *Sermo* 60 (PL 52:366B–367A); cf. the Athanasian Creed, nos. 6–14, as well as the texts that relate to that in Denzinger, B 2d.

[119] Most especially the Confession of the Fourth Lateran Council (Denzinger, 800), to which reference is made in the AC I (*BSLK*, 50.7–14); on this, cf. Maurer, *Historischer Kommentar zur Confessio Augustana*, 2:22–29.

[120] "Nürnberger Kat.-Predigten," Reu, *Quellen*, 1.1:506.29–507.14; Dietenberger makes use of this (Moufang, *Katholische Katechismen*, 7f.). A comprehensive

are addressed to those who are confessing their faith.[121] Luther excludes these references altogether; for him, God's nature and will are demonstrated exclusively in His actions and deeds,[122] in his all-encompassing care.

Along with the tenfold repetition of "all" in the Small Catechism, the substantive attribute "*omnipotens*" is used. The Old Roman Creed can, with ease, use the words: "*Credo in Deum Patrem omnipotentem* (I believe in God the Father almighty)." As is true of Luther's early expositions, creation was included in God's absolute ruling power. The substantive attribute "*omnipotens*" conveys only one aspect of the Greek παντοκράτωρ.[123] The term does not seek to attribute to God a *Potentia absoluta*, for whom nothing is impossible (Luke 1:37); instead, its intent is to convey "a functioning power and constant activity, which incessantly continues in force and accomplishes."[124] But it does not portray an ancient dynamic power, either, drawing everything along and acting without regard for good or evil, which might come closer to some of the somewhat unrefined formulations in *De servo arbitrio* (On the Bondage of the Will)."[125] Instead, it describes a personal lordship, with ancillary emphases on issues of

---

explanation is to be found in the Second Catechism of Erasmus, *Explanatio Symboli*, cols. 1146A–F.

[121] The *Nürnberger Kinderpredigten* proceed as follows: "And it is present in all places, seeing and knowing what we do, speak and think and yet is bound to no place or location. And it is such a lordly, exalted being, so that no human being can investigate and comprehend it, except Christians only, since it is the Lord Christ Himself who reveals Himself in the teaching of the faith" (Reu, *Quellen*, 1.1:506.32–37).

[122] *BSLK*, 647.28f. (LC).

[123] A better rendering would be "*omnitenens*" (holding, controlling, possessing all things); see Augustine, "Gen. ad litt. 4.12" (CSEL 28.1:108.15–19); Rufinus, *Expositio symboli* 5:15 (CCSL 20:140): "ALMIGHTY is applied to Him on account of the dominion He has over the universe. But the Father governs the universe through the Son."

[124] "Magnificat, 1521," WA 7:574.27 (AE 21:295–355); "De servo arbitrio, 1525," WA 18:718.28 (AE 33:189): "By the omnipotence of God, however, I do not mean the potentiality by which he could do many things which he does not, but the active power by which he potently works all in all, which is the sense in which Scripture calls him omnipotent"; cf. also "Ein Sermon und Eingang in das 1. Buch Mose vom 22.3.1523," WA 12:441.23–442.9; "Jona-Ausl., 1526," WA 19:219.31–222.11 (AE 19:33–104); "Daß diese Worte Christi noch fest stehen, 1527," WA 23:133.19–135.11 (AE 37:3–150); Melanchthon, *Catechismus puerilis*, 1532, in Reu, *Quellen*, 1.2.2:10.13–19.

[125] Such as WA 18:709.21–712.38; 724.32–725.6; 752.12–16 (AE 33:3–295), and often elsewhere.

justice and ethics, of politics and state.[126] "All-ruling" or "all-sovereign" or "all-controlling" would likely be the appropriate translation for such a word, coming as it does from "technical vocabulary rooted in the pre-Christian, religious cult."[127]

Already in the Septuagint, the Hebrew terms El Shaddai and Sabaoth are rendered as παντοκράτωρ, and the New Testament stays with that Old Testament shading.[128] The fathers of the second century linked this term with θεός; the Martyrdom of Polycarp connects it with πατήρ;[129] the word to which it is linked is still in flux at the time of Augustine.[130] This corroborates the view that the three words *Deus—pater—omnipotens* were thought to convey one idea.[131] Along with the *Textus receptus* and the way it was translated into German, Luther connects "almighty" with Father, since the words were right together. This is detected, as well, in the rearrangement in the Baptismal Booklet: "Do you believe in God, the almighty Father?"[132]

The terminology "*Creator coeli et terrae*" is not found in the Old Roman Symbol; it found its place only in the *Textus receptus*, surviving several analogous formulations.[133] It is found in the East in Cyril of Jerusalem[134] and in the Niceno-Constantinopolitan Creed;[135] the phrase worked its way to the West via Niceta of Remesiana.[136] Augustine's African Creed is more wide-ranging in its formulation: "*universorum creatorem, regem saeculorum, immortalem et*

---

[126] Cf. Kattenbusch, *Symbol*, 2:526, 533f.

[127] Eichenseer, *Apostolicum*, 180.

[128] 2 Cor. 6:18; Rev. 1:8; 4:8; 11:17, and often elsewhere; cf. Eichenseer, *Apostolicum*, 176; Kelly, *Creeds*, 132f.; Lietzmann, *Symbolstudien*, 243.

[129] *Martyrdom of Polycarp* 19.2.

[130] Augustine, *Epistulae* 238:2.10 (CSEL 57:540.6–9).

[131] Hippolytus, *Contra haeresin Noeti* 8; Irenaeus, *Adversus haereses* 1.1.6; 2.58.1; 4.34.6; further examples are in Kattenbusch, *Symbol*, 2:520–22; 537–40; Kattenbusch translates: "I believe in God as the all-ruling father (ibid., 534); the ecumenical version of the text reads: "I believe in God the Father, the Almighty."

[132] *BSLK*, 540.28; cf. also ibid., 649.2; 555f., n. 5; "Pred. in Schmalkalden über das Symbolum vom 11.2.1537," WA 45:16.8.

[133] See Kattenbusch, *Symbol*, 2:875–78; Kelly, *Creeds*, 372–74; Eichenseer, *Apostolicum*, 187–95; Lietzmann, *Symbolstudien*, 194–98.

[134] Cyril of Jerusalem, *Catechesis* 4.4 (PG 33:460A); Hahn, *Bibliothek*, § 124; Denzinger, 41: "ποιητής."

[135] Denzinger, 150; in the Latin: "*factor*." The ecumenical version renders it: "I believe [up]on God the Father, the Almighty, the creator of heaven and earth."

[136] Niceta, *Explanatio symboli* 2 (PL 52:867f.); cf. Burn, *Niceta of Remesiana*, 39.13f. and Kelly, *Creeds*, 175.

invisibilem" (creator of the universe, ruler of the world, immortal and invisible).[137]

Since God the Father is addressed specifically as the creator of heaven and earth, whatever is involved in being the ruler over everything is articulated *expressis verbis*. The creedal formulations of the second and third centuries expanded the scope of God's fatherly rule to cover everything altogether;[138] the testimony from biblical and salvation history is merged with the cosmic metaphysics of the ancient world.[139] Since the formula "*creator universorum*" could stand alone, the concept of fatherhood could reclaim its Christocentric and salvation-historical accent, which had been there originally.[140] Augustine thus distinguishes between God, Lord, and Father: "*Ipsum quippe habemus et Deum et Dominum et Patrem: Deum, quod ab ipso etiam ex hominibus parentibus conditi sumus; Dominum, quod ei subditi sumus; Patrem, quod eius adoptione renati sumus*" (There is one for us who is God and Lord and Father; God, because we are created by Him, though from human parents; Lord, because we are His subjects; Father, because by His adoption we are born again).[141]

At the same time, the inner movement within the history of the text in early church history is repeated in Luther's explication of this article. As we have noted,[142] Luther started off in the same way with God as our almighty Father. But, for the first time, in his sermon on December 10, 1528, he "emphasizes" the word "creator." It is clear once again in the Large Catechism that God's fatherly nature takes precedence over His nature as creator and as lord.[143] Emphasis is placed there on how He turns toward us in mercy and must thus, of necessity, be understood in terms of the story of salvation. At this point already, Cyril of Jerusalem, Rufinus, Augustine, Peter

---

[137] Augustine, *Sermo* 215.2; on this, see texts in Kelly, *Creeds*, 175f.; Denzinger, 21f.; see also the overview of the content in Eichenseer, *Apostolicum*, 187–99.

[138] The phrases "πατὴρ τῶν ὅλων" or "τῶν ἁπάντων" are based on Eph. 4:6; 3:14f.; 1 Clem. 19.2; 35.2, are amply supported by Justin (cf. how these are placed together in Eichenseer, *Apostolicum*, 190, n. 148), and they are taken up by both Clement and Origen and become part of the standard formula in the East through both Eusebius and Athanasius (according to Kattenbusch, *Symbol*, 2:520, n. 68).

[139] On this, see Scheffczyk, *Schöpfung und Vorsehung*, 30–51; Pannenberg, *Die Aufnahme des philosophischen Gottesbegriffes*.

[140] Cf. Kelly, *Creeds*, 372ff.; Eichenseer, *Apostolicum*, 187–95.

[141] Augustine, *Contra Faustum Manichaeum*, 3.3 (CSEL 25.1:265.12).

[142] Cf. pp. 59–62.

[143] *BSLK*, 649.21–32.

Chrysologus,[144] and the tradition of the Middle Ages which followed them,[145] along with certain of the Reformation-era catechisms,[146] purposely insert reference to the Son at this point: "In an unnatural way, God is the Father of many, but by nature and in truth He is Father of one alone, His only-begotten Son, our Lord Jesus Christ." Nowhere in his catechetical writings can we find Luther stating, in such a succinct way: only through the Son is God our Father; in this sense, Luther preserves a certain measure of the uniqueness of the First Article, staying away from the "twin starting points" by beginning to describe both creation and redemption here already.[147] And yet, in the house sermon at Smalcald on February 11, 1537,[148] he intimates that the little word "father" carries with it more weight than is intimated in the discussion in the catechisms:[149] "The word "creator" tells us about from whence we have come; the word "father" about where we belong and where we are supposed to end up.[150] By contrast with the animals, which cannot call God their father, we human beings are not destined to remain in death, but are

---

[144] Cyril of Jerusalem, *Catechesis* 7.5 (PG 33:609A); Rufinus, *Expositio symboli* 4 (CCSL 20:137f.); Augustine, *Contra Faustum Manichaeum*, 3.3 (CSEL 25.1:264.19–28); Niceta, *Explanatio symboli* 2 (PL 52:867B); Peter Chrysologus, *Sermo* 57 (PL 52:358A); *Sermo* 58 (ibid., 361C); *Sermo* 59 (ibid., 363A, B); *Sermo* 60 (ibid., 366B–367A); *Sermo* 61 (ibid., 370A, B); *Sermo* 62 (ibid., 373A–C); Caesarius of Arles, *Sermo* 9 (CCSL 103:48).

[145] Jocelin of Soisson, *Expositio symboli et orationis dominicae* 4 (PL 186:1482B–C); Hugo of Rouen, *De fide catholica et oratione dominica* (PL 192:1324C); Thomas Aquinas, *De articulis fidei*, § 599f. (in *Expositio in Symbolum Apostolorum*, §§ 887ff., Thomas Aquinas explicates the connection with Christ for the first time in the Second Article).

[146] Before Luther's Catechisms, such was the case with only Wolfgang Capito, "Kinderbericht, 1527," quest. 13–16 (MGP 21:105ff.); Kasper Gräter, "Catechesis" (based on Luther's "Eine kurze Form, 1520," MGP 21:335): Johannes Brenz, "Fragstücke," quest. 6, 11 (22.160f.); but this is not the case with Agricola, Petrus Schulz, Althamer, Sam, and Zwick. When one looks at the later catechisms this happens most frequently in the Geneva Catechism (quest. 22) and in the Heidelberg Catechism (quest. 26). See also Barth, *Credo*, 32; idem, *Dogmatik im Grundriß*, § 6.

[147] Based on how it is formulated by Wingren, *Schöpfung und Gesetz*, 186; idem, *Evangelium und Kirche*, 93, 109.

[148] WA 45:11–20.

[149] Cf. *BSLK*, 648.51–649.2; "Kat.-Pred. vom 10.12.1528," WA 30.1:87.14f. (AE 51:162–169)

[150] WA 45:13.2: "Because you want to know where you and I and all people come from, then listen carefully, for I will tell you: It is God, Father, the almighty creator of heaven and earth, a single God, who created everything and preserves it; now you know it."

to live before God eternally as His children.[151] But even after this time, Luther still places emphasis on the word "creator"; in formulaic renderings, as in commentaries, the attribute "almighty" is connected to creator.[152]

THE CHARACTER OF THE CREATING AND PRESERVING NATURE OF GOD THE FATHER[153]

Luther's interpretation of the First Article is shaped through and through by his astonishment about the character of life as a gift. In this way, the reformer confronts that aspect which Martin Heidegger terms the "foundational question for metaphysics": "Why is there that which exists rather than the more probable nothingness?"[154] But Luther does not consider this as an abstract philosophical question; instead, from the vantage point of the wonderment of a child: "Why is there something and not nothing?"[155] He considers this from the point of view of one who ventures to trust, on the basis of the biblical witness that tells of a God who dispenses life. The dark power of chaos that threatens destruction, from which God called the world to life, continues indeed to lurk all around us as a frightening abyss, but it is within us as well. We could pitch abruptly headlong into this nothingness, above which we are held in every instant, without any

[151] WA 45:16.6: "Beyond that He teaches us more yet, not only who we are and where we are from, but where we are to be born. That is pointed out to us by that little word father, that He wants to be at one and the same time both father and almighty. The animals cannot call him father, but we are to call Him father and are to be known as His children. By means of this word, He shows what He plans to do with us."

[152] As, for example, "Pred. über das Symbolum vom 11.7.1529," WA 29:472.32: "*Deum esse patrem esse creatorem omnipotentem*" (To be God the Father is to be the omnipotent creator), similarly, "Eine einfältige Weise zu beten, 1535," WA 38:373.10 (AE 43:187–211); "Die drei Symbola, 1538," WA 50:263.21 (AE 34:197–229); "Pred. in Schmalkalden über das Symbolum vom 11.2.1537," WA 45:12–16; cf. also Meyer, *Historischer Kommentar*, 278f.

[153] See the literature on the First Commandment, Volume 1, 146–48; in addition, see Buchwald, *Luther über die Welt als "Mitwirkerin Gottes"*; Pedersen, *Schöpfung und Geschichte bei Luther*; Doerne, *Praktischer Schöpfungsglaube nach Luther*; Rost, *Luther's Schöpfungsglaube und Geschichtstheologie*; Althaus, *Der Schöpfungsgedanke bei Luther*; Löfgren, *Die Theologie der Schöpfung bei Luther*; Ludolphy, *Luthers Naturverständnis*; Nilsson, *Simul*, 135–50.

[154] Heidegger, *Was ist Metaphysik?*, 42.

[155] This is how it is formulated by Ernst Bloch, *Tübinger Einleitung in die Philosophie*, 1:16.

effort on our part, indeed, despite our fervid effort. Not a one of us is master of his or her outward or inward existence; we can bungle it, but we cannot guarantee anything on our own and cannot make anything happen completely, on the basis of our own effort. Real life cannot be forced; it is guaranteed to us only as a gift; it can be denied to us and remain closed to us, as well. "Existence means: being preserved within nothingness."[156] But Luther does not proceed from this basic human experience to an existential analysis within the framework of anthropological structures. He confronts the issue existentially and analyses it on the basis of trusting in the witness of the Scriptures and the confession of Christ by the Church; in the midst of the stupor of the individual "I," one gazes upon the overweening power of the creator. He thus summarizes the grand total of what one can learn from the First Article in the Large Catechism in the sentence: "that not a single one of us controls or can preserve life and everything that is now described or could be, no matter how little and slight it is."[157] In the helps for Master Peter, his "beard trimmer," he explains it with this statement: "You are God's creation, production, creature, and work; that is: from you yourself and in you yourself you are nothing, know nothing, comprehend nothing, can do nothing. For what were you a thousand years ago? What was heaven and earth six thousand years ago? In that same way, nothing else but nothing at all, so that nothing was to be created of it at all. But what you are, comprehend, know, set out to do, that is called God's creation, as you confess here with your mouth, so that you have nothing to boast about before God, except that you are nothing and that He is your creator and that He could turn you into nothing in the blink of an eye. Reason knows nothing of such enlightening thoughts, though highly placed people have sought it, what heaven and earth, human beings and the creatures really are, but have not figured it out; and yet, here, what the faith says is stated plainly, that God created everything out of nothing (Heb. 11:3); this is the soul's garden of pleasure, to walk around among God's works."[158]

---

156 Heidegger, *Was ist Metaphysik?*, 35.

157 *BSLK*, 648.27–30.

158 "Eine einfältige Weise zu beten, 1535," WA 38:373.20 (AE 43:187–211); it is much the same in passages such as "Op. in Ps., 1518–21," WA 5:544.18–22; "Sermon und Eingang in das 1. Buch Mose vom 22.3.1523," WA 12:442.1–8; "Gen.-Vorl., 1535–45," WA 43:178.39–179.2 (AE 4:1–409); "Pred. in Schmalkalden über

Since Luther is virtually fascinated when reflecting on the mystery of life, he cannot follow the ancient scholastic intellectual tradition and view the creaturely world as a scenario that has a relatively independent existence over against the creator and that is determined on the basis of fixed orders and laws.[159] The reformer views the creation more in line with the Old Testament, as a history in which God is constantly at work to preserve and lead it. His reflections thus revolve around the substantive attribute "almighty," which gives expression to God's "*omnipotentia actualis*."[160]

As the all-powerful Lord, God does battle, with the help of His creatures, against the princes of this world and their hangers-on; a relentless battle for life in all its dimensions is depicted. In the catechisms, Luther does not describe this in detail in his treatment of the First Article; we need to sketch in the details from his expositions in order to get a comprehensive picture.[161] The creator places His creatures into the battle line: "*Deus creavit istas creaturas omnes, ut stent in milicia et sine fine pugnent contra Diabolum pro nobis*" (But God created all these creatures to be in active military service, to fight for us continually against the devil; AE 1·74).[162] The battle for life is fought on every level: (1) The lowest level is that of the non-human creatures, which God provides to serve us "for the needs and necessities of life,[163] which we by contrariness misuse and thus give over to nothingness.[164] (2) The next level up is that of "the temporal, worldly realm, which includes the realm of the household and the authority of parents over their children";[165] it is the realm of the sword

das Symbolum vom 11.2.1537," WA 45:13.9–21; "Pred. über Joh. 1:3–5 vom 14.7.1537," WA 46:560.4–15 (AE 22:1–530).

[159] Luther acknowledges that this view is correct to a certain extent; "Gen.-Vorl., 1535–45," WA 42:316.21 (AE 2:76): "Nevertheless just as Augustine learnedly states, God governs the things he has created in such a way that he allows them to function with their distinctive activities".

[160] "De servo arbitrio, 1525," WA 18:718.28 (AE 33:3–295).

[161] This is explicated in the commentary on the prophet Zechariah, 1527, WA 23:511–15 (AE 20:153–347), in "Das schöne Confitemini, 1530," WA 31.1:77–92 (AE 51:155–169), and in the "Michaelispred., 1539," WA 47:853–58.

[162] "Gen.-Vorl., 1535–45," WA 42:56.30 (AE 1:1–359).

[163] *BSLK*, 648.19f.

[164] Cf. *BSLK*, 566.20–26 (Large Catechism on the First Commandment); "Das schöne Confitemini, 1530," WA 31.1:72.22–31 (AE 14:41–106); "Michaelispred., 1539," WA 47:857.31–35.

[165] "Sach.-Ausl., 1527," WA 23:513.21 (AE 20:153–347).

and the fist,[166] but also of the hoe and the plow, the economic and political spheres. God seeks to protect and multiply life in this arena as well. In contrast, by means of "agitators, disobedient ruffians, evil and poisonous advice to princes in their castles . . . tyrants, villains and everything that serves to bring war, discord and destruction of lands and people,"[167] Satan seeks to destroy life.[168] (3) God's spiritual realm takes matters to a higher level yet, by means of "Word and mouth,"[169] which points already to the Second and Third Articles; Satan awakens "the heretics, false teachers, hypocrites, and false brothers"[170] against this realm of the Word of God. Above these three levels of conflict, the dimension of the principalities and powers is in play. According to Karl Barth,[171] they are what is meant by the term heavens. Luther refers to them in the catechisms, in the petition in the Morning and Evening Prayers: "May Your holy angel be with me, that the wicked foe will wield no power against me."[172] The angels stand by us; they protect us on the outside and inside, they shield us from harm and disaster and give us good thoughts in our heart and mind; they thus help to "rule Christianity and the world,"[173] in opposition to the dark powers of the realm of Satan.[174]

Such cooperative help is provided for us by the visible and invisible creatures. But the reformer is careful to differentiate clearly between the direct and immediate, internal, creative activity of God and the indirect and mediated help provided by the created beings.[175] For all that they are able to do, one thing they cannot do; they cannot effect or give life itself; this has been reserved for the creator alone.

---

[166] "Sach.-Ausl., 1527," WA 23:513.38 (AE 20:153–347).

[167] "Sach.-Ausl., 1527," WA 23:515.3.

[168] "Das schöne Confitemini, 1530," WA 31.1:83.30 (AE 51:155–161): "that I pay attention to the fact that our present freedom and situation hangs by a silk thread, in fact, it swings precariously in the air, only in the hands of God above and against our own will and thoughts and against all the devil's rage and fury."

[169] "Sach.-Ausl., 1527," WA 23:513.37 (AE 20:153–347).

[170] "Sach.-Ausl., 1527," WA 23:515.4.

[171] Barth, *Dogmatik im Grundriß*, 64: "Heaven is incomprehensible to the human being; the earth is the creature that such a one can comprehend." Cf. Peter Lombard, *Sententiarum* II, dist. 2.

[172] *BSLK*, 521.33–35; 522.17–19 (SC).

[173] "Pred. über Apk. 12:12ff. vom 29.9.1534," WA 37:539.28.

[174] On the service performed by the guardian angels, see the three "Michaelispredigten von 1531," WA 34.2:222–87.

[175] On this, see Seils, *Der Gedanke vom Zusammenwirken*, 177–84 and Nilsson, *Simul*, 78ff.

He wants to have His created beings serve as fellow workers, not fellow creators."[176]

The First Commandment is in play at this point for Luther; he carefully delineates the boundary between creator and created beings with respect to the honor due to the holy ones and to the service of the angels: "Therefore it is necessary that the people are to be taught, so that such a shameful misuse is hindered from ever happening again, whereby the angels and holy ones are addressed in prayer. The one, eternal, living God alone is to be addressed in prayer, the one who forgives sins and who delivers from death; such matters are not the work of angels, creatures, holy ones or even our beloved wives. Instead, this is the work of the one God, who justifies sinners and makes the dead to come alive."[177]

The all-controlling creator draws us astonishingly close to Himself in, with, and under the "masks and masquerades" of His creatures. Taking into account that we are bound to the place where we live, the reformer characterizes this with the shorthand term "ubiquitous";[178] with respect to the way we are inserted into time and history, he uses the shorthand term "momentous."[179] Cutting through space and time, God is uncannily close to us and yet continues to keep Himself away from our clumsy attempts to take hold of Him. Luther depicts God's presence in as real and concrete a way as possible but protects God's overarching sovereignty at the same time.

What does the omnipresence of God mean?: Where God creates and preserves life, it is not just that the creaturely powers are serving Him thereby; He Himself is close at hand as well; He is present "in

---

176 "Michaelispred., 1539," WA 47:857.35; cf. "Sach.-Ausl., 1527," WA 23:511.35ff. (AE 20:153–347), and Seils, *Der Gedanke vom Zusammenwirken*, 157–69. Such an arrangement that attributes to God the inner working and to the creatures the external cooperation was articulated already by Peter Lombard, as for example in *Sententiarum* II, dist. 7.10 (PL 192:666): "None but God can form our mind by justifying it, but men are able to preach the Gospel as an external cause, and not only the good ones in truth, but also the bad ones in pretence. In the same way, it is God who interiorly works in the creation of visible things, but the exterior operations and mixtures or occasions are furnished by good and evil angels, and even by men" [Sileno translation, *Sentences* 2:32].

177 "Michaelispred. vom 28.9.1531," WA 34.2:226.25.

178 On omnipresence, see Genrich, *Die Christologie Luthers im Abendmahlsstreit*; Sommerlath, *Der Sinn des Abendmahls*, 23–62; Metzke, *Sakrament und Metaphysik*; Grass, *Die Abendmahlslehre bei Luther und Calvin*, 57–86; Peters, *Realpräsenz*, 67–113.

179 On "little hour," see Wingren, *Luthers Lehre vom Beruf*, 135–46.

each and every creature in the depth of what is inside, manifest for each one in what is outside, about and about, through and through, beneath and above, in front of and behind . . . so that nothing can be more present and more within in all creatures than God Himself with His power."[180] But God does not position Himself as constantly present and yet at the same time pull Himself away as if He is a stormy wind that blasts through. "The deity is without motion in Himself, is not travelling from one place to another, as do the creatures."[181] When God positions Himself by being present, that does not refer to His movement within space; instead, the exalted creator summons His creatures to come into His presence. He is closer to us than we try to be to our own selves, precisely because He is not caught up in movement within space; instead, He is the sovereign creator and lord of physical space in His nearness.

An analogous relationship holds true for God with respect to time. Here, as well, we ought not to insert Him into a pattern that fits abstract time and eternity. He encompasses all ages with His rule as Lord; "He looks upon time in the same way humans see two things, with their eyes, that are positioned at a great distance from one another, but which are brought together in an instant."[182] Insofar as God holds the creatures within the orders of time, He holds them at the same time in His hands. In order to make sense of this, Luther directs our attention to the mystery of little special moments, the *kairoi.* The wisdom teaching of other nations always circumvented any way to handle this mystery; the proverbs of Solomon elevate the problem to the level of faith in Yahweh; they show "that the realm in which a human being can interact and can make an impact by means of his reason is actually small. No matter where one turns—more properly where one does damage, one stands once again in front of the incomprehensible realm of the activity of God."[183] This incomprehensible situation is described by Luther with an insight that he always has close at hand and which does not change: "God has

[180] "Daß diese Worte Christi noch fest stehen, 1527," WA 23:135.3 (AE 37:3–150).

[181] "Daß diese Worte Christi noch fest stehen, 1527," WA 23:141.13. This is set forth in great detail, and the words of Augustine are preserved by Peter Lombard, *Sententiarum* I, dist. 37.

[182] "Sermon und Eingang in das 1. Buch Mose vom 22.3.1523," WA 12:445.3; cf. "Gen.-Vorl., 1535–45," WA 42:9.27–31; 57.34–58.2 (AE 1:1–359).

[183] Von Rad, *Theologie des Alten Testaments*, 2:438, with reference to Prov. 16:9, 33; 19:21; 21:2f., 30f.; 25:2; 29:26.

made it exactly so and has apportioned everything, so that He wants to have all thoughts and works in His hand, so that nothing can proceed on its own; the hour comes that God has determined for it . . . God has made it thus, so that all things in the world are to have their time and hour; a fine, free little moment in time has been provided for each thing."[184]

Luther's reflections on God's lordship as creator and preserver do not direct our attention to the structures of His existence that endure through time; instead, we are moved to think about our concrete destiny as human beings in our relationship with Him where we live, closely bound to the earth, as well as in the historical realm in which we exist. What one comes to know in this setting is included by Luther as part of the confession about the unseen God, who has disclosed Himself to us in Jesus Christ.[185] This confession about God as creator and preserver within the framework of our daily life is articulated in three statements:

(1) In the midst of life's mysteries, ongoing as they are, which no one can really master, either protecting us wonderfully or taking it all away painfully, in every moment of our existence in our everyday life we come into contact with the Creator God. In all its dimensions, whether the earth that carries us along, or the air that surrounds us, or the rays of sunshine that warm us, the nourishing fruits, the communal existence we share with other human beings, even to the point of the deepest love between two fellow human beings, this bodily life places us before God and bears the character of a gift that is not forced on anyone, "since one word encapsulates it all: Creator."[186]

---

[184] "Pred. über Joh. 7:30 vom 22.7.1531," WA 33:404.37; 405.12 (AE 23:198–422); cf. also "Eccl. sal. cum annotationibus, 1526/32," WA 20:58.5f. (AE 15:1–187); "Wochenpred. über Mt. 6, 1530," WA 32:471.5–22 (AE 21:1–294); "Ausl. von Ps. 101, 1534/35," WA 51:244.18–33 (AE 13:143–224).

[185] "Pred. über Joh. 7:30 vom 22.7.1531," WA 33:404.37; 405.12 (AE 23:198–422); cf. also "Eccl. sal. cum annotationibus, 1526/32," WA 20:58.5f. (AE 15:1–187); "Wochenpred. über Mt. 6, 1530," WA 32:471.5–22 (AE 21:1–294); "Ausl. von Ps. 101, 1534/35," WA 51:244.18–33 (13:143–224).

[186] *BSLK*, 648.31f. (SC). If such statements by Luther are lifted out from the situation of confession before God and projected onto the level of a view of the world couched in wisdom thinking, it is easy to understand how some Roman Catholic interpreters

(2) In this context, however, God is not merely the élan vital, the aboriginal dynamic power for all that lives; He is the refuge and protector of this life against the opposing power of Satan, who seeks to throw us back into aboriginal chaos, against the sinister "drive toward death." As the one who provides and preserves life, God incorporates the creatures into His sphere of influence; as Lord of the heavenly and earthly forces, He is zealous for life in all its dimensions; to carry this out, He makes use of what has been ordained, instituted and mandated,[187] marriage and family, spiritual and temporal realms, and thus household, political, and ecclesiastical estates, but He additionally makes use of the creatures that are not human and the angelic powers. The double commandment to love God and the neighbor, as articulated in the Decalogue, as well as the charge to be in dominion over all the non-human creatures, is the proper framework established by God to deal with the conflict of light and darkness, life and death.

(3) In all such dealings, the Christian recognizes and confesses, with respect to all of the undeserved blessings from the creator, that God as Father is merciful, giving and preserving life by means of direct, internal activity and closeness, as well as through the indirect, external help of His creatures. The believer recognizes and confesses: The world, and everything living within it, continues to exist not merely because the aboriginal material takes shape in an orderly and structured manner; instead, it happens by means of the faithfulness of the creator on behalf of His creatures.[188]

The Human Being in this Physical Existence as the Center of the Creatures by God's Design

God places human beings in the midst of the creation; it seems quite obvious that they are thus the center of the universe. "I believe that

---

of Luther would arrive at a faulty understanding when they apply what they think he says; see Scheffczyk, *Schöpfung und Vorsehung*, 110.

[187] Concerning what is ordained, cf. Volume 1, 197–207, 246–57.

[188] Löfgren, *Die Theologie der Schöpfung bei Luther*, 51: "Luther takes note of the regularity of the laws that govern the creation, as a way of expressing the 'faithfulness' of God over against His creation, and this term can be easily united with thoughts about God's freedom."

God has created me together with all creatures."[189] Though to our mind it is a hasty and naïve way of taking this reality for granted, the believer sees himself at the side of the creator, in the center of the world. In the Large Catechism,[190] Luther merges the creation accounts of the Yahwist and the Priestly Writing and restates both afresh, so that both can apply to those who were living off the land in the sixteenth century. As does the Yahwist, the reformer starts out with "the world that is close to human beings, the world where that person lives life . . . , which God has constructed around the human being."[191] Then, along with the Priestly Writing, he adds the cosmos at large, from the farthest stars to the swarming creatures on the earth, to the soil of the earth that produces its fruits.[192] But the Garden of Eden that stretched out in all directions in the original account becomes now the protecting house of the citizen who dwells on the land. God installs the protecting forces of His worldly rulers, who keep order around this house, the princes and city states, who were ruling as the modern era began to unfold. The reformer thought that God initiated the use of such protecting powers in Gen. 9:6, in the "ancient instruction from the sacral law."[193] "Whoever sheds the blood of a human, by human beings his blood is to be shed, for the human being is made in the image of God." In this passage, God places His majestic right over death and life into the hands of the human community and thereby establishes the political realm, the order of human rule that operates by means of justice and the sword,[194] in an orderly setting, so that thereby, in His temporal realm, peace and security can be guaranteed.[195]

We will not, at this time, analyze the more specific topics of what pertains to the household and political spheres, and we will bypass daily bread as well; at this point, the reader is referred to the

---

[189] *BSLK*, 510.33f. (SC).

[190] *BSLK*, 648.9–24.

[191] Von Rad, *Das erste Buch Mose*, 61; cf. Westermann, *Genesis* 1:48–52.

[192] Westermann, *Genesis* 1:104–30.

[193] Von Rad, *Das erste Buch Mose*, 109.

[194] "Gen.-Vorl., 1535–45," WA 42:361.28 (AE 2:141): "Thus this passage establishes civil government in the world, something that did not exist before the Flood."

[195] *BSLK*, 648.25f. (LC); "Gen.-Vorl., 1535–45," WA 42:360.30 (AE 2:140): "Here we have the source from which stem all civil law and the law of nations"; cf. "Von weltlicher Oberkeit, 1523," WA 11:247.31–248.15 (AE 45:75–129); "Pred. über Gen. 9, 1527," WA 24:203.13–27; "Gen.-Vorl., 1535–45," WA 42:360.9–362.8 (AE 2:1–399).

commentary on the Fourth Commandment, along with the Table of Duties and the Fourth Petition.[196] We reflect here solely on the position that the human being occupies within the cosmos.

The reformer sees the human being as a microcosm and the quintessence of the elements, as well as in the setting of the macrocosm, as remaining directly and immediately in the center of the world. He stays very close to the biblical texts at this juncture. Although Copernicus had broken the notion that depicted the earth in the center of the universe,[197] for Luther the world remained small and subject to observation, both in its spatial and its temporal dimensions. With respect to space, everything seems to revolve around the little domestic setting of the Saxon worker on the land; with respect to time, in his "*Supputatio annorum mundi*" (Computation of the Age of the Earth), Luther counted 5500 years from the creation of the world up to his own time,[198] thus not even 200 generations or, if one were to count the duration of the life of the earliest forefathers [Tr.: such as Methuselah], roughly six generations, one after another. This way to look at life at the time of the Reformation needs to be taken into account in the dogmatic disputes as well. The world is small and one can survey it; the human species is a close community; both the world and humanity are directly dependent on God. Luther paints this picture for us in his sermons about the creation of human beings according to the Priestly Account: "On the last day He (God) made human beings, but before that He built him a house, put a light in the heavens for him, so that he could see, set a boundary for the waters apart from the land, so that he had a place upon which to dwell, and decorated it according to His own pleasure with all sorts of plants, giving him dominion over everything that was alive, so that we are to see that God never forgets us."[199]

Such a naïve viewpoint that considers human beings to be the center of the world has been destroyed for us. The beginning of cosmic evolution, as well as life on our planet, has been pushed back endlessly; the spatial and temporal relationships that have been proposed by scientific activity stretch far beyond our

[196] See Volume 1, 197–207 and Volume 3 on the Fourth Petition of the Lord's Prayer.

[197] Concerning how Copernicus played a role in the Lutheran Reformation, see Elert, *Morphologie*, 1:363–78.

[198] WA 53:22–184.

[199] "Pred. über Gen. 1, 1527," WA 24:58.24.

comprehension.[200] The human being seems to disappear within such dimensions. Another way to conceptualize how everything developed starts with the centrality and complexity of life; it begins with the elements, and then goes on to molecules and viruses, etc., all the way up to the human being.[201] Such a charted course that describes the "inner structure of that which is becoming" would result in similar astronomical numbers, though from this vantage point the numbers would reach still higher orders of power. Only when one takes both types of reckoning into account can one get a suitable view of the position of the human being within the cosmos. The mystery of the biblical thesis is simply intensified thereby, which Luther sketched out in what seems to be a naïve way: The Creator God who is invisible has installed human beings into this cosmos, along with the rest of the creatures, as a visible sign of His majesty.

Luther describes the human beings in his catechism discussions with an equally naïve anthropology; he does not follow the Hellenistic tradition, but reaches back instead into the Old Testament.

In his early writings, with reference to Origen and Jerome,[202] he describes the human being as tripartite: "*Tria sunt in homine, corpus, anima, spiritus; Anima medium utriusque*" (The human has three parts, body, soul, spirit; the soul is between the other two).[203] He

---

[200] Yves Congar sought to make this more comprehensible by using an arbitrary reduction in measurement, letting three seconds stand for every century. In that case "life on our earth began on January 1 . . . ; Jesus Christ made His appearance on December 31, at midnight; but the earth itself had existed then already for four years before January 1 and five years before that December 31. According to this way of measuring, the first vertebrates appeared in the water in July, Sinanthropus-Pithecanthropus about 4 in the afternoon on December 31; Abraham and the origin of the chosen people takes place on that same December 31, at 11:59 PM. And we ourselves today stand just at the end of the first minute of the New Year, which began with the birth of Christ" (Congar, *Kirche und Welt*, 107). Even if these numbers are only approximate, the dimensions indicated are abundantly clear. What Luther said would have lasted for three minutes, the time from the beginning of the world until now, would stretch out to 40,000 hours or more. The spatial dimensions are analogously enlarged as well.

[201] According to Teilhard de Chardin, *Die Zukunft des Menschen*, 133–65; 279–95.

[202] "Gal.-Komm., 1519," WA 2:510.2 (AE 27:151–410); concerning these utterances from the early Church, cf. Joest, *Ontologie*, 142–48.

[203] "Röm.-Vorl., 1515–16," on Rom. 13:1, WA 56:480.18 (AE 25:1–524). It involves primarily the following texts: idem, WA 56:476.20–26; 480.18f.; "Gal.-Vorl., 1516–17," on Gal. 3:3, WA 57.2:77.18–79.2; "Hebr.-Vorl., 1517–18," on Heb. 4:4; 9:2, WA 57.3:158.18–159.1; 197.6–20 (AE 29:107–241); "Gal.-Komm., 1519," on Gal. 3:3; 5:17, WA 2:510.2–5; 585.22–25 (AE 27:151–410); "Magnificat, 1521," WA

bases this biblically on 1 Thess. 5:23. When discussing the Magnificat, he ties this way of thinking back to the viewpoint of Plato and Aristotle.[204] Just as the ark of Noah[205] or, better yet, as Moses' tabernacle, the human being is separated into three portions. When we start to observe a human, we note first of all the forecourt, the body itself, which everyone can see, which is made up of "body parts small and large."[206] But the body does not have life on its own; the soul is the vivifying power of life; it is the holy place, with the lamp stands that have seven arms, "which includes all manner of understanding, discernment, wisdom and knowledge about the bodily, visible things."[207] Then one comes to the Holy of Holies, the spirit as the place where God dwells "in dark faith without light."[208]

This is "the highest, deepest, most honorable part of the human being, by means of which one is capable of comprehending the incomprehensible, invisible, eternal thing."[209] The depiction of the tabernacle or the temple that provides a spatial way to understand the human being could lead us astray if we were merely to add the spirit to the soul, as that specific part that deals with religious abilities. But Luther speaks against this directly: "The soul is the same spirit by its nature, but it has a different job to perform";[210] as spirit, it turns this mysterious life, in faith that loves and hopes, toward the invisible and eternal God; as soul, it directs the body, makes use of the five senses, and rules over the non-human creatures by means of reason and understanding.

But based on his concentrated study of the "most important term" in Hebrew anthropology,[211] Luther uses *nephesh* to modify the tripartite nature of the tradition that is shaped by Hellenism. In his

---

7:550.19–551.24 (AE 21:295–355). The text are explicated by Joest, *Ontologie*, 163–95; Hirsch, *Lutherstudien*, 1:109–28.

[204] On this, see the overview by Duchrow, *Christenheit und Weltverantwortung*, 447–53.

[205] This is pointed out in "Hebr.-Vorl., 1517–18," WA 57.3:158.19 (AE 29:107–241).

[206] *BSLK*, 648.15 (LC).

[207] "Magnificat, 1521," WA 7:551.22 (AE 21:295–355).

[208] Ibid., WA 7:550.28.

[209] Ibid.

[210] Ibid, 550.35; "Röm.-Vorl., 1515–16," WA 56:476.23 (AE 25:468–69): "The 'soul' which is the same as man's spirit, insofar as it lives and works and is occupied with visible and temporal matters"; cf. on this Joest, *Ontologie*, 186f. and Hirsch, *Lutherstudien*, 1:120.

[211] Von Rad, *Theologie des Alten Testaments*, 1:157.

commentary on Gen. 2:7, that *locus classicus* for understanding the human being in the Old Testament, he draws out insights as follows: the word *nephesh*, which can be misunderstood by interpreting it as a reference to the soul, does not refer to the immortal nature of a spiritual person; instead, it is the vital power of life that energizes our existence in our bodies, with the five senses. In this respect, we are one with the animals, that is, with respect to our creaturely existence in bodies;[212] the term is used to describe, at one and the same time, the concrete interrelationship of "body, soul, and life."[213] Like the other creatures, we are taken from mother earth and we live, as do the animals, by means of the breath of life that God bestows. We confront the mystery of existence once again with this breath of life; we do not acquire it by our own power;[214] as the provider, God remains its lord at the same time; if He takes the breath of life back, we then sink once again back into the dust (Ps. 104:29f.; Job 34:14f.). As an "*animal corporeum et sensitivum*" (animal with body and senses),[215] the human being remains tied to mother earth, just as are the animals, and we ought thus to recognize this by bowing in humility.[216]

But because Luther was a careful exegete, he observed at the same time that Gen. 1:26 began afresh, as it distinguished the creation of the human being from that of all other living beings:[217] God's soliloquy announces "that He had desired to create the human being with special effort."[218] Due to the human being's ability to reflect within himself, and because he had the free ability to speak as well, the human being is separated out from communal existence with the

---

212 "Pred. über Gen. 2, 1527," WA 24:67.13: But Moses and the Scriptures identify the soul as everything that lives with the five senses"; cf. "Gal.-Vorl., 1516–17," on Gal. 3.3, WA 57.2:78.6f.; "Pred. über Gen. 2 vom 19.4.1523," WA 14:120.4; "Pred. über 1 Kor. 15:44ff. vom 1.2.1533," WA 36:663.10–664.10 (AE 28:57–213); "Gen.-Vorl., 1535–45," WA 42:65.9–18 (AE 1:1–359).

213 *BSLK*, 648.14f. (LC).

214 "Pred. über Gen. 2 vom 19.4.1523," WA 14:119.25: "The text (Gen. 2:7) wills that that little place for breathing not be under our control."

215 "Disputatio de homine, 14.1.1536," WA 39.1:175, Thesis 1 (AE 34:133–144).

216 In the "Credo-Pred. vom 11.2.1537," Luther comes out sharply against praise of God that is Jewish-heathen, which elevates the individual above the other creatures, WA 45:15.7–16.5. Cf. also Elert, *Morphologie*, 1, § 32 ("Being tied to the earth").

217 On this, see von Rad, *Das erste Buch Mose*, 44; Westermann, *Genesis* 1:198ff.

218 "Pred. über Gen. 1, 1527," WA 24:49.15; cf. "Pred. über Gen. 1 vom 12.4.1523," WA 14:110.1–3; "Ennaratio Ps. 90, 1534–35," WA 40.3:513.8–514.7 (AE 13:73–141); "Gen.-Vorl., 1535–45," WA 42:41.37–43.12 (AE 1:1–359); Hägglund, *De homine*, 55–77.

rest of the animal world, as an "*animal rationale*," and is linked with the angels, the spiritual beings; the human is a "*mixtum animal ex brutali et angelica natura*" (living being compounded of the natures of the brute and of the angels; AE 1:112).[219]

Reason, as the good gift from God, releases the human being from being ensconced within the creaturely realm. The "*potentia intellectiva*" (intellectual power),[220] as "*igemonicon*" (the authoritative part of the soul) and as "*principalis pars hominis*" (principle part of the human),[221] remains yet, even within the fallen creature; God's majesty is reflected even now in this gift that remains with the human being who is enslaved in original sin.[222] God gave this ability to us as human beings "so that they would rule on the earth. That is, so that they would have power to establish law and order for whatever was needed for this bodily existence, such as eating, drinking, clothing, likewise what would be needed to keep external order and an honorable life. Such rule is not reserved solely for Christians; it is most necessary for the heathen and the Turks."[223] Because of reason, the human being is in dominion over the non-human creatures and establishes order to bring about justice and peace even among those who are fellow humans. This independent, upright posture within the cosmos is what characterizes humans over against the other creatures that were made from the earth; the human is thereby singled out from that which is enveloped in the earth and the cosmos. Over against all other powers and forces, such an insistence that this freedom exists binds the biblical and reformational understanding of humanity with that of modern times. The scientific and technological revolution is rooted in and still lives by this presupposition of human freedom.

Luther explicates this freedom on the basis of the relationship with the stars, which threatened to cause a crisis as knowledge of

---

[219] "Gen.-Vorl., 1535–45," WA 42:85.13 (AE 1:1–359); cf. ibid., 34.22–35.7.

[220] Ibid., 85.12.

[221] "De servo arbitrio, 1525," WA 18:741.1 (AE 33:3–295).

[222] "Disputatio de homine, 14.1.1536," WA 39.1:175, Thesis 4 (AE 34:137): "And it is certainly true that reason is the most important and the highest in rank above all things and, in comparison with other things of this life, the best and something divine"; "Ennaratio Jes. 9," WA 40.3:612.31: "Reason is a very great and invaluable gift of God."

[223] "Pred. über Joh. 14, 1537," WA 45:621.5 (AE 24:1–422). On this, cf. Lohse, *Ratio und Fides*, 119–33.

nature progressed during the Renaissance.[224] He notes the "careful attention" in the Priestly Writing that denies any "claim of the starry host to have independent, divine power";[225] he arrives thereby at the enduring insight: "The starry host has not been created to exercise mastery over me; the stars are for my use and service. They are to rule over day and night, but they are not to reign or have power over my soul."[226] Nor are the starry host and the elements, as creatures, to act as lord over life and death; for this reason, we are not to consider them rock solid, to be trusted to give us certainty. "Trust is the purview of God alone; creatures are properly to be used."[227] And yet, with all the creatures, God lets them be there "for use and to serve the needs of life."[228]

Human existence is thus described with respect to its relationship with the world around it; Luther reiterates the philosophical definitions in the cast of popular speech: "*Philosophia, sapientia humana, definit hominem, esse animal rationale, sensitivum, corporeum*" (Philosophy or human wisdom defines man as an animal having reason, sensation, and body; AE 34:137).[229] Luther seems to consider this view to be adequate when he paraphrases the First Article, though he also gives attention to "*homo huius vitae*" (man in relation to this life; AE 34:137).[230] But since he considers earthly life to stem from the hand of the God, the whence and whither is secretly in play at the same time; it goes far beyond purely philosophical observations. Luther raises an objection to such thinking: it concentrates on the *Causa materialis* and points to the *Causa formalis*, the deepest mystery of our emotional and spiritual existence, but hardly from a distance. It does not consider the possibility that a power could help one transcend oneself and does not know of the human being who as a human being can surmount the self to achieve something that has no end. Philosophy goes about its business in this way because it cannot know the *Causa efficiens et finalis*, the whence

---

[224] See Elert, *Morphologie*, 1, § 31; Ludolphy, *Luther über Astrologie*.
[225] Von Rad, *Das erste Buch Mose*, 43.
[226] "Pred. über Gen. 1, 1527," WA 24:44.14; see also the preface to Joh. Lichtenbergs *Weissag- ung*, 1527, WA 23:7–12, but also "Gen.-Vorl., 1535–45," WA 42:30.13–34.21 (AE 1:1–359).
[227] "Das schöne Confitemini, 1530," WA 31.1:114.31 (AE 14:41–106).
[228] *BSLK*, 648.19f. (LC).
[229] "Disputatio de homine, 14.1.1536," WA 39.1:175, Thesis 1 (AE 34:133–144).
[230] Ibid., 175.8.

and whither of our human existence. It does not know that all of us together come from the creative hand of God and that we are to confront Him in judgment. It thus conceives of the human being solely in the way he is involved in the world, but not according to his existence before God. But the human being, in his innermost being, must remain under wraps and hidden, so long as he does not view himself in relationship with God.[231]

For this reason, theology thus defines the human being with reference to God according to one's whence: "*Homo est creatura Dei, carne et anima spirante constans, ab initio ad imaginem Dei facta*" (Man is a creature of God consisting of body and a living soul, made in the beginning after the image of God; AE 34:138)[232] and according to one's whither: the human as "*creatura condita, ut relicta aliquando terra coelestia habitet et aeternam vivat vitam*" (a creature created to inhabit the celestial regions and to live an eternal life when, after a while, he has left the earth; AE 1:46).[233] The path for the human being is thus presented, which ventures to exist before God, as his creator and judge by faith alone, based on the foreign righteousness of Christ. Luther crafts this theological definition of the human being as a paraphrase to describe the way he lives before God in Theses 21—23 of the "Disputatio de homine" of 1536: "*Homo est creatura ad imaginem Dei facta, vitae aeternitate donanda, post lapsum Adae aeterna morte subiecta, per Iesum Christum liberanda*" (Man is a creature made after the image of God, given eternal life; he was subject to death after the fall of Adam, freed through Jesus Christ [Tr.: text has been rearranged; see AE 34:138]).[234]

The Human Being Who Thanks and Serves God as One Remade in the Image of God in Christ[235]

In the concluding discussion in the Large Catechism, Luther places two human beings opposite one another, the godly human being and

---

[231] Ibid., 175, Thesis 17 (AE 34:138): "Nor is there any hope that man in this principal part can himself know what he is until he sees himself in his origin which is God."

[232] Ibid., 176, Thesis 21.

[233] "Gen.-Vorl., 1535–45," WA 42:53.3 (AE 1:1–359).

[234] The summary is cited according to Joest, *Ontologie*, 190; on the *Disputatio de homine*, see idem, 188–93; cf. Peter Lombard, *Sententiarum* II, dist. 16.

[235] *BSLK*, 649.7–650.21 (LC).

the worldly human being. Placing these two types of human beings in opposition transposes, at the same time, the philosophical and theological view of humanity into a description of contrasting views of daily life. The godly human being interacts with his creator in, with, and under the mask of the creatures, by means of thanks and praise; his life and world are not for plundering but for serving God with one's fellow creatures. He shows himself to be in the center of the cosmos precisely in that he lets the Lord of the cosmos be the center of his life. By contrast, the worldly human being misuses the creaturely gifts of God for praise of self and robs thereby the Creator of His honor. But this godly human being and this worldly human being are both stuck in each one of us; they are situated next to each another in the Christian heart in battle. We are both of them at the same time and in the same place: flesh and spirit,[236] *Imago Dei* and *Imago Satanae*. The entire human being is renewed in the image of God in Christ; at the same time, the entire human being carries the image of the satanic fall in his heart and on his body.

Luther seeks to give expression to this differentiation between the godly human being and the worldly human being by using terminology from Paul and John. He differentiates between the Latin prepositions "*per*" or "*in*" and "*ex*"; we ought to live well "*per labores nostros*" (through our labor) and also "*in laboribus nostris*" (by our labor) but not "*ex laboribus nostris*" (because of our labor).[237] When writing in German, he often uses the little word "*von*" (from, by) or even the more pliable "in his hand."[238] No one has life "from himself,"[239] and yet we all live in "the unhappy, distorted world" as if "we have life, riches, power, and honor, etc., from ourselves, so that others ought to fear and serve us."[240] The worldly human being in us exists as if all of life is situated within his own might and power, as if

---

[236] On this, Schott, *Fleisch und Geist nach Luthers Lehre*; Bornkamm, *Äußerer und innerer Mensch bei Luther und den Spiritualisten*; Hägglund, *De homine*, 313–32.

[237] "Dtn.-Vorl., 1523–24," on Deut. 8:17, WA 14:633.10 (AE 9:96): "the godless heart of man . . . nor does it notice that these are simply blessings of God sometimes through our efforts, sometimes without our efforts, but never from our efforts and always given out of His free mercy"; cf. Volume 1, pp. 273–80.

[238] "Sermon und Eingang in das 1. Buch Mose vom 22.3.1523," WA 12:442.1–9; "Röm.-Vorl., 1515–16," WA 56:398.9–399.32 (AE 25:1–524).

[239] *BSLK*, 648.29 (LC).

[240] *BSLK*, 649.23–26 (LC).

he has the world by the tail.[241] The godly human being admittedly lives in the world, with all his efforts and strivings; and yet he does not live because of the world, not by means of his own power; he finds the most important anchorage for his confidence, including his understanding about himself and the world, only in the Creator God who is above and beyond the worldly realm.

The reformer depicts this human being who has the *Imago Dei* and *Imago Satanae* in his commentary on Genesis.[242] He does not concentrate thereby as much on events that took place in the very beginning, but rather on Jesus of Nazareth. Indeed, as the second and final Adam,[243] He is the true image of the heavenly Father and is concurrently "the key for understanding the image of God in Adam."[244] The *Imago Dei* and the *Imago Satanae* are thus also that which is in us as spirit and flesh, as new and old human being, in battle one with the other.

In somewhat of a tension with the Old Testament narratives,[245] Luther describes being in the image of God not so much on the basis of external characteristics, on the basis of a similarity in the way the body looked. Instead, he seeks to describe the inner factors, based on the concept of our conscience that is connected with God in our inner being. And yet, he starts from this center to relate to our physical body and to our relationship with the world. By contrast with church tradition, he does not thereby differentiate between *Imago* and *Similitudo*.[246] Let us sketch out these three aspects, the relationship with God, with the world, and with oneself as *Imago Dei* and examine at the same time the contrasting depiction of the *Imago Satanae*:

---

241 "Das schöne Confitemini, 1530," WA 31.1:109.27 (AE 14:41–106): "For it is true now and will never change; the whole world trusts and relies on human beings and princes, which means, it has doubts about God and tramples on His First Commandment; one can trust all manner of false gods, but not this unique one, the real, true God."

242 On this, Stomps, *Die Anthropologie M. Luthers*, 23–30; Schumann, *Imago Dei*; Hägglund, *De homine*, 77–102; Asheim, *Glaube und Erziehung bei Luther*, 202–25.

243 Cf. 2 Cor. 4:4; Col. 1:15; Rom. 8:29; 1 Cor. 15:49; Phil. 3:21, as well as von Rad/Klein-knecht/Kittel, εικών.

244 Brunner, *Der Ersterschaffene als Gottes Ebenbild*, 88. Barth, *Kirchliche Dogmatik* 3.2.1: "In that the human being Jesus is the revealed Word of God, He is thereby our source of knowledge about the nature of the human being that has been created by God."

245 Cf., on this, von Rad, εικών, 387–90.

246 Cf. Hägglund, *De homine*, 78f. and Asheim, *Glaube und Erziehung bei Luther*, 205.

(1) "The personal relationship between God and the human being, which is established when the human being is created, is at the middle of one's being in the image of God."[247] The reformer thus does not start out using an abstract way of knowing God, but depicts the concrete life in fellowship with God.[248] The complete, full, original image of the human being who is fully open to God, which Adam was to be, is fully visible in Jesus. Such a life, hidden and enfolded within the love of God, was filled with such certainty about the all-encompassing grace of God that there was simply no room left for conflicted doubt, stifling dissatisfaction, and paralyzing fear of death. Because of the fall, this complete obedience to God in loving awe and childlike trust was broken; when that happened, the human being desired to wrap his fist around his own existence, being like God in having life under his own control and charting the future on the basis of his own absolute power. Since the center of power for one's existence shifted from the creator to be located within the creature, greed about things of life and fear of death, passion for this world, and fear of this world grabbed hold.[249]

(2) Because the human being existed originally by knowing God directly, what this meant for the human being was a fearless lordship over his fellow creatures; the innermost nature of the creatures was open to him;[250] he could direct the movements of the strongest animals with a little nod,[251] since he himself

[247] Brunner, *Der Ersterschaffene als Gottes Ebenbild*, 91.
[248] "Gen.-Vorl., 1535–45," WA 42:46 (AE 1:63), note: "The image and likeness of God is true and complete familiarity with God, the supreme delight of God, eternal life, eternal joy, eternal security; cf., ibid., 47.8 11, 33–35; 55.33–35; 63.30–33; 71.31f.; 98.20–24; 124.4–12.
[249] "Ennaratio Ps. 90, 1534–35," WA 40.3:564.4 (AE 13:73–141): "Therefore the old man is restless, wayward, sad, and old"; "Gen.-Vorl., 1535–45," WA 42:47.21 (AE 1:63): "We are never secure in God; apprehension and terror cause us concern even in sleep"; cf. ibid., 86.31–42.
[250] "Gen.-Vorl., 1535–45," WA 42:47.37 (AE 1:63): "a perfect knowledge of the nature of the animals, the herbs, the fruits, the trees and the remaining creatures; idem, 90.29 (AE 1:170): "There was a different light in Adam, who, as soon as he viewed an animal, came into possession of a knowledge of its entire nature and abilities, and, moreover, a far better one than we can acquire even when we devote an entire life to research into these things"; cf. ibid., 49.18–50.41; 87.1–8.
[251] Ibid., 48:1 (AE 1:64): "I believe that Adam could command a lion with a single word, just as we give a command to a trained dog"; cf. ibid., 78:31f.

was still free from fear. By sinfully acting in greed, he distorted the relationship with the earth and with the animal world; the powers of chaos that had been bound broke their fetters and invaded the cosmos once again.

(3) Directing one's attention selflessly toward God had an effect on the physical human body as well. Because of the relationship with God, the human being was guided entirely by the proper ordering of one's desires, feelings, yearnings, and knowledge. The partnering relationship between husband and wife was as yet without battle and conflict, without the desire for the one to rule over the other, without each trying constantly to pull the other one down.[252] The fall broke this harmony apart as well; the desire of the human heart to rise up against God found its echo in the body desiring to rise up against the spirit.[253] The stigma of God's curse brought with it problems for the bodily existence of the human being as well. Because of the judgment of God, sharing life together in a loving way yielded to a one-sided ordering that called for above and below; the "wife was to humble herself before the husband,"[254] and yet, she would have strongly protested such treatment. Chaotic anarchy threatened the human communities of family, tribe, and society; for this reason, God established the temporal realm that ruled with the sword.

It is thus that, through the fall, the *Imago Dei* transitioned to become the *Imago Satanae*;[255] the original image of Adam, in its essential nature, as an unshakable knowledge of God, was lost; we

---

[252] Ibid., 103.8–104.40.

[253] "Pred. über Gen. 3, 1527," WA 24:90.28: "They were fallen and had become disobedient to God, after which everything with respect to the physical body was disobedient as well, so that they were not able to curb it, not in thought and not in one's limbs. That condition has now been inherited by us and thus still remains"; cf. ibid., 90.8–13; "Pred. über Gen. 3 vom 14.5.1523," WA 14:134.2–8, 22–35; "Gen.-Vorl., 1535–45," WA 42:122.20–127.5 (AE 1:1–359).

[254] "Gen.-Vorl., 1535–45," WA 42:151.22 (AE 1:202): "[Eve] has been placed under the power of her husband, she who previously was very free and, as the sharer of all the gifts of God, was in no respect inferior to her husband"; cf. ibid., 151.12–42; 361.19–41; "Pred. über Gen. 3 vom 17.5.1523," WA 14:141.2–6, 20–30.

[255] "Pred. über Gen. 1 vom 12.4.1523," WA 14:111.9: "The image of the devil is made from the image of God"; cf. "Pred. über Gen. 1, 1527," WA 24:50.8f.; "Pred. über Mt. 8:1ff. vom 18.6.1534," WA 37:454.9–12; "Gen.-Vorl., 1535–45," WA 42:47.22; 68.31–42; 166.21–31 (AE 1:1–359).

can catch some glimpse of Adam's original glory only from a distance.[256] But Luther does not sketch out this loss in his discussion of the First Article.[257] By contrast, he depicts in extravagant detail the opposite side; the creator holds onto His creatures without being obliged to do so and with grace. In that sense as well, the reformer teaches about the reason for the image of God, so that human beings would rule over the creatures, that everything that had been created was put under the human beings who were gifted with reason, and that this relationship was not lost completely in the fall.[258] The reason for this, however, was not because of something about the humans, but rather that God was faithful even toward sinners.[259]

The fallen human being is constantly close to the point of enslaving the creature, with the help of reason and the power of the will that remains within, ready to fall headlong into chaos along with the world. But God does not let this happen. He makes it possible for reason to be used to free oneself from one's own false steps; He even uses a person's own self-seeking will to strengthen community with one's fellow citizens.[260] But Luther does not use the catechetical setting to depict how God holds fast to the fallen human beings, from within the depths of its paradoxical nature;[261] he simply points to the

---

[256] "Gen.-Vorl., 1535–45," WA 42:48.31 (AE 1:65): "faith and the Word teach, which as from a distance, point out the glory of the divine image".

[257] It is mentioned in connection with the Second Article, *BSLK*, 651.42, 48.

[258] Von Rad, εικών, 390.30: "The Old Testament gives no indication that the image of God is forever lost for the human being." "Gen.-Vorl., 1535–45," WA 42:48.12 (AE 1:64): "Intellect and will indeed have remained, but both very much impaired."

[259] "Disputatio de homine, 14.1.1536," WA 39.1:175, Thesis 9 (AE 1:65): "Nor did God after the fall of Adam take away this majesty of reason, but rather confirmed it".

[260] On this, see Wingren, *Schöpfung und Gesetz*, 149–74.

[261] In his commentary on Rom. 8:18–23 ("Pred. vom 20.6.1535," WA 41:301–18; "Pred. vom 6.7.1544," WA 49:503–10; presented also by Ellwein, *Epistel-Ausl.*, 1:128–49), Luther also draws in the non-human creatures along with the children of God with respect to the cross of Christ; God had also consigned them to vanity, which means He put them under godless human beings (cf. "Röm.-Vorl., 1515–16," WA 56:372.28 [AE 25:1–524]), until the time when He would exalt them along with the children of God. The reformer thus allows mother earth to speak: "I allow myself to be plowed and cultivated, and yet it is the smallest portion who are Christian, for whom it really comes as a blessing, while the large majority who enjoy my fruits are wicked, evil clods. But what am I to do about that? I will suffer it, will allow myself to be wrecked by plowing and turned over again and again, since that is what my God would have me do and I will hope along the way that it will be different someday, so that I am no longer cast under such vanity, and will be able to serve the friends of God (Ellwein, *Epistel-Ausl.*, 140).

misuse of the gifts of God by referring to this "unhappy, distorted world.[262]

In the final analysis, we do not become aware of the true nature of the image of God that was distorted in Adam in the first pages of the Bible; that comes instead in the New Testament. Jesus of Nazareth, as the second and final Adam, is the true image of the unseen Father.[263] In His Spirit and because of His love, God's majesty and love shine forth upon us. In a renewed sense, He lives for God as the completely open human being and thereby also for His human family; the original concord and harmony are won back in Him for body, soul, and spirit.[264] He defeats the powers of destruction and rules over the creatures that live outside the human realm, in the freedom of the Son of God. He alone fulfills what God stated as His expectations in His commandments. The *Imago Dei* that was lost in Adam is back on track in Him. Moving toward completion at the end of time, it seeks to motivate us as well.[265]

The First Article describes this renewed image of God in Christ; for this reason, the Second and Third Articles are secretly included therein already. Just as we do not have the ability to know God the Father as a well-meaning creator and merciful preserver apart from Christ through the Holy Spirit, it is thus only in the Son through the Spirit that one can fulfill the commandments of the Father and thus love and praise God thereby, without hesitation, thank Him, and serve Him.[266] These insights are part of what Luther has in mind in the First Article already, when he sketches out what is meant by the proper obedience expected from the child of God by using the phraseology: gift and commandment.[267] One might almost use Barth's thought-

---

[262] *BSLK*, 649.26f. (LC)

[263] "Pred. über Gen. 1, 1527," WA 24:50.26: "The heavenly picture is Christ, who was a human being full of love, mercy and grace, humility, patience, wisdom, light and everything good, so that His entire being was directed toward serving every human being and that He would do harm to no one; it is this picture that we are to carry as well, and we will act is the same way as He does"; cf. "Pred. über Gen. 1 vom 12.4.1523," WA 14:110.15–111.3; "Gen.-Vorl., 1535–45," WA 42:48.11–31; 167.14–20 (AE 1:1–359).

[264] Cf. Barth, *Kirchliche Dogmatik* 3.2, § 45.1; § 46.1.

[265] "Gen.-Vorl., 1535–45," WA 42:48.27 (AE 1:65): "In this manner this image of the new creature begins to be restored by the Gospel in this life, but it will not be finished in this life". Cf. "Disputatio de homine, 14.1.1536," WA 39.1:176f., Theses 20–40 (AE 34:133–144).

[266] *BSLK*, 660.38–47; 661.35–42 (LC).

[267] *BSLK*, 650.23–25.

provoking terminology: "Gospel and Law."[268] But Luther concentrates completely on the dimension of creation. Since God has gifted us, along with His creatures, with Himself as Father, we are "obliged"[269] to serve Him, along with this creation. The question about where we can acquire the power for this new obedience has not been posed as yet; the relationship with Christ, which we are inserting into the discussion, lurks hidden within that question.

As far as the obedience itself, Luther depicts it as a summary of the commentary on the commandments,[270] in analogy to the structure in the Small Catechism: "We should fear and love God, so that we do not . . . but . . ." But looking up toward the good creator positions the thankful act of love as that which is most important. Looking at the gifts of the creation focuses us on the material items that we are to use to the praise and honor of God, rather than on fellow human beings who are to be treated on the basis of the fear of God and love of God.[271] At this point, Luther expands the setting in which the Christian is to serve; in addition to parents and other authorities in the Fourth Commandment and other human beings who are mentioned in the rest of the commandments, one's own life[272] comes to the fore here in the First Article, along with the things of the world that are provided for our everyday life. In this sense that is closest to the heart and most expansive, the human being is called to praise and serve God.

Using the structure employed in his commentary on the Commandments in the Small Catechism,[273] Luther positions the First Commandment at this point over the Commandments of the Second Table as well; the relationship with God is to give shape to the way one relates to the self and to the world. In our relationship with God, who created us and gifts Himself to us anew through His creatures

---

[268] In the commentary on Genesis, Luther portrays (WA 42:79.1–83.31 [AE 1:146]) worship of God by the one who was created first and says there, with reference to Gen. 2:16f. (ibid., 110.18): "For Adam this Word was Gospel and Law; it was his worship; it was his service and the obedience he could offer God in this state of innocence"; cf. Brunner, *Zur Lehre vom Gottesdienst*, 119–25. Some measure of the glory of that innocence of Adam hovers in the midst of the presentation on the First Article, particularly in the Small Catechism.

[269] *BSLK*, 511.8 (SC); 649.11; 649.40; 650.25 (LC).

[270] *BSLK*, 649.14f. (LC).

[271] *BSLK*, 650.20f. (Large Catechism).

[272] *BSLK*, 649.35f. (LC).

[273] Cf. Volume 1, 131–34.

each day, one ought to "incessantly . . . love, praise, and thank Him,"[274] so that we do not consider His gifts to be deserved, which would mean that we sense a right to misuse them as if they are to benefit ourselves alone, but rather that we are *thereby*[275] to serve Him by means of our love, as well as in the way we serve the creatures that are entrusted to us. The commandment thus grows immediately out of God's giving of Himself to us; as the "*usus practicus Evangelii*," it carries the gracious act of Christ secretly within it already.

Since the commandment still applies to us in our old sinful nature, however, it still carries with it the form of a demand and a command.[276] The command of the creator brings terror and humiliates us as an accusing law, even though it is in itself life-creating; the First Article works on us the "*usus elenchticus legis* (accusing function of the law [Tr.: others use this term for the paedogogic function])."[277] In this article as well, God wants our innermost heart for Himself and thereby claims our complete human nature in all the ways it relates to the world. This comprehensive demand for faith and obedience conceals the inner schism within each person's heart[278] and the external disobedience manifested in each person's body.[279] This First Article thus draws us, right from the start, into the eschatological battle between the new human being and the old one, the *Imago Dei in Christo* versus the *Imago Satanae in Adam.*

This conflict between the morning of creation that is ascendant, against the night of sin that is descendent,[280] is explicated suggestively according to the "little wreath, wrapped four times around":[281] teaching, praising, confessing, and petitioning. (1) Proper

---

[274] *BSLK*, 649.12f. (LC); cf. 511.6 (SC); 650.19 (LC); "Kat.-Pred. zum 1. Art. vom 10.12.1528," WA 30.1:87.15ff.; 88.6f. (AE 51:162–169); "Das schöne Confitemini, 1530," WA 31.1:76.34f. (AE 14:41–106)

[275] *BSLK*, 649.13 (LC); cf. 649.34–37, the opposite of unthankfulness. Thomas Aquinas, *Expositio in Symbolum Apostolorum*, § 885: "Whatever you have, therefore, either knowledge or wealth, you ought to give it all back and use it to the glory of God."

[276] *BSLK*, 649.14f. (LC).

[277] *BSLK*, 649.32–34.

[278] *BSLK*, 649.21.

[279] *BSLK*, 649.34–38.

[280] "Gal.-Komm., 1519," WA 2:586.19 (AE 27:363): "But it is like a morning twilight, which is neither day nor night yet can be called either one. Nevertheless, day, as that toward which it is tending after the darkness of night, is more appropriate."

[281] "Eine einfältige Weise zu beten, 1535," WA 38:364.31 (AE 51:257–287).

Christians distinguish themselves from the other human beings by recognizing and confessing God as their lord and creator. They are earnest about acquiring a comprehensive and deep understanding of the First Article.[282] For such, it is their "Little Book of Instruction."[283] (2) They do not allow such insight to remain merely in the realm of theoretical knowledge; they practice this article and process what it says for themselves; they take every little gift of God to be cause for praise and thanks.[284] The heart is thus warmed and set afire to sing the song of praise to one's creator and preserver. For such people, the article turns into a "Little Song Book."[285] (3) They allow themselves to be "humbled and awed"[286] by God's absolute demand to love, since they recognize how deeply, in their own heart, their personal "I" remains ensconced and how they sin with all the parts of their own body and with all their goods against their creator and preserver. They subject their old Adam to the judgment of this Article, confess their guilt,[287] and praise the undeserved mercy of the Father. The First Article thereby becomes a "Little Book of Confession" as well.[288] (4) They pray earnestly to be obedient, with thanks and joy, not taking the gifts of God for granted and not misusing them for their own selfish pleasure, but rather accepting them thankfully, protecting them carefully, and using them responsibly, so that here already, the creature can gain the advantage of the lordly freedom of the children of God. This article thus finally becomes also "The Little Book of Prayer."[289] By means of this fourfold little wreath of prayer, we take our life and the gifts of the creation from God's hand and allow ourselves, by means of faith and hope, to go forth in life in the image of the Son as free children of God.

---

[282] *BSLK*, 649.20ff. (LC).

[283] "Eine einfältige Weise zu beten, 1535," WA 38:372.26 (AE 51:257–287).

[284] *BSLK*, 650.10–17 (LC); "Credo-Pred. vom 11.7.1529," WA 29:473.8: "Lead your horse, pull your wagon, etc.; then you will humble yourself and recognize God your creator, in that you do not go back and forth like a cow and an animal without reason."; cf. "Das schöne Confitemini, 1530," WA 31.1:68.16–73.23 (AE 14:41–106).

[285] "Eine einfältige Weise zu beten, 1535," WA 38:372.27 (AE 43:187–211).

[286] *BSLK*, 649.33f. (LC).

[287] *BSLK*, 649.39f. (LC).

[288] "Eine einfältige Weise zu beten, 1535," WA 38:372.27.

[289] Idem; this is not stated with respect to the First Article; but cf. *BSLK*, 682.12–33 (Large Catechism on the Fourth Petition of the Lord's Prayer) and "Eine einfältige Weise zu beten, 1535," WA 38:374.6ff.

What starts with the creation is drawn thereby into the eschatological movement of the history of salvation. Luther points this out sensitively at the conclusion to the First Article in the Large Catechism.[290] But the conclusion[291] demonstrates that, for him as well, the seemingly naïve anthropocentrism of the First Article is oriented toward the central position of Christ. Calvin formulated this in a cogent way that is unsurpassed: "The world is created for the sake of the children of God[292] and even this only because of the head, which is our Lord Jesus Christ."[293] Because God the Father created the cosmos by means of the eternal Son, since the Son took our human nature upon Himself, in order to redeem us and to take us back home under the lordship of God and the goodness of the Father,[294] God's merciful hand holds us in the middle of the cosmos, for which reason we ought to venture forth in childlike confidence, knowing ourselves to be safely protected in the midst of this life where there is no real home, threatened with danger and prone to accidents. We guilt-laden human beings cannot extract ourselves from such a condition by our own spiritual powers and by our own survival techniques in the center of the world; "all without our merits and worthiness," God holds onto us sinners as if He were holding His good creatures, safe within His fatherly mercy. Such awareness summons us to praise God thankfully and to serve God responsibly in the care of all creatures. Not as those who destroy by robbery or as lazy hired hands, but rather as free, fellow shepherds of His nature, we can exist only as those who are protected by God. The seemingly naïve anthropocentrism of the First Article thus shows itself actually to have a theocentric focus that is given its character in Christ.

---

[290] *BSLK*, 650.21–33 (LC).

[291] *BSLK*, 660.18–661.18 (LC).

[292] *As. Mos.* 1:12: "God created the circle of the earth because of His people"; cf. 2 Esd. 6:55–59; 7:11. The tradition of the Church has been summarized by Peter Lombard, *Sententiarum* II, dist. 1.8 (PL 192:653): "And just as man was made for God, that is, to serve him, so the world was made for man, namely to serve him [Sileno translation, *Sentences* 2:6].

[293] CR 51:256, cited according to Niesel, *Die Theologie Calvins*, 63. "Gen.-Vorl., 1535–45," WA 44:781.1 (AE 8:275): "Every creature and whatever there is in heaven and on earth, all this gathered into that sum total, into that one Christ, in such a way that He is the Mediator, whether we seek spiritual or physical things."

[294] Ibid., 66.10 (AE 6:89): "In short, all things in heaven and earth are ordained to this end, that the righteous should be gathered together and the number of those who are to be saved should be filled up."

THE SECOND ARTICLE ON JESUS CHRIST AS OUR LORD AND REDEEMER

LUTHER'S UNDERSTANDING OF THE SCOPE OF THE SECOND ARTICLE AND ITS DIVISIONS[1]

The Second Article portrays God's redemptive activity in Jesus Christ; in that regard, it serves as the center of the Apostles' Creed and of the catechism as a whole;[2] "the entire Gospel, we thus preach," stands upon this; "one is to comprehend this article carefully, since it is on this that our entire salvation and everlasting bliss depend, and it is so rich and expansive that we will always have enough to learn from it."[3]

According to Johannes Meyer,[4] the reformer supposedly developed "four different possibilities for conceptualizing the rich insights of the Second Article "from a single vantage point": (1) Jesus purifies and sanctifies our unclean earthly life by means of His pure body; (2) Jesus the human being is the sign that demonstrates the gracious heart of God the Father; (3) Jesus Christ, as the victorious ruler, frees us from the tyranny of the powers of destruction and brings us back into God's fatherly grace; (4) Jesus enters into the presence of God, on our behalf, as high priest. Such diverse insights are unquestionably all at play, as we must demonstrate, in Luther's understanding of the Second Article. But he lets himself be guided in his commentary by the formal structural arrangement of this article. The reformer knows the clearly dual aspect in one's confession about Christ: The "three substantive titles of honor" provide the essence of what is stated about Jesus of Nazareth; He is the Messiah, the only

---

[1] Literature: Meyer, *Historischer Kommentar*, 295–340 (ibid., 257f., for the older literature); Hardeland, *Katechismusgedanken*, 205–37; Girgensohn, *Katechismus-Auslegung*, 1:124–45; Stallmann, *Der zweite Artikel als katechetisches Problem*.

[2] Cf. pp. 47–56.

[3] *BSLK*, 653.11–15 (LC).

[4] Meyer, *Historischer Kommentar*, 308–10.

Son of God, and our Lord; these central elements are unfolded by means of a series of verbal statements, which take us along the path Jesus traverses, as He saves, starting with the virgin birth and culminating in the parousia.[5] Two levels of narrative are at play as the story unfolds, as indicated at the outset.[6] One would have had an original, actually independent, comprehensive confession about Christ; it would have been inserted into the short, triadic sketch of the baptismal questions. This would likely have taken place somewhere between the middle and the end of the third century in Rome.[7]

Already in the Short Form of 1520, the reformer accentuates the substantival, central confession: I believe "in Jesus Christ, His only Son, our Lord."[8] Both aspects of the article appear in such a way that they focus the application on the "for me" aspect. In his sermon on December 10, 1528,[9] Luther reflects methodically on the structure of the article, in order to arrive at the meaning that is most comprehensible pedagogically. Attacking it from all different angles, he accentuates the central thought, which provides the structure for the commentaries in both the Large and Small Catechisms. He "emphasizes" [Tr.: lit. "urges"] the phrase "my Lord"[10] and links it with the central terminology of redemption: "At this point, Lord means the same as redeemer";[11] if Jesus Christ has become my Lord thereby, it means that He has delivered me from the tyranny of the powers of death. The scope of the article is thus determined already by a first and foundational step forward, and it is formulated with clear intent within the framework "I believe [up]on."[12] The Large Catechism makes this even more precise when it says in the summary: "This is now the summation of this article, that the little word 'LORD,' at its most basic level, means exactly what is meant by redeemer, which refers to the one who brought us from the devil to God, from death to life, from sin to righteousness, and preserves us

---

[5] According to Kinder, *Die soteriologischen Motive der altkirchlichen Glaubensbekenntnisse*, 23.

[6] Cf. pp. 10–13.

[7] On this, Lietzmann, *Symbolstudien*, 223f., 229, 287f.; Kelly, *Creeds*, 147; Eichenseer, *Apostolicum*, 93; Adam, *DG*, 1:195.

[8] WA 7:216.31.

[9] WA 30.1:88–90 (AE 51:162–169).

[10] Ibid., 89.6: "I shall emphasize only the words 'our Lord'."

[11] Ibid., 90.16.

[12] Cf. pp. 27–32.

therein."[13] The Small Catechism seizes on this idea in the central statement of the interpretation: "I believe that Jesus Christ . . . is my Lord, who has redeemed me."[14]

In Luther's sermon on December 10, 1528, the individual scenes that describe the path that brings salvation are arranged around this center, with its leading thought: my Lord = my redeemer; it states "in what way" Christ has become my Lord and redeemer "and at what cost He ventured to accomplish this."[15] The catechisms make use of this description.[16] The catechisms thus probe the historical framework of events so as to give structure to this article and to describe the events succinctly. The chain of verbs tells of the path that Jesus took on Himself to perform, takes on Himself now, and will yet take on, in order to truly become our Lord and redeemer.

Luther's ingenious approach to articulating the entirety of what is in the Second Article in catechetical form is framed initially in the Short Form of 1520[17] and in his sermon on March 5, 1523.[18] At this juncture already, the substantive title of majesty [Lord] is positioned front and center. Luther extracts three decisive insights that will be included in all later interpretations: (a) Jesus Christ is the true, eternal Son of God and concurrently a complete human being. At this point, the reformer makes use of the insights gained from early Church battles. The dual emphasis in the Creed of Chalcedon appears in the Confession of 1528,[19] in the catechisms,[20] and in the Smalcald Articles:[21] "true God, born of the Father in eternity, and also true man, born of the Virgin Mary.[22] Luther unfolds and defends this reality by using the key phrase "*Communicatio idiomatum* (communication of attributes)," initially in his writings on the Lord's Supper, against the Southern Germans and the Swiss between 1526–28, and then once again from about 1539 until the end of his life

[13] *BSLK*, 652.25–30.

[14] *BSLK*, 511.23, 26–28.

[15] WA 30.1:90.17 (AE 51:162–169); cf. ibid., 90.1ff., 16ff.; see, in addition, "Von Jesu Christo eine Predigt, Torgau, 16./17.4.1533," WA 37:53.7–12.

[16] *BSLK*, 652.30–37 (LC).

[17] WA 7:216–18.

[18] WA 11:51–52.31.

[19] "Vom Abendmahl Christi, 1528," WA 26:500.33–501.35 (AE 37:151–372).

[20] *BSLK*, 651.10f., 32, 50; 652:37ff. (LC)

[21] *BSLK*, 414.18–22; Luther gives a more detailed rendering of the double aspect in the Torgau Sermons of 1533, WA 37:35–45.

[22] *BSLK*, 511.23–26 (SC).

concerning the genus that develops, as he explicates this central mystery of Christ's nature.[23] (b) According to His divine nature, Jesus Christ is a co-creator with God the Father and according to His human nature He has been elevated to the Father's right hand; in this way, He is "Lord for me and all things."[24] This points to what occupied Luther's particular attention in his later writings. Christ's lordship is admittedly not narrowed in scope, so that it describes our salvation only in the Second Article; it goes further and deals with the broader issue of our nature as creatures.[25] The catechisms hide the true depth of this connectedness, abbreviating thereby the witness of the Church and Luther's own understanding of the lordship of Christ. (c) No one finds their way to God the Father unless it is through the Son, Jesus Christ; "that is, through faith is His name and lordship."[26] At this point, we encounter the hidden center of Luther's entire theology, which he summarizes once again at the end of the Large Catechism.[27] We find God's gracious, fatherly heart in the Son alone, and—this we must mention as well—we are led there only by the Holy Spirit.[28]

All later expositions are shaped by the central thesis that receives exposition in these three theses, as identified in the Short Form of 1520 and in the Sermons on the Symbol from 1523: Jesus Christ as true man and true God has become my Lord and redeemer, in that He alone has opened for each of us the access point to the heart of the Father.

Already in the Short Form of 1520, the series of verbal statements about the path Jesus took are directed tirelessly by Luther toward the first person "I" of the individual, who is confessing, as well as the "we" of the entire group of those who believe in Christ. Though he uses phrases at times that are to some extent from the late Middle

---

[23] Cf. pp. 134ff.

[24] "Eine kurze Form, 1520," WA 7:217.9; "Pred. über den 2. und 3. Art. vom 5.3.1523," WA 11:51.27; ibid., 52.10: "I believe Christ to be my Lord"; see, as well, "Ein kleiner Unterricht, was man in den Evangelien suchen und erwarten soll, 1522," WA 10.1.1:9.18–22; 10.6–8 (AE 35:113–124).

[25] See p. 44, esp. n. 226.

[26] "Eine kurze Form, 1520," WA 7:217.14; "Pred. über den 2. und 3. Art. vom 5.3.1523," WA 11:52.5: "Through that one, wrapped in flesh, we come to the Father"; ibid., "The First Article lays out the naked God, the Second Article is wrapped therein," 52.7.

[27] *BSLK*, 660.18–661.18.

[28] Cf. pp. 37f.

Ages and from Augustine, such as "blessèd, unsullied and pure, useful and saving, [making] highly serviceable,"[29] he employs them to arrive at the characteristic applications that are employed in the Large Catechism.[30] In his sermon on March 5, 1523, he underscores more sharply our personal faith relationship and that the one and selfsame Lord was at work in all the various stages on His way to bring us salvation.[31] The demons know, as well, that He has taken this path, but they are not able to comfort themselves when observing these various stages.

Luther's sermons on May 23 and September 21, 1528[32] draw the entire Creed together around the central issue: "Who is the God who gave us the commandments, indeed, who gives Himself as well, so that we might fulfill His commandments.[33] The Second Article is visited only briefly thereby.

The Confession of 1528 commences with the "chief article" of the Trinity,[34] unfolding thereby the pattern used in the Short Form of 1520: Christ's person—Christ's office and work. (1) A first section[35] takes up the teaching from the early Church about the two natures, but it is brought into focus by means of the reformational point of emphasis: "for us." (2) A second section[36] depicts Christ's cross and exaltation, from one point of view as the eradication of our guilt before God and, from another angle, as taking away the power of the forces of death.[37] (3) A third polemical section[38] is presented as well; Luther concludes by drawing out the implications of Christ's all-

---

[29] WA 7:217.24, 27, 30; 218.2.
[30] *BSLK*, 652.37–653.3 (LC).
[31] WA 11:52.16: "Not only to believe that He was conceived: I believe [up]on the one who was conceived, [up]on the one who died, so that one is pressed to rely [up]on, '*an*'; just as in Latin and Greek. Said another way, our faith is not greater than that of the devil; His nativity must be our consolation"; cf. on "Von Jesu Christo eine Predigt, Torgau, 16./17.4.1533," WA 37:45.27–46.13.
[32] WA 30.1:9.14–11.7 or else 43.27–46.6.
[33] Ibid., 45.4: "Christ the Son gave all His works and merits so that we may satisfy the Ten Commandments."
[34] "Vom Abendmahl Christi, 1528," WA 26:500.27–32 (AE 37:151–372).
[35] Ibid., 500.33–501.35.
[36] Ibid., 502.18–34.
[37] This way to divide it is used in the Torgau Sermons of 1533; these sermons begin by characterizing Christ's person according to His divine nature and human nature (WA 37:35–45) and then depict Christ's office and work, where they pointedly accentuate the phrase "our Lord" (WA 37:45–53).
[38] "Vom Abendmahl Christi, 1528," WA 26:502.35–505.28 (AE 37:151–372).

availing work of salvation and rejects any trust we might place in our own actions before God. He then articulates the relatedness between faith and love, justification and sanctification, proper works that stem from obedience in faith and false works of the devil that seek self-justification, though he is forging into the territory of the Third Article at this point already.

The Christology of this confession is to be distinguished characteristically from the earlier interpretations of the Creed at three points. The catechisms are affected only minimally by these new aspects. (a) In the first section, Luther includes the virgin birth already at this point in the discussion about the person of Christ;[39] the emphasis is placed on Jesus' complete humanity. The unique treatment in the Short Form of 1520: "conceived for my benefit" by the Holy Spirit and born of the pure virgin, so that He could purify me and make me unsullied, along with all believers, by removing the effects of my sinful conception and accursed birth,[40] this "*Pro nobis*" is given short shrift.[41] At this point, the Large Catechism goes back to the Short Form of 1520; the Small Catechism is shaped by the pattern of the confession; it inserts the incarnation and virgin birth into the central statement: Jesus Christ, my Lord, as he cites the closing phrase of the first section of the confession almost verbatim, which reads: "That is my Lord and that of all others, Jesus Christ, one from God and Mary, actual, natural son, true God and human being."[42] (b) More forcefully than in the interpretations that had been offered up to that point, Luther concentrates in the Confession of 1528 on the office and work of Jesus as these aspects are framed by cross and exaltation. Stating that He is a person assumes that He took on a human nature; His being laid into the grave and His descent into Hades receive no mention, and His final return is mentioned only at the conclusion of the entire confession.[43] What remains thereby, the twin peaks of cross and exaltation, do not concentrate primarily on Christ's becoming

[39] The Schwabach Articles and Marburg Articles, as well as AC III, follow the way the relationship is set forth here, cf. *BSLK*, 54f.

[40] WA 7:217.15–24

[41] "Vom Abendmahl Christi, 1528," WA 26:501.28 (AE 37:151–372). An application of this type, stressing Christ's sinless conception and birth, is thus missing in the Schwabach Articles and Marburg Articles, as well as in AC III, which follows the way it is stated in the Confession of 1528; cf. *BSLK*, 54f. and Maurer, *Zur Entstehung und Textgeschichte der Schwabacher Artikel.*

[42] "Vom Abendmahl Christi, 1528," WA 26:501.34.

[43] This is used, as well, in the later confessions; see the texts in AC XVII, *BSLK*, 72.

Lord with reference to sin, death, and the devil, but concentrate instead on God's own holy wrath.[44]

As the unspotted lamb who was offered, the Lord took our guilt upon Himself and freed us from the eternal wrath of God, [45] as "a true, merciful intermediary, savior, and unique priest and bishop"[46] of our souls, who still approaches God daily on our behalf.[47] The Small Catechism is shaped by this emphasis on Jesus' cross and exaltation; the Large Catechism expands on the topic more considerably. The catechisms do not refer to Christ as the high priest, who functions in an ongoing way, even though the reformer accords greater value to our participation in Christ's high priestly activities than to our participation in His rule as king; and yet, according to The Freedom of a Christian (1520), it remains true for every Christian: "Through His kingly realm He exercises power over all earthly things; through His priesthood He exercises power in the divine realm."[48]

(c) In order to treat this central aspect of the Second Article as completely as possible, Luther inserts the biblical and the Church's view about original sin into the article about Christ as the propitiator of the wrath of God and as the one who subdues the powers of destruction.[49] In both the Large Catechism[50] and the Smalcald Articles,[51] he stays with this approach. By this tactic, he specifically emphasizes the "*peccatum originale, haereditarium, principale et capital* (original, inherited, principal, and chief sin)"[52] in the discussion of our deliverance through Jesus Christ. In AC II, by contrast, Melanchthon discusses original sin separately, before describing our salvation through Christ;[53] he thus separates it more obviously from the collection of phrases that press us on solely to

---

[44] This orientation is likewise reflected most clearly in AC III.

[45] Cf. AC III, *BSLK*, 54:10–12.

[46] "Vom Abendmahl Christi, 1528," WA 26:502.33 (AE 37:151–372).

[47] On Christ's high priestly office, see pp. 195f.

[48] "Von der Freiheit eines Christenmenschen, 1520," WA 7:28.14 (AE 31:327–377); cf. "De libertate christiana, 1520," WA 7:57.24–58.3 (AE 31:327–377).

[49] "Vom Abendmahl Christi, 1528," WA 26:502.25–30 (AE 37:151–372).

[50] *BSLK*, 651.42–48; cf., as well, "Eine einfältige Weise zu beten, 1535," WA 38:374.11–13 (AE 43:187–211).

[51] *BSLK*, 433–35 (SA III).

[52] Ibid., 433.29.

[53] The Schwabach Articles and the Marburg Articles stay with the same sequence of thought as in the Confession of 1528; this is reversed only in the *Confessio Augustana* and in the third formulation (Na) that preceded it, from Nuremberg, *BSLK*, 53–55.

Christ as the pure offering lamb and the high priest who continues to serve on our behalf.

Luther's sermon on December 10, 1528 sets forth what is then reflected in the exposition in the catechism itself. Luther takes to heart the directive that is stated in the visitation articles: "Accordingly, the people are to be instructed about redemption, about how through Christ our sins are forgiven. To that end, all articles about Christ are to be brought together, how He was born, died, rose, etc."[54] Luther singles out the term "*Dominus noster* (our Lord)," characterizes this as referring to the "*Redemptor*" or else "*Salvator*," and interprets the verbal statements as the individual "elements" that show how His becoming Lord "took place" and "what happened to Him."[55] In this sermon, Luther emphasizes exclusively the powers of destruction that are Christ's opposites; they are the kings and lords that Christ conquers. The wrath of God is not discussed; thus also, how those "tyrants and jailers"[56] are to be viewed with respect to God's judgment is not at issue here either. From another vantage point, the reformer underscores how Jesus' physical life is involved; by offering up His own life, the Lord establishes His kingdom.[57]

The Large Catechism follows the pattern of this sermon; it clarifies what was stated, in general and somewhat convoluted terms, eliminates repetitions, goes on to insert a treatment of the wrath of God and our status as slaves because of Adam's original sin, and thus provides the following breakdown:

A. The transition: The Second Person of the Godhead (Trinity) gifts Himself to us entirely so as to effect our salvation[58]

---

[54] Melanchthon, *Studienausgabe*, 1:259.16; "Kat.-Pred. vom 10.12.1528," WA 30.1:88.17 (AE 51:162–169): "The First Article teaches Creation; the Second, Redemption; the Third, Sanctification"; cf., ibid., 89.18; 90.24.

[55] Ibid., 90.2f.; cf., as well, "Torgauer Pred. vom 16./17.4.1533," WA 37:53.7f. and "Eine einfältige Weise zu beten, 1535," WA 38:374.14–20 (AE 43:187–211).

[56] Ibid., 90.2f.; cf., as well, "Torgauer Pred. vom 16./17.4.1533," WA 37:53.7f. and "Eine einfältige Weise zu beten, 1535," WA 38:374.14–20.

[57] "Kat.-Pred. vom 10.12.1528," WA 30.1:90.7 (AE 51:165): "namely, his own body, with which he established his kingdom"; cf. ibid., 90.18f.

[58] *BSLK*, 651.10–15. See, in addition, the reference at the conclusion of the First Article, 650.30–33. By means of this transition, Luther makes use of the trinitarian summary from the Confession of 1528 (WA 26:505.41–506.3 [AE 37:151–372]), as well as the "Kat.-Pred. vom 21.9.1528," WA 30.1:44.37–45.8; he admittedly makes reference in this last text to the fulfilling of the Commandments only at the very end of the interpretation of the Creed, 661.35–42.

B. 1. Summary and scope of the Second Article: Jesus Christ our LORD as our redeemer[59]

(a) Declaration of the scope: Jesus Christ our LORD[60]

(1) First characterization of the scope: our LORD[61]

(2) Catechetical formulation of the scope: "Jesus Christ, true Son of God, *has become* my LORD"[62]

(b) Description of Jesus' becoming Lord by means of His work of redemption[63]

(1) First reference to the successful transfer of lordship[64]

(2) More detailed depiction of Jesus' action to bring freedom, set against the background of original sin[65]

(c) Succinct summary of the scope: Jesus Christ our LORD as our redeemer[66]

B. 2. Development of how Jesus becomes Lord, using the description of salvation in the Creed[67]

(a) The verbs used in the Second Article that describe the stages along the route of Jesus becoming Lord, for our salvation[68]

(b) Treatment of Jesus' humiliation (*status exinanitionis*)[69]

(1) Christ became human, without sin, in order that He "would be" Lord over sin[70]

---

[59] *BSLK*, 651.15–652.30.

[60] *BSLK*, 651.15–33. Section 1 (a) follows the "Kat.-Pred. vom 10.12.1528," WA 30.1:89.5–9 (AE 51:162–169).

[61] *BSLK*, 651.15–22.

[62] *BSLK*, 651.29–33.

[63] *BSLK*, 651.33–652.12.

[64] *BSLK*, 651.33–40. Section 1 (b) (1) follows the "Kat.-Pred. vom 10.12.1528," WA 30.1:89.9–12.

[65] *BSLK*, 651.42–652.12. Section 1 (b) (2) follows the "Kat.-Pred. vom 10.12.1528," WA 30.1:90.13–16; 89.12-14.

[66] *BSLK*, 652.25–30. Section 1 (c) is a free rendering from the "Kat.-Pred. vom 10.12.1528," WA 30.1:90.16 and 89.17–22.

[67] *BSLK*, 652.30–653.3.

[68] *BSLK*, 652.30–37. Section 2 (a) follows the "Kat.-Pred. vom 10.12.1528," WA 30.1:89.22–90.3; see ibid., 90.6ff., 16ff.

[69] *BSLK*, 652.37–47. Section 2 (b) is only generally the same as the "Kat.-Pred. vom 10.12.1528," WA 30.1:90.3–6 (conceived by the Spirit without sin) and idem, 90.18f. (death on the cross, with reference to 1 Pet. 1:18f.); at this point, he relies more heavily on the Short Form of 1520 (WA 7:217.16–218.19) and the "Pred. über den 2. und 3. Art. vom 5.3.1523," WA 11:52.13–26.

[70] *BSLK*, 652.37–40.

(2) He suffered, died, was buried, so that He could purchase me with His blood and thus became my LORD[71]

(c) Treatment of Jesus' exaltation (*status exaltationis*)[72]

(1) He has arisen as the one who overcomes and is Lord over death[73]

(2) He has ascended and has taken lordship over the devil and all power[74]

(d) Treatment of the return of Jesus: He will come for judgment, in order finally to free His own from all powers of destruction[75]

C. Summarizing reflection about the Second Article, as well as its location in proclamation and in the life of the Christian[76]

(a) All the festivals of Christ for the church year are arranged on the basis of the Second Article[77]

(b) Our salvation is rooted in the Second Article as the center of the Gospel[78]

The Small Catechism is arranged somewhat differently. As with the Confession of 1528, Luther includes becoming flesh at this point. He then unfolds Jesus' saving actions for the one who is confessing according to his two points of emphasis, the cross and the exaltation; the believer is held concurrently from below by means of what was offered for him or her and from above by the protection afforded each one by the one who is ruling.

With the Confession of 1528 and the depiction of the scope in the Large Catechism, Luther formulates the key sentence: Jesus Christ—truly God and truly human—has become my LORD. According to Jesus' "being begotten" two times,[79] the Christological controversies from the era of the early Church are reflected in the appositional phrase: "true God, from the Father, born in eternity—and also true

---

[71] *BSLK*, 652.41–47.

[72] *BSLK*, 652.47–653.1.

[73] *BSLK*, 652.47–49.

[74] *BSLK*, 652.49–653.1.

[75] *BSLK*, 653.1–3.

[76] *BSLK*, 653.4–15. The concluding summary is a new construction, though based on the "Kat.-Pred. zum 2. Art. vom 10.12.1528," WA 30.1:90.23; 89.14f.; 90.8–11 (AE 51:162–169).

[77] *BSLK*, 653.4–10. See pp. 163f.

[78] *BSLK*, 653.11–15.

[79] Cf. pp. 172f. with notes 398f.

man, born of the Virgin Mary."[80] The lively positioning of the phrases presses toward three one-syllable words: "is my LORD."[81] These words fall majestically, like a deep-sounding bell that is tolled three times. Already since the time of the Short Form of 1520, "my Lord" forms the secret compass point for Luther's commentaries; for the Small Catechism, this has achieved a form that gives the melody line, a pleasing musical intonation.

As Luther develops this theme, he wants every individual element mentioned in the Second Article to get its due;[82] we modern human beings, impatient as we are, find it hard to tolerate the tensions caused by the elements that scatter in so many different directions. The relative predicate clause pours forth "in full, resonating chords"; attributes, verbs, and adverbial declarations, with adjectives that match up, allow the descriptions to become ever richer. "They transition into the purpose clause and fill it completely, with three-part rhythm"; assessed grammatically, punctuation for the clauses falls by the wayside; but because Luther expands the two-part composition to become three-part, he catches the ideas that could fall by the wayside by having the sentence intensify still more. "And then, remarkably enough, introduced by the coordinating comment 'just as,' it curves upward from the outside, once again using a three-part figure of speech."[83] "That's certainly true"[84] strengthens it all and pulls it together, the likes of which one can seek for in vain in German literature and which has continued to leave many standing in awe. The way one was schooled to use Latin clauses leaves its traces, but the phrases are still constructed more loosely and are divided quite simply. No one gets away with a quick and silent glance; it was designed to be spoken out loud and to be prayed.

With respect to the content as well, the reformer stayed close to the tradition of the Middle Ages; variations are offered repeatedly that refer to the sacrificial death as described in 1 Pet. 1:18f.; they always included the trio: sin, death, and the devil.[85] Admittedly with greater emphasis than the formulas that had been passed down and also to a greater extent than his own earlier expositions, up to the time of the

---

[80] *BSLK*, 511.23–26.

[81] *BSLK*, 511.26.

[82] Meyer provided an overview of this in his commentary, 312f.

[83] Gillhoff, *Zur Sprache und Geschichte des KK*, 39f.

[84] *BSLK*, 511.37f.

[85] Cf. p. 71, n. 97, as well as Meyer, *Historischer Kommentar*, 100f.

Large Catechism, Luther forges ahead already in the Small Catechism by going beyond redemption and forgiveness; he treats justification and deals with new life. The Second Article thus reaches into concepts that are dealt with in the Third Article as well. In a way that seems almost like the enthusiasts, future eschatology seems to have been inserted into the present with the words "everlasting righteousness, innocence, and blessedness."[86] Is our eschatological participation in Christ's lordship in the resurrection age not realized fully already on earth? The astounding statement that accentuates this reality, already in the Small Catechism, must be examined with great care.[87]

THREE TYPICAL DIVISIONS AND APPLICATIONS OF THE SECOND ARTICLE IN THE TRADITION OF INTERPRETATION IN THE CHURCH[88]

The Second Article of faith connects substantives that articulate a brief confession about Christ with verbal statements that describe the way Jesus brought salvation. Such interlacing can be detected already in the New Testament. One vantage point shows how the confession concentrates on the titles of majesty, which the early Church finally summarized by using the symbol of the fish.[89] From another vantage point, one sees various attempts to articulate the *kerygma* about Christ. The central teaching revolves around cross and resurrection, as preserved in the catechetical formula in 1 Cor. 15:3–8.[90] The eucharistic Christ Hymn[91] presents the faith in a rich, variant form, using the concepts: according to the flesh—according to the Spirit or, alternately, humiliation and exaltation. Another approach is preserved in the way the examples of preaching provided in the Acts of the Apostles can be used to teach and to show the undergirding of the Old

---

[86] *BSLK*, 511.35f.

[87] On Luther's eschatology, see pp. 196–202.

[88] No catechetical literature provides a description of the different ways catechisms go about doing what they aim to do.

[89] Dölger, *Ichthys*, 1:248, 259, 318ff., Table 3.7; Cullmann, *Die ersten chrl. Glaubensbekenntnisse*, 36; Lietzmann, *Symbolstudien*, 231.

[90] Cf. 2 Tim. 2:8; Ign. *Eph.* 18:2.

[91] Romans 1:3f.; Phil. 2:6–11; 1 Tim. 3:16; see the later examples in Lietzmann, *Symbolstudien*, 231–35.

Testament.[92] The prehistory of the virgin birth narrative and Jesus' rule over the world, as described in 1 Cor. 8:6, are brought together with exorcism formulas.[93] The two polar aspects of the Second Article are thus crystallized.

Traditions that detail the way the Church interpreted the text never tire of looking to make this rich portrayal obvious to all and to focus on a central theme to be taught in catechisms. As makes good sense, one starts out with that aspect of the Creed that uses substantives, which Luther clearly renders with the words: "and [up]on Jesus Christ, His only Son, our Lord."[94]

Considered schematically, three distinctive statements are presented, no matter which of the three collections of words and titles one seeks to place in the center: Jesus Christ—God's only Son—our Lord. History has clearly dealt with these three statements, as well, admittedly in a complicated interweaving of each aspect with the others: (1) By linking the name of Jesus, which is said to mean "savior," with the title that acclaims Him as the Christ, Calvin derives the teaching that we participate in the threefold office of Jesus. (2) Referring to the only-begotten Son, Augustine introduces the solemn teaching about the two natures; he uses both the death on the cross and Jesus' becoming human to build a bridge that leads to our salvation. (3) Luther is the first to bring the phrase "our Lord" front and center; he elevates this to the cardinal point for interpretation. After we interpret each of these titles of majesty briefly, we will be ready to sketch out the unique aspects that each differentiated phrase offers.

1. Jesus Christ—Our Participation in the Threefold Office of Christ[95]

The formula "Jesus is the Christ" has its source in Peter's confession at Caesarea Philippi (Mark 8:29 par.) and is linked to Peter's

---

[92] Acts 2:14–41; 3:12–26; 4:8–12; 5:29–33; 10:34–47.

[93] Cf. Lietzmann, *Symbolstudien*, 234f.

[94] "Eine kurze Form, 1520," WA 7:216.31; "Betbüchlein," WA 10.2:391.8 (AE 43:3–45); *BSLK*, 511.11f. (SC); 555.37–556.1 (Preface to the Large Catechism); 650.43f. (LC).

[95] On this, see esp. Hahn, *Hoheitstitel*, 133–230; Cullmann, *Die Christologie des Neuen Testaments*, 111–37; Krauss, *Das Mittlerwerk nach dem Schema des munus triplex*; Müller, *Jesu Christi dreifaches Amt*; Weber, *Grundlagen der Dogmatik*, 2:194–203; Pannenberg, *Grundzüge der Christologie*, 218–32; Persson, *Repraesentatio Christi*, 167f. (excursus).

Pentecost sermon (Acts 2:36):[96] Jesus is the messiah who was promised to Israel. The Roman Creed still uses the order "Christ Jesus." "Anointed One" is still treated as an appellative title. Christ is anointed by the Father with the Holy Spirit and thus unifies the Old Testament offices of king and high priest into His own person; Cyril of Jerusalem explicates this in great detail.[97] For the Western tradition, Rufinus charts the course as he produces a succinct summary: "*Christus quoque vel pontificale vel regium nomen est. Nam prius et pontifices unguento christmatis consecrabantur et reges.* (One would use the term *Christus* to refer either to a priest or to a king. In previous times, both high priests and kings were consecrated by being anointed with an ointment.)"[98]

Most of the other Symbols, the *Textus receptus* included, use the opposite word order; Jesus Christ is considered to be a stronger statement, as a "celebratory sounding double name."[99] The introductions to the Synoptic Gospels come close to this phraseology, as do parallel usages in John (John 1:17; 17:3), being supported by Pauline usage as well,[100] even though a messianic tone can still be detected when the word Christ is used without an article.[101]

According to Matt. 1:21 and Luke 2:11, the meaning of the name Jesus is given as σωτήρ and *Salvator*; the Old Testament attribute of God is attached to Him. He is the redeemer of the people; the yearning of the people in the ancient world for deliverance can be detected.[102] Cyril brings the two ideas together: "Jesus is known to the Hebrews as what we call a deliverer, to the Greeks as what we call a savior. For He is the physician for soul and body, He makes it possible for the spirit to get well."[103] His mirror image in the Old

---

[96] Cf. Acts 5:24; 18:28.

[97] Cyril of Jerusalem, *Catechesis* 10.14–16 (PG 33:679f.).

[98] Rufinus, *Expositio symboli* 6.13 (CCSL 20:141); cf. the parallel words from Augustine in Eichenseer, *Apostolicum*, 209–12; Peter Chrysologus, *Sermo* 57 (PL 52:358C); *Sermo* 58 (ibid., 361C); *Sermo* 59 (ibid., 363 B/C); *Sermo* 60 (ibid., 367B); *Sermo* 61 (ibid., 370B); Niceta, *Explanatio symboli* 3 (PL 52:868A); Faustus of Reji [Riez], *hom. de symb.* 1 (Caspari, *Quellen*, 2:189).

[99] Schmid, *Das Evangelium nach Matthäus*, 35.

[100] On this, see Lietzmann, *Symbolstudien*, 199.

[101] According to Hahn, *Hoheitstitel*, 218–25.

[102] Σωτήρ as an expansion of κύριος is used in Phil. 3:20; 2 Pet. 1:1, 11; 2:20; 3:2, 18; cf., as well, Cullmann, *Die Christologie des Neuen Testaments*, 245–52.

[103] Cyril of Jerusalem, *Catechesis* 10.13 (PG 33:677B/C).

Testament is Joshua.[104] Rufinus expands on this: just as that Old Testament *Salvator* led the people out of slavery in Egypt and through life on the edge in the wilderness and on into the Promised Land, this true *Salvator* thus leads the people out of the darkness of foolishness and diversionary paths in this earthly world on into the heavenly kingdom.[105]

Based on this artful connection that brings together the name Jesus with the title Christ, "He is Jesus as redeemer, is Christ as priest,"[106] it first became possible, already in the early Church era, to apply to us what is confessed in the Second Article. As Christians, our baptism affords us the ability to participate in what happened to the Lord when He was anointed with the Spirit of God, and thus to participate in His spiritual office. In the commentaries on the Symbols that were written during the fourth and fifth centuries, one is led to think almost exclusively on the *Munus regale et sacerdotale* (office of king and priest), since the priest and king were both anointed;[107] prophetic anointing is hinted at almost incidentally.[108]

This twofold office of Jesus as a king and as a priest is carried over into the interpretations of the Symbol in the Middle Ages.[109] This emphasis appears in the catechisms of the Reformation that precede Luther's Enchiridion. Johann Agricola writes in his "Christlichen Kinderzucht" of 1527: "Jesus" refers to the savior, "Christ" to the "anointed one, since God anointed Him with His Spirit."[110] Luther knows this tradition as well,[111] but he does not make

---

[104] Cyril of Jerusalem, *Catechesis* 10.11 (PG 33:676); cf. Clement of Alexandria, *Paedagogus* 1:7.60.3; Justin, *Dialogus cum Tryphone* 61; Tertullian, *Adversus Marcionem* 3:16; Lactantius, *Divinarum institutionum libri VII* 4.17.

[105] Rufinus, *Expositio symboli* 6.9 (CCSL 20:141): "So both were called Jesus—both he who, when the people had been brought up out of Egypt and released from their wanderings in the desert guided them into the promised land; and He who brought His people up out of the darkness of ignorance and, recalling them from the distractions of the world, guided them to the kingdom of heaven" [Rufinus, 38].

[106] Cyril of Jerusalem, *Catechesis* 10.11 (PG 33:676A).

[107] Concerning the anointing of the priest, cf. Exod. 29:7; concerning the anointing of the king, cf. 1 Sam. 10:1; 16:13; 24:7, 11; 26:11; 2 Sam. 2:4; 5:3; 1 Kings 11:12; 19:15f.

[108] Cf. 1 Kings 19:16; Isa. 61:1; Ps. 105:15.

[109] Beyond the references on p. 114, n. 98, one might also mention Pseudo-augustine, *Sermo* 252.3 (PL 39:2192); Ivo of Chartres, *Sermo* 23 (PL 162:605B; Jocelin of Soisson, *Expositio symboli et orationis dominicae* 5 (PL 186:1483A).

[110] Agricola, "Christ. Kinderzucht" (MGP 21:48.35); similarly, Capito, "Kinderbericht, 1527," quest. 21 (MGP 21:110); Zwick, *Glaubenserklärung*, quest. 7

use of it in his interpretations of the Creed. When he discusses the priesthood of all believers, He does emphasize the point that absolutely all believers participate in Christ's lordly service as Mediator, contrasting that with a specialized priestly office. He thus writes in his commentary of 1523 on First Peter: "Now Christ is the high, even the most high priest, anointed by God Himself, having offered His own body for us as well, which is the highest activity of the priestly office. After this, He prayed for us on the cross. In the third place, He proclaimed the Gospel and taught all people to recognize both God and Himself. He gave all three offices to us as well. Therefore, since He is a priest and we are His brothers, all Christians are both empowered and commanded to act accordingly; they are to preach and to come before God, they are to pray one for another and are to offer themselves to God."[112]

In this text, Luther hints at what Calvin introduced later into the catechetical and dogmatic tradition after 1543; Osiander's apology (*Schirmschrift*) to the General Council at Augsburg (1530)[113] is given wider circulation by Calvin.[114] One change is that the *Munus regale* and *sacerdotale* (office of king and priest) is expanded now to include the *Munus propheticum* (prophetic office) so that the *Munus duplex* (twofold office) is turned into a *Munus triplex* (threefold office); moreover, our participation in the threefold office of Christ is included within the catechesis of the Second Article.

Concerning the first point, the expansion of the *Officium Christi duplex* to become an *Officium triplex* itself has a long pre-history. The community at Qumran was awaiting an eschatological prophet;[115] the New Testament sees this expectation being fulfilled in Jesus.[116] Thus, here and there in the early Church era, most especially in Eusebius

---

(MGP 23:85); Butzer, *Kat. von 1534 und 1537* (Reu, *Quellen*, 1.1:28.27–45; 70.20–28); Spangenberg, *Kleiner und Großer Kat.*, 1541 (Reu, *Quellen*, 1.2:290.3–10; 309:18–30); Erasmus, *Explanatio Symboli*, cols. 1151E–1152C.

[111] See, for example, "Pred. über Lk. 2 vom 25.12.1529," WA 29:664.4f.; "Pred. über Lk. 2:21 vom 1.1.1531," WA 34.1:13.10ff.; "Post. über Mt. 11:2–10 zum 3. Advent 1522," WA 10.1.2:152.29ff.

[112] WA 12:307.27 (AE 30:1–145).

[113] This portion of Osiander's *Schirmschrift* is replicated in Hirsch, *Hilfsbuch*, 65f.

[114] In the first edition of the *Institutes* of 1536 (Calvin, Opera Selecta, 1:82), as well as in the *Geneva Catechism* of 1537 (Calvin, Opera Selecta, 1:397), Calvin mentions only the kingly and priestly offices of Jesus.

[115] According to Hahn, *Hoheitstitel*, 366ff.

[116] See ibid., 380–404.

and Chrysostom,[117] the prophetic aspect is included when discussing the anointing of Christ. During the Middle Ages, Thomas Aquinas writes, with respect to Christ's priestly office: We humans possess only a few of the gifts of grace, but Christ as our head unites all graces within Himself. "And, for this reason, among people in general, one writes laws, another serves as priest, and a third is king; but these are all unified in Christ, as the source of all graces."[118] The *Munus propheticum* is barely hinted at when one uses the technical term "*legislator*"; at least terminologically, the Gospel appears as the new Law and Christ as the new Moses.[119]

Concerning the second point, that we participate in the threefold office of Christ as well, Chrysostom says: "What does it mean: He who anointed and sealed us? It means: He who gave us the Spirit and through the Spirit has acted by means of this anointing and sealing to make us prophet, priest, and king as well. For these three worthy roles were brought into existence in the distant past through anointing. At present, we possess not just one or the other of these worthy roles, but all three at the same time, in fact in superabundant measure."[120] When he summarizes his comments, he says to each one who has been baptized: "You have now become king, priest, and prophet as well, in the baptismal fountain."[121]

Calvin coalesces such disparate statements to arrive at a catechetical statement. He examines the linkage between the names for Jesus = savior, deliverer and one who brings bliss, and the Christ title = anointed one, to develop a soteriology *in nuce*, sketching out thereby the way we participate in the threefold office of Christ. He sets forth the basic lines of thought in the Geneva Catechism;[122] in the Institutes, he expands on this under the heading: "If we wish to know for what purpose Christ was sent from the Father and what He

---

[117] See the evidence provided by Schmaus, *Ämter Christi*, and Krauss, *Das Mittlerwerk nach dem Schema des munus triplex*.

[118] Thomas Aquinas, *Summa theologiae* III, q. 22, a. 1 to 3.

[119] But concerning the theological understanding of the new Law (*Lex nova*), see Kühn, *Via caritatis*.

[120] John Chrysostom, *Homilae in epistulam ii ad Corinthios*, 3:5 (PG 61:411, cited according to Schmaus, *Katholische Dogmatik*, 4.1:142).

[121] Ibid., 3:7 (PG 61:417).

[122] Calvin, *Genfer Kat.*, quest. 30–45; a short summary is offered in the *Heidelberger Kat.*, 29–32.

brought us, we must pay primary attention to His threefold office, the prophetic, kingly, and priestly [offices]."[123]

Such a catechetical and liturgical reference to our participation in Jesus' *Officium triplex* increasingly became part of dogmatic works as well. Reformed Orthodoxy developed this into a solemn element of teaching; the Lutherans let this shape their views as well. Even the Roman Catechism at least takes note of the *Officium triplex*; it admittedly did not appear in Catholic dogmatic treatments until the nineteenth century. The Fourth World Conference on Faith and Order in Montreal (1963) declared both the priesthood of all believers and the specific office of pastor to be founded upon Christ's threefold office.[124] Quite analogously, the Dogmatic Constitution on the Church, promulgated at Vatican II, speaks of both the "universal priesthood of believers" and the "priestly office of hierarchical service" as participation in Christ's royal priesthood.[125] Karl Barth develops his entire teaching about propitiation on the basis of the pattern of the threefold office.[126]

2. God's Only Son—Inclusion of Teaching about the Two Natures and its Impact on Understanding Jesus' Sacrificial Death and Becoming Human

The confession that Jesus is the Son of God is based on His personal testimony about Himself before the Sanhedrin (Mark 14:61f. par.); as is pointed out in 1 Thess. 1:9f., the phraseology was connected initially with an eschatological expectation of the Messiah and looks forward to Jesus' *parousia*. At the same time, it shows that Jesus was aware of who He was already while He was still on earth. He uses ἀββα as a brand new form of address, the likes of which had never previously been directed toward the unseen God.[127] The claim to have absolute power (Matt. 11:27; Luke 10:22) reflects Jesus' unique

---

[123] Calvin, *Inst.*, 2:15 (Opera Selecta, 3:471): "*Ut sciamus quorsum missus fuerit Christus a Patre, et quid nobis attulerit, tria potissimum spectanda in eo esse, munus propheticum, regnum et sacerdotium.*" A short overview of Calvin's teaching about the offices is provided by Niesel, *Die Theologie Calvins*, 116–20.

[124] "Proceedings of the Fourth World Congress for Faith and Church Order," Montreal, 1963, 56 (Section 3).

[125] *Constitutio dogmatica de Ecclesia*, no. 10.

[126] See the overview concerning the "three forms of teaching about reconciliation," in Barth, *Kirchliche Dogmatik* 4.1:140–70.

[127] See Volume 3 on the Lord's Prayer.

position in Johannine diction: The Son alone is known by the Father, which means that He is the only way to God. The voice of God that makes use of Ps. 2:7 at the baptismal scene in the Jordan (Mark 1:11 par.) and in Jesus' transfiguration (Mark 9:7 par.) comes as prelude to the command to baptize (Matt. 28:19) in the name of the Son. The eternal Father takes us, through baptism, to be His children by the actions of this unique Son.[128]

The unique nature of Jesus as Son is pointed out by the addition of the term "*unicus*, μονογενής." It is absent in the oldest Western textual evidence;[129] later still, it is placed more frequently with "*dominus noster* (our Lord)."[130] The *Explanatio Symboli ad initiandos*, attributed to Ambrose, seeks to put an end to this back and forth.[131] In common speech, μονογενής was taken in a vague general sense to mean "unique in one's genus" or "one of a kind in one's own way." But it is used already in the Old Testament to refer to Israel and is used parallel to "beloved," showing its use in the full sense to suggest "uniquely born" and "firstborn."[132] In the Gospel of John it refers exclusively to Jesus.[133] The parallel term ἴδιος (Rom. 8:32) is used by Paul. "*Unicus filius*" is used only rarely in the post-apostolic age, in the Martyrdom of Polycarp (20:2), in Justin's Dialogue with Trypho,[134] and in the Epistle to Diognetus (10:2).[135] The Gnostic teaching of the Valentinians is based on the Johannine Prologue and hypostasizes "only-begotten," distinguishing this one, as the preexistent Christ, the *Logos*, from the earthly Jesus. Irenaeus holds both elements in tension; God's "only-begotten Word, ever positioned at the side of the human species, is now united with and planted within one of His creatures, having become flesh according to the will

---

[128] Cf. pp. 73–79.

[129] Cf. Lietzmann, *Symbolstudien*, 200; Kattenbusch, *Symbol*, 2:585–89.

[130] References are from Kattenbusch, *Symbol*, 2:591ff., and Eichenseer, *Apostolicum*, 217f.

[131] *Explanatio symboli ad initiandos*, 5:2 (CSEL 73:6f.): "Thus you should say HIS ONLY SON! Not 'only Lord'; God is one, one and Lord. But do they not slander us for saying that we call the Son a separate person: and in [His] only [Son] our Lord?

[132] According to Bultmann, *Das Evangelium des Johannes*, 47, n. 2; the references are there as well.

[133] John 1:14, 18; 3:16, 18; 1 John 4:9.

[134] Justin, *Dialogus cum Tryphone* 105 (PG 6:720C–721A).

[135] Funk, *Die Apostolischen Väter*, 147.25f. (as a citation of 1 John 4:9).

of the Father; this one is Jesus Christ our Lord."[136] This rejection of the Gnostic concept that splits the redeemer into two beings is probably what led to the insertion of the Johannine epithet into the baptismal questions; Origin uses it frequently as well,[137] and Tertullian consciously renders this as "*unigenitus*."[138] But, as is the case with "*dominus noster*" as well, the term remains absent still longer from the confessions in use that had a fixed form; for this reason, it would seem that it migrated only gradually from East to West.[139]

The paraphrases of the Symbols from the Middle Ages[140] speak consistently about the "only-begotten Son"; this terminology continues to resonate in the creedal formulations of the late Middle Ages.[141] Luther consistently renders it as "His only Son."[142] The modern ecumenical text replaces "only-begotten" with "only," since this is a more accurate rendering of "*unicum*."

The phraseology: "*Filius Dei (Patris) unigenitus, id est unicus*"[143] becomes for Augustine the central point that he emphasizes when he anchors his Christological exposition in trinitarian teaching. Even an ordinary member of a congregation ought to know: "The Son possesses the same substance, which means, He has the same existence as the Father, the same almighty power. This means He is the Word of the Father, the only one; and yet, the Father reveals Himself completely through this one. He is immortal, immutable, and thus the power and wisdom of the Father, completely one with Him, since there are not two gods, but rather two persons and one divine being."[144] The words that follow, which describe the birth through the Spirit and the Virgin Mary, are used by Augustine to depict the way

---

[136] Irenaeus, *Adversus haereses* 3:16.6 (PG 7:1.925, Bf., cited according to BKV 3:278).

[137] On Origen, cf. Lietzmann, *Symbolstudien*, 246f.

[138] Tertullian, *Adversus Praxean* 7:1.7–9 (CCSL 2:1165); *Adversus Praxean* 15:6.31–41 (CCSL 2.1179); *Adversus Hermogenem* 18:5.6f. (CCSL 1:412).

[139] It is viewed thus by Kattenbusch, *Symbol*, 2:585ff.; Lietzmann, *Symbolstudien*, 247, 276f.; Kelly, *Creeds*, 141f.; and Eichenseer, *Apostolicum*, 220.

[140] Hahn, *Bibliothek*, §§ 105–16.

[141] Cf. Meyer, *Historischer Kommentar*, 93.

[142] "Eine kurze Form, 1520," WA 7:216.31; "Betbüchlein," WA 10.2:391.8 (AE 43:3–45); *BSLK*, 511.11f. (SC); *BSLK*, 650.43f. (LC).

[143] Augustine, *De fide et symbolo* 3.3 (CSEL 41:6.22); cf. the parallels in Eichenseer, *Apostolicum*, 232.

[144] According to Eichenseer, *Apostolicum*, 231; cf. ibid., 223–32.

that God the Logos becomes human.[145] A new major emphasis is thus crystallized in the commentaries on the Creed. The Christological formula from Chalcedon: Two natures in one person and hypostasis, "unmixed and unchanged, undivided and not separated"[146] works its way into the common confession of the community and its believers; at the same time, it paints a rough picture of the battle for the faith of the Church, along with the heresies that were being rejected. We observe an analogous concentration in the many sermons on the Symbols that were preached in the early Church era.

Sermons 232–46,[147] which have come down to us under the name of Augustine, work hard to accentuate this new point of emphasis, *vere Deus—vere homo*, in a significant way and pass it on to the Middle Ages, as one begins to see references to seven "*articuli divinitatis*" and seven "*articuli humanitatis*."[148] In a most surprising way, in his exposition of the Apostles' Creed, Thomas Aquinas reproduces Augustine's line of argumentation. He offers, in addition, when dealing with the special phrases "*Filius eius unicus*" and "*Conceptus de Spiritu sancto, natus ex Maria Virgine*," a compact overview of the trinitarian heresies that were combated in the early Church, the ones that denied the *Vere Deus* and the Christological heresies against the *Vere Homo*.[149] He explicates the participation of the Son, the Logos, in the divine nature of the Father on the basis of a spiritual conception of our soul.[150]

But when Augustine accentuates God as the eternal Logos, he turns our attention away from our redemption and directs it instead to events within the Trinity that took place before time began and before the world came into being. By necessity, such an emphasis clouds any application of the Second Article to make it apply directly to the one who is confessing. Augustine, and the tradition that follows his interpretation, thus does not bridge the divide for us by using the key phrase "*dominus noster*"; he comes to that point only when he describes Jesus' death on the cross and when he parenthetically links that with His taking on flesh. At this point, a connection is made with how the faith is confessed in the Eastern Church, according to which

---

[145] Cf. Eichenseer, *Apostolicum*, 267–78.
[146] Denzinger, 301f.; cf. the *Catalogus testimoniorum* 1, *BSLK*, 1105.35ff.
[147] PL 39:2173–2220; see also the "3 Sermone de symb. ad catech.," PL 40:637–68.
[148] Cf. p. 16, n. 80.
[149] Thomas Aquinas, *Expositio in Symbolum Apostolorum*, §§ 880–90, 898–904.
[150] Ibid., § 892.

the "only-begotten" Son of God "came for us human beings from Heaven for our salvation" and was crucified "for us" under Pontius Pilate.[151]

By means of apposite terms, Augustine describes succinctly the "*Pro nobis*" aspect of the death of Jesus: "God died for the human being, the righteous one for the sinner, the innocent one for the guilty one, the king for the prisoner, the lord for the slave."[152] He shows us on the cross what we would have had to suffer; in the resurrection, He shows us what we can hope for.[153]

With respect to the incarnation and the virgin birth as well, after long dogmatic explications, Augustine offers brief remarks about the "*Propter nos*" or "*Ad nos*":[154] The Word, who according to His nature is the same as the Father, took on flesh and became a human being; as a result, we are to believe in the only-begotten Son of the almighty Father. He humbled Himself in order to raise us up.

The African sermons that are attributed to Augustine and that are addressed to the catechumens work tirelessly to offer a variety of images to depict this remarkable exchange between Christ and His Church;[155] they are framed so that the Lord is enabled to address the individual Christian personally: I did not die to accomplish something for Myself, but for you. I died so that you may overpower death, not on your own, but through Me. I gave My life for you; now give your life as well, for your fellow human being.[156]

Such statements were expanded during the Middle Ages; two new points of emphasis were added, so as to make explicit what is meant by "*Pro nobis*." The accent is placed on the death on the cross; the incarnation and the virgin birth appear only as they relate to His

---

[151] Nicene Creed, *BSLK*, 26.13f., 17f.; cf. the summary by Lietzmann, *Symbolstudien*, 203f. and the texts, ibid., 205f.

[152] According to Eichenseer, *Apostolicum*, 292; examples, ibid., 290–95.

[153] Augustine, *Sermo ad catech.* 3.9 (PL 40:632): "*Exemplum operis, crux: praemium operis, resurrectio. Ostendit nobis, in cruce quid tolerare, ostendit in resurrectione, quid sperare debeamus.*"

[154] Augustine, *Enchiridion de fide, spe, et caritate* 10.24; *De agone christiano*, 10.11; *De fide et symbolo* 3.6; Morin, *Sermones*, 444.4f.

[155] *Serm. de symb. ad catech.*, 2:6.15; 3:5.5; 4:5.5 (PL 40:644–46; 656; 664f.). [TT-153?]

[156] *Serm. de symb. ad catech.*, 2:6.15 (PL 40:646): "Christ seeks this from you, He says this to you: Because I did it for you, do this for Me; I laid down my life for you, and you lay down your life for your brothers. Do not fear death, because when you could not conquer, I died, so that you would conquer: you are to conquer, not through yourself but through Me, because I did not die for my sake, but for your sake."

death. Peter Lombard deals with the "*causa*" of the passion and the death of Jesus on the cross in the Sentences, Book III;[157] the Lord is the "*hostia*" (victim), not for Himself, but for us;[158] this key term from the Western tradition to explain propitiation is echoed in AC III.[159] Thomas Aquinas uses the exact same two points of emphasis in his exposition of the Apostles' Creed. With respect to becoming human, he speaks of the "*commercium,*" by means of which God became human, in order that the human being could become like God.[160] He describes Jesus' death on the cross initially as that which offers a means of salvation to deliver one from one's own sins, as conveyed through the sacraments;[161] he then makes it function as a pattern that we use to frame our entire life.[162] Augustine's observation about Christ as sacrament and as example is used at this point; Luther himself adopts it consciously and offers reflections on it.[163]

We have thus set forth a second way to offer commentary on the article that deals with Christ. Since it was inaugurated by Augustine, it held the dominant position in the catechetical tradition of the Western Church. It is summarized in a pregnant way in the second verse of Luther's creedal hymn:

> "We believe on Jesus Christ, / His Son and our Lord, / who is eternally by the Father, / truly God in might and honor, / from Mary, the virgin, / He's born a true human / through the Holy Spirit in faith; / for us, since we were lost, / died on the cross and from the dead / rose to life again through God."[164]

This type of interpretation shows movement in two different directions. The phrase "*Filius Dei Patris unicus*" is given special

---

[157] Peter Lombard, *Sententiarum* III, dist. 18.5 (PL 192:794f.): "Regarding the Cause of Death and the Passion of Christ"; concerning becoming human, cf. ibid., dist. 8.2.

[158] Ibid., dist. 18.5 (PL 192:795): "For by dying He was made a sacrifice for our liberation"; cf. Erasmus, *Explanatio Symboli,* col. 1160C.

[159] *BSLK,* 54.10; cf. from earlier still, the Nürnberger Vorform of the AC (Na), *BSLK,* 55.9.

[160] Thomas Aquinas, *Expositio in Symbolum Apostolorum,* § 906: "He makes a certain exchange . . . and thus He was made man so that man should be made God."

[161] Ibid., § 913: "One is as a remedy against sins; another is an example of what to do."

[162] Ibid., § 919: "The passion of Christ suffices to mold our whole life."

[163] See, above all, Jetter, *Die Taufe beim jungen Luther,* 142–59; Iserloh, *Sacramentum und Exemplum.*

[164] *EKG* 132.2 [*LSB* 954.2]; WA 35:451.12 (AE 53:271–273).

attention at first, linked to the virgin birth; both elements highlight the basic teaching set forth in the Creed of Chalcedon. Tne and the same Jesus Christ is "just like the Godhead in relation to the Father and yet, at the same time, just like us with respect to humanity."[165] Augustine and Thomas Aquinas are the most important of those who sketch out, at this point, the trinitarian and Christological implications of the teaching about the two natures and advocate for these connections in response to the heresies of the early Church era. This important point of emphasis is explicated in great detail in Peter Lombard's Sentences, Book III[166] and is reflected later on in dogmatic works in the West. In his "Loci communes" of 1521, Melanchthon writes polemically and considers this aspect to have been overemphasized; he goes in the opposite direction by placing greater emphasis on the soteriological aspect: "*Hoc est Christum cognoscere beneficia eius cognoscere, non quod isti* (most especially John of Damascus and the Peter Lombard) *docent, eius naturas, modos incarnationis contueri* (This is how Christ is to be known, to know His benefits; that is not what they [John of Damascus and Peter Lombard] teach, as they emphasize His nature and the way He became incarnate)."[167] To place the accent here is to underscore the "*Pro nobis*" aspect"; right up to the time of the visitation instructions, the Christological accents remain underexposed in Melanchthon's writings.[168] Luther seems to leave to the side any significant mention of what was learned from the conflicts in the early Church era as well; some appositional comments are all that remain. The other pole is in the center for him as well, which was emphasized far less in the catechetical and teaching tradition inaugurated by Augustine; Luther underscores the "for us" aspect of the saving action of God through Jesus Christ. As is shown in the hymn of faith, what happens on the cross provides the center for Luther.

3. "Our Lord" as Key Term for the Application

From the outset, the reformer placed the greatest emphasis on the last words of this terse confession about Christ, which remains uniquely

[165] Denzinger, 301.
[166] Peter Lombard, *Sententiarum* III, dist. 1–16.
[167] Melanchthon, *Studienausgabe*, 2.1:7, 10. On this, see Maurer, *Der junge Melanchthon*, 2:233–44.
[168] It is barely intimated in the visitation instructions, Melanchthon, *Studienausgabe*, 1:259.16–19.

without accent for both Augustine and Thomas Aquinas, the "*Dominus noster*." Before him, no one attempted to use this last phrase as the key to the entire Article; Luther can let the "for us" provide the underpinning for interpreting the crucifixion and becoming human, but also for interpreting the name of Jesus and the title of Christ.

The word 'Lord' functioned for Palestinian Christianity both in the call for prayer and in the summons to accord honor: μαράνα θά [Marana tha];[169] the community that was gathered for the Lord's Supper calls for the Lord to break into history for the final time. According to Psalm 110:1, as is the messiah, so also the Lord is the one who sits enthroned at the right side of God the creator as the judge of the world. This Old Testament designation for God is applied now to Jesus of Nazareth; this demonstrates "that this particular LORD is not simply a human being; He Himself is God. And as the Scriptures describe Him, He is a LORD of Sabaoth, thus a lord in battle over against all lords, fully armed on the battlefield along with His people, namely, with His beloved angels and with all Christians, who preach and confess Him, for through such means He does battle and wins the victory and preserves His kingdom."[170] And yet, concurrently, such a title of majesty conveys the humble and unpretentious aspect, which shapes how the disciples address their earthly master. The title "our Lord" (ὁ κύριος ἡμῶν) is used in the prescripts, introductory greetings, and postscripts of the New Testament letters: we find it used by Paul most especially in three settings: when Jesus will be coming to judge, when calling upon His name is at issue, and where the "Lord's Supper" is being discussed.[171] Earliest Palestinian traditions are likely reflected when he writes thus; all three settings are intimated when the early Christian *Maranatha* is uttered.

The terse confession "Jesus in Lord!"[172] is offered in adoration before the one who, "equal to God in power and honor," takes part in the lordship and rule of Yahweh. Κύριος χριστός is used in direct opposition to Κύριος Καίσαρ, which has its roots in the ruler cult of

---

[169] 1 Cor. 16:22; *Didache* 10:6; cf. Rev. 22:20 and Kuhn, μαραναθά.

[170] "Torgauer Pred. vom 16./17.4.1533," WA 37:50.35; cf. Foerster, *Herr ist Jesus*, and idem, κύριος.

[171] The texts have been gathered together by Hahn, *Hoheitstitel*, 110; cf., as well, Kattenbusch, *Symbol*, 2:608f.

[172] Romans 10:9; 1 Cor. 8:6; 12:3; Phil. 2:11; Heb. 13:20, and often elsewhere.

late antiquity; it continued to be used later on, as a confession, within the setting of persecution and martyrdom.[173]

The confessions to God the creator and to Jesus of Nazareth are intertwined in the formula used in 1 Cor. 8:6: "No matter how many gods and lords exist, for us Christians there "is only one God the Father, from whom all things come and for whom we exist, and one Lord, Jesus Christ, through whom all things come, and we through Him." The one *Kyrios* appears here as the one "through whom God has reached into this world to save and to act."[174] These words provide the crystallization point for confessions of faith that consist of many parts, most especially the Eastern creedal formulas that are based directly on 1 Cor. 8:6;[175] they draw into the center the "one Lord Jesus Christ" and give witness to His universal reign. But what is admittedly missing there, by and large, is the little word "our," which provides the bridge to the one who is offering the confession.[176] That little word echoes the Aramaic suffix in μαράνα (θά) as well; the controversial comparison to the title applied to Caesar, "our Lord," probably played a role in how it came to be, as well.[177]

By contrast with the Eastern confessions, τὸν κύριον ἡμῶν is tacked on at the end in the Roman Creed. Karl Holl, Adolf von Harnack, and Hans Lietzmann[178] proposed the following thesis: To both titles in the article about Christ, "*Filius Deus unicus*" and "*Dominus noster*," a verbal, descriptive section was added to describe the path that Christ trod; according to Luke 1:35, Jesus became Son of God by means of the virgin birth and according to Phil. 2:6ff., He became Lord by means of the cross, exaltation (and promised return).[179] This thesis has something enticing about it; Luther's

---

[173] *Martyrdom of Polycarp* 8.2; cf. Rev. 17:14.

[174] Foerster, κύριος, 1090.39.

[175] Texts are in Lietzmann, *Symbolstudien*, 235ff.

[176] Cf. the texts, ibid., 198f.

[177] According to Lietzmann, ibid., 199f.

[178] Holl, *Zur Auslegung des zweiten Artikels*; von Harnack, *Zur Auslegung des zweiten Artikels*; Lietzmann, *Zur Auslegung des zweiten Artikels* = idem, *Die Urform des apostolischen Glaubensbekenntnisses*.

[179] This stage for this thesis is set by Rufinus, *Expositio symboli* 7:54 (CCSL 20:144): "Therefore after the order of faith was set forth, [the Creed] set out the ineffable mystery of the nativity of the Son from the Father, who now descends to the dispensation deemed worthy for man's salvation. And this one who was called formerly the only Son of God, it now calls our Lord."

division of the Second Article would be wonderfully substantiated thereby.

But other scholars reject the assumption that "*Dominus noster*" played a "decisive role" when the article about Christ took shape.[180] It is missing from the most ancient Western witnesses, by and large, and likely came into the Roman Symbol only much later.

The commentaries present a similar picture; in contrast to the other titles of honor, "*Dominus noster*" is treated like a stepmother.[181] Augustine admittedly cites it, but he never expands on it.[182] No question needs to be asked about what it means and it does not seem particularly suitable for stimulating dogmatic observations. Thomas Aquinas, who reproduces what Augustine said, passes over it as well, without so much as an additional comment.[183] It receives somewhat greater attention from Cyril of Jerusalem, Rufinus, and Peter Chrysologus,[184] but they use 1 Cor. 8:6 to emphasize the unity between the lordship of Christ and the lordly nature of the Father. Because the only-begotten Son participates by nature in the divinity of the Father, He shares in that sense in the lordship of the Father. Cyril of Jerusalem paraphrases the universality of the lordly rule of the one who mediates creation, very similarly to what Luther says later in the Short Form of 1520: "At the beginning, He created everything according to the will of His Father; He is thus Lord over everything that He created."[185] But, in the entire tradition, the "our Lord" aspect is never "brought front and center" before Luther; it is not used as the chief point of emphasis for the application of the Second Article; that could not happen until "*Pro nobis*" is accentuated on purpose, becoming thus a point of thematic emphasis. This happens in the following sentences in the Short Form of 1520: "I believe that no one can believe in the Father and no one can come to the Father, whether by means of ingenuity, activity, reason or any other way that human beings can identify in heaven or on earth,

---

[180] Thus, for example, Kelly, *Creeds*, 120–26; Eichenseer, *Apostolicum*, 235.

[181] According to Kattenbusch, *Symbol*, 2:594f.; Eichenseer, *Apostolicum*, 232f.

[182] See the evidence gathered together by Eichenseer, *Apostolicum*, 232.

[183] Thomas Aquinas, *Expositio in Symbolum Apostolorum*, §§ 887–96.

[184] Cyril of Jerusalem, *Catechesis* 10:1ff.; Rufinus, *Expositio symboli* 7:47–58 (CCSL 20:144); Peter Chrysologus, *Sermo* 59 (PL 52:363C); *Sermo* 60 (ibid., 367B); *Sermo* 61 (ibid., 370B); *Sermo* 62 (ibid., 373C); cf. Augustine, *Enchiridion de fide, spe, et caritate* 10:35.

[185] Cyril of Jerusalem, *Catechesis* 10:5 (PG 33:668A, cited according to BKV 41:148).

except only in and through Jesus Christ His only Son, that is, through faith in His name and lordship."[186] Luther articulated the "our Lord" aspect most forcefully in the Torgau sermons of 1533;[187] when speaking of "our Lord," we confess "that everything that that man is and does happens for our benefit; in that He was thus born, suffered, died, has been raised, He is OUR LORD."[188]

Catechisms that are written later on no longer accentuate this aspect. Already in the Nuremberg Children's Sermons, the Western point of emphasis, as clearly stated by Anselm, returns to accentuate even more strongly the concept of satisfaction and to reemphasize early Church teaching on the two natures. And yet, the phrase "our Lord" still forms the concluding bracket around the Second Article; these words are to be noted "with particular diligence," for therein lies "our highest comfort, that Christ is our Lord."[189] This phrase is repositioned and placed at the beginning in the Heidelberg Catechism, and it forms the gateway to all that follows, though under the key term "Savior": "What then is your one comfort in life and in death? That I, with body and soul, both in life and in death, properly belong not to myself but to my faithful Savior Jesus Christ."[190] Question 34 takes up Luther's comments from the Small Catechism, right down to Luther's exact words. In the Geneva Catechism, "our Lord" is just one point of emphasis among many; Calvin thereby paraphrases the lordship of Christ to include all the aspects Augustine included: At the same time, as "Lord of Sabaoth," Jesus is "installed by the Father in order to reign over us, to administer the kingdom and the lordship of God both in heaven and on earth, and to be head over both the angels and the believers (Eph. 5:23; Col. 1:18)."[191]

We have thus set forth three attempts to make sense of the Second Article. Bringing the discussion to a close, it must still be pointed out once again that these three treatments do not stand awkwardly, one

---

[186] WA 7:217.11. This is taken up by J. Bader in the *Gesprächsbüchlein* (MGP 20:269.16–21), by J. Agricola in "Christl. Kinderzucht, 1527" (MGP 21:49–51) and by W. Capito in the "Kinderbericht" (MGP 21:111).

[187] WA 37:45–53.

[188] Ibid., 49:17.

[189] Reu, *Quellen*, 1.1:515.20, 26; cf. ibid., 515:16–42.

[190] *Heidelberger Kat.*, quest. 1.

[191] Calvin, *Genfer Kat.*, quest. 54 (Calvin, Opera Selecta 2:81.18–21, cited according to Jacobs, *Reformierte Bekenntnisschriften*, 19).

next to one another; they are each aware of the others and depend on each other.

(1) The decisive point of emphasis is shaped by Augustine and is passed on by the tradition of those who follow Peter Lombard and Thomas Aquinas: The "*Filius Dei Patris unicus*" is positioned to have central importance and is linked to the virgin birth; both points are then explicated on the basis of the teaching about the two natures. More comprehensive teaching about "*De persona Christi*" follows then in the dogmatic treatments. "*Pro nobis*" is treated in greater detail only when one comes to the death on the cross; afterward, it is used when discussing what it means that He became human. The teaching about propitiation, Christ's role as intermediary, is drawn out from these initial points of emphasis; the path of Jesus is portrayed, starting with His becoming human and ending with His return. These two points of importance, Christ's person and then Christ's office and work, leave their mark on Luther's interpretations as well. But the reformers lay the greatest importance concerning the teaching about the two natures on the redeeming work of Christ.

(2) The redeeming actions of the Lord are implicit in the commentaries of the early Church, already when they discuss the name Jesus and its meanings. The "Christ" title makes it possible to set forth the work of Jesus and our participation in Him according to the pattern of the *Officium duplex* or even *triplex*. These aspects are inserted, in the development of both the Geneva and Heidelberg Catechisms, into the overall framework of interpretation that was given shape by Augustine and that was adopted by Luther. The application of the name of Jesus and the title of Christ, upon us, appears as a doublet, in terms of the content; it parallels the more comprehensive application of the individual stages of the life of Jesus that are applied to us.[192] It is only at the time of the orthodox Scholastic dogmaticians that the teaching about the *Officium propheticum, regale et sacerdotale* pushes the teaching of Christ's humiliation and exaltation (*status exaninationes–exaltationis*) once more into the background, though it was dealt with extensively in the *Summa* by Thomas Aquinas.[193]

---

[192] In the Geneva Catechism, what is discussed briefly in quest. 30–48 is dealt with in greater detail in quest. 49–87; the relationship is analogous in the Heidelberg Catechism between quest. 29–34 and quest. 35–52.

[193] Thomas Aquinas, *Summa theologiae* III, quest. 27–59.

(3) Since Luther brings "*Dominus noster*" front and center, he does not so much treat new content in the Second Article as much as that he concentrates on that aspect of the pattern set forth initially by Augustine, making sure that it is applied to the believers. The *Dominus* aspect was always equated with *Salvator* or *Redemptor*.[194] Luther offers somewhat of a paraphrase in the Torgau sermons: "Take note, for one ought thus to get to know it, that He is that kind of LORD who helps, protects, and saves us, so long as we live, not only in situations of external danger and need, but also against the gates of hell and the loathsome devil."[195] By necessity, an application that centers on those who are confessing leads to less emphasis on the teaching about the two natures of Christ, as tradition had passed it down. This leads us to the question: What is the connection between the teaching about Christ that Luther received from the early Church and the new central point about redemption and justification, with emphasis placed now on "my Lord and redeemer"?

What Happens to the Early Church's Christology When "For Us" Is the Central Point of Emphasis?[196]

The Small Catechism formulates it classically: "I believe that Jesus Christ, true God, born of the Father in eternity, and also true man, born of the Virgin Mary, is my Lord, who has redeemed me."[197] Three points are made thereby: Jesus Christ: true God—true man—my Lord and redeemer; but the way in which these three points relate to one another has been disputed in Luther scholarship.[198] In "Drei Symbola oder Bekenntnis des Glaubens Christi," from 1538, the reformer depicts Satan's attack against the "Chief Article about Jesus Christ"[199]: The devil "does battle against Christ with three vanguards

---

[194] *BSLK*, 652.27f. (LC).

[195] WA 37:51.3.

[196] For sources and literature that deals with the way Luther makes use of the teaching of the early Church on the two natures, see pp. 202–204.

[197] *BSLK*, 511.23–28.

[198] See especially the presentations by Wolf, *Die Christusverkündigung bei Luther*; Congar, *Regards et réflexions sur la christologie de Luther*; Althaus, *Theologie Luthers*, 159–95; Nilsson, *Das Miteinander von Göttlichem und Menschlichem*, 151–260; Peters, *Luthers Christuszeugnis*; Lienhard, *Luther, Témoin de Jésus-Christ*; and Vorlander, *Deus incarnatus*.

[199] WA 50:266.33 (AE 34:197–229).

(dividing wedges); one does not want to let Him be God; the second does not want to let Him be human; the third wants to keep Him from effecting what He has accomplished."[200]

In each case, it deals with the one and entire Christian faith. The conflicts in the early Church revolved around the issue of the *Vere Deus* and *Vere homo*; the new battle raised the question about how redemption was effected. The battle for Luther's own day focused on the thrust of that third wedge; Christ's office and work were endangered, which resulted in the new concentration on "my Lord." Luther writes from the perspective of being engaged in the battle as one of the members of Satan's forces: "And what do we have, to set forth before the most important, greatest holy ones in the papacy? We have confessed that He is God and man. But that He is our savior, the one who has died and risen for us, etc., that we have denied and disputed with all might, and have no intention of stopping even now."[201] We have no intention of permitting the "for us" to be true, in its final ultimate sense and consequence. We consign Christ to the past; He seems no longer to be our present and future Lord. Luther points out that it is here on this third front that the total rejection of the Christian faith becomes the scene of the battle; the modern human being of Luther's time, depicted in what it meant to be a Renaissance man, works with all his might to concentrate absolutely on what goes on in this world, denying thereby, with vehemence, Jesus' resurrection: "From that third crowd, there are those that will come forth, and many are at the point already, that they will not believe that Christ is resurrected from the dead, to say nothing of His being seated at the right hand of God, nor do they follow anything else connected with Christ in faith. They want to knock the floor out from under the barrel and to put an end to the whole game. For it is thereby that the entire Christ goes down, and the world will have no thought about the life to come; at that point, Christ is no more. For if one no longer hopes for the life to come, one has no more need of Christ than does the cow and the other animals of Paradise."[202] Luther knew perfectly well that belief [up]on Jesus' living reign as Lord makes everything else perfectly clear for us human beings who live out this earthly

---

[200] Ibid., 269.1.

[201] Ibid., 268.21.

[202] Ibid., 269.21; cf. "Pred. über 1 Kor. 15:1ff. vom 11.8.1532," WA 36:478.1–482.2; "Gen.-Vorl., 1535–45," WA 43:363.21 (AE 4:317): "The denial of a future life completely does away with God."

existence, even though "on earth, such a foolish, impossible, dubious thing has never been heard or seen, that a human being who died should now not only be alive but should be functioning as Lord as well, distributing life, and going to awaken all the dead."[203]

Because of the conflict that had to be waged on this battlefront, which had appeared so recently, centering on whether "for us" has meaning in the present, the reformer could no longer merely reiterate the formulas of the Council of Chalcedon;[204] he renewed, and brought into contemporary application, the teachings that were implicit in these formulas. He intimated what was at issue in simple terms in the catechisms; he explicated these points in further detail in festival sermons, treatises, most especially those that discussed the Johannine prologue, disputations, and polemical writings. The formula from Chalcedon: "one and the same Jesus Christ, the Son, the Lord and only-begotten, two natures in the one person and hypostasis, unmixed and unchanged, undivided and unseparated,"[205] remained there formally. To be sure, some possibilities were excluded thereby and clear borders were marked out, though what is circumscribed in that wording does not call for an analysis of the inner relationships within the Godhead. "In this way, place is left for testimony about the uniqueness of Jesus Christ, which dogma can describe but cannot probe in detail."[206] But this formalized, fourfold pattern was not adequate for articulating the real points that the two parties in the conflict wanted to emphasize, the Alexandrians who were allied with Cyril and the Antiochenes who were allied with Theodoret of Cyrrhus. What they sought to articulate was taken up by Luther, being transposed at the same time into the realm of the personal aspects of the faith. The main issues can be divided to express three central points.

(1) According to the formulas of the Creed of Chalcedon, it could seem as if the Lord were something of a third type of being, the result of the flowing together of a divine being and a human being; but this would be a fundamental misunderstanding. We do not analyze the two natures becoming one person as we might watch two fluids becoming one in a reagent beaker; much rather, we ourselves are

---

[203] "Weihnachtspred. über Jes. 9:2–7 vom 26.12.1525," WA 19:154.4.
[204] On this, see most especially the three-volume work: *Das Konzil von Chalkedon, Geschichte und Gegenwart*.
[205] Denzinger, 302; cf. *BSLK*, 1104f.
[206] Adam, *DG*, 1:337.

caught up within this Christ event; we give our allegiance to this one and the same Lord as our redeemer; in Jesus' actual life, God Himself turns toward us. [Without taking time to reflect deeply], Cyril praises this sure statement of the faith in his twelfth anathema against Nestorius,[207] which was taken up by the Fifth Council of Constantinople in 553: "Whoever does not confess that our Lord Jesus Christ, who was crucified in the flesh, is true God and Lord of Lords and is one of the Holy Trinity, such a one is excluded."[208] Luther never tires of seizing on this central issue: If God Himself had not actually stepped in on our behalf and died in the person of Jesus of Nazareth, we would not as yet be saved. This holds true for Jesus' entire existence; "all actions, words, suffering, and what Christ does, the true Son of God does, accomplishes, speaks, and suffers, and it is correct to say that God's Son died for us, God's Son preaches on earth, God's Son washes feet for the disciples."[209] With respect to worship, this meant: "When we worship that particular human being who was born of the Virgin Mary, we do not worship just any human being who has been singled out, who is his own unique person, without God and apart from God; instead, we worship the one, true God, who is one God with the Father and the Holy Spirit and who is a unique person with respect to humanity."[210]

(2) At the same time, along with the Alexandrians, the reformer emphasizes the other aspect of God and a human being existing as one in Christ. In Jesus of Nazareth the eternal God, the Logos, actually enters into our existence, takes on our humanity completely, not only the undamaged human existence of Adam before fall apart from the guilt of sin, but our human existence that includes what is ours as sinful human beings under God's curse. "The Word . . . became flesh, in order to show the weakness and mortality of the

---

[207] Denzinger, 245; *BSLK*, 1104.32–34, 47–50.

[208] Denzinger, 432, cited according to NR 263.

[209] "Vom Abendmahl Christi, 1528," WA 26:320.31 ; cf. ibid., 319.27–324.35 (AE 37:151–372); "Von den Konziliis und Kirchen, 1539," WA 50:590.5–22 (AE 41:3–178).

[210] "Von den letzten Worten Davids, 1543," WA 54:91.10 (AE 15:265–352). Concerning worship, cf. the utterances from the early Church in the *Catalogus testimoniorum* 3, *BSLK*, 1116–19. Peter Lombard, *Sententiarum* III, dist. 9.2 (PL 192:776): "What is worshiped is neither the humanity, by itself or naked, but what is united with the Word." This is taken up by Thomas Aquinas, *In Sententiarum* III, dist. 9, q. 1; Duns Scotus, *Opus Oxoniense* III, dist. 9, q. un.; idem, *Reportata Parisiensia* III, dist. 9, q. un.

flesh. Christ took on human nature, which is mortal, which has been placed under the horrifying wrath and judgment of God because of the sins of the human race; this weak and mortal nature in Christ felt and suffered the wrath."[211] For this reason, in a radical and unabbreviated way: "The God who created all things and still preserves them . . . does not let Himself be found, let Himself be embraced and encountered, except in this flesh and blood of the Son";[212] only in the concrete, physical life of His Son does the invisible and eternal God permit Himself to be found by us mortal human beings, in order to be saved. Whoever comes into contact with this physical human being comes into contact with God Himself; "whoever encounters *this* flesh encounters God."[213] The concrete, physical nature of this human being, along with the physical means of grace that He instituted, provides the organ by which God proffers salvation. Cyril describes it this way in his eleventh anathema: "Whoever does not confess that the flesh of the Lord provides life, and that this is the actual flesh of the Word who comes forth from God the Father . . . , that person is excluded."[214]

This lively way to take part in and to be given a connection with the deity and the humanity in the one person Jesus Christ was described by the Cappadocians, Gregory of Nazianzus and Gregory of Nyssa, as the *Communicatio idiomatum* (ἀντίδωδις τῶν ἰδιωμάτων); Leontius of Byzantium, Maximus the Confessor, and John of Damascus cast this in the form of a solemn teaching.[215] In his dispute with Zwingli, Luther underscores the inner unity of the natures; in the one person, the one hypostasis, the divine nature and human nature permeate as inwardly as one can possible conceptualize.[216] Obviously,

---

[211] "Pred. über Joh. 1:14 vom 1.9.1537," WA 46:632.22 (AE 22:1–530); "Gen.-Vorl., 1535–45," WA 43:580.7 (AE 5:219): "Therefore both things are true: the highest divinity is the lowest creature, made the servant of all men, yes, subject to the devil himself. On the other hand, the lowest creature, the humanity or the man, sits at the right hand of the Father".

[212] "Pred. über Joh. 6:51 vom 25.2.1531," WA 33:185.15 (AE 23:1–197).

[213] "Pred. über Joh. 6:52f. vom 4.3.1531," WA 33:194.23 (AE 23:1–197).

[214] Denzinger, 262, cited according to NR 244; this anathema is taken up into the SD VIII, 76 (*BSLK*, 1043.2–6) and in the *Catalogus testimoniorum* 3 (*BSLK*, 1119.36–47).

[215] See Forster, "Idiomenkommunikation."

[216] "Ennaratio Jes. 53, 1544," WA 40.3:707.29: "The faith teaches that this is not abstract, but concrete, joining and coupling both natures"; "Gen.-Vorl., 1535–45," WA 43:580.23 (AE 5:220): "Here there is God and man, the highest and the lowest, infinite and finite in one person, emptying and filling all things"; "Vom Abendmahl

the initiative for this proceeds from God, the Logos; He alone is the one who carries the majesty of the divine-human hypostasis. John 1:14: "The Word became flesh and took up dwelling among us and we saw His glory"[217] conceptualizes this dual focus of the Alexandrian *Logos-Sarx* Christology, as Luther reiterates it and as the Lutheran Confessions present it in fixed form.[218]

(3) But Luther also wants to do complete justice to the biblical emphases that are protected by the Antiochenes. The Alexandrian formula, "a hypostasis" or even "the nature of the God-Logos who became flesh," adopted by Cyril from Apollinaris of Laodicea,[219] aimed to allow something to remain unclear, though that was very important to the Antiochene group that included Diodorus of Tarsus, Theodore of Mopsuestia, and Theodoret of Cyrrhus: the unity of God and this human life became complete not in the setting of what was natural and involuntary but rather by what God alone accomplished in the setting of grace and in the economy of salvation and with respect to the human nature by what was freely willing and personal;[220] it is a unity that is grounded at the deepest level in God's free and unforced grace and is completed willingly and freely in the offering of a human life. At the same time, along with the formally and historically standard framework that was developed on the basis of John 1:14: λόγος—σάρξ, the Pauline witness speaks of the Son of God coming into the flesh according to the seed of David,[221] which is given in

Christi, 1528," WA 26:324.19 (AE 37:151–372): "They cry against us that we merge the two natures into one being. That is not true. We do not say that divinity is humanity or divine nature is human nature, which would merge the nature into a being. Instead, we merge the two distinguishable natures into one person and say: God is human and human is God."

[217] Grillmeier, *Die theol. u. sprachl. Vorbereitung der christol. Formel von Chalkedon*, points most especially to John 1:2; 4:2; 1 Tim. 3:16; Tit. 2:11; 3:4. On John, in addition to Bultmann, *Das Evangelium des Johannes*, see also Käsemann, *Aufbau und Anliegen des johanneischen Prologs*, as well as idem, *Jesu letzter Wille nach Johannes 17*, 14–52, with the corrections provided by Bornkamm, *Zur Interpretation des Johannes-Evangeliums.*

[218] One ought to consult, in this connection, the *Catalogus testimoniorum*, *BSLK*, 1101–35.

[219] Concerning him, see Mühlenberg, *Apollinaris von Laodicea.*

[220] A good overview is provided by Grillmeier, *Die theol. u. sprachl. Vorbereitung der christol. Formel von Chalkedon*, 130–53.

[221] Grillmeier, *Die theol. u. sprachl. Vorbereitung der christol. Formel von Chalkedon*, 27: "John speaks of the Logos *becoming flesh*, Paul of an *indwelling* of the fullness of the deity in the man Christ or else of a *taking on* of the form of being

concentrated form in the Letter to the Colossians (1:19; 2:9), which speaks of the indwelling of the fullness of God in this living body; using these ideas, the Antiochenes came up with the pattern: λόγος—ἄνθρωπος, God and human being.

Luther seizes upon that which was central to the Antiochenes, but without thereby constricting the living unity of the natures in Jesus Christ, as they did. Drastically and robustly, Luther supports his statement by using Luke 2:40, 52: Jesus grew in age and wisdom before God and human beings. The Alexandrians admittedly spoke of the humanity of Christ as "a creation and house for the divinity,"[222] but one ought not to interpret this to mean that the Lord was lord from the first moments of His conception and birth, completely "filled with wisdom and Spirit, so that nothing else had to be added, as if the soul were a wineskin that one would fill until nothing more could be added."[223] Even Jesus, as a true human being, grew up completely in obedience to God; though the Spirit of God "was in Him from the moment of His conception, even still His body grew and His reason developed in a natural way, as it would in any other human being, as if the Spirit sank into Him deeper and deeper and moved Him more intensively as time moved on."[224]

The formula from Chalcedon: "one person and hypostasis in two natures" does not really make the intentions of the Alexandrians, as well as the Antiochenes, explicit; the reformer seeks to articulate these afresh and to unite them. He accentuates the Johannine pattern: λόγος—σάρξ, and confesses with the Alexandrians: The eternal Son of God Himself is in the bodily existence of this Jesus of Nazareth, among us, and following a plan; the invisible, exalted God uniquely and exclusively allows Himself to be comprehended by us mortal human beings by faith. At the same time, Luther inserts the stronger Pauline statement into the Johannine pattern and articulates once again the concern of the Antiochenes, as well as their pattern λόγος and ανθρωπος: the eternal, invisible God and creator reveals Himself to us only in the free, undeterred life of faith and obedient suffering of this true human being before His heavenly Father.

---

of human nature. John emphasizes more the inward nature of the unity of being, Paul much more the entirety of both states of being."

[222] "Weihnachtspost. 1522 über Lk. 2:33–40," WA 10.1.1:447.12 (AE 52:102–148).

[223] Ibid., 446.13.

[224] Ibid., 447.15. See below, p. 174f.

But when Luther makes use of the decisions from the early Church, as these formulations demonstrate, the connection with the confessing community is consciously in play and is made part of the statements of faith. Luther uncouples the teaching of the early Church about the two natures from the conceptual framework that is mythological and Docetic, so that he can connect his observations with applications to daily existence. For this reason, the challenge for an interpretation in his own day and age called for appropriate existential Christological categories that would match the early Church's ontological categories.[225] But a corresponding issue appeared at the same time, as Luther points out in his commentary on the "Three Symbols": the phrase "for us," without a concrete reference back to the Christ event, remains empty; the ontological and existential point of entry for what is meant by "*Pro nobis*" must be grounded once again in the insights from the Christology of the early Church and cannot in any case be surrendered. With respect to each of the three elements: Jesus Christ—true God–true man—my Lord and redeemer, it is finally always about the same issue, that of the chief article of our confession. Christ's person and Christ's work cannot be divided, one from the other. Without this two-sided apposition: "true God, born from the Father in eternity, and also true man, born of the Virgin Mary,"[226] "my Lord and redeemer" matters not at all; pure and simple, this is the reason the reformers solemnly take hold of and pass on the Christology of the early Church. Even though the reformer barely hints at the decisions of the early Church in his reference in the Large Catechism, when he uses the phrase "the second person of the Godhead"[227] and "true Son of God,"[228] these briefly mentioned references still carry decisive weight. This can be demonstrated in his comments on the *Communicatio idiomatum*.

---

[225] This is claimed most especially by Rahner, *Chalkedon—Ende oder Anfang?*

[226] *BSLK*, 511.23f. (SC).

[227] *BSLK*, 651.10f. (LC).

[228] *BSLK*, 651.32 (LC).

OUR REDEMPTION THROUGH JESUS CHRIST AS VICTORY OVER THE POWERS OF DESTRUCTION AND AS PROPITIATION WITH GOD[229]

Since we do not discuss the cross and resurrection of Jesus as a separate topic within the framework of the sequence of festivals that give shape to Christology, the notes concerning Luther's translation of the Apostles' Creed into German are inserted here.

The words "*passus sub Pontio Pilato, crucifixus, mortuus et sepultus*" are translated by the reformer in the same consistent way as follows: "suffered under Pontius Pilate, crucified, dead, and buried";[230] admittedly, the introductory text to the Large Catechism reads: "(who) *had* suffered under Pontius Pilate, "*is* crucified, dead, and buried."[231] Originally, "*passus*" was translated as "martyred,"[232] concentrating particularly on the scourging under Pontius Pilate, with a brief expansion to depict the earthly path that Jesus took. From the end of the fifteenth century, that was replaced with "suffered,[233] which, from His perspective, takes Jesus' earthly path as the suffering He endured when He made an offering.[234] This "suffered" includes at the same time the spiritual dimension, as He stood under the judgment of God and was in the grasp of the powers of death as well; the paraphrases of the Symbols in the Middle Ages, by contrast, brought into the center those events that took place on the human level; "I believe that the same Son of God was betrayed and was sold by one of His own disciples, Judas, imprisoned, and martyred, nailed upon the holy cross, and died thereon, with respect to His humanity but not according to His divinity."[235]

The words: "*tertie die resurrexit a mortuis*," from the *Textus receptus*, are rendered in a clear manner by Luther as "resurrected on

---

229 For a selection of the most important texts, and the literature that deals with them, see pp. 204f.

230 "Eine kurze Form, 1520," WA 7:216.33; "Betbüchlein," WA 10.2:391.10 (AE 43:3–45); *BSLK*, 511.14f. (SC); *BSLK*, 651.1f. (LC).

231 *BSLK*, 556.3–5.

232 Hahn, *Bibliothek*, §§ 93, 100, 108, 111, 112, 114–17.

233 Cf. the examples in Meyer, *Historischer Kommentar*, 93.

234 Capito, "Kinderbericht, 1527" (MGP 21:126.5): "His entire life was suffering"; cf. Calvin, *Genfer Kat.*, quest. 55; idem, *Inst.*, 2:16.5; *Heidelberger Kat.*, quest. 37.

235 Hahn, *Bibliothek*, § 117.

the third day from the dead";[236] admittedly, the introductory text to the Large Catechism and the Torgau sermons insert an "again."[237] At first, "*resurrexit*" was translated into German with a simple "arisen (*erstanden*)."[238] In addition, one also finds "rose up (*aufstehen*)" or "resurrected (*auferstehen*)."[239] Instead of the literal "from the dead' that is kept by Luther, some texts render it "from death,"[240] which is what Luther uses in his commentary: "just as He is raised from the dead."[241]

Admittedly, commentary on the Second Article in the Catechisms clearly accentuates the redeeming work of Jesus, not His person as divine and human. But, at the same time, Jesus' office and work are not described in intellectual terms; instead, the dramatic action of a battle unfolds in narrative fashion, by means of which Luther extols the "for us" aspect. In which way, by what actions, did Jesus Christ become my Lord? That question guides the discussion. By this means, the reformer seizes upon the central confessional statement of early Christendom: "Jesus is Lord!" (Rom. 10:9; 1 Cor. 8:6; 12:3; Phil. 2:11) and interprets what is described in the Second Article as an explication of that earliest *kerygma*; testimony is provided to show that Jesus Christ is the one who rules over us as Lord, in the here and now, as the Lord of the one who is making confession. The direction one looks with this interpretation must be observed carefully. At this point, the reformer presents independent movement, but in two directions; he starts out by allowing the Christ event that overarches every time and space relationship to focus on the here and now of the one who is making confession: "I believe that Jesus Christ . . . has *become* my Lord."[242] He gave Himself, at that time and in that place, and died under Pontius Pilate, so that He could redeem me and "*would become* my Lord."[243] What is attested in the Second Article, as the saving action of Christ that encompasses the world, comes upon us, concentrated in our experience as we are confronted in the

---

[236] "Eine kurze Form, 1520," WA 7:217.1; "Betbüchlein," WA 10.2:391.13 (AE 45:11–49); *BSLK*, 511.16f. (SC); *BSLK*, 651.3–5 (LC).
[237] *BSLK*, 556.7; WA 37:36.2; 45.21; 62.28.
[238] Hahn, *Bibliothek*, §§ 93, 95, 100–04, 106, 108, 109, 111, 112, 114–17.
[239] Hahn, *Bibliothek*, § 110; Meyer, *Historischer Kommentar*, 94.
[240] Hahn, *Bibliothek*, §§ 116, 117; Meyer, *Historischer Kommentar*, 94.
[241] *BSLK*, 511.36f. (SC).
[242] *BSLK*, 651.31–33 (LC).
[243] *BSLK*, 652.46 (LC).

here and now: Jesus Christ, my Lord, is my redeemer. But Luther takes another step as well, when in a colossal way he expands that here and now of my little existence; it is taken up and enfolded within the space and time of Christ's victory that, by means of what He does, explodes our confinement in this world of death.[244]

This second step marks out for us so-called modern human beings something that alienates us from Luther's understanding. In the Small Catechism, Luther permits the one who is making confession to be enwrapped completely by the Christ who rules. From below and from time past, the one who was humiliated now holds onto the believer; from above and from future time, the one who is elevated at the right hand of the Father holds that same believer. By means of His humiliation, which culminates in His death as an offering, Jesus Christ freed us from the tyranny of those powers of destruction: sin, death, and devil. The event on the cross at Golgotha has seized the one who is making confession and has transferred that believer into a new status through Holy Baptism; in our baptism, we were taken up into the event on Golgotha and were buried with Christ in His death as an offering. This redeeming activity of Christ, for me, opens at the same time a new path into an eschatological future, "*so that* I might be His own and live under Him in His kingdom and serve Him in everlasting righteousness, innocence, and blessedness."[245] And this newly revealed path of life under the lordship of Christ, at the very same moment, from above and from the future, is encompassed by Christ's exaltation: "*just as* He is risen from the dead, lives and reigns in eternity."[246] Christ's lordship encompasses my existence in the here and now, not only from the then and there of the offering upon Golgotha, but simultaneously from the here and now of His on-going lordship, and it opens to me the future of a life in God that overcomes death. The here and now of my existence, which is confined to the earth, has all the strictures of such existence removed eschatologically in this way; already now, in Him, even though still hidden under the cross of Jesus and open only to the eyes of faith, the final lordship that Christ is to exercise in the Kingdom of God begins to dawn. "If you believe on Christ, everything is cleared away for you already, hell

---

[244] This second step is hardly carried out fully by those who interpret Luther existentially, as for example in Ebeling, *Luther*. The presentation offered by Joest, *Ontologie*, is not sufficient here either.
[245] *BSLK*, 511.33–36; cf. 652.2–12 (LC).
[246] *BSLK*, 511.36f.

is extinguished already, sin is gone already, death is conquered, and you have eternal righteousness, blessedness, and life."[247]

The reformer expands still more in the Large Catechism on this battle against the powers of destruction that encompass the world, and in which we are involved in our relationship with God, as he calls attention to events that take place at the very beginning and eschatologically. He appears to speak in a "naïve" way, by seeming to include us in the history of the fall into sin: "Then, when *we* were created and had received all manner of good things from God the Father, the devil came and moved *us* to disobedience, sin, death, and all misfortune, so that *we* were under His wrath and displeasure, condemned under the judgment of eternal damnation, for which we were responsible and which we had deserved."[248] More strongly than Paul, in Rom. 5:12–21, Luther writes us into Adam's original sin. "Adam" is not the first person to form the chain of humanity, lost back in the darkness of the prehistoric era; Adam, that is we ourselves.[249] We are the ones who were overpowered by the devil; we are the ones who are enslaved thereby under the lordship of sin and death and who have fallen under God's wrathful judgment. The reformer does not go into great detail, at this juncture, to describe the connection between that original sin, into which all of us were born under the sentence of judgment;[250] this distinguishes the Catechisms from the confessions. In the Confession of 1528 he discusses both aspects at the same time "in a more objective manner": "For I confess and know how to demonstrate from the Scriptures that all human beings have come from one human being, Adam, and by means of one's birth one receives the fall, guilt and sin from this same person, which this same person Adam set in motion in Paradise through the evil of the devil, and thus together with him every single person is born in sin, lives and dies and would have to be under the judgment of

[247] "Pred. über Joh. 6:45–47 vom 11.2.1531," WA 33:162.13 (AE 23:1–197); WATR 1:111.31 (no. 267) (AE 54:3–114): "Christ is made Lord through the resurrection, receives power and rule through the ascension."

[248] *BSLK*, 651.42–48. Earlier than that, the status was described, in *BSLK*, 651.38–40: "seized by the devil's power, damned to death, ensnared in sin and blindness"; cf. "Kat.-Pred. zum Credo vom 10.12.1528," WA 30.1:89.11f., 18f (AE 51:162–169).

[249] Kierkegaard, *Der Begriff Angst*, 26: "Adam is the first human; at the same time he is himself and the species"; concurrently, Kierkegaard sets up a warning, idem, 25: "as soon as Adam is positioned outside, as a phantasm, all manner of confusion results."

[250] For texts and literature dealing with Luther's view of sin, see pp. 205.

eternal death, if it were not that Jesus Christ came to help us."[251] But even here, the reference to the sin that is connected to Adam is enwrapped in an overarching way by the soteriological connection with Jesus Christ, in contrast to the treatment in the Augsburg Confession.[252] The imprisonment, from which He has freed us, is apparent only after Jesus Christ comes to be known as our Lord and redeemer. The Nuremberg Children's Sermons link the catechetical tradition with the confessional tradition: they describe the fall into sin in an expanded way and construct the bridge that comes from Adam to us, aided by the teaching about original sin. The original sin is paraphrased, with the aid of AC II: "They do not trust God; they do not love God, they are stuck full with fear and hold fast to evil desires."[253]

The jailhouse of original sin, from which Christ has torn us free, is not something that lies once and for all in our past, which we can leave behind as a child does its mother's womb. This jailhouse and its tyrants, such remain as a sinister opposing force, which constantly oppresses those who are living under the lordship of Christ. For this reason, the original fall into sin corresponds to the eschatological judgment day and to Christ's final and complete lordship over the powers of death. This is envisioned in the Large Catechism as the *telos* of the lordship of Christ: "until the time that He (Christ) finally cuts us off and separates us from the evil world, the devil, death, sin, etc., on the last day."[254] To that "etc." belongs also the old Adam in us, which will be eradicated completely only through death and the fire of judgment.

The commentaries offered by the Small and Large Catechisms are characterized by this movement in two aspects. They concentrate the

---

[251] "Vom Abendmahl Christi, 1528," WA 26:502.25 (AE 37:151–372).

[252] "Disp. de iustificatione, 1536," WA 39.1:84, Theses 7–11 (AE 34:154): "7. Not one of all men could think that it was a sin of the world not to believe in Christ Jesus the Crucified. 8. This is original sin born in us after Adam's fall, and not only something personal but also natural. 9. Not to believe in Christ is to be unbelieving, ignorant, and estranged from God, who promised Christ the Savior. 10. For this reason Paul rightly declares: all are consigned to unbelief, so that God may have mercy upon all. 11. This unbelief brings with it all the other sins, since it is the principal sin against the first commandment."

[253] "Nürnberger Kat.-Predigten," Reu, *Quellen*, 1.1:512.47; cf. ibid., 512.1–513.20, esp. 513.13f.; Dietenberger follows the "Kat.-Predigten," (Moufang, *Katholische Katechismen*, 15f.).

[254] *BSLK*, 653.1–3.

Christ event, which is worldwide in scope, on the "for me" aspect, as the one who is making confession. But the individual making confession is located, as well, within the events at the beginning of time and within the eschatological dimensions of the battle between the Lord and the satanic opponents. By necessity, both aspects belong together for Luther. "All Christological statements are "*pro me*" statements and, conversely, all "*pro me*" statements must be interpreted Christologically."[255]

The work of Jesus to effect salvation, Christ's becoming Lord, is depicted in a lively manner, by the one who is confessing, as a dramatic battle action; by this means, Christ's opponents are viewed as personal powers and presented in a unique way, employing language customarily used in myths. The actions of Christ, as a whole, are applied in the Large Catechism according to the various stages that deal with the other "persons"; completion is signaled by a final "so that."[256] (1) Christ became human without sin, so that He "would be" lord over sin; (2) He suffered, died, and was buried, so that He might purchase me by means of His blood and "would become my LORD"; (3) He is risen as lord over death; (4) He has ascended and has taken control of His kingdom as lord over Satan and all powers; (5) He will come again, in order to separate His own once and for all from the powers that do battle against God. But this arrangement must be understand only in a general way, as a loose appropriation of the stages, since the entire path that the Christ took is present at every step of the way; at each individual stage, the opponent of the moment is primarily in view. At the same time, this way to view the stages could result in a misunderstanding, as if "my LORD,"[257] written with capital letters, is simply another stage in the sequence that chronicles Christ's lordship over sin, death, and the devil. But Christ's lordship over the believers is opposed diametrically to his lordship over those powers that do their wasting work;[258] whereas those powers are to be banished far from God, when all is said and done, the believer will be brought once again, from their tyranny, into a gracious relationship with God the Father. This characterization of opposing forces is stated more clearly in the Small

[255] Iwand, "*Wider den Mißbrauch des 'pro me'*," 121.
[256] Iwand, "*Wider den Mißbrauch des 'pro me'*," 121.
[257] *BSLK*, 652.46.
[258] "Torgauer Pred. vom 16./17.4.1533," WA 37:52.27: "that one indeed separates the actions, so that He acts against the devil and our enemy, and against us."

Catechism: Jesus Christ delivered me "from all sins, from death and from the power of the devil."[259]

Turning back to the Large Catechism, one notes that it is more successful at being able to underscore the relationship with God the Father; whereas God is mentioned in the Small Catechism solely as the Father of Jesus, the Large Catechism points out that Christ's redemptive actions and His becoming Lord mean, at the same time, that fallen human beings are brought once again "into the Father's favor and grace."[260] Within that context, Luther depicts this as one united activity; Christ brings us "from the devil to God, from death to life, from sin to righteousness,"[261] and preserves us in that relationship.

And yet, we distinguish between two aspects of this singular action of Jesus that brings about redemption. A very helpful way to articulate these two aspects is provided by Karl Heim; he identifies them as the solutions to the question of guilt and the question of power.[262] The question of guilt would read: By what means is my guilt expiated before God? The question of power would read: By what means am I rescued from the tyranny of the powers of destruction? The holy God Himself appears as the opponent in that work of Christ that resolves the question of guilt; the question of power brings the sinister powers of Satan, death, and sin front and center. Luther treats what is unique with respect to God and Satan, and unique to each question, when he interprets the Second Article, but he still treats the discussion as one issue; the accent admittedly rests more heavily on Christ becoming lord over the opposing forces. He handles the expiatory work with respect to God Himself only indirectly in the Small Catechism, with the phraseology that had ties to previous catechetical tradition, by referring to 1 Pet. 1:19: "won me . . . with His holy, precious blood and His innocent suffering and death."[263] Luther articulates this more clearly in the Large Catechism: By means of Satan's seduction, we fell under God's wrath and displeasure, being condemned to eternal damnation;[264] by the saving

---

[259] *BSLK*, 511.29f.
[260] *BSLK*, 652.8f.
[261] *BSLK*, 652.28f.
[262] Heim, *Jesus der Weltvollender*, 40ff.; taken up by Tiililä, *Das Strafleiden Christi*, 4.
[263] *BSLK*, 511.28, 31–33.
[264] *BSLK*, 651.42–48.

work of Christ we are brought back once again into the grace and favor of the Father.[265] At the same time, he accentuates the expiatory function of Jesus' sacrificial death; the Lord took death upon Himself, "so that He would do enough and would pay that for which I was responsible."[266] It must be admitted that the opponent that is placated by the action of satisfaction, and who receives the payment for the guilt, is not identified *expressis verbis*. We must therefore briefly sketch out Luther's view about propitiation; we will thereby see his views within the development of this teaching in the Church at large.

Luther picks up two senses of καταλλαγή, of "*reconciliatio*"; both are suggested already in the New Testament and are accentuated in the Church's tradition.

(1) According to the New Testament,[267] Jesus Christ is presented as the covenant propitiatory offering, as is evidenced chiefly by the traditions passed down about the Lord's Supper; He was offered in our place, put under the Law (Gal. 4:4), so that He could purchase our freedom from its curse (Gal. 3:13; Rom. 8:3f.; 2 Cor. 5:21).

(2) Jesus Christ has saved us from the old existence that consigns us to death and has transferred us into life before God; the rulers (archons) of this world, which are on their way out, put Him to death on the cross (1 Cor. 2:8), and yet He was victorious over them in the resurrection and exultation; He took their power away and made them march after Him in His triumphal victory march (Col. 2:15). By the power of His resurrection, the cross has become the sign of victory, from which the demons take to flight.

Christ's death is thus both elements, at the same time and wrapped up one with the other, "an offering that does away with the guilt of sin, which means the punishment that is commensurate with the sinning," and "the means whereby one is freed from the powers of this aeon, law, sin, and death."[268] It is thus appropriate to say about Christians: "The fruit of the death of Jesus is that a person is won

[265] *BSLK*, 652.2–12.

[266] *BSLK*, 652.42f.; "Vom Abendmahl Christi, 1528," WA 26:502.30 (AE 37:151–372): "if Christ had not come to help us and taken such guilt and sin upon Himself as an innocent little lamb, on our behalf, through His suffering."

[267] On this, see Bultmann, *Theologie des Neuen Testaments*, §§ 31, 33, 37–40; Käsemann, *Erwägungen zum Stichwort, 'Versöhnungslehre' im NT*; idem, *Die Heilsbedeutung des Todes Jesu bei Paulus*; Stuhlmacher, *Zur paulinischen Christologie*, idem, *Vom Verstehen des Neuen Testaments*, 225–47.

[268] Bultmann, *Theologie des Neuen Testaments*, 297.

again to become a child of God; the lordship of God is exercised on earth once again, and the cosmic powers are thereby disarmed."[269]

Both aspects, the death offering and the exaltation of Jesus, have been accentuated differently in the Church's tradition. Norwegian scholars differentiate between the "classic" Eastern Church and the Latin-Western Church typology for teaching about the atonement. A rich variety of sermons on the Creed can help one to crystallize the points that are emphasized, without forcing the issue too much.

What Gustaf Aulén identifies as the "classical" established typology brings front and center the conquest of the powers of destruction; success here is demonstrated in a "dualistic-dramatic depiction of battle." The almighty God Himself, in the person of Jesus Christ, enters our human existence in order to overcome the powers of death as the eternal God, the Logos, hidden within our mortal flesh. The cross becomes the "*Tropaeum triumphi salvatoris* (trophy of the Savior's triumph)"[270] because the resurrection light shines all over it. The Lord stretches His arms out on the accursed tree in order to redeem old Israel, along with the elect, from the heathen world; He hovers between heaven and earth in order to cast down the devil, to purify the air, and to provide the pathway to heaven; He hung in the center of the cross that pointed in all four directions, in order to bring the entire universe into unity.[271] Christians are not ashamed of the cross because its power to exorcise has taken effect for them. According to Cyril of Jerusalem, it still had the power "even to this present day [to heal] diseases, and to the present day it can drive out demons and put to naught the deceptive work of magic and sorcery."[272] The exorcistic formulas thus concentrated on using the name of the one who was crucified under Pontius Pilate.[273] For the purpose of our overview, the catechetical instruction about the Symbols from the early Church concentrates chiefly on Cyril of

---

[269] Käsemann, *Die Heilsbedeutung des Todes Jesu bei Paulus*, 82.

[270] Rufinus, *Expositio symboli* 12.12ff. (CCSL 20:149, App.).

[271] According to Athanasius, *De incarnatione Verbi* 25 (PG 25:140A/B); cf. idem, *Expositio fidei* 1 (PG 25:202A/B); Gregory of Nyssa, *Catechismus magn.*, 32:2 (PG 45:80D–81A); John of Damascus, *De fide orthodoxa* 4:11.

[272] Cyril of Jerusalem, *Catechesis* 13:40 (PG 33:821A); cf. also *Catechesis* 4:10, 14.

[273] See the examples in Kattenbusch, *Symbol*, 2:288–93.

Jerusalem and Gregory of Nyssa, Rufinus and Nicetas of Remesiana.[274]

From Gnostic and Marcionite sources, Origen posited the concept that Christ offered His soul, which lived within His blood, to Satan as ransom money; but since it remained inextricably bound to His divinity, the powers of death were not able to hold onto it and they were thus craftily tricked.[275] Leo, as well as Gregory the Great, goes to great lengths to depict the cunning way that Satan was deceived.[276] Gregory of Nyssa and Augustine both underscore Satan's legal claim to humanity;[277] Gregory of Nazianzus, however, rejects such a treatment.[278] In his overview of this typology, John of Damascus leaves out any discussion of paying ransom money to the princes of this world.[279] Peter Lombard formulates the issue dialectically: To be sure, the devil holds human beings in his grasp without a just reason, and yet humanity was justifiably placed under the devil.[280]

"Latin" atonement teaching, which held sway over the theology of the Western world right up to the time of Reformation Orthodoxy, sees Christ primarily as the God-*man*, who in our stead silenced the holy wrath of the heavenly Father and reconciled us with God. The reflections commence with our impotence before God; they seek to explain the actions of the one who had propitiating our guilt in mind. Christ, as the human being who is Himself identical with God, is brought into the center as the subject of the satisfaction; God the Father appears more in the role of the one who receives the action that brings about propitiation. Such a treatment is oriented toward a righteousness that is based on a legal form of Holy Ordinance. This

---

[274] Cyril of Jerusalem, *Catechesis* 13; Gregory of Nyssa, *Catechismus magn.*, 32; Rufinus, *Expositio symboli* 14; Niceta, *Explanatio symboli* 5.

[275] Cf. Aulen, *Den kristna försoningstanken*, 86–100.

[276] Leo the Great, *Sermo* 22.3f.; 60.3; 61.4; 62.3; 64.2f.; 69.4; Gregory the Great, *Expositio in Librum Job, sive Moralium libri xxv* 17:30.46f.; 33:7.14ff.

[277] Gregory of Nyssa, *Catechismus magn.*, 22–26; Augustine, *De libero arbitrio* 3:9.29–31; *De Trinitate* 4:13, 17; 13:12, 16–19. Cf. Riviere, *Le dogme de la Rédemption chez St. Augustin*, 261–91.

[278] Gregory of Nazianzus, *Orationes* 45:22.

[279] John of Damascus, *De fide orthodoxa* 3.27.

[280] Peter Lombard, *Sententiarum* III, dist. 20.2 (PL 192:799): "Therefore the devil unjustly holds man to himself with such power, yet man is held justly, for the devil never deserved to have power over man, but man deserved to suffer the tyranny of the devil because of sin." See, as well, Anselm, *Cur Deus homo*? 1:6f., 22.

comes close to characterizing the action of salvation in legalistic-moralistic terms and in an abbreviated, anthropocentric way.[281]

The central terms that are used in this treatment include "*reatus, culpa, poena, satisfactio, pretium, compensatio*,"[282] as used by Tertullian the lawyer in his instruction about penitence. It is Gregory of Nyssa who initiates the process of applying these penitential terms to the work of Christ.[283] Anselm uses such terms to arrive at a solemn teaching about atonement. *Cur Deus homo?* expands on the rational beauty such terms provide. Since the human being robbed God of honor when he fell originally, the creator must either punish him or demand restitution. It would not be fitting simply to erase the guilt and to let sinful human beings, without further ado, replace the fallen angels; this would not square with Him being the majestic one who ordered the cosmos.[284] Since human beings, enslaved under the demonic forces, were not in a position to achieve full obedience, the God-man stepped in, in their place. As a human being, Christ was indeed completely obedient, and yet, because He was sinless, He was not guilty and worthy of death.[285] Since He offered His life freely, He achieved satisfaction (*satisfactio*) of God's demand for righteousness, accomplished a service (*meritum*), and could expect a reward (*praemium*). Since, as God, He did not need any more than what He was already, He gifted His brothers with the Father's action (*retributio*), all who are bound to Him by their common sharing in the body of flesh.

In the Great Catechism, Gregory of Nyssa already deals extensively with the rational beauty of our redemption and that the redeeming actions are appropriate to God's expectations.[286] But Gregory stays with concentrating on the fact that Christ took on flesh and mentions His offering unto death only in passing;[287] in this way, he orients himself by using the contrasting terms: death—life, giving less attention to the contrast between transgression and satisfaction.

---

[281] This is the critique used by Aulen, *Den kristna försoningstanken*, 143, 151, 153f., 157.

[282] Concerning Tertullian's teaching on contrition, see Poschmann, *Paenitentia secunda*, 283–367, as well as idem, *Buße und letzte Ölung*, 18–26.

[283] Cf. Loofs, *DG*, 2:359f.

[284] Anselm, *Cur Deus homo*? 1:12–19.

[285] Ibid., 2:10.

[286] Gregory of Nyssa, *Catechismus magn.*, 14–32.

[287] Ibid., 32.

With respect to the offering that led to Christ's death, his thoughts revolve much more around the secret that the one who alone is living stoops down to be part of our nothingness,[288] though He at the same time wills to be "the one who lives forever . . . who comes so close to death that He drank up all of the deadliness and used His own body to provide the resurrection for all humanity; by means of His power He will awaken the entire human race."[289]

Cyril of Jerusalem discusses Christ's offering of death on the cross, which took control from the demons, within a song of praise, showing the tension between God's truth and mercy, which neither a human being nor an angel could have done, but only the "God who became flesh" and ventured to undergo complete suffering.[290] About Him alone it can be said: "The unrighteousness of the sinner was not as great as the righteousness of the one who died on our behalf."[291] Such formulations pave the way for Anselm's closed system of argumentation. None of the commentaries from the Middle Ages reflect intensively on this aspect. Peter Lombard considered this as little more that a convenient way to show what had happened; God could have saved us in another way if He had so chosen.[292] Even for Peter Lombard, the answer to the question to "*Cur Deus homo et mortuus*"? was oriented primarily toward bringing judgment upon the powers of destruction: "*Factus est ergo homo mortalis, ut moriendo diabolum vinceret* (A man was therefore made mortal, so that by dying He would conquer the devil)."[293] And yet, the reconciliation (*reconciliatio*) with God receives a stronger accent.[294] As both priest (*sacerdos*) and sacrificial offering (*hostia*), at one and the same time, the Lord brings Himself onto the altar of the cross, not before the devil but before for the Holy Trinity; indeed, the Trinity itself puts Him into that position.[295] The sacrificial moment effects, however, a

---

[288] See esp. ibid., 24.

[289] Ibid., 32 (PG 45:80B; cited according to BKV 56:63).

[290] Cyril of Jerusalem, *Catechesis* 13:33.

[291] Ibid. (PG 33:813A); cf. idem, *De Trinitate* 13:14, 18.

[292] Peter Lombard, *Sententiarum* III, dist. 20; see, in addition, Bonaventure, *In Sententiarum* III, dist. 20, a. un., q. 4; Thomas Aquinas, *Summa theologiae* III, q. 46, a. 2.

[293] Peter Lombard, *Sententiarum* III dist. 19.2 (PL 192:796).

[294] See esp. ibid., dist. 18.5.

[295] Ibid., dist. 20.3 (PL 192:799): "Christ is thus the priest, as well as the sacrificial price for our reconciliation, who offered Himself on the altar of the cross, though not

turnabout in the direction toward which one looks: Christ does not break so much into the darkness of our world of death as the *God*-man from God's heaven; instead, He brings Himself as the God-*man* at the same time from below to be in the heights, in the presence of the enthroned Trinity. With reference to 1 Tim. 2:5, the mediatory office gives pride of place to the human nature of Christ,[296] which at the same time accomplishes what He Himself had to do for Himself.[297] This brings to Christology an inner tension and unevenness, which remains right up to the time of the Reformation era; Peter Lombard hold fast to the early Church's teaching about the way in which the hypostasis occurred; Christ is not a human being who became godly, but is "God who has taken on human flesh";[298] the place where the transaction of business occurs to unify the two natures is not in the human nature, but in the hypostasis of the God-Logos; and yet, Augustine and Anselm step forward from the other side to advocate that the completion of the propitiation takes place at the same time within the human nature; an independent person who acts and accomplishes what is necessary and comes forth opposite the Trinity that acts as a Unity.[299]

Such a tension, which can hardly be reconciled, is carried over into the expositions of Thomas Aquinas. He depicts the victory of Christ over the powers of destruction initially at the point of the descent into hell[300] and thus brings the death of Jesus solely within the purview of propitiation with God. Christ accomplished the satisfaction for sins[301] for God the Father, opened the gates of Paradise once again, and opened free admission into the heart of the Father, who is appeased now.[302] These gracious actions of Christ are

---

to the devil but to the Trinity on behalf of all, enough for the sufficient price; but for the elect, this is so efficacious that it works salvation for those that are predestined.

296 Ibid., dist. 19.7 (PL 192:798): "He is therefore the mediator inasmuch as He is human"; Bonaventure, *In Sententiarum* III, dist. 19, a. 2, q. 2; Thomas Aquinas, *Summa theologiae* III, q. 48, a. 5.

297 Peter Lombard, *Sententiarum* III, dist. 18; Thomas Aquinas, *Summa theologiae* III, q. 49, a. 6; on this, see the critical objections by Calvin, *Inst.*, 2:17.1–6.

298 Peter Lombard, *Sententiarum* III, dist. 7, 11 (PL 192:774): "*Deus humanatus, non homo deificatus.*"

299 Ibid., dist. 17f.; on Augustine, see the texts in Eichenseer, *Apostolicum*, 290–95, as well as Anselm, *Cur Deus homo*? 1:18 (with a certain sense of self-correction).

300 Thomas Aquinas, *Expositio in Symbolum Apostolorum*, §§ 928f.

301 Idem, § 915.

302 Idem, § 928 (with reference to Luke 23:43 and Heb. 10:19); cf. Bonaventure, *In Sententiarum* III, dist. 18, a. 2, q. 3: "It is, however, the heavenly Paradise, the vision

conveyed to us by means of the sacraments, which achieve their effective power in the blood of Christ that was offered and on the basis of His passion.[303]

Anselm's rational argumentation is used first in the teaching about the two natures that appears in the Nuremberg Children's Sermons.[304] The following theses are placed into the center of the commentary on the Second Article: Only a real human being can take upon Himself everything necessary, including death on the cross and the descent into hell; only the true God can remain sinless while accomplishing this and in the end burst forth from hell and rise from the dead. The Heidelberg Catechism places both this *a priori* and Scholastic argumentation under the key word "On Human Redemption," as the most important point[305] and underscores, at the same time, the "burden of the eternal wrath of God."[306] The considerations that are summarized in Ursinus's doctoral disputation[307] function in a uniquely constructed manner; at first, the God-man, due to logical necessity, is presented as the only possible mediator and redeemer; only thereafter is the message about the historical Jesus presented.

The two ways of stating the teaching about redemption, for the early Church and Eastern Church and for the Western and Latin Church, both of which are interwoven in the catechetical tradition, are discussed by Paul Althaus on the basis of the following basic motifs:

---

of God revealed." In the "question about the effect of the passion of Christ" in the *Summa* (*Summa theologiae* III, q. 49), Thomas Aquinas sees the freedom from the tyranny exercised by the powers of devastation ("liberation from sin, from the power of the devil, from the penalty of sin") and the reconciliation with God ("reconciliation to God, opening the gate of heavenly kingdom") tied together more closely.

[303] Thomas Aquinas, *Expositio in Symbolum Apostolorum*, § 916: "the grace of God, which is bestowed in the sacraments, which have their efficacy from the passion of Christ." Erasmus writes with more forcefulness about the example of Christ, *Explanatio Symboli*, col. 1160F: "The whole of philosophy, the whole solace, the whole strength of the Christian mind is in the cross of Christ."

[304] Reu, *Quellen*, 1.1:513.24–515.15.

[305] Questions 12–21.

[306] Questions 14, 17.

[307] Goeters refers to these "Theses about the office and person of the only mediator between God and humans, our Lord Jesus Christ," written in 1562, in his study *Christologie und Recht-fertigung nach dem Heidelberger Katechismus,* 40f. An analogous foundational statement concerning the wondrous way the divine and human natures of the mediator are united was set forth by Melanchthon in his *Enarr. Symb. Nic.*, 1550 (CR 23:338f.; Hirsch, *Hilfsbuch*, 66f.). Argumentation that has its roots in the Scholastic tradition forced its way into the catechism in this way.

"Ancient Greek Christianity was influenced most especially by the question about the life of God that could never die, which redeems from corruptibility, from death. For this reason, Greek Christology understands Christ most especially as the one who conveys the immortal life of humanity through the incarnation and resurrection. . . . Western Christianity is framed by the question about how to be freed from the guilt and the power of sin. For this reason, Christ is honored decisively as the one who provides the propitiation for sin and affords the gracious power for holy living through the sacraments."[308]

Luther unites both constellations of motifs, inasmuch as he applies both aspects to our personal existence before God. Thus, what lurks behind the issue about whether one resolves the issue "according to God's unfading, incorruptible life, or according to His power, or according to His propitiating and saving grace" is the question "about God Himself, according to His will and heart."[309] In the catechisms, especially in the Large Catechism, along with the dominant early Church tradition, the reformer accentuates the battle motif. As "Christus-Victor,"[310] the Lord of life breaks in, into the tyranny of the powers of death, and extracts those who have been enslaved. Luther portrays this battle in his Easter songs and sermons with bloody colorings; in this way, he personifies the opposing, satanic powers.[311] They pounce upon the man who has been delivered

---

[308] Althaus, *Theologie Luthers*, 161.

[309] Ibid.

[310] Aulen, *Die drei Typen der christlichen Versöhnungslehre*, 505: "The central theme of reflection about reconciliation in the early Church is Christus-Victor."

[311] The motif of battle and trickery is shown is a rather formative way in the following texts: "Pred. über Mk. 16:1ff. vom 31.3.1521," WA 9:661.10–35; "Pred. über Rom. 10:9ff. vom 28.4.1522," WA 10.3:100.17–24; "Pred. über Mk. 16:14ff. vom 14.5.1523," WA 12:564.28–565.8; "Pred. über Ex. 9 vom 26.12.1524," WA 16:137.8–139.7; "Pred. über Ex. 15:1–12 vom 25.3.1525," WA 16:199.1–7; "Pred. über Mt. 27:51ff. vom 8.3.1525," WA 17.1:78.14–80.2; "Pred. über Mk. 16:1ff. vom 16.4.1525," WA 17.1:188.11–190.11; "Pred. über Gen. 3:15 vom 2.4.1526," WA 20:334.8–335.22; "Pred. über Eph. 4:8–10 vom 31.5.1527," WA 23:699–725; "Osterpred. vom 12.4.1528," WA 27:116.18–117.20; "Osterpred. vom 28.3.1529," WA 29:262.2–269.2; "Osterpred. vom 17.4.1530," WA 32:39–47; "Osterpred. vom 9.4.1531," WA 34.1:273.11–275.10; "Gal.-Komm., 1535," on Gal. 3:13 u. 4:5, WA 40.1:417.8–11; 438.5–443.11; 564.5–570.12 (AE 26:1–461); "Ennaratio Jes. 53, 1544," WA 40.3:741.22–744.34; "Gen.-Vorl., 1535–45," on Gen. 48:15f., WA 44:697.21–35 (AE 8:1–333); "Viel fast nützlich Punkt: Pred. über Lk. 23:27ff., 1537," WA 45:367.14–34; "Pred. über Joh. 1:1f. vom 7.7.1537," WA 46:556.25–40 (AE 22:1–530); "Pred. über Mk. 16:14ff. vom 30.5.1538," WA 46:391.7–393.3.

to them; they seem to have overpowered Him eventually, on Good Friday; but on Easter the one who had been put to death breaks forth by means of the power of the Godhead that holds Him fast, coming forth from the abyss of hell; He drags forth with Himself the powers of death as prisoners in His triumphal march. As was the case for the early church fathers, Luther is not reticent about saying that God acts with wise cunning. According to Job 40:19f., God hangs the little worm that comes forth with the rain, that of the human existence of Christ, on the sharp hook of His Godhead. The line is made up of those who descended from the patriarchs, prophets, and kings, from Adam and Abraham.[312] Satan and his thugs rub their hands together gleefully and boast: Should we not indeed be able to swallow down this little rainworm!? They open their gullets wide and press forward toward the hidden opposing hook of the Godhead, choke to death on it themselves, and have to throw up everything that they had swallowed down. This fighting and choking is depicted most drastically when considering what happens with death: "From this we see what a blessed, restorative and powerful death is the death of our Lord Christ, how He with all power and might chops away at and stabs death, whose prisoners we once were, grabs him by the chops, knocks out all the teeth, and blunts his javelin and stinger, so that we who believe in Him cannot be bitten, poked or choked in the future."[313] That is the meaning of the phrase: "swallowed and devoured death."[314]

The motif about cunning reaches its highpoint over against Satan; it resonates in the hymn: "Nun freut euch, lieben Christen gmein": ["Dear Christians, one and all, rejoice," lit.:]

"Most secretly He uses His power;

Luther bases what he says on Gregory the Great (cf. p. 151, n. 276) and his interpretation of Job 40:19f. ("Osterpred. vom 17.4.1530," WA 32:41.14f. [AE 51:193–208]), as well as on Pliny and his report of the battle of Ichneumon with the whale or else crocodile ("Pred. über Lk. 23:27ff., 1537," WA 45:367.18; Pliny, *Naturalis historia* 8:24). With these portrayals as well, he stands in the catechetical tradition of the late Middle Ages; cf. Zellinger, *Der geköderte Leviathan im Hortus deliciarum des Herrad von Landsperg.*

312 Cf. "Pred. über Mk. 16:1ff. vom 31.3.1521," WA 9:661.26f.; "Pred. über Röm. 10:9ff. vom 28.4.1522," WA 10.3:100.26f.; "Pred. über Gen. 3:15 vom 2.4.1526," WA 20:334.24f.

313 "Pred. über Eph. 4:8–10 vom 31.5.1527," WA 23:715.17.

314 *BSLK*, 652.48f. (LC).

He went forth in my poor form;

He wants to catch the devil."[315]

But the burlesque motif of the devil being cheated has an inner side to it as well, which points beyond itself to the *Theologia crucis*. Leo the Great and others already spoke of the Lord going up against His opponent clothed in our weak and feeble nature, indeed, that the lord of the entire world took the form of a servant; God Himself, who is unable to suffer, bows Himself low as a human being who can suffer and places Himself under the law of death.[316] And Peter Lombard summarizes the elements of this tradition in the dictum: The Lord did not desire to overcome the opponent by means of mighty power, but through obedient and self-denying righteousness.[317]

Luther makes use of these observations in two ways: viewed from the outside, he shows that the Lord did not redeem us with gold or silver; instead, He yielded up His living body,[318] as He defeated Satan's tyranny and established His lordship and needed "no other weapon than His body" to gain victory.[319] Viewed from the inside, he points out how the Lord defeated the opposing forces precisely by suffering their best thrust right into the heart of His existence. The reformer deals with this inner aspect in his commentaries on the Psalms and in his sermons on the passion:[320] In the Garden of Gethsemane and on Golgotha, Christ, as a "fine, pure, real human

---

[315] WA 35:424.22 = *EKG* 239.6 [*LSB* 556.6].

[316] Leo the Great, *Sermo* 62.3 (PL 54:351A/B); *Sermo* 22.2 (ibid., 195A–196A).

[317] Peter Lombard, *Sententiarum* III, dist. 20.1 (PL 192:799): "Justice therefore frees men from humiliation, whom only the most equitable power is able to free"; according to Augustine, *De Trinitate* 13:14, 18, 44 (CCSL 50A:407): "For Christ was crucified, not through immortal power, but through the weakness which He took upon Him in mortal flesh" [Nicene and Post-Nicene Father, 1st Series, 3:177]. "Pred. über Lk. 2:20 vom 26.12.1533," WA 37:243.23: "Even with the weakness, sickness, humiliation, He tears open the devil's belly and breaks hell wide open, opens heaven and alters the whole earth"; ibid., 242.22: "This is the great power of God, who makes strength from weakness."

[318] Cf. "Kat.-Pred. vom 10.12.1528," WA 30.1:90.7, 18f. (AE 51:162–169).

[319] "Osterpred. vom 17.4.1530," WA 32:43.1.

[320] On this, see passages such as "Op. in Ps., 1518–21," WA 5:325.25–34; 458.8–27; 601.5–606.28; "Pred. über die Passionsgeschichte vom 18.4.1522," WA 10.3:72.32–75.13; "Pred. über Mt. 27:45ff. vom 6.3.1525," WA 17.1:72.10–73.11; "Pred. über die Passionsgeschichte vom 27.3.1529," WA 29:244.2–15; 249.5–250.14; "Pred. über die Passionsgeschichte vom 30.3.1537," WA 45:64.5–23.

being" using His pure reason,[321] suffered this horrendous assault of Satan's mockery because He had been abandoned by God. Both aspects are at play in the phraseology: "He became the absolute least and most scorned, so that He could never have gone down into the depths any further, and no human has ever gone to greater depths than He did. . . . For He gave Himself into the deepest depths, under the Law, under the devil, death, sin, and hell, which is, in my view, the final and deepest depth."[322]

The phrase "under the Law" points to the following: Going beyond what was said by the early church fathers and the teachers of the Middle Ages, the reformer inserts the Law, as well, into the list of the powers of destruction, using the insights provided by the apostle Paul. Christ overcame even this "horrendous tyranny"[323] on our behalf;[324] "He purchased our liberty from the curse of the Law, in that He came under the curse on our behalf" (Gal. 3:13).[325] Luther sketches out the implications of Christ submitting Himself to the Law and taking the Law upon Himself, from the very beginning days of His life, in sermons that he preached for New Year's Day when he dealt with His name being given and with His circumcision. And yet, the Law weighed heavily on Him, cast Him into confusion and anguish to the point that He sweated blood in the Garden of Gethsemane, and affixed Him to the cross where God's curse was poured out on the one who alone was without guilt. "Finally victorious, cries out the Law; but it did not know that it had taken

---

[321] "Pred. über die Passionsgeschichte vom 18.4.1522," WA 10.3:73.2; 74.20; "Pred. über die Passionsgeschichte vom 27.3.1529," WA 29:249.12: "This is the best, that He does not distrust, but prays. What it is to be abandoned, I am not able to say, since even yet you will not all understand."

[322] "Pred. über Eph. 4:8–10 vom 31.5.1527," WA 23:702.12.

[323] Ibid., 709.20.

[324] Concerning the positioning of the Law under the destructive powers, see: "Gal.-Komm., 1519," WA 2:534.30–535.3 (AE 27:151–410); "Gal.-Komm., 1535," WA 40.1:564.5–570.12 (AE 26:1–461), as well as the commentary on these passages by Karin Bornkamm, *Luthers Auslegung des Galaterbriefes*, 127–56; in addition, "Pred. über Eph. 4:8–10 vom 31.5.1527," WA 23:706.12–710.5; "Ennaratio Jes. 53, 1544," WA 40.3:741.22–744.34; see, as well, the New Year's sermon on Gal. 4:1–7: "Weihnachtspost. 1522," WA 10.1.1:365.12–367.6; "Vom 4.1.1540," WA 49:6–11; "Neujahr 1531—Hauspost., 1544," WA 52:78.12–80.29; and the New Year's sermons on Luke 2:21: "Weih-nachtspost., 1522," WA 10.1.1:515.17–518.4 (AE 52:149–158); "Vom 1.1.1525," WA 17.1.2:2.23–3.30; "Vom 1.1.1528," WA 27:4.15–5.7.

[325] Cf. Gal. 4:5; 2 Cor. 5:21.

hold so despicably, had damned God's Son and thus had judged so despicably, and by means of the death on the cross had committed murder as one who blasphemed God and acted as an insurrectionist. Because it had now judged, as guilty and condemned, the very one who was innocent and on whom it had no claim, the very one who was lord over the Law and was creator of all creatures, it would now be on the other side and have to pay the price, would itself have to be taken into custody and be lifted up onto the cross, and let itself be condemned and would lose all of its power and lie for all eternity under the feet of the one it had condemned."[326] Luther makes no mention of Christ's battle against the Law in the catechisms.

In terms of content, this establishes the crossing point from the battle motif emphasized by the early Church and the Eastern Church over to the satisfaction motif that was articulated by the Western Church and during the Middle Ages. Behind and above the powers of death, as the stinger of the Law, the holy wrath of God stood against the sins of all human beings; Jesus had to suffer the full consequences of that wrath in the Garden of Gethsemane and on Golgotha.[327] Luther explicates this by using traditional terminology in the Large Catechism: "With His own precious blood" the Lord accomplished "for me what was sufficient, . . . and paid that for which I was responsible."[328] In his Church Postil of 1522, Luther freely uses the terminology of Anselm's teaching on satisfaction: The price of redemption was paid to the holy divine justice of God and the sufficient activity that was necessary for divine justice was accomplished: "Despite the fact that our sins are not to be reckoned against us before God, and that purely by grace, He still did not wish to have this happen apart from His Law and His righteousness, which

---

[326] "Pred. über Eph. 4:8–10 vom 31.5.1527," WA 23:709.26; cf. "Gal.-Komm., 1535," WA 40.1:565.18–567.12; esp. ibid., 565.21 (AE 26:370): "Here Christ says: "Lady Law, you empress, you cruel and powerful tyrant over the whole human race, what did I commit that you accused, intimidated, and condemned Me in My innocence? Here the Law, which once condemned and killed all men, has nothing with which to defend or cleanse itself. Therefore it is condemned and killed in turn, so that it loses its jurisdiction not only over Christ—whom it attacked and killed without any right anyway—but also over all who believe in him. Here Christ says: "Come to me, all who labor under the yoke of the Law."

[327] "Passionspred. vom 30.3.1537," WA 45:64.8: "The spiritual passion of Christ in the Garden . . . there He feels the wrath of God, that He wills for Him that His body and life will pass away."

[328] *BSLK*, 652.42–45.

existed before all things and was more than sufficient. His righteousness had to be bought off and demanded on our behalf before we could be afforded such grace."[329]

The reformer thus takes up both constellations of motifs: on the one hand, Christ as the one who vanquishes all the powers of destruction and powers of death and, on the other hand, Christ as our substitute and as our propitiatory offering over against God's holy, judging wrath. Luther links both aspects in such a way that the hidden emphasis from the Western Church and the Middle Ages, on the punishing suffering of Christ, persists. The propitiation of God's wrath[330] remains the center, in terms of content, in the catechisms as well; at the deepest level, it is God's curse of judgment that delivers us over to the powers of destruction. These powers stand in a unique relationship with God; according to the Large Catechism, on the one hand, they are our "tyrants,"[331] caught up in rebellion against God, and yet, on the other hand, they are the "harsh schoolmasters"[332] that God Himself put in place, which means that they are the authorities who run the prison; the real prison came into existence for us when God gave us over under the condemning wrath of His Law. "Death, sin, hell, all of these come from the wrath of God; they are its harsh schoolmasters."[333] Even among these ominous allies, Luther intimates that there is a pecking order; Satan stands at the top; he "clearly is to be identified as a prince over sin and the prince of death."[334] This is the specifically theological dimension; to it corresponds an

---

[329] "Über Gal. 3:23–29," WA 10.1.1:470.18; cf. "Über Hebr. 1:1–12," ibid., 162.5: "There must be as great a payment for sin as God Himself is, who is so weighed down by sin"; "Über Mt. 2:1–12," ibid., 719.20: "But it worked on Him in a bitter way, gave Him a great burden. For that God's wrath, judgment, conscience, hell, death and all sorts of evil things would be laid aside and all good things would be inherited would not have been able to happen, since God's righteousness had to have something sufficient take place so that sin would be paid for, death would be overcome in just measure." A few corrections are to be found in Cruciger's "Sommerpostille zu Lk. 24:36–47," WA 21:264.27–35. Still other passages are in Seeberg, *DG*, 4:1.244–47 and Althaus, *Theologie Luthers*, 178, esp. n. 5.

[330] Cf. *BSLK*, 651.46f.; 652.8f.; 660.41ff.; 661:14.31f. (LC).

[331] *BSLK*, 652.2

[332] *BSLK*, 652.3.

[333] "Pred. über Joh. 14:23 vom 20.5.1526," WA 20:339.31: "*Mors, peccatum, infernus, omnia veniunt ex ira dei, quae sunt ein Stockmeister.*"

[334] "Osterpred. vom 17.4.1530," WA 32:40.8; Meyer, *Historischer Kommentar*, 319: "This alludes to the fact that the powers of sin and death that cause such great fear in our life are really rays that come forth from a single power of evil."

anthropological aspect. As we are free, in heart and conscience, from the accusation of the Law and from the wrath of God that thereby brings its onslaught, we are free, as well, with respect to the battle against the satanic demons;[335] for us, these have been rendered harmless, because the wrath of God no longer stands behind them.

By means of these insights, Luther deepens and personifies both the "classical theory of the atonement" of the Christus Victor model as well as Anselm's teaching about satisfaction. By means of his hyper-realistic and drastic images of Christ's victory over the dark comrades, sin, death and the devil, he reaches back into the tradition of the early Church and the Eastern Church and renews its emphasis on the motif of a battle that encompasses the entire earth. But because he points out, in, with and under the onslaughts of the powers of death, how Christ fully suffers the deepest, holy wrath of judgment from God that hangs over all human guilt, and inserts the Law at this point as well, into the list of the powers that effect the curse, the reformer deepens the early Church's confession about Christus Victor by means of insights that are set forth initially by Paul: precisely by suffering the full consequences of the divine curse of judgment upon the guilt of human sin, Jesus Christ overcomes the original power of those that destroy.

Since Luther serves as a forerunner of the modern existential interpretation of Jesus' sufferings unto death by being struck down by the Law of God in one's conscience, he frees the Latin teaching and Anselm's motif of Christ's suffering as punishment, at the same time, from a type of moralism that is contractual and legal. Finally, in Jesus' cross and resurrection, the merciful love of God breaks right through God's own holy judgment. God does battle here with God.[336]

---

[335] "Gal.-Komm., 1535," WA 40.2:4.11 (AE 27:4): "Therefore the freedom by which we are free of the wrath of God forever is greater than heaven and earth and all creation. From this there follows the other freedom, by which we are made safe and free through Christ from the Law, from sin, death, the power of the devil, hell, etc."

[336] Tiililä, *Das Strafleiden Christi*, 265f.: "The 'classic' teaching about propitiation comes with the danger of making Christ into a hero, who stays far from the suffering human being with respect to His divinity; in the form that describes this as a dramatic battle, there is not enough room to deal adequately with the question of guilt. The 'Latin' teaching about propitiation, for its part, leads away from a proper theocentric point of origin toward legalism and moralism, since it views God as one who can be calmed down by means of a good enough action. The properly important points of emphasis that are connected with each are deepened by Luther against the

Such depths and abysses within the propitiatory event are hinted at only briefly in the Catechisms. Luther initially makes use of catechetical tradition and remains therewith in the realm of mythic and symbolic language. Christ engages in conflict with the opponents as if they were physical adversaries; He pays for the guilt with His "precious blood,"[337] as one would with a material gift. This image-filled and mythological language stays in the center in his sermons to congregations.[338] And yet, even by means of such traditional imagery, something exemplary comes forth; one can conceptualize redemption from the tyranny of the powers of death and the propitiation with God as a single, unified act of God; as our Lord and redeemer, Christ "brought us from the devil to God, from death to life, from sin to righteousness," and He preserves us in that relationship.[339]

UNFOLDING THE SECOND ARTICLE WITHIN THE CHRISTOLOGICAL CIRCLE OF FESTIVALS

The Gospel of the Second Article finds its center in the cross and resurrection of Jesus; for this reason, we included Luther's treatment of the passion and Easter in the depiction of the redemptive event. But the Good News of our salvation unfolds within the circle of festivals that celebrate Christ; thus, Luther's sermons for various festival occasions consciously expand and deepen[340] the catechism's "short

---

background of taking with utter seriousness the righteousness of God and are linked to the punishing sufferings of Christ."

[337] *BSLK*, 652.45 (LC).

[338] Late in life, Luther still held to the traditional teaching about blood and wounds; "Gen.-Vorl., 1535–45," WA 44:768.22–31 (AE 8:257–8): "Among the papists this word has remained: 'The sacraments flowed out of the sides of Christ.' For the sacraments have their efficacy from the wounds and the blood of Christ. Therefore this is a good and godly saying ... Those who hear the Word of the Gospel concerning Christ are sprinkled with the blood of the Son of God. It is all the beautiful red blood of Christ"; "Ennaratio Jes. 53, 1544," WA 40.3:717.27: "The person is certainly eternal and infinite, of whom even one little drop would have been enough to save the whole globe of the earth. For so great and so incalculable is the worth of this person, that the whole world must not be given for one little drop of His blood, and still, if so much as one drop should be poured out, this would free the whole globe of the earth." Cf. passages such as "Pred. über Ps. 110 vom 5.6 u. 13.6.1535," WA 41:192.4f.; 200.3–10; 203.12–21; 233.36ff. (AE 13:225–348).

[339] *BSLK*, 652.28f. (LC).

[340] A reference to the church year sermons is found in passages such as "Kat.-Pred. vom 21.9 u. 25.9.1528," WA 30.1:46.4f.; 54:20; "Pred. über Lk. 24:13ff. vom 18.4.1530," WA 32:65.14ff.; "Pred. über Lk. 1:23ff. vom 25.3.1531," WA

children's sermons."[341] The reformer orients the individual sermons for festivals, time and again, on the basis of the appropriate sections from the Apostles' Creed;[342] indeed "these words . . . are truly and in an orderly way stated in the form of and simply a calendar for the whole year, so that we celebrate all the festivals of the Lord Christ, commencing with cradle night, when we rock the little baby and play with our beloved Lord who is in the lap of His mother. Thereafter we come to martyrdom week, when we celebrate and reflect on the passion, going on from there to the Easter festival, Ascension, and Pentecost, etc.; all of our festivals are summarized in this short article."[343] The garland of the Christ festivals decorates and makes real the chief article of our redemption. Even in his festival sermons, Luther tirelessly reiterates the "for us" aspect; he deepens a practice from the late Middle Ages that used the church year to impress the Creed on the minds of the listeners."[344]

1. Incarnation and Virgin Birth[345]

The "*qui conceptus est de Spiritu sancto, natus ex Maria virgine*," from the *Textus receptus*, is rendered consistently by Luther: "who is conceived by (the) (*vom = von dem*)[346] Holy Spirit, born of the Virgin Mary."[347] All earlier German renderings kept the Latin word order, "*ex Maria virgine*"; Luther is the first to reverse the position of the word virgin.[348] "Virgin, maiden" replaces the earlier "maid," which had been used since the fifteenth century. In about 1450, "*natum ex*,"

34.1:170.9ff.; "Pred. über Christi Auferstehung vom 31.3.1532," WA 36:159.2ff.; cf., as well, Hardeland, *Katechismusgedanken*, 205f.

[341] *BSLK*, 653.5f. (LC).

[342] *BSLK*, 653.7–10 (LC).

[343] "Torgauer Pred. vom 16./17.4.1533," WA 37:48.39.

[344] Weidenhiller, *Untersuchungen*, 17 (Teaching on the Five Words): "The people who seek to speak about the faith who are not good at learning and speaking should believe according to the orderly teaching of holy Christendom: thus, at Christmas, that God was born, at Easter, that He was martyred, died, and was buried, arose on the third day, ascended into the heavens as God and man, sent the Holy Spirit and will come again to judge on the last day." [Tr.: Old German]

[345] For texts and literature, see pp. 205–206.

[346] "Eine kurze Form, 1520," WA 7:216.32; "Betbüchlein," WA 10.2:391.9 (AE 43:3–45); *BSLK*, 556.2 (Preface to the Large Catechism).

[347] *BSLK*, 511.12–14 (SC); 650.44–46 (LC).

[348] The Preface to the Large Catechism (*BSLK*, 556.3) still reads "out of Mary the virgin"; the "Torgauer Pred. vom 16./17.4.1533" reads "from Mary the virgin," WA 37:35.33; 53.16.

the literal rendering "born out of (*geboren aus*)" replaces "born of (*geboren von*)"; along with several texts from the late Middle Ages,[349] Luther stays with the "born of" translation.[350] The new ecumenical translation reads: "conceived *through* the Holy Spirit, born *of* the Virgin Mary"; the intention is to note how the Spirit, in a serving capacity, participates in the incarnation of the God-Logos, while simultaneously emphasizing Jesus' fully human nature.

In the Small Catechism, the virgin birth is inserted appositionally: "true God, born of the Father in eternity, and also true man, born of the Virgin Mary."[351] Christ's "twofold going forth" is pointed out only briefly, "the first is from God the Father in eternity before the world began, the second, when He goes out into the world from the virgin."[352] In the Large Catechism, Luther discussed the virgin birth only when mentioning the "elements" that clarify and unfold our redemption; he takes note of the virgin birth when discussing Christ's becoming lord over sins: "conceived and born from the Holy Spirit and the virgin without any sin, so that He could become lord over sin."[353] Luther had accentuated this already in the Short Form of 1520: Christ is "conceived for my benefit . . . by the Holy Spirit," without the sin-besmirched cooperative activity of humans, "so that He could purify the sinful and damnable conception that is a reality for me and all believers"; for me, he is "born . . . from the pure virgin Mary without doing any damage to her physical and spiritual virginity, so that He . . . could bless my birth and that of all believers, sinful and already under damnation, making it innocuous and pure."[354] The Confession of 1528 reaches back more intentionally to the discussions of the early Church and underscores Jesus' full humanity—"in every way and form a real human being, as I myself am and all others"[355]—but Luther interjects, at the same time, that He was kept separate from our inherited sin because He was born from the Spirit of God and the virgin—"except for the fact that He alone

[349] Cf. Meyer, *Historischer Kommentar*, 93.
[350] Only the Preface to the Large Catechism (*BSLK*, 556.3) reads "*out of* Mary the virgin."
[351] *BSLK*, 511.23–26.
[352] "Pred. über Mt. 2:1ff. vom 6.1.1532," WA 36:60.8, 25; 77.4.
[353] *BSLK*, 652.38–40.
[354] "Pred. über Mt. 1:18ff. u. Lk. 1:26ff. vom 24.12.1528," WA 27:217.16; WA 27:485.10: "He had to be conceived without sin so that sin would not be His Lord."
[355] WA 26:501.27 (AE 37:151–372); cf. "Vom Abendmahl Christi, 1528," ibid., 500.33–501.35.

came forth from the virgin through the Holy Spirit without sin."[356] In his Torgau sermons about the Second Article, Luther provides illustrations to characterize the scope of the Large Catechism and the Short Form of 1520 and provides details for this seminal thought through all the stages of Jesus' journey.[357] As the one who alone is pure and holy, Jesus trod our path through life before we did and took the journey for us, beginning with conception and birth and ending up dying the martyr's death and being laid in the tomb; in this way, He has made our journey in the presence of God both holy and pleasant, whether we speak of our life or our death, not primarily through the message of Good News that He proclaimed, but through His physical participation in our human lot in life. Luther thus allows himself to be guided by the Apostles' Creed[358] and depicts Jesus' earthly path neither chronologically nor psychologically, but describes it instead under the "*Pro nobis*," as the categorical nature of our existence. "This now is the path of the LORD Christ, from birth on, through our whole life, that He indeed has experienced all things and has acted as we do and therefore, because He Himself has touched it all, He has accomplished and sanctified all things; nothing can make us unclean, no food, no eating nor drinking, no clothing, no sleeping, waking, going, standing, and a Christian cannot see, hear, touch, etc., anything that would cause him to sin, so long as he remains in faith; for it is through Him that everything has become pure and has been made holy by His holy eyes, mouth, hands, feet, and all body parts, indeed clothing and His whole life."[359] No compartment of our life, whether it be an internal or external situation, no banality of physical existence and no abyss of psychic suffering exists where we would be alone with our doubts and struggles, desires and joys; He has already been everywhere we will go, before we go there, and He is therefore with us. It is at this point that Luther inserts the virgin birth, as he sets forth the thrust of his application of the entire Second Article.

The birth of Jesus Christ from the Virgin Mary does not belong to the *kerygma* from the first, as did His death on the cross, His resurrection, His exaltation at the right hand of God, and His coming again to judge; it is recorded for us only at the end of the prehistory

---

356 Ibid., 501.28.
357 Most especially WA 37:53–62.
358 Ibid., 55.12–16; 54.10ff.; 58:11.
359 Ibid., 59.1.

that precedes Jesus' public ministry in Matthew (1:18–25) and Luke (1:26–38); the other New Testament witnesses report nothing. On their part, these prehistories cannot be viewed as being passed down as a literary unit; the witness to Jesus' being a Son of David belongs to the earliest level; the confession of divine sonship carries with it adoptionistic overtones (Luke 1:32, 36); the reference to Isa. 7:14 (Matt. 1:22f.) interrupts the flow of the narrative.[360] This complex of concepts, including the virginity of Mary, is prefigured in Jewish and Palestinian passages, which means that it makes sense when it is set within Jewish Christianity. Within the Hellenistic setting of Diaspora Judaism, the symbolic world that speaks of a god begetting anyone is most apparent in Philo, in which the human male plays no role.[361] In contrast to the heathen theogamies[362] and to later Christian embellishments,[363] Matthew and Luke preserve the mystery. Luke reports that the angel announces the event that is to take place immediately;[364] the verb ἐπισκιάζειν (to overshadow) indicates, with brevity, the procreation through God's Spirit-Power and hides, at the same time, the way this takes place. Matthew assumes the virgin birth and defends it apologetically by means of Joseph's dream.

The demarcation over against heathen reports of marriages between gods and humans is clear. The announcement by the angel, as well as the accession on Mary's part to the will of God, stays within the framework of the way a prophetic call is described.[365] In the center, one notes obedient submission under God's gracious promise and directives that convincingly move a person to follow; that someone is chosen, made holy and set apart through God's Spirit-Power, within the womb of the mother, belongs, as well, to the call of a prophet. But God's creative overshadowing goes way beyond the conceptual framework of those scenarios, going all the way back to connect with the creation narrative (Gen. 1–2); "even by Jesus' very coming into existence one is dealing with a creative act of God that

---

[360] See the presentation by Dibelius, *Jungfrauensohn und Krippenkind*, as well as the overview in Hahn, *Hoheitstitel*, 274–77, 304–08, 314f.

[361] References in Dibelius, *Jungfrauensohn und Krippenkind*, 32ff.

[362] Cf. Brunner-Traut, *Die Geburtsgeschichte*.

[363] Cf. Dibelius, *Jungfrauensohn und Krippenkind*, 49–54.

[364] On ἰδού in Lk.1:31; cf. Hahn, *Hoheitstitel*, 276, n. 5.

[365] Cf. Audet, *L'annonce à Marie*; Gewiess, *Die Marienfrage*.

sets forth something new";[366] by means of this new beginning, God establishes the divine Sonship of the child who brings redemption.

The Old Roman Symbol still read: "*qui natus est de Spiritu sancto et Maria virgine*."[367] This would present the Spirit as Jesus' father, analogous to Mary being the mother; Justin thus identifies the Spirit with the Logos.[368] Formulas of an as yet "naïve" Spirit-Christology are still to be found in Irenaeus and even as late as Ambrose.[369] Ambrose and Augustine consciously insert the conception and birth of Jesus from the Spirit of God into their teachings that delve deeper into and explain the Trinity and the incarnation.[370] The Spirit is in no way the father of the Son; instead, in conjunction with the Father and the eternal Son-Logos, He would have prepared the virgin womb of Mary for the reception of the "*Virtus Altissimi* (power from on high)" (Luke 1:34) of the Logos.[371] These and other attempts to state things more precisely might have led to more distinct differentiation of the prepositions "*de*" and "*ex*," as well as also between the conception and birth. This is what led to the phraseology of the *Textus receptus* "*qui conceptus est de Spiritu sancto, natus ex Maria virgine* (who was conceived by the Holy Spirit, born of Mary the virgin)" which is attested first by Jerome and later by Faustus of Reji (Riez).[372]

In his commentaries, Augustine compares the mystery of the human birth from the virgin, in time, with the mystery of the divine

---

[366] Delling, παρθένος, 834.9f.

[367] Denzinger, 11; concerning the formulation of the other confessions, cf. Lietzmann, *Symbolstudien*, 200–05.

[368] Justin, *Apologia* 1:33.6.

[369] See the examples provided by Kattenbusch, *Symbol*, 2:616–25 and Eichenseer, *Apostolicum*, 249f.

[370] Ambrose, *De Spiritu Sancto* 2:59; Augustine, *Enchiridion de fide, spe, et caritate* 12.38–40; *Sermo* 214.6; *De Trinitate* 5:12.13; *Collatio cum Maximino Arianorum* 2:17.2. Cf., as well, the Pseudo-augustine *Sermo* 234.5 (PL 39:2178): "For Christ was not conceived by the substance of the Holy Spirit, but instead by the power, not by begetting, but by decree and blessing."

[371] Rufinus, *Expositio symboli* 8:33 (CCSL 20:145f.): "You observe, then, the Trinity operating in unison. The Holy Spirit, it is said, comes upon the Virgin, and the Power of the Most High overshadows her. But what is the Power of the Most High, if not Christ Himself, who is the power of God and the wisdom of God? And to whom does this Power belong? To the Most High, says Scripture. So we have here the Most High, the Power of the Most High, and the Holy Spirit" [Rufinus, 43].

[372] Jerome, *dialogus contra Luciferianus* 17 (PL 23:179B); Faustus of Reji [Riez], *Epistulae* 7 (CSEL 21:205.6ff.); Denzinger, 25; in addition, see Kattenbusch, *Symbol*, 2:879–87 and Kelly, *Creeds*, 369, 376ff.

birth from the Father, in eternity;[373] the incarnation draws into the light the "*Pro nobis*"; with it, Christ begins His lordship.[374] Ambrose and Augustine admittedly set their gaze initially on the then and there of Jesus' birth, by means of which they underscore two elements at the same time and in an interrelated way; one element emphasizes that Jesus is fully a human being, the other, the enduring virginity of Mary. Against the Gnostic and Docetic emphases of Manichaeism, but concurrently against movements such as that of Apollinarius, they argue the point that the God-Logos took on human flesh, with soul and spirit, from the body of Mary, without Himself thereby being overcome by the powers of destruction.[375] Against Tertullian and Helvidius, they oppose Jerome for advocating Mary's perpetual virginity,[376] a position the latter based on an alternate way to read the biblical texts. Along with Peter of Alexandria, such a reading states that the "one who brought God to birth" was also glorified as the "perpetual virgin:[377] "*Illa enim virgo concepit, virgo peperit, virgo permansit* (She indeed conceived as a virgin, gave birth as a virgin, remained a virgin)."[378]

As the first of the Western thinkers, Ambrose constructed the bridge between the virginal conception and Jesus' status as one whose nature was free from original sin;[379] Augustine bases his teaching at this point very clearly upon what Ambrose had articulated.[380] Mary

---

[373] Augustine, *Sermo* 214.6; *De Trinitate* 15:27.48.

[374] Cf. the passages in Eichenseer, *Apostolicum*, 239ff.

[375] Cf. the texts in Eichenseer, *Apostolicum*, 252ff., 274f.

[376] According to Huhn, *Das Geheimnis der Jungfrau-Mutter Maria nach Ambrosius*, 192–221, 227ff. and Eichenseer, *Apostolicum*, 263ff.; Luther bases his observations on this determination in passages such as "Pred. über Joh. 1:51 vom 19.1.1538," WA 46:723.16–35 (AE 22:1–530) and "Vom Schem Hamphoras und vom Geschlecht Christi, 1543," WA 53:640.18–22.

[377] Peter Alexander, *fragm.* VII (PG 18.517B); additional texts are in Schmaus, *Katholische Dogmatik*, 5:136ff.

[378] Augustine, *Sermo* 51:11.18 (PL 38:343); cf. idem, *De catechizandis rudibus* 22:40; *De symbolo ad catechumenos* 3:6 (PL 40:630) and Pseudo-augustine, *Sermo* 240:1 (PL 39:2189); Peter Chrysologus, *Sermo* 62 (PL 52:374A): "*Virgo concipit, Virgo parit, permanet virgo post partum.*"

[379] Ambrose, in *Expositio Evangelii secundum Lucam* 2:56 (CCSL 14:55.760–64); *in Ps. 37:5* (CSEL 64:139f.); *Expositio Psalmi 118* 6:22 (CSEL 62:119); *De paenitentia* 1:13 (PL 16:490f.); cf. Huhn, *Das Mariengeheimnis beim Kirchenvater Ambrosius*, 133ff.

[380] Augustine, *De peccato originali* 41:47 (CSEL 42:205f.); *De nuptiis et concupiscentia ad Valerium comitem* 1:35.40 (CSEL 42:251f.); *Contra duas epistulas Pelagianorum ad Bonifatium* 4:11.29 (CSEL 60:559–61).

did not conceive because of fleshly desires, but in submissive slumber as a result of the message of the angel. The passion of the flesh reduces to nothing when and where the Spirit of God throws His holy shadow over a human being.[381] In his conflict with the Pelagians and semi-Pelagians, Augustine places greater emphasis on the gracious character of this creative activity of God. Without having done anything special beforehand, Mary was chosen, and she acquiesced to receiving Jesus' human existence from the God-Logos. Thus, for Augustine, the incarnation and the virgin birth become the pattern of the way God acts graciously, though under no obligation and without reason.[382]

The paraphrases of the Symbol from the Middle Ages insert the biblical narratives in, at times, into the way they render the Apostles' Creed. This is the source for the threefold phraseology: announced by the angel Gabriel, conceived by the Holy Spirit, born by the Virgin Mary.[383] Or else, with Ambrose and Augustine, they underscore the perpetual virginity of the mother of God, on the one hand,[384] and Jesus' unrestricted fully human nature, on the other; this latter aspect is characterized in great detail.[385] With reference to Jesus Christ, they bring both elements together in the phrase that has echoes in Luther: "*Credo quod in hoc saeculo fuit sicut alius homo praeter peccato solo* (I believe that in this world He was just as another human being except for sin alone)."[386]

Bernard of Clairvaux intensifies the way that Mary participates in our salvation and Bonaventure follows him in this regard; Mary is

---

[381] Augustine, *Sermo* 287:3.4 (PL 38:1302): "*Non erit aestus, ubi umbra facit Spiritus Sanctus*"; Ambrose, *De mysteriis* 3:13.51–59 (CSEL 73:94); Peter Lombard, *Sententiarum* III, dist. 12.2 (PL 192:780): "And yet, from the virgin, who conceived by the Spirit, not the flesh, what preceded was faith, not desire; nor did concupiscence of the flesh come between, which seizes all others who bear original sin; instead, virginity was made fertile by believing, not by lying with [someone]."

[382] Augustine, *Enchiridion de fide, spe, et caritate* 11:36; 12:40; 28:108; *De correptione et gratia* 11:30; *De praedestinatione sanctorum* 10:31; This is taken up by Thomas Aquinas and modified, *Summa theologiae* III, q. 2, a. 10–12; q. 6, a. 6. On this entire section, see additionally von Campenhausen, *Die Jungfrauengeburt in der Theologie der alten Kirche.*

[383] Hahn, *Bibliothek*, §§ 109, 114–17.

[384] Ibid., §§ 105, 106, 108.

[385] Ibid., § 105: "I believe that the holy Christ lived thus on this earth as any other man," expanded extensively; similarly see additionally §§ 106, 108.

[386] Ibid., § 108.

elevated to the role of being the *mediatrix* of all grace.[387] Thomas Aquinas reins in these Mariological excesses and concentrates solely on the incarnation in his commentary on the Symbol.[388] By using the analogous relationships between inner thoughts and articulated words, or else by using the concept of the spoken and written word, he seeks to make the incarnation of the eternal God-Logos comprehensible; only as the "*Verbum Dei carne indutum*" (Word of God clothed in flesh) does God allow Himself to come down to us, to be heard, seen, and comprehended.[389] Thomas Aquinas thus recapitulates the Christological heresies, right up to the time of the Creed of Chalcedon, and offers support for the many decisions that were made by the Church during those times, by means of Scripture citations.[390] Based on a third approach, he explains the incarnation by using the Athanasian motto: "*Factus est homo, ut hominem faceret Deum* (He was made man, so that He might make man God)."[391] Already at this time, he speaks of a "*commercium*" between God and humanity; Luther's imagery from The Freedom of a Christian, the concept of a "happy exchange and battle,"[392] of a "happy transaction,"[393] between Christ and our soul, resonates here.[394] The late Middle Ages puts the image of the virgin mother of God front and center once again; most especially, it was the order of the Augustinian Eremites who advanced the veneration of Mary. It arrived at a new highpoint with Johann of Paltz. A sermon on Mary in the *Supplementum* to the *Coelifodina* has the characteristic title: "*DE HUMILITATE gloriose virginis Marie, qua deum traxit de celis, tria vota emisit pro omnibus religiosis et omnia monasteria, immo totam fidem christianam fundavit* (On the glorious humility of the Virgin Mary, who carried

---

[387] Bernard of Clairvaux, *In nativ. Beat. Virg. Mari* 5:5–7 (PL 183:440ff.); see, in addition, the Pseudo-augustinian tractate, *De assumptione b. Mariae virg.* (PL 40:1141–48), as well as the sermon ascribed to Anselm, no. 50 (PL 158:952–59); additional texts are in Schmaus, *Katholische Dogmatik*, 5:366ff., 401ff.

[388] Thomas Aquinas, *Expositio in Symbolum Apostolorum*, §§ 897–909; Mariology remains connected with the incarnation of the Savior in the *Summa* as well, *Summa theologiae* III, q. 27–30.

[389] Thomas Aquinas, *Expositio in Symbolum Apostolorum*, § 897.

[390] Ibid., §§ 898–904; cf., as well, Thomas Aquinas, *De articulis fidei*, § 606, and *Summa theologiae* III, q. 2, a. 1–6; q. 5, a. 1–4.

[391] Thomas Aquinas, *Expositio in Symbolum Apostolorum*, §§ 905–09.

[392] "Von der Freiheit eines Christenmenschen, 1520," WA 7:25.34 (AE 31:327–377).

[393] Ibid., 26.5.

[394] Cf. ibid., "De libertate christiana, 1520," 55.7–37.

God from heaven, who established three vows for all the religious and all monasteries, more than that, who founded the entire Christian faith)."[395] All piety that is connected with the faith is concentrated in Mary.[396]

The reformer called for Christ to be brought back front and center. He understood that his sermons for the festival cycle of Christmas were to furnish commentaries on the article of faith: "conceived from the Holy Spirit, born from the Virgin Mary."[397] In this regard, in his sermon on January 6, 1532, on Micah 5:1, just as Ambrose and Augustine had explained it, he depicts the dual nature of how Christ goes forth as king and confesses, with the Creed of Ephesus, concerning the woman who bore God:[398] "This king thus goes forth twice, the first time from God the Father in eternity, before the world came to be, the second time, when He went forth from the virgin into the world, who is a lord and who is born in Bethlehem, but who is born before the world as well, that is: one unique person, not two persons, and yet true God and a real human being; Mary is thus not only a mother of the flesh and blood of the one whom she nursed and cared for, but is also the mother of the one who was born before the world came to be, since it is exactly this very same person who was born before the world, who came to be from the Father, who is the one born of the virgin in the world, and is thus baked together to be

---

[395] Cited from Düfel, *Marienverehrung*, 41; cf. ibid., 33–69, 140ff., 219–46.

[396] Here is what Luther says, in "Ein merklicher Sermon von der Geburt Marias über Mt. 1:1–17 vom 8.9.1522," WA 10.3:325.5: "We want to accord to her the honor that God gave to her, but we are not willing to make her into a false goddess; we do not want to have her as an advocate, but we want to have her as an intercessor, as is the case with the other saints"; cf. also Ap XXI (*BSLK*, 319.45–322.53), as well as the expansive assemblage of citations gathered by Tappolet, *Das Marienlob der Reformatoren*, 17–160, 357–64, and the critical evaluation in Düfel, *Marienverehrung*.

[397] Passages such as "Weihnachtspost. über Lk. 2:1–14, Christmesse, 1522," WA 10.1.1:93.13ff. (AE 52:7–31); "Pred. über Lk. 1:26ff. vom 25.3.1522," WA 11:71.3ff.; "Pred. über Mt. 1:18ff. u. Lk. 1:26ff. vom 24.12.1528," WA 27:474.3f.; 475.1f.; "Pred. über Lk. 2:1ff. vom 25.12.1528," WA 27:487.1f.; "Pred. über Lk. 2:1ff. vom 25.12.1529," WA 29:642.4f.; "Pred. über Lk. 1:26ff. vom 24.3.1532," WA 36:138.5; "Torgauer Pred. vom 16./17.4.1533," WA 37:54.25ff.; 55:12ff.; "Pred. über Lk. 1:26ff. vom 25.3.1538," WA 46:225.2.

[398] On the Creed of Ephesus, see "Von den Konziliis und Kirchen, 1539," WA 50:581.15–592.15 (AE 41:3–178), as well as the texts in Tappolet, *Das Marienlob der Reformatoren*, 358, and the treatment by Düfel, *Marienverehrung*, 213–16.

one person, true God and true human being.[399] In his treatise on the Three Symbols of Faith (1538), Luther treats both births together by using the concept of a sign;[400] as the Spirit demonstrates His eternal procession from the Father and the Son through His physical procession into the world, thus also the Son, through His physical birth, demonstrates His eternal birth from the Father; "each one has for His inner nature an external comparison or image."[401]

Just as Luther established the rule in his "Sermon on the Observation of the Holy Suffering of Christ" in 1519:[402] "Climb up through Christ's heart to God's heart,"[403] in the same year, in a Christmas sermon, he offers the challenge:[404] sacramental mediation must begin with Christ's humanity; one is to recognize God's turning toward us thereby, by faith, for salvation, and we are to appropriate it for ourselves with love;[405] we are to say: mother, the little child is mine!"[406] The reformer never grows weary of steering us away, even in his later sermons, from the Areopagite meditations on the mysteries of God, by turning us to the child in the manger.[407] High forms of speculation confront us with the "*Deus absconditus in majestate sua* (God who is hidden in His majesty)," which can cast us down into the abyss of temptations about predestination; by contrast, the child gets us on the correct path to the heart of the Father. Luther returns again

---

399 WA 36:60.25; cf. the parallels, ibid., 60.3–10; 77.4–12, 22–31; 79:5–20, 25–42; in addition, "Vorl. über Micha, 1525," WA 13:325.4–19 (AE 18:205–277); "Disp. de divinitate et humanitate Christi vom 28.2.1540," WA 39.2:101.4–23; "Ennaratio Jes. 53, 1544," WA 40.3:708.20ff.

400 WA 50:274.31–275.26 (AE 34:197–229); cf. Peter Lombard, *Sententiarum* III, dist. 8.2.

401 WA 50:275.25.

402 WA 2:136–42 (AE 42:3–14).

403 Ibid., 140.36.

404 WA 9:439–42.

405 Ibid., 442.32: "consider Christ sacramentally, that is, trust that He Himself may be this gift for you"; "Weihnachtspost. über Lk. 2:1–14, Christmesse, 1522," WA 10.1.1:68.6 (AE 52:7–31): "the more deeply we associate Christ with [our own] nature and flesh, the more comforting it is for us."

406 "Weihnachtspred., 1519," WA 9:440.28.

407 In passages such as "Weihnachtspost. über Joh. 1:1–14, 1522," WA 10.1.1:202.2–204.8 (AE 52:41–88); "Symbolpred. vom 5.3.1523," WA 11:51.4–52.13; "Pred. über Lk. 2:8ff. vom 25.12.1527," WA 23:730.25–732.33; "Pred. über Lk. 2:1ff. vom 26.12.1529," WA 29:671.17–673.10; "Pred. über Mt. 2:1ff. vom 6.1.1532," WA 36:61.17–62.24; "Gal.-Komm., 1535," WA 40.1:77.28–78.26 (AE 26:145–49); "Pred. über Lk. 1:26ff. vom 25.3.1538," WA 46:226.9–228.21.

and again to John 14:8f.[408] and lets Christ speak: "*Ego sum positus signum, in quo contempleris patrem* (I am the sign that is provided, by means of which you can contemplate the Father)."[409] The basic rule of thumb is preserved hereby, which we demonstrated in the trinitarian formulation of the Symbol: "*In confessione oportet, ut a supremo incipias, in instructione, a Christi humana natura* (When confessing, you ought to start with the Most High, when teaching, with Christ's human nature)."[410]

Concerning the incarnation and the virgin birth, with the paraphrases of the Symbol from the Middle Ages, Luther underscores the complete humanity of Jesus. Our Lord was "a true, natural human being with flesh and blood and with all limbs, powers and the mind's ability to think, just as you and I and every single human being have since Adam."[411] "He ate, drank, slept, awoke, was tired, sad, happy, cried, laughed, got hungry, thirsty, cold, sweated, chatted, worked, prayed."[412]

More forcefully than all theologians who preceded him, Luther lets the Lord participate in our weaknesses and ignorance; by this means, he pushes back against the "naïve Docetism," which had been making its mark on the Christian tradition ever since the Gospel of John.[413] According to the tradition of the early Church, which was clarified more completely by Scholasticism, from the first moment that it was united with the divine Logos, Jesus' soul lived in a beatific vision of God; it existed, therefore, on the other side of faith and hope and had the ability to be omniscient. Thomas Aquinas therefore went to great pains in the *Summa* to carve out some small place for Jesus to have truly possessed the ability to learn through experience, but this

---

408 "Pred. de testamento Christi vom 8.4.1520," WA 9:449.9: "Therefore divinity put on flesh, so that we should now have some certain sign, to which we should fasten our souls"; cf. Mülhaupt, *Ev.-Auslegung*, 4:379–98; Nilsson, *Simul*, 153–71.

409 "Pred. über Joh. 16:5 vom 6.5.1520," WA 9:449.19.

410 "Symbolpred. vom 5.3.1523," WA 11:51.29; cf. 36–47.

411 "Torgauer Pred. vom 16./17.4.1533," WA 37:54.27.

412 "Pred. über Joh. 1:10f. vom 18.8.1537," WA 46:598.32 (AE 22:1–530); "Pred. über Joh. 1:13f. vom 5.1.1539," WA 47:637.2: "The Word, which has been made flesh, has lived among us, has become our fellow citizen, has acted just as any other human being, exists as a child; He carried the ax after Joseph, carried water for His mother."

413 The unique phrase comes from Käsemann, *Jesu letzter Wille nach Johannes 17*, 51f., 83, 118, 124, 137. On the tradition, see texts such as Schulte, *Die Entwicklung der Lehre vom menschlichen Wissen Christi*; Landgraf, *DG der Frühscholastik*, 2.2:44–131; Ternus, *Das Seelen- und Bewußtseinsleben Jesu*.

was admittedly limited to the manner and means of the way it was acquired; with respect to content, even with respect to the initial knowledge of what He later would have acquired concerning the natural world, Jesus would actually have known everything. Luke 2:52 was consequently understood not in the sense that Jesus Himself was gaining in knowledge, but only that it seemed to the eyes of the world and to the disciples that He grew in wisdom.[414] Luther cuts through Docetic speculative activity of this sort. The unity of the two natures in Christ's person could not be understood to mean that Jesus' bodily needs would not have been real or that His lack of knowledge only seemed to be the case. Even Jesus had "not, though such is the case for any other holy, natural human being, thought, spoken, willed, or accomplished everything at all times . . . ; instead, He was filled with grace and wisdom as God let that happen and as it came to Him, so that He could evaluate and teach that which had come to Him."[415]

And yet, at the same time, Luther admits specifically concerning the article: "born from the Virgin Mary," that indeed this took place "without any evil lust and desire, additionally without birth pangs and pains. There was no reason for the days of labor to have come, since that was laid by God on the wives as punishment; this child was conceived not in sin by a human male but by the Holy Spirit."[416] The reformer never gave up on the notion of Mary's perpetual virginity:[417] "*Virgo est et fit mater et manet virgo* (She is a virgin and is made a mother and remains a virgin)";[418] and yet, he argued that Mary was to be venerated in only a limited way. Our salvation does not depend on her virginity[419] or even upon the fact that she was a unique coworker

---

[414] Thomas Aquinas, *Summa theologiae* III, q. 12; Peter Lombard, *Sententiarum* III, dist. 13f.; ibid., dist. 13.2 on Luke 2:52 (PL 192:782): "*In alliis ergo non in se proficiebat sententia et gratia.*"

[415] "Weihnachtspost. über Hebr. 1:1–12, 1522," WA 10.1.1:149.13; cf. "Dict. super Psalt., 1513–16," WA 4:266.24–267.5 (AE 11:1–553); "Pred. über Mt. 1:1ff. vom 25.12.1519," WA 9:441.32–442.21; "Weihnachtspost. über Hebr. 1:1–12, 1522," WA 10.1.1:148.19–151.6; "Weihnachtspost. über Lk. 2:33–40, 1522," WA 10.1.1:446.7–448.17 (AE 52:102–148).

[416] "Torgauer Pred. vom 16./17.4.1533," WA 37:56.39.

[417] On Mary's perpetual virginity, cf. Düfel, *Marienverehrung*, 135ff., 190ff.

[418] "Pred. über Lk. 1:46ff. vom 2.7.1533," WA 37:96.15.

[419] "Pred. über Lk. 1:26ff. vom 19.3.1524," WA 15:477.5: "*nostra salus non consistit in virginitate matris, sed in filio* (our salvation does not depend on the virginity of the mother, but in the Son)"; Luther bases this on the thinking of Bernard concerning the threefold advent of Christ (Bernard, *Sermones*, PL 183:35–56), but turns such an

when God became a human being; our salvation is grounded in God's condescending.

Luther's observations about Mary accord her honor for her faithful obedience, since she bowed in humility under the promise of the angel.[420] He reaches back to make use of the term used in early Church tradition: "*conceptio per aurem* (conception through the ear)"[421] and garners support from the biblical narratives to provide links to prophetic call narratives. Mary received the Lord from the message of the angel (Luke 1:31): "When she comprehended the Word and became pregnant in the heart through faith, she physically became pregnant as well, with the one about which the word in her heart spoke."[422] As the antitype of both the Church and the individual believer, Mary received her Lord only on the basis of trust in the Word of God against all appearances; as an image of the Church and of each Christian in the sight of the world, indeed standing before her husband to whom she is engaged, she stands in dishonor until God uses His messenger to reveal to him what He had done to her.

---

analysis against the call of Bernard there-by to exalt Mary, in "Pred. über Joh. 1:17 vom 6.10.1537," WA 46:663.32–36 (AE 22:1–530).

[420] "Pred. über Lk. 2:1 vom 25.12.1520," WA 9:517.23: "Moreover, it is no difficult matter for God to have a boy born to a virgin. It is a very great thing, however, that God may become a human being and that the virgin herself may be the mother of God. The greatest thing comes at the end, that the virgin herself believed that she was a mother; it is necessary for us to consider how reason was embarrassed by it all"; cf. WA 7:188.22–189.7 and "Pred. über Lk. 2 vom 25.12.1520," WA 9:517.14–26; "Pred. über Lk. 1:46ff. vom 2.7.1533," WA 15:480.32–37; "Pred. über Lk. 1:26ff. vom 25.3.1525," WA 17.1:150.23–152.32; "Pred. über Lk. 2:1ff. vom 25.12.1529," WA 29:650.10–651.9; "Pred. über Lk. 1:46ff. vom 2.7.1533," WA 37:96.13–97.17.

[421] Cf. Barth, *Kirchliche Dogmatik* 1.2:219f.

[422] "Wider die Schwarmgeister, 1527," WA 23:185.20 (AE 37:3–150). Concerning conception on the basis of the message of the angel, see "Pred. über Lk. 2:14 vom 25.12.1520," WA 7:189.2–20; "Sermon von dem Sakrament des Leibes und Blutes Christi wider die Schwarmgeister vom 28.3.1526," WA 19:490.24–35 (AE 36:329–361); "Wider die Schwarmgeister, 1527," WA 23:185.7–29 (AE 37:3–150); "Pred. über Lk. 1:26ff. vom 24.3.1532," WA 36:142.19f.; "Torgauer Pred. vom 16./17.4.1533," WA 37:56.2–10; "Pred. über Lk. 1:39ff. vom 1.7.1535," WA 41:354.7–28. In his letter to Amsdorf from March 11, 1533 (WABr 7:37.335–54, no. 2093), Luther comes out strongly against Erasmus, *Explanatio Symboli*, cols. 1154E/F, who refers back to Rufinus, *Expositio symboli* 9, to identify the heathen divine marriages and the births of heroes as the antitype, pointing instead to examples in the Old Testament: "Why should we not also call the conversation of God with Moses and the other prophets a sexual union, and portray angels as bridesmaids, with the Holy Spirit acting as the seed, unless one would consider it obscene?"

Along with Ambrose and Augustine, Luther testifies as well: By means of the conception by the Spirit in the virgin, Jesus Christ was removed from the context of original sin.[423] No human being, on his or her own, can escape from the cursed circle of that original enslavement; our human way of looking at one another is contaminated down into the roots by evil lust and sinful desire. For that reason, God Himself has to initiate a new beginning by means of "the pure hands and fingers of the Holy Spirit."[424] This creative, new beginning on God's part is visible in that human being who has the form of the virgin mother; erotic love is changed into subservient acquiescence to the promises of God.[425]

Luther's words about Jesus' true development as a human being, but particularly his insights into Jesus' standing under the wrath of judgment of the God who hides Himself, are encouraging: The conception and birth from the virgin, without the action of a man, ought not to be explained away by some sort of quasi-medical spin job that refers to the generic nature of Jesus' life and death for the many. Luther does not conceptualize some automatically functioning solution on Jesus' part to escape from the slavery of sin, not some sort of external, physical barricading of the floods of original sin. Jesus' lordship over sin, which characterizes Him, from His origin, is truly at work throughout His entire life; it is protected against all external attacks of the enemy, and against internal temptations, right up to the hour of death and is, in the final analysis, ratified by God Himself and manifested in the resurrection and exaltation. "In the language of an age that took magic seriously, the wonder of Christmas is a kerygmatic statement about where Jesus comes from, not about His

---

[423] By referring time and again to Psalm 51, Luther explicates the reference to the original sin already in connection with the conception by Mary, "Pred. über Lk. 11:27 vom 8.12.1517," WA 4:625f., and "Roths Festpost. über Lk. 11:27f., 1527," WA 17.2:282.14–287.26; cf., as well, "Vom Schem Hamphoras und vom Geschlecht Christi, 1543," WA 53:640.3–10.

[424] "Pred. über Lk. 1:16ff. vom 24.3.1532," WA 36:143.13; cf., as well, "Sermo de testimonia scripturae Gen. 3:15 und Ex. 3:1–6 vom 2. u. 3.4.1526," WA 20:330.1–40; 358.17–25; "Pred. über Lk. 1:26ff. vom 24.3.1532," WA 36:143.7–144.4; "Torgauer Pred. vom 16./17.4.1533," WA 37:55.17–56.42; "Pred. über Lk. 1:26ff. vom 25.3.1538," WA 46:203.3–232.7.

[425] The human being takes part "only in the form of a human being who is not willing, who cannot bring something to completion, cannot be creative, cannot act in a sovereign way, only in the form of a human being who can do nothing but receive, who can merely be ready, who can do nothing but allow something to happen to him and with him (Barth, *Kirchliche Dogmatik* 1.2:209).

forebears. 'Eschatological history' is directed toward Jesus' point of origin."[426]

2. Jesus' Journey into Hades[427]

Luther initially translated "*descendit ad inferna*" from the *Textus receptus* as "descended to hell (*niedergestiegen zu der Helle*),"[428] parallel to "ascended into heaven (*aufgestiegen zum Himmel*)." Only when he got to the catechisms did he permit the alteration in these little books for the laity and children to read "went up heavenwards (*aufgefahren gen Himmel*),"[429] which affected the description of the journey to Hades with the formulation: "went down to the infernal regions (*niedergefahren zur Hellen*)."[430] The paraphrases of the Symbols from the Middle Ages preferred to use the simple verbs "climbed" for the one[431] and almost always "went" for the other.[432] In the late Middle Ages, the prefixes emphasized the direction of travel: "climb off, go off, climb down, travel down (*absteigen, abfahren, niedersteigen, niederfahren*)."[433] The literal "to the infernal regions" was treated consistently, by Luther as well, as a singular; the singular would also more intensely replicate the topography of the nether region as it was conceptualized during the Middle Ages. The modern ecumenical text suggests: "climbed down into the depths of death"; this demythologized, new rendering seeks to capture both elements, Christ's deepest deprivation, as well as His victory over the powers of darkness.

The text of the Symbol that first includes "*descendit in (ad) inferna*" is recorded by Rufinus in the Confession of Aquileia, his hometown."[434] Rufinus remarks about this: This addendum is missing in the Eastern Symbols, as well as in the Roman Creed, but its intent

---

426 Weber, *Grundlagen der Dogmatik*, 2:121; cf. ibid., 118–21; Barth, *Kirchliche Dogmatik* 1.2:187–221; Pannenberg, *Grundzüge der Christologie*, 140–50.

427 For texts and literature referred to here, see p. 206.

428 "Eine kurze Form, 1520," WA 7:217.1; "Betbüchlein," WA 10.2:391.11 (AE 43:3–45); cf. the "Büchlein für die Laien und Kinder," (MGP 20:203.31).

429 MGP 20:203.32.

430 *BSLK*, 511.15f. (SC); 556.5f. (Preface to the Large Catechism); 651.3 (LC) and "Torgauer Pred. vom 16./17.4.1533," WA 37:62.28; 36:1: "to Hell."

431 Hahn, *Bibliothek*, § 93.

432 Ibid., §§ 100–03, 108, 110, 112, 114, 116, 117.

433 Cf. Meyer, *Historischer Kommentar*, 94; Hahn, *Bibliothek*, §§ 95, 106, 111.

434 Denzinger, 16; cf. Caesarius of Arles, *Sermo* 9 (CCSL 103:47) and the Athanasian Creed, *BSLK*, 30.13f.

is apparently to underscore the "*sepultus* (buried)."[435] The trip to Hades is mentioned already some decades before Rufinus, in clarifications offered by three synods that are linked together: Sirmium, in 359; Nicea[436] in Thrace, in the same year; and Constantinople, in 360. As formulated at Sirmium by Bishop Marcus of Arethusa, it was cast originally in Latin, with the words about the trip to Hades supposedly reading originally: "(*qui*) *in* (*ad*) *inferna descendit* ([who] descended into [to] the infernal regions)."[437] In his summary of the teaching about the faith, Cyril of Jerusalem formulates it similarly: "He climbed down into the underworld, in order to redeem the righteous there as well."[438] Since the seventh century, "*descendit ad inferna*" is used in the Spanish and the Gallic formulations,[439] and since the eighth century in the Germanic Symbol formulas as well.[440] In the Irish *Antiphonar* (Tr.: collection of antiphons) from Bangor, the article reads: "*Qui crucifixus et sepultus descendit ad inferos* (who, crucified and buried, descended to the infernal region)."[441]

Though reference to Jesus' descent into Hades appears only late in the texts of the Symbols, this train of thought developed into its full form between the New Testament era and the third century. Three main points of emphasis are intertwined: (1) Jesus took full part in our destiny in death; (2) Jesus demonstrated that He was Lord even at the "place" of the dead; (3) Jesus overcame the satanic opposing powers and broke their strength. But, from the outset, the desire to add fabulous details interposed within the elements that were important to the faith; mythological elements were adapted from both late Jewish apocalyptic and from Hellenistic Gnosis. As a result, Jesus' participation in our destiny of death was thoroughly interlaced with emphasis on His victory over the powers of destruction.

The question about the destiny of the dead from Israel is at issue in 1 Pet. 3:18f. and is unfolded in a Jeremiah Apocryphon that has been transmitted to us by Justin and Irenaeus: "The Lord, the holy

---

[435] Rufinus, *Expositio symboli* 16.4–7 (CCSL 20:152f.).

[436] Hahn, *Bibliothek*, §§ 163f., 167; cf. Kattenbusch, *Symbol*, 2:896.

[437] According to Kattenbusch, *Symbol*, 2:897.

[438] Cyril of Jerusalem, *Catechesis* 4.11 (PG 33:469A).

[439] Hahn, *Bibliothek*, §§ 54–56; Denzinger, 23, as well as Hahn, *Bibliothek*, §§ 66f.; Denzinger, 27.

[440] Hahn, *Bibliothek*, § 92; Denzinger, 28.

[441] Hahn, *Bibliothek*, § 76; Denzinger, 29.

God of Israel, remembered His dead, those who slept in the graves in the earth, and He climbed down to them, in order to bring to them the happy message of His salvation."[442] 1 Peter 4:6 already seems to intimate that there was a sermon in Hades for everyone; the light of Christ would shine forth even on the heathen forebears.[443] The New Testament itself proclaims Christ's victory over the demonic powers. All knees are to bow before the Lord and all tongues are to confess Him as the *Kyrios*, not only those who are on the earth, but also those who are in the heavenly and nether regions.[444] As the one who was exalted to be in the presence of the Father, He shows Himself to be ruler, as well, over those who had fallen asleep. He holds the insignias of power in the underworld in His right hand and thus possesses complete power, "to open the gates of the world of the dead and to call the dead to resurrection."[445]

Christ's lordly invasion into the region of power known as *še'ol* is depicted in colorfully brilliant form by Cyril,[446] carefully discussed by Augustine, [447] and given only a brief summary by John of Damascus: "The deified soul climbed down into the underworld. . . . And thus He released those who had been in fetters from time immemorial, rose again from the dead, and prepared for us the path to resurrection."[448] In the West, the Council at Sens (1140) rejected the thesis of Abelard that Christ's soul forced its way down into the world of Hades, though only the power to effect something really got there;[449] the Fourth Lateran Council (1215) states explicitly: Christ "*descendit in anima, et resurrexit in carne: ascendit pariter in utroque*" (descended in soul and rose in flesh: He ascended equally in both).[450] The paraphrases from the Middle Ages once again formulate

[442] Justin, *Dialogus cum Tryphone* 72.4 (cited from BKV 33:119); Irenaeus, *Adversus haereses* 3:20.4; 4:22.1; *Apostol. Verkündigung*, 78. In addition, see Ignatius, *Magn.* 9:2; Hermas, Herm. *Sim.* 9:16.7; *Ep. Apost.* 27 (38); *Gos. Pet.* 10:41f.

[443] Cf., additionally, the Christological interpolations in the *Testaments of the Twelve Patriarchs* and in the *Odes of Solomon* 24:13.

[444] Phil. 2:10f.; cf. 1 Tim. 3:16; Col. 2:14f.

[445] Jeremias, κλείς, 746, concerning Rev. 1:18; cf. Reicke, *The Disobedient Spirits and Christian Baptism*; Bieder, *Die Vorstellung von der Höllenfahrt Jesu Christi*; Grillmeier, *Der Gottessohn im Totenreich.*

[446] Cyril of Jerusalem, *Catechesis* 14:19 (PG 33:848C–849A).

[447] Augustine, *Epistula 164 an Evodius* (CSEL 44:521–41).

[448] John of Damascus, *De fide orthodoxa* 3:29 (PG 94:1101A, cited according to BKV 44:186).

[449] Denzinger, 738.

[450] Denzinger, 801.

this with more flowery language: "I believe that His holy soul went to hell, shattered it, and took from there the righteous and the good, who had accomplished His will."[451] Early and High Scholasticism was occupied with the question about whether or not Christ remained truly human, even between the time of His death on the cross and His resurrection.[452] Peter Lombard helped clarify it for himself by differentiating between "*Christus totus* (the whole Christ)" and "*Christus totum* (the entire Christ)," which would play a role later during the Reformation era debate about Christ's real presence in the Lord's Supper.[453] In His physical flesh, bound to the Logos-hypostasis, the Lord lay in the grave; and yet, His soul that was bound to the God-Logos pressed its way into the realm of the dead. In the grave, as in Hades, He was one and the same Lord in His hypostasis, and yet not in His completely human nature.[454] All such speculations envision the trip to Hades from the viewpoint of Christ's victory over the demonic powers.

Only with the mysticism of the late Middle Ages was there a change in emphasis; the trip to Hades was interpreted anew on the basis of the suffering on the cross, and concurrently, on the tempted human being. This new understanding was offered by Eckhart, Tauler, and Suso; the *Theologia Germanica* and Nicholas of Cusa allude to it.[455] Christ's *Descensus ad inferos* (descended to the nether regions) becomes the model for our "*Resignatio ad infernum* (resignation to what is below)." "Christ's soul had to go into hell before it could come into heaven; the same holds true for the human

---

[451] Hahn, *Bibliothek*, § 116 (congregational confession on the basis of a Baumgartenberger handwritten copy from the fourteenth century); similarly, ibid., § 117; see also §§ 102, 105, 106, 108, 109, 110, 112, 114.

[452] Landgraf, *DG der Frühscholastik*, 2.1:273–319; Peter Lombard, *Sententiarum* III, dist. 22; Alexander, *Summa* IV, no. 165; Thomas Aquinas, *In Sententiarum* III, dist. 22, q. 1, a. 1; idem, *Summa theologiae* III, q. 50, a. 4; Bonaventure, *In Sententiarum* III, dist. 22, art. un., q. 1; Duns Scotus, *Opus Oxoniense* III, dist. 22, q. un.; idem, *Reportata Parisiensia* III, dist. 22, q. un.

[453] Peter Lombard, *Sententiarum* III, dist. 22.3 (PL 192:804): "From this it appears that Christ was, at the same time, completely in the tomb, completely in hell, completely everywhere, and in just that way He is entirely wherever He is, but not wholly; wholly refers to nature, but entirely refers to the hypostasis."

[454] Erasmus, *Explanatio Symboli*, col. 1161F–1163D, sets forth the nature of the problem, and formulates cautiously: "It suffices for you to profess your belief in Christ's descent to the nether regions as the Scriptures and the Church perceive it" (ibid., col. 1162F).

[455] See the evidence in Vogelsang, *Höllenfahrtsstreitigkeiten*, 91ff.

soul."[456] Christ's trip to Hades now becomes a part of the punishment He suffered and, with support from the theology of the cross, bears fruit for our justification.

Both ways of interpreting the descent are intermingled in Luther's commentaries on *Descensus Christi*; the teaching about propitiation comes to the fore once again in concentrated form. The reformer views the trip to Hades from the aspect of Christ's suffering death, and yet, he brings it as well into the context of the resurrection and ascension into heaven; for him, there are concurrent issues: the conflict with God's punishing judgment because of our sins is in the center, but vanquishing the powers of destruction is there too. For those making confession, both aspects are bound together and applicable; Luther resorts eagerly to Phil. 2:10 at this point: "That is our article of faith, that we know: we have one Lord, in life, in death, and after death."[457] In Luther's comments about the trip to Hades, what receives the stronger accent is admittedly adjusted; the elements that were still held together by the reformer were separated afterward; this led to dogmatic controversies.

In *Operationes in Psalmos*, Luther links Psalm 16:10 christologically and tropologically with Acts 2:24 and sees the words of Peter's sermon that the Lord "suffered the pangs of death" to be a reference to the Church's teaching about the descent.[458] In order to excel beyond all of us, Christ did not have to suffer physical death alone, but had to stand, as well, under the actual death that was under God's judgment of wrath. This journey of the soul into hell is not limited by Luther to the Garden of Gethsemane and to Golgotha; he expands it to include the death of Jesus and beyond, even to include the *Triduum mortis* (three days of death). In that mysterious time in between, between the cross and resurrection, the Lord would have been undergoing the complete suffering of the pangs of *še'ol* in His soul. Luther stuck with this interpretation later on, that Christ "had overcome not only the maggots and the separation of the soul from the body, but also the anguish of the pain of hell and doubt about

---

[456] *Theologia Deutsch*, 11:140.36.

[457] "Pred. über Christi Höllenfahrt vom 20.4.1538," WA 46:313.9: "That is our article of faith, *ut sciamus dominum habere in vita, in morte et post mortem*"; "Coburger Ausl. d. ersten 25 Pss, 1530," WA 31.1:318.17: "*Inferna* means everything that it means, that we go there, after life, whether to the grave or somewhere else."

[458] WA 5:462.29–463.35.

God."[459] But this is proscribed completely, being viewed solely as part of Jesus' sufferings unto death.[460]

Calvin and the Heidelberg Catechism later seek to limit the trip to Hades in the Apostles' Creed to just this aspect.[461] The confession of faith starts out with those aspects of the suffering of Christ on the cross that are visible and comprehensible, in order to accentuate the sufferings that His soul underwent, which remain hidden from sight. As the redeemer of our souls, Christ had to "experience the entire harshness of the divine judgment, in order to turn away God's wrath and to satisfy His righteous judgment. For this reason, He also had to do battle and be victorious over the powers of hell, with the terrors of eternal death, as if man against man,[462] even though God the Father, in the final analysis, was not standing opposite the Son as an enemy.[463]

And yet, even Calvin does not limit the trip to hell to be solely about Jesus' abandonment by God; he agrees easily with Abelard that the power of Jesus' death offering was able to reach back even to those who fell asleep under the old covenant, so that even they were able to perceive that "the grace that they had merely tasted in hope was visible now to the world."[464] Luther accentuated this aspect of the trip to Hades in his later interpretations. Already in the Short Form of 1520 he writes: "I believe that He climbed down to hell, to suffocate and to imprison the power of the devil and all his minions, all craftiness and evil, for me and for those who believe in Him, so that the devil cannot do damage to me in the future, and He redeems me from the pain of hell, rendering such powers harmless and servile."[465] In the later sermons on the descent into hell, he uses Phil. 2:10 and Eph. 4:10 to place the descent into hell within the light of the

---

[459] "Pred. über Christi Höllenfahrt vom 20.4.1538," WA 46:311.10.

[460] Ibid., 311.14: "Others say that He suffered after death; but I say that He descended to . . . , which means that He is Lord over the infernal region."

[461] Calvin, *Genfer Kat.*, quest. 65–70; idem, *Inst.*, 2:16.8–12; *Heidelberger Kat.*, quest. 44.

[462] Calvin, *Inst.*, 2:16.10 (Calvin, Opera Selecta, 3:495.5–9; cited from Calvin, *Unterricht*, 320). Cf. Agricola, "Christl. Kinderzucht, 1527" (MGP 21:54f.).

[463] Cf. Calvin, *Genfer Kat.*, quest. 67; idem, *Inst.*, 2:16.11.

[464] Calvin, *Inst.*, 2:16.9 (Calvin, Opera Selecta 3:494.5ff., 12f.; cited from Calvin, *Unterricht*, 320).

[465] WA 7:217.31.

exaltation, as the victory of Christ over the powers of death.[466] He thereby makes foundational statements about the possibility that one can demythologize certain biblical statements. From one vantage point, it is true: We can conceptualize the mystery of the victory of Christ only by using the rough pictures of His invasion into the realm of Satan; but from another angle it is true as well: In, with, and under those mythological symbols, we must turn our gaze to the "for us" aspect.[467] Since Luther seeks to hold these statements in tension throughout, he admittedly was driven to use the Hades topography current in the Middle Ages.

In one sense, he is at pains to emphasize that Jesus did not press onward, down into the realm of the death, solely with His soul that was bound to the God-Logos, or merely that the power of His offering on the cross went there;[468] no, the "entire person, God and man, with body and soul undivided" pressed on into the satanic realm of power.[469] But he looks at this another way as well, pointing out: This admittedly took place "not bodily or comprehensibly,"[470] since hell is not a "special" place, where the souls are supervised until the Day of Judgment. As an actual spatial place, "the real hell . . . will come into being only on the last day";[471] if one wants "to speak completely accurately about this," then Christ "never really went down."[472]

Is there not a threat at this point, similar to what took place for the mystics of the late Middle Ages and in full form in Reformed teaching, that the focus is narrowed when dealing with the lordship of Christ, which is part of the Gospel proclamation? In his earlier interpretations of 1 Pet. 3:18 and 4:6, Luther goes full bore with this

---

[466] "Pred. vom 31.3.1532," WA 36:161.15–17; "Torgauer Pred. vom 16./17.4.1533," WA 37:66.37–42.

[467] Cf. esp. "Pred. vom 31.3.1532," WA 36:160.26–161.17; "Torgauer Pred. vom 16./17.4.1533," WA 37:65.13–66.9; "Pred. über Christi Höllenfahrt vom 20.4.1538," WA 46:306.9–307.2.

[468] "Pred. vom 31.3.1532," WA 36:159.16f.; "Torgauer Pred. vom 16./17.4.1533," WA 37:63.14–17; "Pred. über Christi Höllenfahrt vom 20.4.1538," WA 46:306.6f.

[469] Cf. "Pred. vom 31.3.1532," WA 36:160.22–26; "Torgauer Pred. vom 16./17.4.1533," WA 37:65.3–12; this is used in SD IX (*BSLK*, 1052.15f.).

[470] "Torgauer Pred. vom 16./17.4.1533," WA 37:65.15.

[471] "Pred. über Christi Höllenfahrt vom 20.4.1538," WA 46:311.18; ibid., 312.4: "Therefore, the actual Hell does not exist; it will be there on the last day, but Christ has conquered it"; cf. "Pred. über Lk. 16:19–31 vom 22.6.1522," WA 10.3:192.11–23; "Pred. über Apg. 2:24ff. vom 30.5.1531," WA 34.1:496.12f.

[472] "Pred. vom 31.3.1532," WA 36:161.16.

"spiritualizing."[473] Later, he is admittedly not so willing to limit the lordship of Christ to this earthly life, nor to limit the Gospel that is proclaimed here. According to Phil. 2:10, Christ alone has the right to wear the threefold tiara; He is truly Lord, not only here on earth, but also over everything in the upper and lower regions, all of what has been kept from our control.[474] No heaven is too high, no hell too deep, that He cannot be by us there as our Lord and redeemer. We realize this because we can pray to Him about those who have died and we commend them into His hands.[475]

The Formula of Concord seeks to smooth over the disputes that arose after Luther's death, especially concerning the theses of the Hamburg superintendent Johann Aepinus, by citing Luther's Torgau sermon;[476] but handling it in this way passes over the way Luther demythologized the topography of the soul, as advocated in the Middle Ages,[477] and therefore strengthens the newer efforts to come up with quasi-mythical speculations about the trip to Hades.

3. Christ's Ascent into Heaven and His Being Seated to the Right of the Father[478]

The *Textus receptus* conceptualizes the ascension and rule of Jesus together, by using the words "*ascendit ad coelos, sedet ad dexteram Dei, patris omnipotentis* (He ascended to heaven; He sits at the right of God, the Father almighty)." Luther does not translate this in a uniform way. In the Short Form of 1520 he still renders it "climbed up to heaven";[479] the Little Book for the Laity and Children (1525) already chooses to translate it "gone up toward heaven";[480] this is how

[473] "Pred. über 1 Petr. 3 u. 4, 1523," WA 12:367–71; 375f. (AE 30:1–145); ibid., 376.16: "I cannot accept the viewpoint that the Gospel is to be preached to the dead and deceased."

[474] Cf. "Pred. über Christi Höllenfahrt vom 20.4.1538," WA 46:307.1–11; 312.2–10; "Gen.-Vorl., 1535–45," WA 42:322.19–323.17 (AE 2:1–399).

[475] Cf. passages such as "Pred. über Lk. 16:19–31 vom 22.6.1522," WA 10.3:195.21–27; "Ein Trost den Weibern, welchen es ungerade gegangen ist mit Kindergebären, 1542," WA 53:205ff. (AE 43:243–250).

[476] FC IX (*BSLK*, 1052.6ff.); concerning these disputes, see esp. Frank, *Die Theologie der Concordienformel*, 3:397ff.

[477] It is simply stated: we ought not to use our reason to try to comprehend the way in which the descent into Hades took place, SD IX (*BSLK*, 1053.4–12); Ep IX (*BSLK*, 813. 28–33).

[478] For texts on the ascension and reign of Christ, see p. 206–207.

[479] WA 7:217.2; "Betbüchlein," WA 10.2:391.12 (AE 43:3–45).

[480] MGP 20:203.32; cf. ibid., 203.8: "ascended into heaven."

it is translated in the catechisms.[481] The singular form "heaven" is used in the Lord's Prayer as well; this phraseology is probably what influenced the song: "Christ went up toward Heaven."[482] The words "sitting at the right of God, the almighty Father"[483] are generally always rendered the same way; only in the text that introduces the Large Catechism is the word "hand" added, as had been customary in most of the earlier translations.[484] The participial form "sitting" is without precedent. The modern ecumenical text formulates this: "and elevated to the right of God"; it is rendered thus in an effort to preclude a misunderstanding that would suggest a solid, spatial place, pointing instead to Christ's coregency.

In the Small Catechism, Luther deals with the rule of Christ concurrently with the resurrection; the one who arose back then and over there "lives and reigns in eternity."[485] The one who believes is incorporated into the lordship of the one who has been exalted, since he lives "in His kingdom, under Him" and serves Him.[486] The Large Catechism views the ascension as Christ's ascendancy, when He takes up His rule, and concurrently, as draining the power from the satanic forces; Psalm 110 resonates in the background.[487]

The Short Form of 1520 and the Confession of 1528 expand on the short references in the catechisms. At the ascension, the crucified one received from the Father "power and honor over all angels and creatures"[488] and sits to the right of the Father as "a lord over all lords, king over all kings and over all creatures in heaven, on earth, and under the earth, over death and life, over sin and righteousness."[489] The reformer does not limit the rule of Christ to being over the

---

[481] *BSLK*, 511.17f. (SC); 556.7f. (Preface to the Large Catechism); 651.5 (LC).

[482] *EKG* 90.1; cf. also the echoes in *EKG* 91.1 and *EKG* 92.1.

[483] "Eine kurze Form, 1520," WA 7:217.3; "Betbüchlein," WA 10.2:391.13 (AE 43:3–45); *BSLK*, 511.18f. (SC); 651.6f. (LC).

[484] *BSLK*, 556.8f. (Preface to the Large Catechism); cf. Meyer, *Historischer Kommentar*, 94.

[485] *BSLK*, 511.37.

[486] *BSLK*, 511.34.

[487] *BSLK*, 652.25–653.3.

[488] "Eine kurze Form, 1520," WA 7:218.9; ibid., 218.10: "A king and lord over all God's possessions in heaven, hell, and on earth"; "Von der Freiheit eines Christenmenschen, 1520," WA 7:27.8 (AE 31:327–377): "for everything is placed under His control in heaven, earth, and hell, even if no human being can see it, which means that He rules spiritually and invisibly"; cf. "De libertate christiana, 1520," WA 7:56.22–26 (AE 31:327–377).

[489] "Vom Abendmahl Christi, 1528," WA 26:502.23 (AE 37:151–372).

Church as the body of Christ; the exalted one takes part in the almighty, creative activity of the Father. Not only are human beings and the creatures of the earth placed under His authority, but the angelic powers and the powers of death are specifically under Him as well.

The reformer makes use of New Testament evidence at this point, with Old Testament prophecies in the background. Christ's exaltation is positioned by both Paul and John in close proximity to the cross and resurrection. The one who is offered is elevated thereby, by God the Father, to His right side.[490] Using the background furnished by Ps. 110:1, the exaltation, which can be characterized as the installation or the session of Jesus,[491] at the right of the Father, furnishes a characteristic topos for the early Church's proclamation. Jesus' existence to the right of God is formally linked with the ascension in 1 Pet. 3:22 and in the addition to the Gospel of Mark (Mark 16:19); the Church uses this specific phraseology in crafting the confession.[492]

The ascension of the redeemer corresponds to when He descended into the earthly realm (Eph. 4:8–10). Both aspects are developed as a description of an enthronement;[493] it describes not only how He seized lordly control over the powers but also how He enters before God in His role of serving as a priest. Since God allowed Christ, in His presence, to penetrate through into the realms of the cosmic powers, God cast under His control all those sinister, intermediary powers and demonic rulers in the world;[494] all dimensions of the cosmos must bow down before the exalted one (Phil. 2:10f.), in whom everything has become reconciled (Col. 1:20), which are now thoroughly under His rule (Eph. 4:10). In this sense, Christ steps forward as the Paraclete (1 John 2:1) and as the intercessor (Rom. 8:34), pushing Satan aside, who is the accuser

---

[490] On what follows, cf. Kretschmar, *Himmelfahrt und Pfingsten.*

[491] Cf. Acts 2:33; 5:31; 7:55f.; Rom. 8:34; Eph. 1:20; Col. 3:1; Heb. 1:3, 13; 8:1; 10:12f.; 12:2. In addition to Ps. 110:1 (cf. also Mark 12:36 par.; 14:62 par.), Pss. 2:7; 8:6f.; and 68:19 are used as well. Discussion about Christ's exaltation and ascension has a theological explication available already on the basis of the textual references from the Old Testament.

[492] See the texts in Lietzmann, *Symbolstudien*, 206ff.; Kattenbusch, *Symbol*, 2:648–55; Eichenseer, *Apostolicum*, 315f.; 322f.

[493] Cf. Acts 13:33; 2:36; Phil. 2:9ff.; Heb. 1:5; 5:5; Rom. 1:4; 8:17; 1 Pet. 1:21; 1 Tim. 3:16.

[494] 1 Peter 3:22; Eph. 1:21; Col. 2:15.

(John 12:31; Rev. 12:7ff.); according to the Letter to the Hebrews, He has pressed on into the heavenly sanctuary, as the eternal high priest, bearing the sacrifice of His entire life that is all-sufficient (Heb. 7:25f.; 9:24). He sends the Spirit down upon His own and prepares for them a way to come before the gracious visage of the heavenly Father.

Luke admittedly describes the date, place, completion, and witness of the journey into heaven (Acts 1:9–12; Luke 24:51) in a most unsentimental, "almost unsettling brevity."[495] He underscores two elements thereby; the first is the certainty of the return—the Lord will come down for judgment in the same way that He was raised up into heaven—and the second is that those left behind were to wait patiently for the exalted one to commission them to go forth: having been told not to look for the signs that presage when He will return, the witnesses are commissioned to concentrate on acting in the here and now.

The Festival of the Ascension was accorded a permanent place in the liturgy from the fourth century on.[496] This caused the Church to differentiate more radically between the resurrection and Christ's reception to the right of the Father; based on Acts 1:3, it occasioned the reference in some creedal formulations: "*Post quadraginta dies ascendit in caelum coram oculis discipulorum* (After forty days He ascended into heaven in the sight of the disciples)."[497]

Due to disagreements with both Gnostic and Manichaean elements, who denied a physical ascension, Augustine steadfastly advocated the exaltation of Jesus' glorified human nature.[498] We obviously ought not to pose the question about the way in which this took place, but certainly ought to trust with certainty that we also, as is true of the Lord already, will be able to function in sinless purity with our physical bodies, permanently freed from suffering. To the right of God thus does not serve to describe a spatial location either,

---

[495] Haenchen, *Die Apostelgeschichte*, 115–19; the number 40 is likely more a marker for a theological than for a historical time period (according to Ratzinger, "Himmelfahrt Christi," 362).

[496] Kretschmar, *Himmelfahrt und Pfingsten*, 209ff.; Rheinfelder, *Kultsprache und Profansprache*, 73f.

[497] Augustine, *Sermo* (Morin, *Sermones*, 204.32); cf. *Apostolic Constitutions and Canons* 8:12.34 (Funk, *Die Apostolischen Väter*, 508.13).

[498] See the texts in Eichenseer, *Apostolicum*, 316–18; 323–26.

but rather the totality of joy in God and in divine peace.[499] In like manner, "sitting" to the right does not describe bodily positioning, but rather Christ's worthiness to be Lord and His full right to exercise the office of judge.[500] As the head over His own people already, Christ draws after Himself the remaining members of His body, inasmuch as He addresses them with the "*Sursum corda* (Lift up your hearts)!"[501] Since He is our solicitor, intermediary, and advocate before the Father, we are to lift our hearts and minds up to Him.

The insistence that one press on toward God, as articulated in the admonition of the Letter to the Colossians: "Seek what is above, where Christ is, sitting to the right of God!" (Col. 3:1) concentrates one's gaze toward the community that is lovingly drawn toward God by its Lord; at the same time, however, the exalted one seems to have been pulled far away from His own, if one surveys the numerous earthly conflicts. Christ's renewed presence here below, on the earth and until the world comes to an end (Matt. 28:20), is accentuated anew by Augustine; and yet, at least with respect to commentaries on the Creed, less emphasis is placed on the Lord's participation in the reign of God and on how He is hindering the powers of death.[502]

The paraphrases of the Symbols from the Middle Ages paint the picture of the ascension in great detail and underscore the miraculous elements of the biblical narratives. The resurrected one ate and drank with His own, in order to document the resurrection; after forty days, He exalted Himself before the eyes of His disciples toward heaven

---

[499] Augustine, *De agone christiano* 26.28 (CSEL 41:128.10): "The right hand of the Father means perpetual blessing, which is promised to the holy; in the same way, the left hand is most correctly described as perpetual misery, which is given to the wicked"; cf. idem, *De symbolo ad catechumenos* 4.11 (PL 40:634).

[500] Augustine, *De fide et symbolo* 7.14 (CSEL 41:16.21–17.9).

[501] Augustine, *Sermo* 261.1: "What do you recite in the Creed? On the third day, He rose from the dead, ascended into heaven, was seated at the right hand of the Father. Therefore, in heaven, He is our head. For this reason, when 'Lift up your hearts' is said, your response is to be 'We have [lifted them] to the Lord!' "; Morin, *Sermones,* 507.6: "Therefore He ascended in order to protect us from above."

[502] Morin, *Sermones,* 485.16: "Our Lord Jesus Christ did not indeed thus descend from the Father in order to leave the Father; when He ascended from us He did not leave us either. When He was about to ascend and to sit at the right hand of the Father, He said long ago to His disciples: 'Behold, I am with you always, even to the end of the age'."

and now sits up there, to the right of His Father, participating fully in God's eternity and almighty nature.[503]

According to Thomas of Aquinas, Christ returns to the Father in the ascension by going back to His original position; as a human being, He acquired for Himself this exaltation precisely because of His humble obedience, to the death, as well as by His victory over the satanic temptations.[504] In His ascent, He pressed upward through all the spatial heavens, as well as above all spiritual angelic powers, all the way to the Father's seat; the right side must be understood not physically but "metaphorically."[505] His human nature has a claim, as well, on God's majesty as judge and on God's eternal blessedness.[506]

With respect to what could be said about the believers, Thomas of Aquinas finds three helpful elements about Christ's ascension:[507] He constructs the path and gives us confidence that the reign of God is a gift (John 14:2); He enters into the presence of His Father as our advocate (Heb. 7:25; 1 John 2:1); He draws our hearts upward to Himself, so that we can scorn things temporal (Col. 3:1). As is the case with Scholastic tradition in general, the reign of Christ appears as the reign of grace over the mystical body, in which the exalted head permits the streams of blessing to flow into the parts of His body through the organic elements of the sacraments. Christ's participation in the creative majesty of God is given short shrift; the opposing forces, against whom the Lord sets forth on the field of battle, are mentioned when His descent into hell is discussed, but no defined and

---

[503] Hahn, *Bibliothek*, § 107: "*Et post resurrectionem comedit et bibit cum suis discipulis ad probandam veram suam resurrectionem. Et postea in quadragesima die sursum ad coelos ivit suis discipulis inspicientibus. Et ibi sedet ad dexteram dei patris omnipotentis, ei coaeternus et compotentialis*"; the same is said almost word for word in ibid., §§ 108, 110, 112, 114–17. Luther values the importance of the forty days as a confirmation of the resurrection of Jesus, as well, "Pred. über Apg. 1:1ff. vom 17.5.1531," WA 34.1:402.5–403.3.

[504] Thomas Aquinas, *Expositio in Symbolum Apostolorum*, § 946.

[505] Ibid., § 945: "*Non autem accipitur in Deo dextera corporaliter, sed metaphorice*"; cf. idem, *Summa theologiae* III, q. 57, a. 4f.

[506] Thomas Aquinas, *Summa theologiae* III, q. 58, a. 2: "Whence to sit at the right hand of the Father is nothing other than to have divine glory with the Father (according to John of Damascus, *De fide orthodoxa* 4:2), and blessedness (according to Augustine, *De symbolo ad catechumenos* 4:11) and the power to judge (Augustine, *De fide et symbolo* 7:14), and such never change and are regal."

[507] Thomas Aquinas, *Expositio in Symbolum Apostolorum*, § 947; idem, *Summa theologiae* III, q. 57, a. 6.

clear contours are sketched out at this juncture with respect to Christ's exaltation.

In the first Ascension Day sermon he preached in 1520,[508] Luther still follows the tradition of the Middle Ages. As the exalted head, Christ draws all of His own, together with their minds, upward to Himself;[509] as the one who first traversed the path and as the one who accompanies them, He brings them through the river of death to be on the saving shore of eternal life.[510] Christ's lordly rule over everything (Eph. 4:10) concentrates itself upon the—sacramental—streams of grace, which pulse through the mystical body of the Church.[511] One hardly penetrates the Stoic-pantheistic worldview, to say nothing of the Hellenistic-Gnostic worldview.[512]

And yet, already in his commentary on Psalm 110 (1518), "De regno et sacerdotio Christi,"[513] the reformer operates from within the thought world of the Old Testament, with its use of the language of warfare; according to Christ's humanity as well, all powers in heaven and on earth have been delivered over to Him, and He is involved in both realms of God, the spiritual as well as the temporal, right up to the last day, positioned on the battlefield and opposing all the forces that seek to destroy.[514] In the center stands Christ's spiritual regiment: "The right side of God means that the Lord Christ's kingly reign is a spiritually hidden kingdom,"[515] whose scepter and kingly power are only and exclusively the Gospel.[516] The impotent and powerless word

---

[508] WA 9:453–59.

[509] Cf. esp. ibid., 453.8–25; 456.15–22.

[510] Ibid., 453.26–454.3; 456.23ff. It is as "leader on the journey, supporter," in fact as the "ferryman" that Luther depicted Christ on the basis of Heb. 10:19 ("Hebr.-Vorl., 1517–18," WA 57.3:224.10); he follows tradition ("*quod vulgo diceretur*") more closely when he depicts Him, in light of Heb. 2:10, as "the instrument and means by whom God brings His children" (ibid., 125.6).

[511] "Himmelfahrtspred. vom 18.5.1520," WA 9:459.7: "He ascended above all the heavens, so that He might fill everything, that is, in order to fill the whole Church with His goodness, so that for all the members, as it were, the head trickles and flows down."

[512] See the passages selected by Schlier from Philo, *Der Brief an die Epheser*, 193f.

[513] WA 1:690–710; cf., in addition, the interpretation of Psalms 2 and 8 in the "Op. in Ps.," WA 5:47–74, 249–84, esp. 279.17–36 (AE 14:279–349).

[514] Especially WA 1:693.1ff., 37ff.; cf. "Pred. über Ps. 110 vom 8.5. u. 12.6.1535," WA 41:96.8–17; 226.19–227.20 (AE 13:225–348).

[515] WA 1:692.8.

[516] Ibid., 693.32ff.; cf. "Pred. über Ps. 110 vom 10.5.1535," WA 41:123.21–124.12 (AE 13:225–348).

is used by the Lord to seize seemingly invincible powers of destruction; He overpowers them precisely by means of the suffering on the cross.[517] This paradox is reflected in the existence of the Christian: "As far as the left side is concerned, according to the outer nature, Christ and His people are suffering and unsettled under the enemies, and God is not with him but abandons him; but, as far as the right side is concerned, according to the inner human nature, he is among friends in comfort and peace, and God is with him and stands by him."[518]

In his numerous sermons on the ascension, based on the additions to the Gospel of Mark (Mark 16:14–20), in which he consistently refers back to the words from the psalms of the Old Testament, Pss. 2:7; 8:6; 68:19; 110:1,[519] as well as in the corresponding commentaries on the Psalms,[520] the reformer sketches out the ramifications of the "*Pro nobis*," as it applies to the ascension: Christ "has gone up toward heaven, not that He Himself can take a seat there, but so that He can reign there, all for our benefit, so that we have comfort and joy thereby."[521] He had to remove Himself from our sight physically precisely so that He could be completely close to us, in order to continue to wage the battle with us and in us against the powers of death. He comes to us through the open proclamation of the Gospel, which runs its course throughout the entire world until the last day, and He summons all human beings to come face to face with Him, leaving none free of responsibility, so that even the non-human creatures are placed under His lordship.[522] The exalted one thus does

---

[517] WA 1:693.37–695.7; "Pred. über Ps. 110 vom 8.5.1535," WA 41:109.8–115.7 (AE 13:225–348).

[518] WA 1:704; cf. "Himmelfahrtspred. vom 17.5.1520," WA 9:457.1–16.

[519] See the texts on pp. 206–207.

[520] Especially the explication of Psalm 110 in sermons from 1535, WA 41:79–239 (AE 13:225–348).

[521] "Pred. über Mk. 16:14–20 vom 14.5.1523," WA 12:563.27; cf. ibid., 562.19–27; 564.16–21; 565.18–21; "Pred. über Lk. 1:26ff. vom 23.3.1521," WA 9:631.26ff.; "Pred. über Mk. 16:14–20 vom 5.5.1524," WA 15:553.27–554.14; "Pred. über Mk. 16:14–20 vom 10.5.1526," WA 20:382.25–383.22; "Pred. über Mk. 16:14–20 vom 30.5.1538," WA 46:390.14–20.

[522] On Mark 16:15: "Pred. vom 14.5.1523," WA 12:556.9–24; "Pred. vom 5.5.1524," WA 15:550.20–25; "Pred. vom 25.5.1525," WA 17.1:257.19–258.4; "Pred. vom 10.5.1526," WA 20:384, 19–23; "Pred. über Mk. 16:15ff. vom 18.5.1531," WA 34.1:412–22; "Pred. über Mk. 16:15ff. vom 18.5.1531," WA 34.1:412–22; "Pred. über Ps. 110 vom 5.6.1535," WA 41:196.36–197.14 (AE 13:225–348); ibid., 197.9:

not "slumber" and "is not idle, but is working down below, gifting to His own the Holy Spirit, so that one can preach, baptize, forgive sins, comfort the people, which causes the devil to break out in a sweat."[523] At the same time, the Lord preserves the temporal estates and orders against the attack of the powers of chaos, "to the consternation of the devil."[524]

This emphasis on the actively engaged nearness of the God-Man, here below on earth in our Christian life, provides for Luther a foundation for his disputes with Zwingli and Oecolampadius, by means of the so-called "doctrine of ubiquity."[525] As was the case already with Augustine, being followed by the Scholastics of the Middle Ages, the right [hand] of God is not to be identified as a cosmographic place without borders, but as the "almighty power of God, which can be simultaneously nowhere and yet everywhere."[526] Christ Himself, in His human nature, participated in this majestic nearness of the creator. This "divine, heavenly manner"[527] of being present is depicted by Luther by means of a unique substitution of one subject for another. He asks: according to this, is it not possible that Christ could "be so wonderfully in all creatures, not so that they can measure or comprehend Him, but rather, that He is present and can measure and comprehend them?"[528] The mediator of creation does not present Himself to His creatures; He brings the creatures into His own presence and summons them, one might say, to appear before Himself. The unique reversal of direction is coupled with the thesis

---

"Just as He physically wandered from one city to another and preached . . . , He has thus not ceased to wander throughout the world with His Gospel, up to the last day."

[523] "Pred. vom 30.5.1538," WA 46:394.6.

[524] WA 46:394.11.

[525] On this, see "Sermon von dem Sakrament des Leibes und Blutes Wider die Schwarmgeister vom 28. u. 29.3.1526," WA 19:486–501 (AE 36:329–361); "Daß diese Worte Christi noch fest stehen, 1527," WA 23:129.20–153.20 (AE 37:3–150); "Vom Abendmahl Christi, 1528," WA 26:326.22–342.27 (AE 37:151–372). In addition to the literature mentioned on p. 83, n. 178, see also Elert, *Morphologie*, 1:220ff., 363–93; Mahlmann, *Das neue Dogma der luth. Christologie*, esp. 167–75; Lienhard, *Martin Luthers christologisches Zeugnis*, 156f., 164, 172–75, 185–89, 250, 284, 287.

[526] "Daß diese Worte Christi noch fest stehen, 1527," WA 23:133.21 (AE 37:3–150).

[527] "Vom Abendmahl Christi, 1528," WA 26:329.27ff.; 336.8ff (AE 37:151–372).

[528] WA 26:336.13; cf. ibid., 337.15–31 (AE 37:151–372).

that God and Christ are "immovable."[529] Even at this point Luther follows the tradition that was expressed precisely by Thomas Aquinas[530] and he transfers that over to Christ: The exalted one does not present Himself, time and again, before us, only to disappear again; His presence is not linked to movement within space and time. By means of His Word and Sacrament, He reveals Himself and gives of Himself freely, more in the sense of the present *Kyrios* who is present already in His creative majesty.

This understanding of the real presence of Christ works backward to influence Luther's view of the ascension. Luther does not shy away from speaking about a physical journey upward for Jesus; as a "down feather," He was taken upward, out of the view of His own.[531] But from another angle, the ascension for Luther is not specifically about that physical disappearance of Jesus; this is only an "external manifestation" and a visible sign for the lordly rule of Christ that remains invisible.[532] The reality that is manifested in such signs, the life of Christ in His human nature, before and in God, as well as the participation of His human nature in the worldwide reign of God, was present already before His resurrection, in fact already at the time of His incarnation. Luther refers at this point to the gloss in John 3:13:[533] "who is in heaven," which played a certain role in the tradition already.[534] Luther thereby ameliorates to some extent the Augustinian tension implicit in the *Sursum corda*!; the upper sanctuary, the "place of the Trinity," loses its luster as the source from which creation,

---

[529] "Daß diese Worte Christi noch fest stehen, 1527," WA 23:147.25 (AE 37:3–150): "Do not think so much about up and down, not about going here and there, since God is immovable and Christ also sits at the right side of God and does not move about."
[530] See the summary by Martensen, "Ubiquitätslehre."
[531] "Pred. über Apg. 1:1ff. vom 17.5.1531," WA 34.1:406.3: "That would have been a strange appearance and sight and would have seemed adventuresome, that one would go up thus into the air, as a down feather, in the flesh and even up to the clouds"; ibid., 409.9: "It is a fine appearance, because He would have ascended externally. And the trip would not have taken all that long, until He came into heaven, for when He comes into the cloud, He is away already."
[532] Ibid., 406–11; "Pred. vom 10.5.1526," WA 20:382.10–19; "Pred. vom 30.5.1538," WA 46:390.14–20; 392.1–4; "Pred. über Apg. 1:1ff. vom 22.5.1544," WA 49:418.1–20.
[533] On this, see passages such as "Pred. über Joh. 3:1ff. vom 22.5.1524," WA 15:569.21–34; "Pred. über Joh. 3:13ff. vom 27.5.1526," WA 20:428.3–38; "Daß diese Worte Christi noch fest stehen, 1527," WA 23:147.28–149.14 (AE 37:3–150); "Vom Abendmahl Christi, 1528," WA 26:343.35–346.27 (AE 37:151–372).
[534] Cf. Landgraf, *DG der Frühscholastik*, 2.1:138–46.

redemption, and new creation stream forth.[535] Christ's journey is recast by Luther almost into a new form of incarnation; as lord of all lords and king of all kings, Christ establishes His rule from the cross right here, down below on earth, among us human beings; over and over again He drives back the destroying forces of sin, the world, the law, death and the devil, which have been robbed of their power already, until on the last day He will cast them down, once and for all, into the abyss of destruction.[536]

"Heaven," as the spiritual "place" where Christ is present at the right side of the Father, does gain in importance for the reformer when it comes to unfolding the priestly role of the exalted one.[537] In the final analysis, Christ's constant intercession before the holy God is more important for Luther than is Christ's victory over the powers of death, as we pointed out earlier; the question of power is finally resolved when the question about guilt is resolved.[538] Christ did not merely take our guilt upon Himself one time only and "pay with His suffering" for us. He comes forward daily for us before God "as a faithful, merciful intermediary, savior, and unique priest and bishop of our souls."[539] Because He "offers and shows His body and blood . . . before God daily, on our behalf, we may obtain grace."[540] His sacrifice is not something in the past; it protects us still, in the here and now, from the accusation of the holy law and opens for us free

---

[535] At this point, Barth, *Kirchliche Dogmatik* 2.1:495–551, esp. 534f.

[536] "Pred. vom 14.5.1523," WA 12:563.16–29; 565.1–11; "Pred. vom 5.5.1524," WA 15.553.31–554.14; "Pred. vom 10.5.1526," WA 20:382.25–32; "Pred. vom 21.5.1528," WA 27:139.2–141.8; "Pred. vom 18.5.1531," WA 34.1:428.6–430.3; "Pred. vom 30.5.1538," WA 46:394.3–12.

[537] On Christ's ongoing office as priest, see "Hebr.-Vorl., 1517–18," on Hebr. 9:14, 24, WA 57.3:207.7–209.27; 215.15–218.15 (AE 29:107–241); "Ausl. von Ps. 110, 1518," WA 1:702.20–704.18; "Pred. 'nova et vetus lex' vom 21.12.1519," WA 9:439.1–12; "Ein Sermon von dem neuen Testament, 1520," WA 6:368.26–370.34 (AE 35:75–111); "Von der Freiheit eines Christenmenschen, 1520," WA 7:27.3–16 (AE 31:327–377); "De libertate christiana, 1520," WA 7:56.18–34 (AE 31:327–377); "Grund und Ursach aller Artikel, 1521," WA 7:345.1–8 (AE 32:3–99); "Pred. über 1 Petr. 2, 1522/23," WA 12:306–22 (AE 30:1–145); "Fastenpost. zu Hebr. 9:11–16, 1525," WA 17.2:227–31; "Pred. über Eph. 4:8–10 vom 31.5.1527," WA 23:715f.; "Pred. über 1 Tim. 1:5ff. vom 24.11.1532," WA 36:366.6–367.37 (AE 51:257–287); "Gal.-Komm., 1535," on Gal. 2:20, WA 40.1:297.7–299.2 (AE 26:1–461); "Pred. über Ps. 110 vom 30.5 u. 5.6.1535," WA 41:174–203 (AE 13:225–348); Kinder, *Christus als Hohepriester*.

[538] Cf. pp. 161f.

[539] "Vom Abendmahl Christi, 1528," WA 26:502.32 (AE 37:151–372).

[540] "Deutsche Messe, 1526," WA 19:100.1 (AE 53:51–90).

access to God's fatherly heart, now by means of confident prayer and, in the future, when by sight we will offer up our adoration. Christ, as the exalted high priest, provides protection from the divine wrath of the holy God.[541] This is the only way He can shelter us, as the exalted king, at the same time, from the onslaughts of the powers that bring destruction; this sequence is not reversible,[542] since the powers of death were able to win access and power over us only because of the wrath of God. Despite this, Christ's service as priest receives slight mention in the catechisms, where Luther places Christ as victor front and center.

The tension between the "heaven" above, as the "place" of the enduring priestly service of Christ, and the earth here below, as the battle ground for His kingly rule, as well as that between the wandering of the faithful, far from the Lord, and their rights as citizens now already, up above in heaven, is bridged by Luther when he uses the following paradoxical dictum: "He is here by us and therefore is seated in heaven, so that He can be close by us; we are thus by Him up there and He is by us down here: through the sermon He comes down, and thus, by faith, we come up."[543]

4. Christ's Return for Judgment[544]

The Lord's return is articulated in the *Textus receptus* by means of the phrase: "*inde venturus est iudicare vivos et mortuos* (from there He will come to judge the living and dead)." Luther initially translates this similarly to the way it is rendered in Mirror of the Christian Man from (1510): "From there He is to judge the living and the dead in the future";[545] it is only in the reworked text of the catechisms that he

---

541 "Pred. über Ps. 110 vom 5.6.1535," WA 41:192.6 (AE 13:225–348): "and does not stop even until the last day, who sits at the right hand of the Father and presents the same offering, His body, to the Father, without pause. In eternity our Lord God will look upon that offering."

542 This corresponds to the fact that the document about freedom says that the participation of the Christian in His priestly office is of more import than is that of His royal rule, WA 7:28.6–25; 57.24–58.3 (AE 31:327–377).

543 "Pred. vom 14.5.1523," WA 12:565.18.

544 For texts and literature about Jesus' return, see p. 207.

545 "Eine kurze Form, 1520," WA 7:217.3; "Betbüchlein," WA 10.2:391.13 (AE 43:3–45); cf. Melanchthon's *Enchiridion* (MGP 20:32.32); the "Buchlein für die Laien und Kinder"; ibid., 203.34, and *BSLK*, 556.10 (Preface to the Large Catechism). For other ways to express the "*inde*," see Meyer, *Historischer Kommentar*, 94.

formulates it:[546] "from there He will come to judge the living and the dead."[547] Already in the fourteenth century, older German translations that had rendered "*iudicare*" as "pass sentence"[548] were either expanded to include, or replaced that with, "judge"[549]; Luther does the same. The new ecumenical rendering in German breaks the statement into two parts and starts afresh: "From there He will come, to judge the living and the dead."

Christ's return to judge is given some slight mention in the Small Catechism; Luther concentrates thereby almost solely on the one who believes and confesses, who in one respect is living already under the lordship of Christ and who is already serving "in eternal righteousness, innocence, and blessedness,"[550] but who in another respect is still living among all the dead, yearning in hope for the physical resurrection and hoping to receive eternal life "with all the dead in Christ."[551] According to the Large Catechism, the lordly rule of Christ reaches its full form on the Day of Judgment. Luther interprets Christ's return, in connection with the question of power, as the final time when the faithful will be torn away completely from the onslaughts of the powers of chaos, which thus serves as the *telos* of Christ's becoming Lord.[552]

In the Short Form of 1520, just as in the Confession of 1528, the reformer places greater emphasis on both sides of the judgment character, by means of which God will either welcome in or cast out; this corresponds to the confessional tradition from which sprang forth the *Regula fidei*.[553] "Finally, I believe in the resurrection of all the dead on the last day, both the pious and the evil, so that each one receives in his own body that which he deserves, and thus the pious will live eternally with Christ and the evil will die eternally with the

---

[546] Meyer, *Historischer Kommentar*, 94, refers at this point to the "reflective book" that the laity could use to guide one in confessing, from ca. 1498; Geffcken, *Bildercatechismus*, 148ff.

[547] *BSLK*, 511.19–21 (SC); 651.7–9 (LC).

[548] Hahn, *Bibliothek*, §§ 95, 100–03, 105, 106, 108, 109, 111, 112, 114, 115.

[549] Ibid., §§ 116, 117.

[550] *BSLK*, 511.35f.

[551] *BSLK*, 512.11f.

[552] *BSLK*, 652.25–653.3.

[553] Irenaeus, *Adversus haereses* 1:10; Tertullian, *De praescriptione haereticorum* 13; Denzinger, 443, 485, 801, 859, and often elsewhere.

devil and his angels."[554] Whereas Luther takes more time in his confessions to deal with the "objective elements of the faith," in the catechisms he concentrates more on the conflict of Christ with the powers of chaos. Within this framework, as is described in John 5:24, the believer appears as one over whom the Lord has spoken His final Yes already;[555] judgment applies to such a person no longer. About such a one, it is more correct to say that Christ hurries in as his legal defender to afford aid and to drive back his opponents.

Behind this interpretation of how the New Testament describes the judgment stands Luther's curt rejection of the sermons preached concerning that judgment during the late Middle Ages. The form taken when referring to judging the living and the dead appears to have been fixed already in the New Testament.[556] Irenaeus's depiction of this scene in his summary of the *Regula fidei* left a lasting impression, and it has been passed on through the tradition of the Church: Christ "will hold a just judgment for everyone. He will send to the eternal fire the spirits of evil and the disobedient angels that fell away from God, along with the godless and unrighteous and criminals and those who mock God. With His grace, however, He will give eternal life as a gift to the righteous and the pious and to those who obeyed His commandments and who remained in His love, some from the beginning and some after they repented, and He will freely give them eternal life by grace and clothe them with eternal glory."[557] Based on the model of the *Regula fidei*, the confessions that were written later for the purpose of instruction characterize the *eschata* in terms of an apocalyptic vision of the end time, when Christ returns for judgment;[558] the dogmatic Scholastic explanations of the faith put this

---

[554] "Vom Abendmahl Christi, 1528," WA 26:509.13 (AE 37:151–372). "Eine kurze Form, 1520," WA 7:218.13–19, connects the judgment with our deliverance from the tyranny of the destructive powers; cf., as well, AC XVII and Schwabach Article 13 (*BSLK*, 72).

[555] "Pred. über Joh. 6:54 vom 1.4.1531," WA 33:222.40 (AE 23:1–197): "The number of hours yet to pass make no difference, if you dare to believe it, as this relates to the last day; the point is that one cannot yet see it or feel it, and you will have no more on the last day than now. For the flesh and blood of Christ are mine in this hour already; such is present and lives, as it will be alive on the last day as well; it is my food in the present already, though I do not detect it, for it is hidden in faith and is still in secret."

[556] Especially Acts 10:42; 1 Pet. 4:5; 2 Tim. 4:1.

[557] Irenaeus, *Adversus haereses* 1:10 (cited according to BKV 3.33).

[558] See the texts cited on p. 196, n. 541 and passages such as AC XVII (*BSLK*, 72); *Confessio Belgica*, art. 37.

into fixed form within the framework of the following topics: *de mortuorum resurrectione* (*ad vitam—ad iudicium*) —*de consummatione mundi—de iudicio extremo—de damnatione et de vita aeterna.* (Concerning the resurrection of the dead [for life—for judgment]—concerning the consummation of the world—concerning the last judgment—concerning damnation and eternal life). By contrast, the sermons on the Creed concentrate more extensively on the apostolic message about Christ's role as judge; they differentiate both aspects thereby: acceptance and rejection, judgment and grace. Irenaeus thus had written already: "The same God who judges is also the Father who summons to be saved; to one He gives the gift of eternal light and allows those who wear no wedding garment to be cast out into outer darkness. The same Lord, who is the Father of our Lord, who sent the prophets, on account of His unending goodness, calls those who are unworthy, but also looks to determine whether those who are called are wearing a suitable garment, as is appropriate for His Son's marriage.[559] Augustine accentuates this tension more on the description of Christ as our judge and advocate.[560] He teaches: the same one whom we await as our Lord and judge at some time in the future is the one who serves already as our defender and advocate before the Father, for which reason we dare to have hope.[561] But he underscores, as well, the enduring fear: The Lord will openly reveal His final, all-encompassing judgment, for which reason we are to live in fear because of His judgment and thus live, as is appropriate because of our baptism, so that we may obtain the blessing of the Father.[562]

The sermons passed down under the name of Augustine place greater emphasis on the aspect of judgment.[563] The paraphrases of the Symbols from the Middle Ages thus place their emphasis on the

---

[559] Irenaeus, *Adversus haereses* 4:36.6 (cited according to BKV 4:129f.).

[560] See the summary in Eichenseer, *Apostolicum*, 327–36.

[561] Augustine, *Sermo* 215.7; 213.5 (Morin, *Sermones*, 446): "*Advocatum eum (Christum) habemus, et iudicem time(a)mus? Immo, quia advocatum praemisimus, secure iudicem venturum speremus.*"

[562] Cf. Eichenseer, *Apostolicum*, 334.

[563] Pseudo-augustine, *Sermo* 249–51 (PL 39:2206–10). Looking up to the judge drives us to penitence and to acts of love; God through Christ will help us thereby: "He who created us assists us, so that we will be worthy to come through to the heavenly kingdom, through Christ our Lord." (*Sermo* 250.2, PL 39:2210). And yet there are mere hints (esp. *Sermo* 249.3) that direct our attention to the fact that the judge is the one who offers Himself for us.

accounting that we are to render before God, as well as on the contrite confession of sin: I believe that I am to stand and am to give a reckoning about everything that I have ever done, for which reason I have come to confession and have been given acts of penance, and have a desire for grace and for righteousness."[564] Thomas Aquinas says nothing about the joy of that "beloved final day" as the day of our deliverance;[565] in his exposition of the Apostles' Creed, by contrast, he enumerates four reasons to come in fear because Christ is our judge, His wisdom and might, His unchanging righteousness, and His holy wrath;[566] opposite these he places four means for salvation, good works and acts of contrition, alms, and love for God and the neighbor.[567] Even though Thomas Aquinas knew, as well, that the poor in spirit would not come under judgment,[568] he concentrated instead on Augustine's preaching that was based on the dictum: time for us now is a time for divine mercy; in the future, there will be only God's time, as the time of His strict judgment.[569] Such a juxtaposition—now grace—then judgment—is found frequently in the creedal interpretations of the late Middle Ages;[570] the proclamation bears down directly on the Christians when handled thus.

This type of sermon—Christ at this point is still the gracious provider of mercy, in the future the strict judge!—cast Luther to the depths during his horrific agonizing struggles; future judgment based on our works seemed to call into question once again the deliverance to be afforded by Christ's grace from the perspective of the eschaton.[571] Unlike what is taught by Neo-Protestantism, Luther held

---

[564] Hahn, *Bibliothek*, § 117; cf. ibid., §§ 106, 107, 109, 110, 112, 115.

[565] Pesch, *Rechtf. bei Luther u. Thomas*, 838f., points this out.

[566] Thomas Aquinas, *Expositio in Symbolum Apostolorum*, §§ 953–56.

[567] Ibid., § 957.

[568] Ibid., § 952.

[569] Ibid., § 955: "*Nunc enim est tempus misericordiae; sed tempus futurum erit solum tempus iustitiae: et ideo nunc est tempus nostrum, sed tunc erit solum tempus Dei*"; cf. idem, *Summa theologiae* III, q. 59.

[570] As in Dietrich Koldes, *Christenspiegel*, 56.11: "I believe also that God is wonderfully gracious during this time as well. I believe as well that He is now in this time a very strict judge over the four corners of the earth."

[571] This has not been sufficiently recognized in the analyses of the so-called "tower experience"; In the Scholien [Tr.: marginal notes] to Psalm 71, Luther still sees the future advent of Christ solely as He comes "as a severe judge and with eternal vengeance" ("Dict. super Psalt., 1513–16," WA 3:462.6 [AE 10:1–464]); cf. Lohse (ed.), *Der Durchbruch der reformatorischen Erkenntnis bei Luther*.

fast to what is taught in the New Testament and in the Church's tradition. The exalted one will summon all flesh to appear before Him, face to face. But this Lord and judge will differ in no way from the one and the same person who gave His life over, once for all, in order to save His own. He holds the offering He made on the cross, which is completely satisfactory for sin, continuously before the holy God. Christ's eternal, condemnatory judgment is upon every creature at enmity with God, surrounding us but within us as well; but to those who believe in Him He appears as an advocate and as a legal defender to afford aid. Luther describes this without any flowery language, quite drastically: "Even though He will be a judge, yet He is a comfort and salvation for me too, so that He can protect me against my enemies and can damn those who refuse to believe and who do not consider Him to be their Lord. Briefly stated, this means that there is one who can cast all wrath, judgment, and punishment away from us as well, to be imposed upon His enemies, the devil and all his arrows and against your own evil thoughts about Christ."[572] We thus ought not to set up a dichotomy that separates the here and now from the then and there. Whoever claims Christ as his Lord in the here and now will be welcomed in by Him in the then and there; whoever spurns Christ in the here and now will be cast out by Him then.[573] The day of eternal judgment is the day of complete mercy, since the Lord will rush in to aid His own when everything is on the line and will rip them completely from the grasp of Satan. "It is our comfort that, in the twinkling of an eye, we will be removed from the godless host, physically as well, as we are spiritually removed already at this time from the power of the devil, and He will say to us: Here is your patron, your Father, which will be pure joy and delight."[574]

---

[572] "Torgauer Pred. vom 16./17.4.1533," WA 37:51.21; cf. ibid., 51:14–37; "Eine treue Vermahnung, sich zu hüten vor Aufruhr und Empörung, 1522," WA 8:677.20–678.3 (AE 45:51–74); "Pred. über Joh. 6:37–39 vom 14.1.1531," WA 33:87.22–90.22 (AE 23:1–197); "Pred. über Joh. 8:12–15 vom 7.10.1531," WA 33:538.31–543.9 (AE 23:198–422); "Gal.-Komm., 1535," WA 40.1:92.2–93.8; 297.7–299.2 (AE 26:1–461); "Ennaratio Jes. 53, 1544," WA 40.3:719.7–720.22; "Pred. über Ps. 110 vom 5.6.1535," WA 41:197.5–203.5 (AE 13:225–348).

[573] Cf. passages such as "Pred. über 1 Thess. 4:15ff. vom 11.5.1525," WA 17.1:221.11f.

[574] WA 17.1:226.5; "Pred. über Joh. 6:37–39 vom 14.1.1531," WA 33:90.17 (AE 1–197): "The rainbow on which He will ride helps me toward salvation; He will take hold of you and will not cast you away and will also protect you against the devil"; "Pred. über Joh. 8:12–15 vom 7.10.1531," WA 33:540.17 (AE 23:198–422): "On the

For this reason, true Christians must tirelessly beseech their Lord to return, as we do in the Lord's Prayer;[575] with heads held high, they are to run as fast as possible toward that day of judgment (Luke 21:28), which even Christ Himself describes as our redemption, "that is, not death, but eternal life, no wrath, but pure grace, no hell, but the kingdom of heaven, neither terror nor danger, but pure comfort and joy."[576]

Texts and Literature on How the Early Church's Teaching about the Two Natures is Used

WA 10.1.1:142–80, 180–247: Weihnachtspostille 1522 on Hebr. 1:1–12 and Joh. 1:1–14 (AE 52:41–88)

WA 10.1.1:443–48: Weihnachtspostille 1522 on Lk. 2:40 (AE 52:102–148)

WA 20:344–48, 353–63: Predigten über die testimonia scripturae zu Gen. 22:18 u. Ex. 3:1–6, from 2. and 3.4.1526

WA 20:348–53: Predigt über Lk. 24:36ff., from 3.4.1526

WA 23:131.7–149.14; 155.7–159.19: "Daß diese Wort Christi noch fest stehen wider die Schwarmgeister," 1527 (AE 37:3–150)

WA 26:317.21–346.27: "Vom Abendmahl Christi," 1528 (AE 37:151–372)

WA 39.2:3–5: Thesen zur Disputatio de sententia: Verbum caro factum est (Joh. 1:14), from 11.1.1539 (AE 38:235–277)

WA 39.2:92–121: Disputatio de divinitate et humanitate Christi, from 28.2.1540

WA 40.3:702.33–708.35: Enarratio 53. cap. Esaiae, 1544 (1550)

WA 43:579.7–582.29; WA 44:93.34–94.5: Genesisvorlesung, 1535–1545 (AE 5:1–386)

WA 46:541.1–562.3: Auslegung des 1. u. 2. Kapitels Johannis in Predigten, 1537–38 (AE 22:1–530)

WA 50:262–83: Drei Symbola oder Bekenntnis des Glaubens Christi, 1538 (AE 34:197–229)

WA 50:581–605: "Von den Konziliis und Kirchen," 1539 (AE 41:3–178)

---

last day He will judge, but as a savior, who will help me and will turn everything that gave me grief upside down."

[575] See Volume 3 on the Last Petition of the Lord's Prayer.

[576] "Pred. über Lk. 21:25–29 vom 10.12.1531," WA 34.2:478.27; cf. ibid., 479.20–30.

WA 54:49.5–50.12; 89.5–91.14: "Von den letzten Worten Davids," 1543 (AE 15:265–352)

LITERATURE

Althaus, *Theologie Luthers*, 159–95.

Asendorf, *Gekreuzigt und Auferstanden. Luthers Herausforderung an die moderne Christologie.*

H. M. Barth, *Der Teufel und Jesus Christus in der Theologie Martin Luthers.*

Bohlin, *Der korsfästa Skaparen.*

K. Bornkamm, *Luthers Auslegungen des Galaterbriefes von 1519 und 1531.*

Buchrucker, *Nullus Diabolus—Nullus Redemptor. Die Bedeutung des Teufels für die Theologie Martin Luthers.*

Burba, *Die Christologie in Luthers Liedern.*

Congar, *Regards et réflexions sur la christologie de Luther.*

Ellwein, *Summus Evangelista: Die Botschaft des Johannesevangeliums in der Auslegung Luthers.*

_____. *Die Christusverkündigung in Luthers Auslegung des Johannes-evangeliums.*

Gennrich, *Die Christologie Luthers im Abendmahlsstreit.*

Th. Harnack, *Luthers Theologie*, 2.

Iserloh, *Sacramentum und Exemplum. Ein augustinisches Thema lutherischer Theologie.*

Iwand, *Rechtfertigungslehre und Christusglaube.*

Josefson, *Christus und die hl. Schrift.*

Kadai, *Luther's Theology of the Cross*

Kantzenbach, *Christusgemeinschaft und Rechtfertigung. Luthers Gedanke vom fröhlichen Wechsel.*

Lienhard, *Martin Luthers christologisches Zeugnis. Entwicklung und Grundzüge seiner Christologie.*

_____. *Les cantiques de Luther et leur témoignage christologique.*

Lohse, *Luthers Christologie im Ablaßstreit.*

Mahlmann, *Das neue Dogma der lutherischen Christologie.*

Maurer, *Von der Freiheit eines Christenmenschen.*

_____. *Die Anfänge von Luthers Theologie. Eine Anfrage an die lutherische Kirche.*

_____. *Die Einheit der Theologie Luthers.*

Müller, *Luthers Christusverständnis.*

Nilsson, *Das Miteinander von Göttlichem und Menschlichem in Luthers Theologie*, 151–260.

Peters, *Luthers Christuszeugnis als Zusammenfassung der Christusbotschaft der Kirche.*

Ritschl, *Die christliche Lehre von der Rechtfertigung und Versöhnung.*

Schwarz, *Gott ist Mensch. Zur Lehre von der Person Christi bei den Ockhamisten und bei Luther.*

E. Seeberg, *Luthers Theologie*, 2.

Siggins, *Martin Luther's Doctrine of Christ.*

Thomasius, *Christi Person und Werk.*

Vogelsang, *Die Anfänge von Luthers Christologie.*

_____. *Der angefochtene Christus bei Luther.*

Vorländer, *Deus incarnatus. Die Zweinaturenchristologie Luthers bis 1521.*

Wolf, *Die Christusverkündigung bei Luther.*

TEXTS AND LITERATURE ON "JESUS CHRIST AS THE REDEEMER" (Since it would not be possible to cite a large number of texts, only some are mentioned, primarily those that deal with the battle against the powers of death)

WA 10.1:365.12–367.6: Weihnachtspostille 1522 on Gal. 4:1–7

WA 23:699–725: Predigt über Eph. 4:8–10 (Christi Kampf mit den Gewalten), from 31.5.1527

WA 32:39–47: Predigt über den Kampf Christi mit den Gewalten, from 17.4.1530

WA 40.1:438.5–443.11; 564.5–570.12: Galaterbriefkommentar, 1535 (AE 26:1–461)

WA 40.3:741.22–744.34: Enarratio 53. cap. Esaiae, 1544 (Christ under the law)

LITERATURE (see what is above, as well)

Alpers, *Die Versöhnung durch Christus.*

Aulen, *Den kristna försoningstanken.*

_____. *Die drei Typen der christlichen Versöhnungslehre.*

Billing, *Försoningen.*

Bring, *Dualismen hos Luther*

Lindroth, *Försoningen. En dogmhistorick och systematisk undersökning.*

Tiililä, *Das Strafleiden Christi.*

Turner, *The Patristic Doctrine of Redemption.*

TEXTS AND LITERATURE ON LUTHER'S VIEW ABOUT SIN

WA 56:157.1–159.24; 259.8–261.9; 286.11–291.14; 312.1–317.12; 339.4–357.26: Römerbriefvorlesung, 1515–16 (AE 25:1–524)

WA 1:224–28: Disputatio contra scholasticam theologiam, from 4.9.1517 (AE 31:3–16)

WA 1:185–94: Sieben Bußpsalmen, 1517, on Ps. 51

WA 8:43–128: Rationis Latominianae . . . confutatio, 1521 (AE 32:133–260)

WA 10.1.1:507.14–509.16: Weihnachtspostille 1522 on Lk. 2:21 (AE 52:149–158)

WA 18:683.11–691.39; 733.22–764.34; 770.20–785.19: "De servo arbitrio," 1525 (AE 33:3–295)

WA 31.1:538–43: Entwurf zu Ps 51

WA 39.1:109–18: Disputatio de iustificatione, from 14.1 (10.10.) 1536 (AE 34:145–196)

WA 39.1:175–80: Disputatio de homine, from 14.1.1536 (AE 34:133–144)

WA 40.2:322.6–327.10; 378.5–385.10: Enarratio Ps. 51, 1538 (AE 12:197–410)

BSLK, 433.11–435.16: from the Smalcald Articles, 1537

LITERATURE

Althaus, *Paulus und Luther über den Menschen.*

Hermann, *Zu Luthers Lehre von Sünde und Rechtfertigung.*

Iwand, "Sed originale per hominem unum."

Kinder, *Die Erbsünde nach der Lehre der ev.-luth. Bekenntnisschriften.*

Ljunggren, *Synd och skuld i Luthers teologi.*

Schott, *Fleisch und Geist nach Luthers Lehre.*

TEXTS AND LITERATURE ON THE INCARNATION AND THE VIRGIN BIRTH

Luther texts are most importantly to be found in Mülhaupt, *Ev.-Auslegung*, 1 (Weihnachts- und Vorgeschichten bei Mt und Lk); 4 (Joh.-Ev.), 1–86.

Düfel, *Luthers Stellung zur Marienverehrung.*

Ellwein, *Summus Evangelista.*

Hendry, *The Gospel of the Incarnation.*

Von Loewenich, *Luther als Ausleger der Synoptiker.*

Pittenger, *The Word Incarnate*

TEXTS AND LITERATURE ON THE JOURNEY TO HELL

WA 5:462.29–463.35: *Operationes in Psalmos* 1518–21, on Ps. 16:10

WA 7:217.31–218.3: "Eine kurze Form des Glaubens," 1520

WA 12:367–71, 375–76: Predigten über 1 Petr. 3f., 1523 (AE 30:1–145)

WA 31.1:318.15–36: Coburger Auslegung der ersten 25 Psalmen, 1530, on Ps. 16:10f.

WA 36:159–161.17: Predigt über Christi Auferstehung, from 31.3.1532

WA 37:62–67.13 (= WA 36:159ff.): Torgauer Predigt von Jesu Christo, from 16/17.4.1533

WA 42:322.19–323.17: Genesisvorlesung, 1535–45, on 1 Pet. 3:19 (AE 2:1–399)

WA 46:305–13: Predigt über Christi Höllenfahrt, from 20.4.1538

LITERATURE

Althaus, *Niedergefahren zur Hölle.*

Lindroth, *Descendit ad inferna.*

Peters, *Glaube und Werk*, 240–49.

Vogelsang, *Luthers Torgauer Predigt von Jesu Christo.*

_____. *Weltbild und Kreuzestheologie in den Höllenfahrtsstreitigkeiten der Reformationszeit.*

_____. *Der angefochtene Christus bei Luther*, 44ff., 80ff.

TEXTS ON THE JOURNEY TO HEAVEN AND THE RULE OF CHRIST

WA 1:690–710: Auslegung des 110. Psalms, 1518

WA 9:453–59: Predigt über Apg. 1, from 17/18.5.1520

WA 12:555–65: Predigt über Mk. 16:14ff., from 14.5.1523

WA 17.1:256–59: Predigt über Mk. 16:14ff., from 25.5.1525

WA 20:382–85: Predigt über Mk. 16:14ff., from 10.5.1526

WA 27:131–41: Predigt über Mk. 16:14ff., from 21.5.1528

WA 34.1:412–30: Predigt über Mk. 16:15ff., from 18.5.1531

WA 37:77–82: Predigt über Mk. 16:15ff., from 22.5.1533

WA 46:389–94: Predigt über Mk. 16:14ff., from 30.5.1538

WA 41:79–239: 8 Predigten über Ps. 110, from 8.5. to 13.6.1535 (AE 13:225–348)

A selection of these can be found in Mülhaupt, *Ev.-Auslegung*, 5:458–71, 478–83; cf. idem, *Ps.-Auslegung*, 3:192–256 (on Psalm 110); 1:26–44 (on Psalm 2); 123–44 (on Psalm 8); 2:316–49 (on Psalm 68).

Texts and Literature on the Return of Jesus

WA 8:676–680: "Eine treue Vermahnung . . . sich zu hüten vor Aufruhr und Empörung," 1522 (AE 45:51–74)

WA 17.1:196–227: Predigt über 1 Thess. 4:13ff., from 10/11.5.1525

WA 33:87.22–90.22: Predigt über Joh. 6:37, from 14.1.1531 (AE 23:1–197)

WA 33:538.31–543.9: Predigt über Joh. 8:14f., from 7.10.1531 (AE 23:198–422)

WA 34.2:459–82: Predigt über Lk. 21:25ff., from 10.12.1531

WA 45:324–29: Predigt über Mt. 25:31–46, from 25.11.1537

Literature

Asendorf, *Eschatologie bei Luther* (see literature citations!).

Düfel, *Luthers Stellung zur Marienverehrung*, 65–69.

Hardeland, *Katechismusgedanken*, 234–37.

Joest, *Ontologie der Person bei Luther*, 320–53.

Meyer, *Historischer Kommentar*, 306ff.

Modalsli, *Das Gericht nach den Werken*, 128–37.

THE THIRD ARTICLE ABOUT GOD'S SPIRIT AS THE ONE WHO MAKES US HOLY IN THE PROPER FAITH IN CHRIST

LUTHER'S QUEST FOR AN APPROPRIATE CATECHETICAL FORM OF COMMENTARY ON THE THIRD ARTICLE[1]

The Third Article of the faith was crystallized in the early Church era only late in time; the situation is similar for Luther, whose catechetical interpretation achieves a sharply detailed form for the first time in the sermon preached on December 10, 1528. Luther transfers the structure that he used to interpret the Second Article to provide the framework for the Third Article. The early Church had inserted into the Creed its teaching about the story of salvation; when discussing the answer to the second baptismal question, Luther says that what was articulated at that point in the Creed provides the unique "elements by means of which" Christ became our Lord, along with further teaching about what He "endured" for our salvation.[2] In the same way, when interpreting the Third Article, he mentions those "elements" that are attributed to the Spirit: the Church, forgiveness of sins, and physical resurrection, as the means by which the Spirit carries out His work of salvation.[3] Whereas he gave brief mention concerning the individual stages of Jesus' journey in the article about Christ, referring to the "quite extensive sermons preached throughout

---

[1] Literature on this: Reischle, *Die katechetische Behandlung des dritten Artikels von Luthers KK*; Meyer, *Luthers Ringen um ein Gesamtverständnis des dritten Artikels*; ibid., *Historischer Kommentar*, 340–74 (258, n., provides references for the older literature); Hardeland, *Katechismusgedanken*, 237–69; Girgensohn, *Katechismus-Auslegung*, 1:146–62; Bohne, ". . . *nicht aus eigener Vernunft noch Kraft* . . . "

[2] "Kat.-Pred. zum 2. Art. vom 10.12.1528," WA 30.1:89.9; 90.1–3, 6–8 (AE 51:162–169); *BSLK*, 652.30–37 (LC); cf. pp. 106–107.

[3] "Kat.-Pred. zum 3. Art. vom 10.12.1528," WA 30.1:91.8 (AE 51:162–169): "*Spiritus Sanctus sanctificat* per *sequentia membra*"; cf. ibid., 91.18; 94.1; in addition, "Pred. über Joh. 14:23ff. vom 17.5.1529," WA 29:366.3–8 and *BSLK*, 654.6–13; 654.51–655.2 (LC).

the church year for more explicit instruction,"[4] he not only offers a comprehensive summary for the Third Article here; he even "goes into great detail" concerning the individual elements, since they are "not all that clear for the uninitiated."[5] The commentary on the Third Article, in the sermon on December 10, 1528,[6] as well as in the Large Catechism,[7] thus reached a length equal to the treatment of the first two articles together.

With the aid of Rufinus and Faustus of Reji[8] [Riez], as well as the tradition that was influenced by the two, the reformer had stated already in the Short Form of 1520: Along with the Son, the Holy Spirit is to be strictly distinguished from all other creatures because of the phrase "I believe *in*"; He is positioned at the side of the Creator and placed in charge of the passionately holy watchfulness of God over the First Commandment.[9] The Spirit is also to be confessed as "a true God . . . with the Father and the Son."[10] In contrast to Augustine and to his successors who passed his teaching on during the Middle Ages,[11] Luther does not mention the Holy Spirit as an initial effort to teach about the immanent Trinity; he highlights the work of the Spirit in God's act of salvation as this impacts the one confessing the faith: "With the Father, through Christ and in Christ, this is the one who works everything and makes alive,"[12] drawing all to Himself. At the conclusion, Luther summarizes what he considers must be said about the trinitarian structure of the work of salvation as expressed in this article: I do not doubt that "the Father, through the Son Jesus Christ

---

[4] *BSLK*, 653.6f. (LC).

[5] *BSLK*, 655.35f. (LC).

[6] WA 30.1:91–94 (AE 51:162–169) on 86–90.

[7] *BSLK*, 653.26–660.13 on 647.24–653.15.

[8] Rufinus, *Expositio symboli* 33:20 (CCSL 20:169): "At the same time, to emphasize the unity and identity of the Godhead in the Trinity, just as we say we believe IN GOD THE FATHER, prefixing the preposition IN, some use the form IN CHRIST HIS SON, and also IN THE HOLY SPIRIT" [Rufinus, 71]; ibid., 34:15 (CCSL 20:170): "Thus the effect of this monosyllabic preposition is to distinguish the Creator from His creatures, and to draw a boundary line between things divine and things human" [ibid., 72]; Faustus of Reji [Riez], *De Spiritu Sancto* 1f. (CSEL 21:103.10–105.11).

[9] WA 7:215.11–22.

[10] WA 7:218.25.

[11] Cf. pp. 14–20.

[12] "Eine kurze Form, 1520," WA 7:218.31.

our Lord, with and in the Holy Spirit, permits all of what is described here to be done for my benefit."[13]

In any case, the individual "elements" are placed together, one next to the other, like blocks, introduced each time afresh by "I believe that. . . ." It is not hard to see how such elements are related. The Church is gathered, preserved, and ruled by the Spirit;[14] salvation and the forgiveness of sins are provided through the Church alone, because Christ has entrusted it with the Office of the Keys;[15] the *Spiritus Creator* will awaken the dead in the future.[16]

The Creedal Sermons of 1523[17] unfold the pattern used in the Short Form of 1520 and connect thereby the individual elements more forcefully with the Spirit. Luther begins by setting forth the central thought: The Spirit leads us through Christ to the Father, in that externally He allows the Gospel to be preached to us and inwardly He inflames our heart to believe;[18] in this manner, He shows Himself to be the "*Spiritus vivificans* (the Spirit that makes alive)."[19] The reformer proceeds thereafter to discuss the further elements of the article; even at this point they are placed next to each other like blocks; and yet, the Church, forgiveness, and resurrection are considered already as the three works of the Spirit,[20] with special emphasis placed on the Church as the "*proprium opus Spiritus sancti* (proper work of the Holy Spirit)."[21] The Spirit is shown to be the "*vivificator*"[22] in the resurrection, which is exactly what happens when the heart is inflamed. In a threefold way in these sermons, Luther wraps the Third Article into God's trinitarian activities of creation and redemption: (1) When the Gospel and faith apply the benefits of the Christ event, culminating in the forgiveness of sins,

---

[13] WA 7:220.2.

[14] WA 7:219.4.

[15] WA 7:219.6ff., 17–25.

[16] WA 7:216:26ff.

[17] WA 11:52.31–54.36.

[18] WA 11:53.12: "The proper work of the Holy Spirit is to apply the Gospel, so that it bears fruit"; cf. WA 11:52.31–53.4; 53.6–16, as well as the references to the Second Article, WA 11:51.12–15.

[19] WA 11:53.10.

[20] WA 11:53.32: "The proper work of the Holy Spirit is to establish the Church"; WA 11:54.1: "'the forgiveness of sins,' that is the second work of the Holy Spirit"; WA 11:54.25: "the third work of the Holy Spirit: 'the resurrection of the dead'."

[21] WA 11:53.32.

[22] WA 11:54.26.

God the Father, through the Son, in the Spirit, turns toward us; we recognize thereby the structure of revelation that is at work in the Scriptures.[23] (2) At the same time, however, the Spirit is at work in the First and Second Articles as the *Spiritus Creator: "Pater creavit caelum et terram cum Spiritu sancto. Filius fit homo et facit Christianos cum Spiritu sancto* (The Father created heaven and earth along with the Holy Spirit. The Son became a human being and makes Christians along with the Holy Spirit)."[24] (3) The *Spiritus vivificans* plays a role in the "*Creatio ex nihilo*," for He calls us into being, comforts our conscience in the faith, and inflames our heart to love God and the neighbor, for at some time in the future He will summon us from death into eternal life.[25] In all such actions, He demonstrates Himself to be one God with the Father and the Son.[26]

The Confession of 1528[27] follows the pattern of the Apostles' Creed as well, but it admittedly takes false teachings that had been rejected and recasts them to depict what is positive; the downside is that the individual elements of the Third Article are separated thereby from one another, all over again. Between the treatment of the Spirit and the Church, Luther discusses how the triune God turns to us through Word and sacrament, rejecting the "Anabaptists and Donatists," along with those who deny the real presence of Christ among the gifts of the Lord's Supper.[28] Since he knows that the physical Church, scattered throughout the world, shares "spiritually in one Gospel and faith," under Christ as the head, he understands bishops to be servants of the Church and rejects the papal claim of authority as anti-Christian.[29] By means of an "addendum," he then deals with confession;[30] between that discussion and the resurrection of the dead, he inserts his rejection of indulgences, prayers for the dead, purgatory, appeal to the saints, his viewpoint on whether there are seven sacraments, rejection of the sacrifice of the mass, rejection

---

[23] WA 11:51.12–15; 52.36f.; 54.7f.
[24] WA 11:53.30.
[25] WA 11:51.10f.; 53.17.
[26] WA 11:53.11f., Luther allows the words of Hilary, *De Trinitate* 2:1 (PL 10:51A) to be heard: "infinity in the Eternal, the form in the Image, and the use in the Gift" [Hilary, 36], which picks up the phraseology of Augustine, *De Trinitate* 6:10.11 ("*aeternitas – species – usus*" [eternity – form – use]).
[27] "Vom Abendmahl Christi, 1528," WA 26:505.29–509.18 (AE 37:151–372).
[28] WA 26:505.38–506.29 (AE 37:151–372).
[29] WA 26:506.30–507.6 (AE 37:151–372).
[30] WA 26:507.17–27 (AE 37:151–372).

of vows of the holy orders as a good work before God, and concludes by offering his viewpoint that the adornment of churches is an adiaphoron.[31] Because he handled the issues in this way, the elements of the Third Article are treated in isolation, one from the other. Admittedly, the central aspect that glorifies the Spirit as the "one who makes present" is fully explicated here, as in the Short Form of 1520 and in the Creedal Sermons of 1523.[32] Luther actually adds to the importance of the Spirit in that He inserts a discussion about Him into the context of the entire work of God's salvation; this resumé is incorporated at the conclusion of the commentary on the Creed in the Large Catechism.[33]

The sermons preached on the catechism on May 23 and September 21, 1528[34] clearly enumerate the content of the article, which means that the emphasis falls on the Church.[35] The visitation articles accentuate the key word "sanctification" as "the activity of the Holy Spirit";[36] Luther encapsulates the entire article under this motto in his sermon on December 10, 1528.[37] The commentary is divided into three main parts, with the middle one of those sections being further subdivided into three points:

(a) The scope of the article: The Spirit makes holy in the following ways:[38]

(b) The individual characteristics of the work of the Spirit are seen in the following points:[39] (1) The Spirit makes holy

---

[31] WA 26:507.28–509.12 (AE 37:151–372).
[32] WA 26:505.29–506.12 (AE 37:151–372).
[33] *BSLK*, 660.18–661.18.
[34] WA 30.1:10.31–37 and 45.9–14.
[35] "Kat.-Pred. vom 23.5.1528," WA 30.1:10.33: "The Holy Spirit holds the Christian Church in a harmony of experience and faith. It is thus *una* ecclesia Christiana [*one* Christian Church], in which there is forgiveness of sins"; "Kat.-Pred. vom 21.9.1528," WA 30.1:45.12: "Christ brought forth the benefit of His passion, which then brings forth the Holy Spirit, through His Church. The work of the Church is thus the forgiveness of sins"; "Pred. über Apg. 2:1ff. vom 18.5.1529," WA 29:374.19: "Summary of that book: by His works and the teachings of the apostles, the Holy Spirit gathers the Church, builds it up in one mind, and guards it in its faith in Jesus Christ."
[36] Melanchthon, *Studienausgabe*, 1:259.10, 20.
[37] WA 30.1:91–94 (AE 51:162–169).
[38] WA 30.1:91–94 (AE 51:162–169).
[39] WA 30.1:91.19–93.8.

through the Church;[40] (2) The Spirit makes holy through forgiveness;[41] (3) The Spirit makes holy through resurrection and eternal life.[42]

(c) Recapitulation of the overall scenario,[43] the individual aspects are explained,[44] and reference is made to the contemporary effect of the article.[45]

The Large Catechism follows not only the overall pattern of this sermon, but replicates the specific elements as well, staying away from repetition, and filling in the brief outline by means of insights and formulations used in the Short Form of 1520, the Creedal Sermons of 1523, and the Confession of 1528.[46] At this point Luther inserts an even stronger accent on the Word and faith as the foundational means by which the Spirit of God works, differentiating at the same time, on the basis of the Confession of 1528, between the external and internal ways the Spirit works; the Spirit approaches us externally "through the Gospel, through baptism and the Sacrament of the Altar,"[47] while working within us "through faith and the other spiritual gifts."[48] This results in the following structure:

I. Summary and scope of the Third Article: The Spirit makes (us) holy according to the following elements of the Creed:[49]

(a) The Spirit of God as the one who makes (people) holy in the Church[50]

(b) The Spirit as the one who brings (people) to Christ through Word and faith[51]

---

40 WA 30.1:91.19–92.18, taken up into WA 30.1:93.11–14; 94.1–5 (AE 51:162–169).
41 WA 30.1:92.18–93.4; taken up into WA 30.1:94.5f. (AE 51:162–169).
42 WA 30.1:93.4–8, 15–20; 94.6f. (AE 51:162–169).
43 WA 30.1:93.8–11 (AE 51:162–169).
44 WA 30.1:93.11–94.9 (AE 51:162–169).
45 WA 30.1:94.10–13; 94.14–22 (AE 51:169–176) summarizes the entire commentary on the Creed and is used next to the section on the trinitarian and 'economy of salvation' section in the Confession of 1528 (WA 26:505.38–506.12 [AE 37:151–372]) to form the center point at the concluding section of the commentary on the Creed in the Large Catechism (*BSLK*, 660.18–662.4).
46 See also Meyer, *Historischer Kommentar*, 357.
47 "Vom Abendmahl Christi, 1528," WA 25:506.10.
48 WA 25:506.8.
49 *BSLK*, 653.32–655.37 (according to WA 30.1:91.2–92.4 [AE 51:162–169]).
50 *BSLK*, 653.32–654.17 (according to WA 30.1:91.2–10 [AE 51:162–169]).

(c) The Spirit as the one who makes holy through the mother Church[52]

(d) There is no Holy Spirit and no Church outside of the preaching about Christ[53]

II. Unfolding the "elements" mentioned in the Third Article for the uninitiated[54]

(a) The Church[55]

1. The Church as holy Christendom[56]

2. The Communio sanctorum as "holy community"[57]

3. Our own being incorporated into it through the Spirit[58]

(b) Daily forgiveness of sins through Word, sacrament, and office, only within Christendom[59]

(c) Ever more thriving sanctification because of daily forgiveness, pressing beyond death toward the resurrection of the body from the dead[60]

III. Eschatologically oriented summary of the Third Article: The Spirit carries out His eschatological work on human beings in the Church[61]

This overview of Luther's interpretations of the Third Article permits us to recognize three points:

---

[51] *BSLK*, 654.22–42 (according to WA 30.1:91.10–15 [AE 51:162–169]).
[52] *BSLK*, 654.46–655.8 (according to WA 30.1:91.15–21 [AE 51:162–169]).
[53] *BSLK*, 655.11–37 (according to WA 30.1:91.21–92.4 [AE 51:162–169]).
[54] *BSLK*, 655.44–659.31.
[55] *BSLK*, 655.44–658.2 (according to WA 30.1:92.4–18 [AE 51:162–169]).
[56] *BSLK*, 655.44–656.26 (according to WA 30.1:92.4–8 [AE 51:162–169]).
[57] *BSLK*, 657.1–32 (according to WA 30.1:92.8–13 [AE 51:162–169]).
[58] *BSLK*, 657.33–658.2 (according to WA 30.1:92.13–18 [AE 51:162–169]).
[59] *BSLK*, 658.10–42.
[60] *BSLK*, 659.1–31 (only connected in a loose way with WA 30.1:92.4–8; 93.14–20 [AE 51:162–169]).
[61] *BSLK*, 659.44–660.13 (according to WA 30.1:94.10–13; and yet the expansion furnishes new accents about the Church that encompasses the entire world).

(1) The reformer envisioned what form his later observations would take already in the Short Form of 1520 and in the Creedal Sermons of 1523: (a) He starts out by depicting the office and work of the Spirit as the way the sacred activity of God in Christ through Word and sacrament is applied to individuals, as this was taking place around the world; (b) he follows this by turning to the specific elements of the article, in order to interpret this work of the Spirit for us and to us.

(2) But we observe, at the same time, how what is accentuated in these two earlier discussions proceeds forward now in different directions: (a) In the Creedal Sermons of 1523, Luther is most insistent about linking the Third Article very explicitly into the overarching activity of the triune God for salvation; at the same time, he begins to interweave the Church, forgiveness, and resurrection together, attributing them to the "*Spiritus vivificans*." (b) By contrast, in the sermon of December 10, 1528, these three elements in the article are subordinated under the Spirit, with a deft catechetical move; at the same time, the connection of the Spirit to God the Father, and also somewhat to the Son, is less manifest.

(3) The Large Catechism proceeds (a) to go even more deeply into treating the article as a unity, in that it sets forth its eschatological focus in greater detail; the sanctifying work of the Spirit takes on a greater role, beyond affording daily forgiveness; its trajectory presses on toward the "new immortal and glorified body."[62] (b) And yet, in its summary statement[63] about the Office of the Spirit, the Large Catechism sketches out once again the overarching work of the creating, redeeming, and sanctifying activities of the triune God.

Luther's deft artistic shift, which organizes the elements of the article by identifying them as the means whereby the "Sanctifier" carries out His work, admittedly forces the situation a bit. He goes a different route and does not carry this through in the Small Catechism. A careful analysis shows a more nuanced relationship:

---

[62] *BSLK*, 659.15f.

[63] *BSLK*, 660.18–661.18.

(1) The elements of the article are not all treated as equally important. The Christian Church is both the "place or space" where the believers encounter their Lord;[64] the Church becomes the "mother that gives birth to each and every Christian and nourishes each through the Word of God."[65] The Church is characterized in the Small Catechism as well, coming for those who confess and accompanying each one, as a hidden community of faith and forgiveness, on into the *eschaton*. The "I . . . together with all creatures"[66] in the First Article is now recast in the Third Article to read "I . . . together with all believers in Christ."[67] In the first paragraph of the explanation, individual Christians and the Christian Church seem to be arranged in parallel; in the second paragraph, the Church shows itself to be one, comprehensive flock of those who have been redeemed.

(2) If, according to Luther, "The Holy One is none other than the one who brings us to the LORD Christ,[68] the primary "manner" and the foundational "means"[69] by which this takes place, the Gospel and the faith, need to be accentuated in detail in the Third Article. Luther did this unceasingly in the Large Catechism already, most especially in the first[70] and the last of the sections[71] by means of constantly varying turns of phrase, all of which have something to do with the key terms "Word of God" and "faith,"[72] naturally making mention of the forgiveness of sins as well,[73] at which point "Gospel (*Evangelion*)" becomes the key term.[74] In the Small

---

[64] See below, pp. 288f..

[65] *BSLK*, 655.4f. (LC).

[66] *BSLK*, 510.33f. (SC).

[67] *BSLK*, 512.11f.

[68] *BSLK*, 654.39f. (LC).

[69] *BSLK*, 654.52f.

[70] *BSLK*, 653.32–655.37.

[71] *BSLK*, 659.44–660.13.

[72] *BSLK*, 654.25: "through the preaching of the Gospel"; *BSLK*, 654.35; 655.5; 659.9: "(through) the Word (of God)"; *BSLK*, 657.35: "God's Word"; *BSLK*, 658.27: "through Word and sign"; *BSLK*, 660.8: "through the same Word and forgiveness of sins"; *BSLK*, 655.29: "from the preaching of Christ"; *BSLK*, 658.1: "in faith and its fruits"; *BSLK*, 660.7: "Word and faith."

[73] *BSLK*, 658.10–42.

[74] *BSLK*, 658.14, 17, 36.

Catechism, faith, as the key term, pushes the word 'sanctification' to the side. That term admittedly stands as the motto above the article as a whole,[75] but it is mentioned in its explanation only two times, briefly identifying a station within the chain of salvation.[76] Faith, with second place going to Gospel,[77] is drawn front and center; one does not come to Christ because one is holy but because one comes in "faith,"[78] a term that summarizes the entire happening; this leitmotif is detected as the substantive turn of phrase appears twice, "in the (one) true faith"[79] as well as "for me and all believers,"[80] or "me, together with all believers in Christ."[81]

(3) Because of what had become apparent during the visitations, Luther urged that the word "sanctification" be used, both in his sermon on December 10, 1528 and in the Large Catechism, since he wanted to hold steady over against an antinomian and libertine misunderstanding of the "grace alone"; he wanted to accentuate the necessity of new obedience: "Christ did not provide us just with *gratiam*, grace, but also with a *donum*, the gift of the Holy Spirit, so that we do not have just forgiveness of sins, but also have the power to cease from sinning."[82] Whoever wants to attain forgiveness in an underhanded way, without wishing to undergo the sanctifying work of the Spirit of God for oneself, falls back under condemnation. But the battle against works righteousness, as advocated by the Roman Church,[83] moved the reformer to accentuate that true sanctification grows from

---

75 *BSLK*, 511.39.
76 *BSLK*, 512.4, 6.
77 *BSLK*, 512.3.
78 *BSLK*, 512.1.
79 *BSLK*, 512.4, 7.
80 *BSLK*, 512.8f.
81 *BSLK*, 512.11f. The way the divine works of salvation are connected to one another is pointed out in the Large Catechism most specifically in the summary conclusion, *BSLK*, 660.3–13; it had been substantially stated already in the Short Form of 1520, where Luther paraphrases the work of the Holy Spirit, "through whom the Father and the Son stirs me and all who are His, awakens, calls, draws, and makes one alive, holy, and spiritual in Christ and thus brings one to the Father" (WA 7:218.28).
82 "Von den Konziliis und Kirchen, 1539," WA 50:599.32 (AE 41:3–178).
83 Cf. *BSLK*, 655.22–29; 658.38–42 (LC).

faith alone, faith in the all-sufficient sacrifice of Christ.[84] Luther thereby directs his attention to articulating, with precision, the confession of the Church, through an affirmation of the forgiveness of sins. He does this in order to distinguish between true Christendom, which lives on the basis of daily forgiveness, and the hypocritical church, which accentuates deeds of sanctification, by placing acts of obedience of one's own choosing alongside the cross of Christ. This comes to the fore in the Small Catechism as well, in the phrase: "sanctified and kept in the true faith."[85]

(4) The new key term, 'faith,' also made it possible to link the Third Article to the Second Article without doing it in a forced way; here as well Luther mentions what is most foundational. In the final analysis, what is most crucial is for one to believe in Jesus Christ as our Lord and Savior.[86] This is articulated for each individual who is making confession and is then reiterated for Christendom as a whole;[87] it is taken up at the point where Luther envisions pressing on to come before Christ in the *eschaton*.[88]

These four observations, as well as the insight that the article that was dealt with so expansively in the Large Catechism could in no way be summarized by means of a few brief phrases without radically reducing its content, make it clear that, with respect to the formal parallelism between the Large and Small Catechisms, Luther has to give up much more in this article than was necessary for the earlier two articles. When he fashioned the phrases for the Small Catechism he turned more directly to his first commentaries, most especially to the Short Form of 1520.

The artfully constructed sentences are divided into two major parts, each of which is divided two times further; the first and the last of those four subdivided elements are divided still again into two parts. Luther sought in this way to make reference to all the statements found in the Third Article.

---

[84] *BSLK*, 655.17–21.
[85] *BSLK*, 512.4f.
[86] *BSLK*, 511.47 (SC).
[87] *BSLK*, 512.7.
[88] *BSLK*, 512.12.

I. The foundational event for the faith, both for the individual person who is confessing, as well as for Christendom as a whole: The Spirit sanctifies me, as He does this for the entire Christian Church, in that He brings me to Christ in faith through the Gospel and keeps me close to Him.

(a) 1. My faith in Christ is not based on my own reason or strength,

2. but comes through calling, enlightening, sanctifying and preserving through the Spirit,

(b) in just the same way as the calling, *gathering*, enlightening, sanctifying, and preserving takes place for the whole Christian Church.

II. The eschatological unfolding of the faith event for the one who is confessing within the Christian Church: The Spirit affords forgiveness at present, as a gift, and will give resurrection and eternal life in the future:

(a) In (this) Christian Church He daily forgives sins for me and all believers;

(b) on the Last Day in the future:

1. resurrection comes for me and all the dead,

2. eternal life comes for me and all believers.

Such a structure, wonderfully composed throughout, demonstrates only the slightest unevenness. The phrase "in which Christian Church"[89] seems to frame the entire sentence, right to its conclusion; and yet, at the same time, Luther acts as if he is inserting brackets around "and on the Last Day will raise me and all the dead,"[90] so that the introductory phrase can resume once again to govern "me with all believers in Christ."[91] In this way, one sees the loose and free manner in which the reformer inserts various phrases.

[89] *BSLK*, 512.8.
[90] *BSLK*, 512.10f.
[91] *BSLK*, 512.11f.

THE PROCESS OF GROWTH FOR THE THIRD ARTICLE AS WELL AS THE ARRANGEMENT OF ITS ELEMENTS WITH RESPECT TO THE HOLY SPIRIT

Luther's efforts to characterize the way the article is formed, in his effort to present a comprehensible, catechetical structure, will make more sense when we reflect on how the article itself came to be. One can detect a hesitation about attaching this article to the confession that originally had two parts (according to 1 Cor. 8:6), and it took a long time for it to reach a fixed form.[92] The Creed took shape as a way to answer baptismal questions, which are themselves rooted in the command to baptize (Matt. 28:19); those questions suggest that reference was being made to the Spirit already at the time of Justin (died about 165), phrased something like: Do you believe in the Holy Spirit, who spoke through the prophets?[93] According to the Church Order of Hippolytus (215, or else 217), the Holy Spirit was confessed in the Holy Church, and the resurrection of the flesh was mentioned as well.[94] According to letters from Cyprian (died 258) to Firmilian of Caesarea, a person about to be baptized in the Church in Africa would be asked: "*credis in remissionem peccatorum et vitam aeternam per sanctam ecclesiam* (Do you believe in the remission of sins and life everlasting, through the Holy Church)?"[95] Thus, in rich variation and in uniquely stated formulations, the further elements of the article appeared alongside the Spirit. The Old Roman Symbol positions four such elements so as to form a double chiasm and it makes use of alliteration: "*in Spiritum sanctum, sanctam ecclesiam, remissionem peccatorum, carnis resurrectionem* (in the Holy Spirit, the Holy Church, the remission of sins, the resurrection of the flesh)."[96] Though "*vita aeterna* (eternal life)" appears already about 340, in an apology of Marcellus of Ancyra to Julius I,[97] it is missing in Rufinus[98]

---

[92] See the texts gathered together by Lietzmann, *Symbolstudien*, 240ff.

[93] Based on the reconstruction by Kelly, *Creeds*, 73; cf. Eichenseer, *Apostolicum*, 62.

[94] See the assemblage of texts in Eichenseer, *Apostolicum*, 64–66, and the presentation by Lietzmann, *Symbolstudien*, 260–70.

[95] Cyprian of Carthage, *Epistulae* 69:7 (CSEL 3.2:756.14f.); cf. idem, *Epistulae* 70:2 (CSEL 3.2:768.7), as well as Denzinger, 21f.

[96] Von Dobschütz, *Das Apostolicum in biblisch-theologischer Beleuchtung*, 14: "πνεῦμα ἅγιον, ἁγίαν ἐκκλησίαν, ἄφεσιν ἁμαρτιῶν, σαρκὸς ἀνάστασιν"; set forth abstractly, this would read "a:b, b:a, c:d, d:c."

[97] Denzinger, 11; Epiphanius, *Panarion (Adversus haereses)* 72:3.1 (PG 42:385D). Kattenbusch, *Symbol*, 1:72, assumes therefore that a later copiest inserted this.

and in two old handwritten copies of the Symbol.[99] It seems to have made its way into the West from the East; it is contained in the Symbol of Jerusalem that can be reconstructed on the basis of the catechetical teaching of Cyril of Jerusalem;[100] Niceta of Remesiana uses it[101] and brings it near to the West; even the African confessions likely used it.[102] Thus the phrase "*vita aeterna*" makes its appearance initially in Gaul, in the predecessor text that eventually became the *Textus receptus*.[103]

The gradual growth of the Third Article can be properly located within the development of the framework surrounding baptism. The command to baptize, and the baptismal questions and doxologies that took shape in the effort to properly carry out this command, caused the Spirit of God to be positioned before and above the other elements of the article. Rufinus was the first to establish the course for how it was worded.[104] He wanted to make sure that "Credo *in*" was reserved for the three persons of the Godhead alone and he thus separated the Spirit, as the divine Creator, from the Church as His creature, as well as from the statements about forgiveness and resurrection as His works; those were clearly articulated with *Credere* plus the accusative. The elevated positioning of the Spirit of God, over against His works, is articulated with utmost clarity in the Small Catechism; He alone is the majestic subject of the entire article.

But the problem that we encountered already when examining the arrangement of the three articles still remains;[105] it can be articulated here by posing the question: How can one justify biblically the one-sided arrangement of the elements of the Third Article to connect them to the Spirit alone?[106] Does Scripture not more correctly

---

[98] Denzinger, 12; Rufinus, *Expositio symboli* 34.

[99] See the texts in Kelly, *Creeds*, 102, and Eichenseer, *Apostolicum*, 100.

[100] Cyril of Jerusalem, *Catechesis* 18:29 (PG 33:1049A/B); Hahn, *Bibliothek*, § 124; Denzinger, 41.

[101] Niceta, *Explanatio symboli* 10 (PL 52:871C): "Consequently, you believe in the resurrection of your flesh and in eternal life"; cf. Hahn, *Bibliothek*, § 40; Denzinger, 19.

[102] Ravenna, Denzinger, 15 (Kelly, *Creeds*, 174); Hippo, Denzinger, 21 (Eichenseer, *Apostolicum*, 474); Carthage, Ruspe, Denzinger, 22 (Kelly, *Creeds*, 176).

[103] Denzinger, 26–28; cf., as well, Denzinger, 23, 29.

[104] See p. 210, n. 8; cf. the texts in Eichenseer, *Apostolicum*, 71, n. 51.

[105] See pp. 47–56.

[106] Girgensohn, *Katechismus-Auslegung*, 1:146: "In all three articles, the great work of God's love is described, which comes to its completion in the forgiveness of sins,

demonstrate, as is emphasized by Luther in the Short Form of 1520 and in the Creedal Sermons of 1523,[107] that the Church, forgiveness, and resurrection are to be attributed conceptually to the comprehensive action in the world by God the Father, through the Son, in the Spirit, and not just to one person?[108]

The Church seems most immediately connected to the Spirit who is active at Pentecost, who brought it into existence;[109] Luther says additionally that this is the "*opus proprium*"[110] of the Spirit, who directs His holiness toward the Church. But the other connections deserve immediate attention as well; is not the Christian Church first and foremost the people of God who are hastening toward the heavenly house of the Father, "the assembly of God in Christ,"[111] the only bride of Christ and His spiritual body?"[112] To remain true to the subject, the Church must thus be described as the product of the triune God as a whole; it is "the family of God the Father that extends to every corner of the world, which shares brotherhood with Christ and participates with Him thereby as sons and daughters of the Father. . . . The Church is the community of the reconciled, since God eradicated enmity and sin in Christ, which separated us from Him, and gave us His Spirit. The Church is the community of the Holy Spirit, the congregation of the saints. It is the temple of the Spirit, where spiritual offerings are being brought continually; it is the sanctuary of God upon earth. . . . The Church exists because of the faithfulness of the one God, Father, Son, and Holy Spirit; it is grounded in the love that God has in Himself eternally, and in the consubstantial community of the Father and the Son in the Holy Spirit. As such, the

---

resurrection of the flesh, and the life everlasting as its goal and completion; faith confesses this love and praises it."

[107] Cf. pp. 209–212, 216.

[108] "Pred. über die Dreieinigkeit vom 4.6.1531," WA 34.1:503.6: "My faith says: I believe in the Father, etc., in the Holy Spirit for eternal life, resurrection from the dead, and forgiveness of sins; I wait for this from the Father, Son, and Holy Spirit."

[109] Schweizer, "πνεῦμα," 407–10 ("The Spirit as the characteristic sign of the age of the Church,"); Kretschmar, *Himmelfahrt und Pfingsten*, 244: "Even this oldest level of tradition understood the pouring out of the Spirit as the action of God or else of the exalted Christ, which established the Church."

[110] "Pred. über den 3. Art. vom 6.3.1523," WA 11:53.32f.

[111] Schmidt, ἐκκλησία; *BSLK*, 509.24; 511.37; 534.15.

[112] "Vom Abendmahl Christi, 1528," WA 26:506.32 (AE 37:151–372).

Church is the product of the three divine persons."[113] Tertullian already designates it therefore as the "*corpus*" of the triune God.[114]

The forgiveness of sins was closely identified with the Spirit as well, at an early time already, but this was mentioned especially in the eastern Symbols in connection with baptism: "the one baptism of repentance for the forgiveness of sins."[115] For this reason, the absence of any mention of baptism can be clarified in the Apostles' Creed; when the baptismal questions were posed, and answers were articulated, it was simply anticipated that the forgiveness of guilt would become real in the action that would follow. From the middle of the fourth century on, reflection increased about the ongoing blessings that were promised to the Church, which come with forgiveness; most especially in commentaries by Augustine, the foundational baptismal act that provided the means of propitiation, with the unique declaration of sins, was to be accompanied by daily humility.[116] Baptism removed the original sin and the false steps that were taken when one lived in one's old heathen life; a single opportunity for a public confession of sins in the future left one with the chance to have a way out, when one publicly admitted lapses of the sort that Paul identified in his catalogue of serious offenses; the Lord provided a way to confess the smaller sins of everyday life in that petition of the Lord's Prayer that asks for forgiveness; in addition to those avenues, one had fasts, works of love and church discipline.[117] Those who came later put the insights of the church fathers into a schematic pattern and provided specific details about how this would be addressed in catechetical instruction.[118]

---

[113] *Christus und die Kirche*, 57; cf. *Constitutio dogmatica de Ecclesia*, 156–75 (Chap. 1: "Concerning the mystery of the Church") as well as *Bericht aus Uppsala 1968*, 8–16 ("The Holy Spirit and the Catholicity of the Church").

[114] Tertullian, *De baptismo* 6:2.11–14; idem, *De corona militis* 3:3.15–17; cf. Cyprian of Carthage, *De dominica oratione* 23; Augustine, *Sermo* 71:20.33.

[115] Cf. Denzinger, 41, 42, 44, 46, 48, and often elsewhere; Lietzmann, *Symbolstudien*, 208–11, 277f.

[116] Augustine, *Enchiridion de fide, spe, et caritate* 64–83, as well as the presentation by Barbel, in *Augustinus, Enchiridion*, 227–29, n. 102, and Eichenseer, *Apostolicum*, 410–24.

[117] A list of seven is found in Pseudo-augustine, *Sermo* 240:1 (PL 39:2189): "Seven ways of forgiveness are provided: first, baptism; second, penance; third, divine piety; fourth, indulgences of enemies; fifth, true charity; sixth, alms; seventh, by that preaching that converts those who have strayed."

[118] Ivo of Chartres, *Sermo* 23 (PL 162:606C): "Not only those that are forgiven through baptism, but also those that are cleansed through the light of confession by

Based on the earliest statements in the New Testament that precede the Symbols,[119] which can be detected still in the Eastern confessions,[120] the forgiveness of sins is coupled with Christ's sacrificial death, as one can read in the Words of Institution (Mark 14:22–25 par.), and in the original *kerygma* (1 Cor. 15:3); it is in His death that the "treasure" was acquired, and is linked, as well, with baptism,[121] which is the most excellent means used to deliver this treasure. Paul brings two insights together in Rom. 6:3[122]; the forgiveness of sins was acquired once and for all for us in Christ's sacrificial offering on the cross and that very forgiveness is available to us, ever new, in baptism. Since Luther interprets the article that deals with the "*remissio peccatorum*" as our existential point of entry to interpret the Creed as a whole, he considers the forgiveness of sins to be the specific way that the Trinity in its entirety turns toward human beings; "Christ forgives the sins, so what about the Father? The Father desires it, the Son has accomplished it; as for the Holy Spirit, He is the one who delivers it."[123] Where the signs of grace that have been established by the Son are to be found, the entire Trinity is present there as well, for our salvation.[124]

Something analogous is true for the resurrection of the dead, and for life everlasting as well. Both Ambrose and Augustine extol each of these as works of the Creator Spirit,[125] and Luther follows them at this point. But each element achieves its actual reality in light of Christ's resurrection. Neither element can be shown to be different from an earthly resuscitation, as the Lord afforded to Lazarus, until Christ's return. This forced church teachers of the fourth and fifth centuries to interpret the eschatological hope expressed in 1

---

worthy satisfaction"; this was taken up by Jocelin of Soisson, *Expositio symboli et orationis dominicae* 17 (PL 186:1488C).

[119] See the presentation by Lietzmann, *Symbolstudien*, 229–42.

[120] See ibid., 203–06.

[121] Passages such as 1 Cor. 6:11; Acts 2:38; 10:43; Heb. 6:1f.

[122] Cf. *BSLK*, 654.27–38 (LC).

[123] "Pred. über den 3. Art. vom 6.3.1523," WA 11:54.2.

[124] "Vom Abendmahl Christi, 1528," WA 26:507.10 (AE 37:151–372): "And so also is Christ and His Spirit and God the same."

[125] Ambrose, *De Spiritu Sancto* 2:3.27 (PL 16:779C): "But where the Spirit is, eternal life is there"; Niceta, *Explanatio symboli* 7 (PL 52:870B): "without whose working the creature is in no way able to reach eternity"; Augustine, *Sermo* 215:8 (PL 38:1076): "Through Him (the Holy Spirit) we believe in the resurrection of the flesh; through Him we hope for eternal life."

Corinthians 15 by emphasizing the Christological connection; they thus establish the foundation for "eternal life" once again in the Second Article, where it had been located already in the *Regula fidei.*[126] In his series of sermons on 1 Corinthians 15, even Luther speaks about the "article of resurrection in Christ":[127] "Just as Adam is the beginning and the first one, through whom we must all die as he died, thus Christ is also the first one, through whom we are all to rise to new life, as He is the first one who rose from the dead."[128]

We thus ought not to place too great a weight on the fact that the reformer by and large subordinates the various elements of the Third Article under the Spirit in his creedal interpretations.[129] He relates the same elements to the "office and work of Jesus Christ" in the Smalcald Articles.[130] But, at one point, the reformer mentions the Spirit there as well, in a side comment that rejects enthusiasm.[131] Concerning that issue, he points out specifically that it is through the Spirit of God that we are united with Christ and drawn up into the saving work of God. God Himself turns toward us as the gracious Father, through the Son, in and with the Holy Spirit.[132] The Father and the Son unite with us in the Holy Spirit, insofar as He gives witness to us that the Scripture is "a living, eternal, divine gift and present."[133] And yet, in that He takes possession of us within our very being, the Spirit is the true and majestic God with the Father and with the exalted Lord.

---

[126] Lietzmann, *Symbolstudien*, 248: "The Greek phrase that is used frequently at this point (in the Third Article) in the East, "ζωὴ αἰώνιος," is used by Irenaeus, 1:10, and Tertullian, *De praescriptione haereticorum* 13, as part of the discussion about 'Christology'."

[127] "Pred. über 1 Kor. 15:20ff. vom 13.10.1532," WA 36:550.25 (AE 28:57–213).

[128] Ibid., 551.15; cf. ibid., 550.6–551.3.

[129] This danger poses a threat in the noteworthy presentation by Maurer, *Studien über Melanchthons Anteil an der Entstehung der CA*, esp. 171–78.

[130] *BSLK*, 415.4.

[131] Ibid., 453.16–456.18.

[132] See pp. 33–47.

[133] "Vom Abendmahl Christi, 1528," WA 26:505.32 (AE 37:151–372).

THE SAVING ACTION OF THE SPIRIT OF GOD ON THOSE WHO BELIEVE

1. THE OFFICE AND WORK OF THE SPIRIT[134]

The office and work of the Holy Spirit are hard for us to conceptualize; the Spirit takes on personal characteristics and His own personhood for us only with difficulty. By contrast, the reformer made use of what was taught in the Middle Ages to brighten the depiction of the Spirit as the third person of the Trinity, whose majesty is acclaimed in songs of praise and who is besought in prayer to come down upon all flesh. One is reminded of the three Pentecost hymns: "Come, Holy Ghost, Creator Blest" based on the Latin hymn of Hrabanus Maurus; "Come, Holy Ghost, God and Lord," itself based on the antiphon: "*Veni sancte Spiritus*"; and "To God the Holy Spirit Let Us Pray," in which Luther makes use of and refashions how it was handled in the twelfth century.[135] The reformer paraphrases the office and work of the Spirit with the following words in the Confession of 1528: "In the third place, I believe [up]on the Holy Spirit, who is true God with the Father and Son and who proceeds eternally from the Father and Son, and is still a distinct person with respect to His divine being and nature."

Through this same one, as a living, eternal, divine gift and endowment, all believers are adorned with faith and with other spiritual gifts, awakened from the dead, freed from sins, made happy and comforted, and made free and confident in their conscience. That is our assurance, so that we feel the witness of this Spirit in our hearts: God desires to be our Father, forgives sins, and has given us eternal life as a gift."[136]

---

[134] For literature on this, see Otto, *Die Anschauung vom heiligen Geiste bei Luther*; Schmidt, *Luthers Lehre vom Heiligen Geist*; Heintze, *Luthers Pfingstpredigten*; Gerdes, *Zu Luthers Lehre vom Wirken des Geistes*; Schott, *Fleisch und Geist nach Luthers Lehre*; Prenter, *Luthers Lehre von der Heiligung*; Watson, *Luther und die Heiligung*; Schwarzwäller, *Delectari assertionibus*; von Loewenich, *Luthers Auslegung der Pfingstgeschichte*.

[135] *EKG* 97, 98, 99 [*LSB* 498/499, 497, 768]; cf. the introduction to the Pentecost hymns by W. Lucke in WA 35:161–72, as well as Schlisske, *Handbuch der Lutherlieder*, 210–27; 249–59.

[136] "Vom Abendmahl Christi, 1528," WA 26:505.29 (AE 37:151–372); "Das 14. u. 15. Kap. S. Johannes gepredigt u. ausgelegt, 1537/38," WA 45:727.28 (AE 34:1–422): "Christ is mine with His suffering, death, and life, the Holy Spirit with His comfort, in addition the Father Himself with all His graces, which the Holy Spirit

The Spirit is thus two things, concurrently and in an interrelated way: true and eternal God, of the same nature with God the Father and the Son, and the one who gives us the gift of surety about God. He is the indwelling power, which gives us the freedom to make confession of faith in Jesus Christ as well as to call upon the Father; in that very action shows Himself to be no other God than is our Lord Himself. Once again, this involves the full meaning of that foundational statement "I believe [up]on."[137]

When we cast our glance into the Scriptures, we recognize numerous revelatory figures already in the Old Testament, through whom the sovereign Creator God reveals Himself to the world, in whom He makes it possible for Himself to be recognized, without merging Himself into them thereby.[138] This is where His "attributes" belong, such as righteousness, goodness, faithfulness, but also wrath, with even more emphasis on concepts that deal with body parts, such as arm, right hand, hand, face, and angel, but most especially His Word, as well as in the unique plural "we, us"; these two latter aspects appear in concentrated form in the name as well as in the covenant. As the Old Testament draws to a close, these ciphers that describe God's turning toward the world themselves achieve their own unique role between Him and His creatures, as for example in Wisdom, and later in the Logos. In the New Testament, God consolidates His self-revelation in Jesus of Nazareth, as the only Son; Jesus takes such figures that brought revelations to apply to Himself; they are appropriated to Him later on, in the teaching of the Church; as the Son, the Logos, He is also wisdom and the visible manifestation of the unseen Father.

Only one figure remains, the *Pneuma*. That is God's creative breath already in the Old Testament, which is shown to be active most especially in the prophets.[139] Even though it carried connotations of the demonic in an earlier time, breaking forth in an eruptive manner in the rustlings within a group that was experiencing collective

---

sends so that He can preach Christ for me in the heart and can fill me with His comfort; that is the first glory and title of the Holy Spirit."

[137] Cf. pp. 27–32.

[138] A summary is provided by Deissler, *Gottes Selbstoffenbarung im Alten Testament*; cf., in addition, Barth, *Kirchliche Dogmatik* 1.1:332–38; Schmaus, *Katholische Dogmatik*, 1:382–88.

[139] See Kleinknecht, Baumgärtel, Bieder, Sjöberg, Schweizer, "πνεῦμα," etc.; cf., in addition, *RGG* 2:1268–90; *LTK* 5:108–14.

ecstasy, as well as in charismatic leadership settings, it thus also "appears in a refined form" in connection with the great writing prophets, as the religious and ethical pronouncement of the will of a personal divine power. He is described distinctly as a person already in later Judaism; He speaks, cries out, admonishes, and comforts, suffers, sighs, and is happy. Both the messianic king (Isa. 11:1ff.) and the suffering servant (Isa. 42:1ff.) are characterized as those who bear the Spirit; the Spirit of God is to be poured out onto all members of the populace in the promised time of salvation.[140]

According to the Synoptic Gospels, the Spirit appears in the New Testament as the eschatological power of God, which bursts forth in the works of Jesus, taking hold of human beings with signs and wonders and thus expropriating them for God. He is not so much His own person as He is the *Pneuma*-power of God that rested in an exceptional manner on Jesus; whoever slanders Him cannot be forgiven (Mark 3:28–30 par.). The Spirit does appear as personal and as one who has a unique existence at Jesus' baptism and birth,[141] but also at the point where He goes forth from Jesus to dwell in those who belong to Jesus;[142] on this side, He builds the bridge between God and His Son; on that side, He builds it between the exalted Lord and His empowered witnesses. For Paul and John, the *Pneuma* is essentially the form taken by the one who is exalted at the right hand of the Father as He carries out His work among His own here below.[143] These two leading figures thus take hold of the promises of the Old Testament and the hopes articulated by Jewish prophecy, in order to appropriate them to refer to Jesus Christ: "Spirit refers to the Spirit of prophecy, not the phenomenon that happened in the distant past, but the power of God that is present in the proclamation of the community, giving shape to the life of the people of God living in the end times, but concurrently summoning and judging the world."[144] "In the Spirit . . . the Resurrected One manifests Himself with His resurrection power, which is more than just the power of ecstasy and

[140] Isaiah 44:3; Ezek. 36:27; 39:29; Joel 2:28ff.

[141] Mark 1:10 par.; Matt. 1:18, 20; Luke 1:35.

[142] Acts 2:4; John 20:22; 7:39.

[143] See Hermann, *Kyrios und Pneuma*; Stalder, *Das Werk des Geistes in der Heiligung bei Paulus*; Bornkamm, *Der Paraklet im Johannes-Evangelium.*

[144] Schweizer, "πνεῦμα," 433.3; cf. ibid., 431f.

miracles; it reaches out to the world and brings into existence the new creation."[145]

The specifically theological question that deals with the Trinity, how God, Lord, and Spirit relate, one to the other, how they are to be worshiped as one and the same God and yet as three differentiated "persons," has not as yet been posed at this juncture. Even the Apostles' Creed had not as yet posed such a question; one could summarize its teaching simply as "that the one God had one Son, whom He sent into the world, and a Holy Spirit, through who He works in the Church."[146] And yet, the issue of the Trinity is intimated already, just by the reference to the Spirit. One must start out by saying: in contrast to Yahweh in the Old Testament and to Jesus in the Gospel of John, the Spirit is not revealed in the New Testament by means of the personal pronoun "I."[147] He appears especially at those points where one observes the activity of God, as well as Christ, among human beings, admittedly as the dynamic force at work as each work uniquely in the world. But one can state as well: Where the Spirit serves in the stead of the exalted one among us as the "other Paraclete" (John 14, 16), and as He utters the "Abba" within us (Rom. 8:15, 26; Gal. 4:6), He appears as God in His own unique way, differentiated from the Father and the Lord Jesus Christ.[148]

Within Christianity, the Spirit is referred to at all times in terms of His relationship with the Father and the Son; Augustine's classic definition unfolds this by using His name: "In a certain sense, the Holy Spirit is thus the inexpressible community of the Father and Son. He possibly has His name because one can use the same designation when turning to the Father and to the Son. He is thus addressed in a unique sense as the other two are identified in a general sense. The Father is also Spirit, the Son is Spirit as well; the Father is holy, the Son is holy as well. Thus, in order to use a name that is appropriate both to the Father and Son, so that the Holy Spirit can give us a way to depict the communion between the two, the gift from both is called the Holy Spirit."[149]

The Holy Spirit is the gracious gift of God to us and God is in us thereby; as He gives Himself, He remains the free, majestic Lord, the

[145] Käsemann, "Geist und Geistesgaben im NT," col. 1274.
[146] Schmaus, *Katholische Dogmatik*, 1:368.
[147] Cf. Mühlen, *Das Christusereignis als Tat des Heiligen Geistes*, 514.
[148] Cf. passages such as Rom. 8:26f. and 1 Cor. 2:10 with 1 Cor. 3:16; 2 Cor. 6:16.
[149] Augustine, *De Trinitate* 5:11.12, cited according to BKV Erg.-Bd. 13:204.

God for us but also opposite us, for He is the Lord over us. In the short, intense conflict about the divinity of the Spirit, between the Synods of Alexandria (362) and Constantinople (381), the Cappadocians took the central thoughts of Athanasius that are part of the Second Article and applied them to the Third Article as well: If the Holy Spirit were simply a creature, He could not provide us with the full confidence that we are brothers of Christ and sons of God in baptism;[150] were the Spirit of God not there for us in this world, with sighs that words cannot express, we would be left on our own to trust in the exalted Lord and to call out our 'Abba' to the unseen God-Father, caught in a hubris that leaves us powerless, in the hubris that leaves us teetering on the brink.

Luther makes use of this insight in the Large Catechism:[151] According to the Scriptures, there are many spirits, our own human spirit as well as heavenly spiritual powers, but also the satanic spiritual powers; and yet there is only one Spirit that is called holy. He is not just the "living" Spirit; He is the "life-giving" Spirit too,[152] described majestically as *Spiritus creator*, *vivificator*, *sanctificator*.

In its confession about the Spirit, the Apostles' Creed reflects on the work done by that same one in the Church after Pentecost. The reformer concentrates in the catechisms in the same way, focusing on the internal workings of the spiritual realm, though he underscores, at the same time, the eschatological direction on which faith embarks. The Spirit brings us to Christ; in the confidence of our assurance in the faith, He is so close to us that we can sense His witness in the innermost part of our being;[153] we thereby experience and offer our confession: in the final analysis, it is not some creaturely power that is at work to provide such spiritual confidence in our heart, nor some human, yet transcendent power of our own making, nor some spiritual powers known to tradition and custom. Though such forces are

---

[150] Cf. Schmidt, *Heiliger Geist, dogmengeschichtlich*, col. 1280, and the overview by Scheffczyk, *Lehramtliche Formulierungen und Dogmengeschichte der Trinität*, 161–87.

[151] *BSLK*, 653.39–654.4.

[152] Cf. Lietzmann, *Symbolstudien*, 208ff.

[153] Brunner, *Dogmatik*, 1:218: "But whereas the faith in Jesus is proclaimed in the form of a confession, witness is given about the Holy Spirit as a reality that has been experienced"; Bohne, ". . . *nicht aus eigener Vernunft noch Kraft* . . . ," 128: "The Holy Spirit can be perceived by the young man as the author of truth only in retrospect, on the basis of experience, that in Christ the divine truth is truly perceived as correct."

present, the 'Spirit of Christ' of the Creator God is also at work according to His own plan, at cross purposes to all human solutions. Luther consciously touches on the mystery of life once again; when the Spirit gives us the confidence to believe, the *Spiritus Creator* gives Himself to us as a gift, that very one who awakens from the dead.[154] He is the one who effects all things and makes alive, with the Father, through Christ and in Christ."[155] At this point, the reformer provides the bridge from faith that uses the forgiveness of sins to cross over to resurrection from the dead. In this context, the Holy Spirit shows Himself first and foremost to be Creator and not a creature, since He awakens us from the death of slavery to sin and gives us the gift of a comforted conscience. This faith of ours is thus not a human effort, based on our own reason or strength; from its first blossoming and all the way to its last confirmation, in the hour of death, it is not a product of our own human effort, in, with, and under our efforts to carry out what we desire and to claim that we are in control. The office and work of the Holy Spirit is responsible for the faith and is involved in the faith.[156] The daily work of the Spirit to effect justification and sanctification presses on through death to resurrection, as well as to eternal life in God's presence; in the Spirit, the human being who is in Christ is restored to the image of God and is thus already living out what is planned for the future, no longer merely as a human being confined to this bodily life. By means of these special terms we have circumscribed the innermost circle of the work of the Spirit, as it stands in the center of the Western confessional tradition.

The more expansive Symbols of the East do not concentrate so exclusively on the activity of the Spirit in the Christian Church after Pentecost. Their bridge arches back toward the old covenant. The Confession of Epiphanius (about 374) reads roughly as follows, in its most expansive form: "We also believe in the Holy Spirit, who spoke in the Law and preached through the prophets and came down to the Jordan, who spoke in the apostles and who lives in the believers."[157] And in the commentaries on what was created on each of the six days

---

[154] Cf. Barth, *Kirchliche Dogmatik* 1.1:470–514 and *Kirchliche Dogmatik* 1.2:222–304; Tillich, *Systematische Theologie*, 3:21–337 (Part 4: "Life and the Spirit").
[155] "Eine kurze Form, 1520," WA 7:218.31.
[156] Cf. "Promotionsdisp. von Palladius und Tilemann vom 1.6.1537," WA 39.1:202f., Theses 1–15.
[157] Denzinger, 44, cited according to NR 833.

(Tr.: generally titled *Hexaemeron*), the early fathers themselves go beyond the realm of the Old Testament salvation history and frame the creation as the work of the *Spiritus Creator*;[158] as God's creative Spirit, He hovered, brooding over the waters of the original chaotic flood,[159] and He continuously renews the face of the earth (Ps. 104:29f.; Job 34:14f.). The Western scholastic tradition provides a schematic arrangement to position the ways that the presence of the Spirit of God is at work in the present by means teaching about the three stages of the presence of God in His creatures. According to Peter Lombard, God is present in all creatures by means of the power of His almighty presence, in the souls of His holy ones by means of the power of the grace that comes when He adopts them, and in the human existence of Jesus by means of the grace that makes Him one unity.[160]

The reformers, most especially Luther and Calvin, make use of these differentiations[161] and link them with the teaching about the two realms. The *Spiritus Creator* is at work not only among the non-human creatures and in the Christian Church, but also within all human beings in general, and the benevolent Father overshadows His creatures, which are able to reason, with the charisms that are needed

---

[158] Thus by authors such as Basil, *Hexaemeron, homilia* 2:6; Ambrose, *Hexaemeron* 1:8.29; Augustine, *De Genesi ad litteram imperfectus liber* 1:6.

[159] This interpretation of *merachefet* is taken up by Basil, who got it from Ephraim the Syrian; on this, see the critical observations of Westermann, *Genesis* 1:147ff.

[160] Peter Lombard, *Sententiarum* I, dist. 37.1 (PL 192:621): "And so it is to be known that God, existing everywhere unchangeably in Himself, by presence, power, and essence, is in every nature or essence without limitation of Himself, and in every place without being bounded, and in every time without change. And moreover He exists more excellently in the holy spirits and souls, namely indwelling through grace; and most excellently in the man Christ, in whom the fullness of the divinity dwells corporally. . . . For in Him God dwelt not by the grace of adoption but by the grace of union" [*Sentences*, 1, 202]. Thomas Aquinas, *Summa theologiae* I, q. 43, a. 3: "For there is one mode of communion by which God is in all things by essence, power and presence, as the cause of participating in the effects of His own goodness. Above this mode of communion, however, is a special one that applies to rational creatures, in which God is said to be as the thought in thinking and the love in loving."

[161] "Promotionsdisp. von Bachofen vom 24.4.1543," WA 39.2:239.29: "The Holy Spirit is in human beings in a twofold way. This comes in a certain general activity that preserves them, along with other creatures of God. But the Holy Spirit is given to the righteous as well, by Christ, He who purchased them Himself"; cf. ibid., 248.34–249.4, as well as Prenter, *Spiritus Creator*, esp. 187–204, 297–300; Krusche, *Das Wirken des Hl. Geistes nach Calvin*, esp. 95–125; 338–43.

to construct and to establish a human community made up of people and state, politics and economics, arts and knowledge. Old Testament insights into the power of God's blessing[162] hint at what was later promoted in the humanistic emphasis that became the genius of the Renaissance. The Creator Spirit is also carrying out the plan that provided charisms for His temporal realm, overshadowing us with His gifts but yet holding in His hand the overall rule that is kept distant from us; it is He who provides, or withholds from us, the charisms as well as the *kairos* that provides the right time for success in our activities.[163]

Luther consciously makes connections with all three areas, the creaturely, the communal-political, and the ecclesiastical, *cosmos*, *polis*, and *ecclesia*, by referring constantly to the character of life as a gift. God remains the majestic Lord of all life in all the aspects of our existence; and yet, the reformer still points to the opposing tensions of Law and Gospel. The Holy Spirit thus claims a threefold manner of relating as well; He shows Himself to be the benevolent one who provides the charisms, as the holy lawgiver, and as the gracious provider who effects faith in Christ; in such differentiated actions He is and remains, however, one and the same *Spiritus creator*, *vivificator*, *sanctificator*.

We did not bring about our own birth, and our life does not continue under our own power; we cannot manage either the bodily or the spiritual gifts on our own; our only role is to discover, use, and develop them; our hands do not control the timing for when things will succeed; all such things are given to us as a gift, despite the exertions of our spiritual, emotional and physical powers. This is all within the realm of what the *Spiritus creator* effects as the *Spiritus gratiarum*.

We lack the ability to control our conscience; even when the summons to act in a certain way seems to come from within ourselves, it still comes above us. We cannot control or force the conscience, which means that the call of the Law touches us in the heart and exposes us on the inside, to prepare us for grace. The Law

---

[162] Cf. Baumgartel, "πνεῦμα," 363–66; Procksch, *Theologie des Alten Testaments*, 459–68; Westermann, *Der Segen in der Bibel und im Handeln der Kirche*, 9–66.

[163] The most important collection that refers to the earthly charisms: "Promotionsthesen für Bachofen vom 24.4.1543," WA 39.2:235–37, Theses 1–32, and "Ausl. von Ps. 101, 1534/35," WA 51:207.21–210.21; 240.7–254.12 (AE 13:143–224).

comes down upon us only where and when the Spirit of God burns His original writing in our hearts once again.[164] This is the office and work of the Holy Spirit as the "*Auctor legis.*"[165]

We have no power to unravel the meaning of the Gospel of our deliverance in Jesus Christ; we ourselves cannot conceptualize it. In truth, we cannot really forgive ourselves; we do not baptize ourselves, we do not provide the Lord's Supper for ourselves. The Gospel is proclaimed to us from within the Christ event, the forgiveness of sins is promised to us, the sacraments are proffered to us. We cannot force ourselves to believe God's promises and cannot plot out how to make it our own; it becomes ours when we hear it in the deepest place where it can confront us, in the enlightenment of the heart. We are not able to hold ourselves in the faith by our own powers; we are saved and pulled through the onslaught of the enemies that attack from without and the temptations that threaten from within, brought in fact through the abyss of our own impotence. All of that is the office and work of the *Spiritus vivificator* and *sanctificator* as the "*Donum per Christum* (gift through Christ)."[166] Finally, and in conclusion, we cannot awaken ourselves from the dead; this will happen to us, as well, through the *Spiritus renovator*.

We are not our own creator and preserver, lord and redeemer, cannot justify, sanctify, or awaken ourselves from the dead. The turn of phrase from the First Article "all without my merits and worthiness"[167] is taken up in the Third Article with the words "not by my own reason or strength";[168] both phrases serve as a bridge and are held together by the broad arch that stretches from the creation to the new creation. In all dimensions of our life we experience the sinful impotence of our creaturely existence; our attention is directed to the overweening power that erects it all once again, the *Spiritus creator* and *gratiarum*, the *Spiritus Auctor legis* and *Donum per Christum*, the *Spiritus vivificator*, *sanctificator*, *renovator*.

---

[164] "1. Antinomerdisp. vom 18.12.1537," WA 39.1:371.1: "The Law does not show sin to be what it is without the Holy Spirit. God the legislator makes this happen."

[165] Ibid., 370.3–371.16; 389.2–391.20.

[166] Ibid., 391.17: "In summary, God is with the Holy Spirit in His nature, He is the author of the Law, without whom the Law does not show sin to be sin; but when He is given as a gift through Christ, He gives us life and makes us holy"; cf. ibid., 370.18–20.

[167] *BSLK*, 511.5 (SC).

[168] *BSLK*, 511.46f.

But this mysterious Spirit directs us away from Himself to the Father and to the Son; He speaks no individualistic "I am," and thus, according to the observations of the early church fathers who reflected on it deeply, ought not to be depicted as a person having human form. He brings us, in the Son, to the Father, in the very sense that we experience Him as the 'Christ Spirit' of God, completely opposite to all human spiritualities and created spirits. Thus, following Hrabanus Maurus, Luther pleads: "Teach us to know the Father well,/ and also Jesus Christ, His Son,/ that we of the faith will be full,/ you, both Spirits, to understand."[169]

But in what manner and through what means does the Spirit gift us with Himself, and how does He bring us thereby to the Son, as to the Father? Luther provides an answer to these questions in the catechisms by means of a twofold line of argumentation. In a foundational way, in exact analogy to the First Article,[170] he starts out by differentiating between the external and internal work of the Spirit of God: externally, He works through the Word and the sacraments, internally, by means of faith and the charisms. Then, secondly, the reformer sketches out the path the believer takes from the point when he comes to faith until he is awakened from the dead; this is where the key phrases are set forth: called through the Gospel, enlightened with the gifts of the Spirit, sanctified and kept in the true faith; this is true of each individual believer and of the Christian Church as a whole. We start by depicting not only the external but also the internal workings of the Spirit of God and then come to the "proper path" of the Christian walk.

2. The Gift of the Christ Event through the External and Internal Workings of the Spirit of God

The Holy Spirit bridges the gap between the Christ event from past time under Pontius Pilate, as well as what happened in Palestine, and my existence in the here and now, in that He calls me "through the Gospel."[171] This bridging function seems to be His essential task,

---

[169] *EKG* 97, st. 6 (= WA 35:447.3ff. (AE 53:263–264); *LSB* 498/499). The stanza reads as follows in the hymn: "*Per te sciamus da Patrem / noscamus atque filium / Teque utriusque Spiritum / credamus omni tempore*" (literally: that we may know the Father through You / and that we may know the Son as well / and you also, O Spirit / may we believe at all times).

[170] Cf. pp. 82–86.

[171] *BSLK*, 512.2 (SC)

though in his discussion in the Large Catechism Luther paraphrases what he entitles "to sanctify" in the Third Article as "to bring to the Lord Christ";[172] in the Small Catechism, he expands on the almost furtively inserted new technical term "*gläuben* ([I] believe)" with "come to the Lord Christ."[173] The Spirit of God contemporizes the Christ event for us.

Luther describes the redemption that took place then and there, once for all, as well as its appropriation for the here and now, with one new turn of phrase after another. That the redemptive act needed to be completed once only, he says: "The deed has taken place and is accomplished";[174] "Christ has gained and won for us the treasure";[175] "God's grace (is) acquired through Christ";[176] or, with reference to the Lord's Supper: "the deed (has) taken place on the cross and the forgiveness of sin has been accomplished."[177] With reference to the appropriation in the present he writes: "Such treasure and redemption" is "brought home and made fit" for us,"[178] it is "provided and made beneficial,"[179] it is "comprehended in the Word and presented to us,"[180] it is "given and gifted" into our lap."[181] Concerning the means through which this takes place, the following are mentioned: the holy Word of God[182] of the "*Evangelion*,"[183] or the "proclamation of the Gospel";[184] as both "Word and sign,"[185] this includes both the sacraments and the "offices of the Christian Church" that are established for proclamation and distribution of the sacraments.[186] The faith that the Spirit works is the organ by means of

---

[172] *BSLK*, 654.39; "Weihnachtspost., 1522, 'Ein kleiner Unterricht . . .'," WA 10.1.1:13.22: "For to preach the Gospel is nothing other than Christ comes to us or brings us to Himself."

[173] *BSLK*, 512.1f.

[174] *BSLK*, 654.27f. (LC).

[175] *BSLK*, 654.28f.

[176] *BSLK*, 658.19f.

[177] *BSLK*, 713.36f.

[178] *BSLK*, 654.37f.

[179] *BSLK*, 654.34f.

[180] *BSLK*, 698.27f. (Large Catechism on Baptism); cf. 673.36–39; 713.40–44; "Kat.-Pred. zum 3. Art. vom 10.12.1528," WA 30.1:91.11–15 (AE 51:162–169).

[181] *BSLK*, 654.26f.

[182] *BSLK*, 654.35; 655.5; 657.35; 658.21; 660.6; 673.37.

[183] *BSLK*, 512.3 (SC); 658.14, 17, 36; 713.47.

[184] *BSLK*, 654.25; cf. 672.32; 713.42.

[185] *BSLK*, 658.28.

[186] *BSLK*, 658.10–18.

which we receive this gift.[187] This fourfold interrelationship is summarized in the statement: "the LORD Christ, on the cross, is not a work, but is rather a treasure, comprehended in the Word, provided for us, and received through faith."[188]

The reformer admittedly alludes in brief to that tension-filled back and forth between the past and the present and the external and internal aspects; the most significant depictions of that relationship are to be found in his writings on the sacraments.[189] When Luther describes the relationship between the Christ event that took place "back then" and current preaching, he distinguishes between the "acquisition" and "distribution" of forgiveness,[190] between the "*meritum Christi*" and the "*distributio meriti*,"[191] between the "*factum passionis*" and the "*usus passionis*."[192] The action that brought about our salvation was completed on the cross on Golgotha; Christ accomplished what was necessary for the forgiveness of our guilt once for all, then and there. And yet, without the proclamation of the Spirit of God, the reconciliation between us and God would remain hidden.[193] Thus, in opposition to Karlstadt's resuscitation of the practice of meditating on the cross, which was so common in the late Middle Ages, Luther places all the emphasis on the Word from the cross; if we lose the "for us" aspect of the sermon, Christ remains hanging on the gallows; it would do us no good if He had been crucified a thousand times over; without the proclamation about the cross we remain under judgment.[194] In light of such a way to interpret

[187] *BSLK*, 511.1, 4, 6 (SC); 655.14; 660.7; 673.38.

[188] *BSLK*, 698.26–29 (LC on Baptism).

[189] "Wider die himmlischen Propheten, 1525," WA 18:202.34–205.28 (AE 40:73–223); "Sermon von dem Sakrament des Leibes und Blutes wider die Schwarmgeister vom 28.3.1526," WA 19:510.21–26 (AE 36:329–361); "Vom Abendmahl Christi, 1528," WA 26:294.23–26; 296.30–297.26 (AE 37:151–372); cf. also "Auslegung deutsch des Vaterunsers, 1519," WA 2:113.35–114.4 (AE 42:15–81); "Pfingstpred. vom 24.5.1523," WA 12:571.20–27; 572.6–9; "Vorl. über 1 Tim., 1528," WA 26:40.2–41.23 (AE 17:1–416); "Pred. de sacramento vom 24.3.1529," WA 29:198.5–202.6.

[190] "Wider die himmlischen Propheten, 1525," WA 18:203.28–38 (AE 40:73–223).

[191] "Vom Abendmahl Christi, 1528," WA 26:294.23 (AE 37:151–372).

[192] Ibid., 297.13; "Vorl. über 1 Tim., 1528," WA 26:40.5 (AE 17:1–416): "*factum—usus facti*"; ibid., 40.25: "*usus, applicatio.*"

[193] Cf. *BSLK* 660.44–47 (LC).

[194] "Vorl. über 1 Tim., 1528," WA 26:40.10 (AE 28:268): "Had Christ been crucified a hundred thousand times and had nothing been said about it, what profit would the act of His being taken to the cross have brought?"; "Pred. de sacramento vom

the cross event, Luther seems to be oblivious to having to reckon with the "hideously broad expanse"[195] of fifteen hundred years; he seems not even to notice its presence. Karlstadt's mystical treatment of the cross, rooted in the late Middle Ages, is not rejected by Luther because the intervening cultures and worldviews drive such a deep wedge between the Christ event and the present; for him as well, it is a given that one can "run" to "the cross" on Golgotha.[196] But for him a categorically much deeper abyss must be negotiated, the abyss between the holy God and the sinful human being. We cannot acquire forgiveness on our own, not even if one would make an ardent effort to sink down into the depths of Jesus' sacrificial suffering; all such efforts do nothing to help us extract ourselves from the strictures of works righteousness; we would still be trying "to achieve our grace and to become . . . blessed through our works."[197] The divine righteousness of Christ, which is foreign to our nature, must be imparted to us from the outside, placed on our head with a promise. We are not the ones who climb upward, because of fervent meditations of our human spirit, to comprehend the mystery of the cross of Christ; instead, the offering of Christ is appropriated to us through the Spirit of God in the message about the cross.[198]

At this juncture, the tension between 'back then' and the 'present' transitions to the deeper issue concerning whether the chasm is bridged by the inner spirit of the human being or by the external Word of God. Luther is no proponent of the view that one moves from inside to outside, as does Karlstadt; his starting point is precisely where the external Word is at work, as he states that inward faith begins when that proclamation occurs. The external Word and the internal faith are the two pillars of the proper bridge provided by the Spirit of God. God works externally through seemingly weak human words to achieve the proper result that causes faith to work internally.

24.3.1529," WA 29:200.3: "If Christ were crucified a hundred times in one day and no one were to proclaim it, the forgiveness of sins would be without effect"; ibid., 201.8: "If you make something of the Word from the cross as being '*pro nobis*,' reflect on Christ and the thief on Golgotha."

[195] Lessing, *Über den Beweis des Geistes und der Kraft*, 84.

[196] "Wider die himmlischen Propheten, 1525," WA 18:203.31 (AE 40:73–223).

[197] *BSLK*, 655.26–28 (LC).

[198] Luther warns others about Karlstadt: that one teaches "not that the Spirit [comes] to you, but that you are to come to the Spirit" ("Wider die himmlischen Propheten, 1525," WA 18:137.16 [AE 40:73–223]).

In "Against the Heavenly Prophets" (1525), the reformer writes: "So God has let His holy Gospel go forth now; as far as we are concerned, it works on us in two ways, in the one sense externally and in the other sense internally. He deals with us externally by means of the verbal Word of the Gospel and through physical signs, baptism and the sacrament. He deals with us internally through the Holy Spirit and faith, together with other gifts. But instructions about masses and ordinances are external only, and are not of the essence. The internal things thus come about by means of external things; He decided to give nothing inwardly, without the change happening through external means."[199]

The external and internal workings of God are thus to be distinguished and are yet inextricably bound together. At the beginning comes the summons of the Gospel; God Himself makes use of human beings to help Him. God has not just bound us to this means of grace; He has bound Himself as well. He desires to give us saving faith, but that is delivered through the means of grace alone. In this way, Word and sacrament, but most especially the proclamation of the Gospel, are necessary for salvation. And yet, at the same time, it must be freely acknowledged that the Lord does not stay on the outside only; He remains sovereign and free when He binds Himself to such means of grace. He gives, as a gift, the proper means of grace, "where and when He wants to."[200] Insofar as grace is involved, the means of grace are and remain absolutely indispensible for salvation.[201] We confront once more, at this point, the mysterious boundary between the Creator and the creature. Not any one of us has the ability to "pour [the true faith] into the heart"[202] of another, nor can we acquire such faith by ardent devotion to acts of meditation. Our possibilities of influence upon others remain circumscribed to the

---

199 WA 18:136.9 (AE 40:73–223); cf. "Vom Abendmahl Christi, 1528," WA 26:506.3–12 (AE 37:151–372); *BSLK*, 58.2–15; 59.1–14, 22–25 (AC V, Schwabach Article 7 and Marburg Article 8); *BSLK*, 453.16–20; 456.1–18 (SA C, VIII, on Confession).

200 *BSLK*, 58.6 (AC V).

201 Concerning the tension between the necessity of the Word and its insufficiency, cf. Schempp, *Luthers Stellung zur hl. Schrift*, 49ff.; Bornkamm, *Das Wort Gottes bei Luther*, 918; Prenter, *Spiritus Creator*, 254–64; Beisser, *Claritas scripturae bei M. Luther*, 158–73.

202 "2. Invocavit-Pred. vom 10.3.1522," WA 10.3:15.5 (AE 51:75–78): "I can come no closer than to the ear; I cannot get into the heart, since I . . . cannot pour faith into the heart."

level of physical, worldly existence; the transcendent depths of the human heart, by contrast, remain under the control of God. Thus, based on our own powers of reason, we are never able to arrive at faith in Christ that is not just a put on; despite all such efforts, we each remain caught up in our own selves, enslaved under the tyranny of the princes of this world.[203] The Holy Spirit Himself has to break this prison open and bring us to Christ through the external Word and through faith in our inner being, give to us the treasure of forgiveness that has been achieved on the cross, and unite us with our Lord.[204]

Luther summarizes the external activity of the Spirit by using one key word: Gospel. At this point he initially has in mind the verbal proclamation,[205] not the Bible as a written document. In the introduction to the Church Postils, he articulates it as follows:[206] In the sense that Paul speaks of the letter of the law, Scripture refers only to the Old Testament, which has the character of legal material. The Gospel is essentially a lively word from the mouth to the ear; the necessity to begin afresh and write the New Testament in a literal form came about when a need arose to oppose heretical distortions. Christ Himself had written nothing; He proclaimed the message; the apostles left very little in written form. This external state of affairs demonstrates that the Lord did not wish Himself to be known primarily from a legal perspective, as one who was teaching a model for life (*Exemplum*), but in a sacramental dimension (*Sacramentum*), as one who was bringing joy. This framework makes the Gospel "a chronicle, a history, stories about Christ . . . , that He is God's Son and became human on our behalf, died and rose, a Lord who is over all things."[207] The Gospels and the Epistles of the New Testament

[203] *BSLK*, 655:25 (LC); Augustine already bears witness, in *De praedestinatione sanctorum* 8.16 ("Writings against the Semipelagians," 272): "Faith . . . , in its beginning as well as in its completion, is God's gift."

[204] The controversial question concerning whether the reformer merely intimates a unity with Christ, as well as an appropriation of the gifts acquired on the cross (*BSLK*, 654.27–38, LC), or whether a representation of the cross itself is the central salvific event, will be postponed until the teaching on the sacraments is dealt with in Volume 4.

[205] Cf. Oestergaard-Nielsen, *Scriptura sacra et viva vox*.

[206] "Ein kleiner Unterricht, was man in den Evangelien suchen und erwarten soll, 1522," WA 10.1:1.8–18 (AE 52:3–6).

[207] Ibid., 9.16, 19 (AE 35:113–124); cf. "Post. über Joh. 1:19–23 zum 4. Advent 1521," WA 7:526.10–24; "Weihnachtspost. 1522 über Mt. 2:1–12," WA

thus point us back to the writings of the prophets, as well as to the Law of the Old Testament, so that we can learn to find the Promised One in them as well, but, at the same time, find Him "wrapped in swaddling cloths and laid in the manger."[208] The New Testament is thus, in its innermost nature, "nothing other than . . . a disclosure and revelation of the Old Testament."[209]

Luther uses the traditional rendering to describe the internal activity of the Spirit as "*illuminatio*," with "*praedicatio*" serving as an additional descriptor.[210] The Spirit of God enlightens hearts and fires them up, so that they take hold of the Word.[211] The internal and external activities of the Spirit are not differentiated to any great extent in the Small Catechism; Luther wants to initiate us into the lively dynamic, which carries through from our being called to the time of fulfillment. Based on the formulations that he uses most regularly, something like the following could have been articulated in the Small Catechism: The Spirit enlightened and inflamed my heart in the true faith.[212] The terminology: "enlightened [me] with His gifts"[213] reminds one of the hymn to the Spirit from the Middle Ages that was inspired by 2 Cor. 4:4: "Ignite in us a light for understanding / put

---

10.1.1:625.12–628.8 (AE 52:159–286); "Pred. über 1 Petr. 1, 1522/23," WA 12:259.5–19; 275.5–15 (AE 30:1–145); ibid., 259.8: Gospel means nothing other than a preaching and crying aloud about the grace and mercy of God, gained and acquired by the Lord Christ with His death, and is actually not that which is written in books and which is put together with alphabet letters; instead, it is rather a verbal preaching and a living Word and a voice that resounds throughout the entire world and is shouted out in the open, so that people everywhere will hear it."

208 "Ein kleiner Unterricht, was man in den Evangelien suchen und erwarten soll, 1522," WA 10.1.1:15.4 (AE 35:113–124).

209 "Weihnachtspost. 1522 über Mt. 2:1–12," WA 10.1.1:626.2 (AE 52:159–286).

210 "Pred. über den 3. Art. vom 27.5.1531," WA 34.1:452.14: "The Holy Spirit does this through preaching and illumination"; "Pred. über Mt. 9:1ff. vom 5.10.1529," WA 29:580.8: "But the Spirit preaches in a spiritual way, whether in an external sense or in an internal way."

211 *BSLK*, 655.6 (LC); cf. 673.38f.; but the same is said of Christ, "Von beider Gestalt des Sakraments zu nehmen, 1522," WA 10.2:23.12 (AE 36:231–267): "Christ the Master teaches in the heart, though it is done through His preachers with the external Word, who drive this into the ears, but Christ drives it into the heart."

212 "Pred. über den 3. Art. vom 5.3.1523," WA 11:53.2: "The Holy Spirit . . . , who kindles the heart and makes one alive . . . , who inflames the heart"; "Pred. über Mt. 20:1ff. vom 28.1.1526," WA 20:236.18: "But it is proper for the Holy Spirit to illumine the heart and set it on fire."

213 *BSLK*, 512.3f. (SC).

burning love into our heart."[214] And yet, in contrast with Thomas Aquinas,[215] the enlightening for Luther was characterized not by its effect on the intellect, but by what it did to the heart. Luther thus goes farther back than the tradition set in motion by Plato, by reaching into the Scriptures. Based on Scripture's use of the term, he understands "heart" in a comprehensive sense as "the location not only for everything connected with one's emotional life, but also the place where understanding and the will are located,"[216] as the "chief organ for the emotional-spiritual life," and thereby as "the place within the human being where God reveals Himself,[217] as well as "that place where decisions about the entirety of one's standing in the *coram Deo* (presence of God) are made."[218]

If it is the Spirit who enlightens our heart in faith, it is He who enlightens our understanding of the message of the Scripture as well; the physical written letters of the alphabet are dead until the gracious Father addresses us directly; the Spirit breaks through the shield of our heart that resists penetration and lets the joyous good news press on into our innermost being.[219] If the Spirit allows that gracious good

---

[214] *EKG* 97, st. 3 (= WA 35:446.10; *LSB* 498/499).

[215] Thomas Aquinas, *Expositio in Symbolum Apostolorum*, § 967: "Second, it illuminates the intellect, so that everything that we know, we know from the Holy Spirit."

[216] Von Rad, *Theologie des Alten Testaments*, 1:157; cf. Baumgärtel, καρδία.

[217] Behm, καρδία, 614.31; cf. ibid., 614–16.

[218] Joest, *Ontologie*, 213. Concerning how Luther understands the heart, cf. ibid., 212ff.; Genrich, *Die Christologie Luthers im Abendmahlsstreit*, 94ff.; Metzger, *Gelebter Glaube*, 86ff.

[219] "Op. in Ps., 1518–21," WA 5:505.10: "With regard to the spiritual nature of the wind (Ps. 18:11 [Engl.: 18:10]), it says that that very Word is the Spirit, interpreting the Law and demonstrating grace. For this Word comes quickly, just as the wind does, blowing where it will, and you do not know or hear His voice, whence it comes or whither it goes. The wings of this wind, however, are themselves spoken words, by which this spirit flies. . . . Therefore, it flies above the wings of the winds, which is the ministry of the spoken word, by which faith is taught; it flies above us, so that where the spoken word is, faith is received there through the Spirit, where without doubt the Lord is and flies above them"; "Pfingstpred. vom 24.5.1523," WA 12:571.20: "For this reason God gives the Holy Spirit, who presses such a sermon into the heart, so that it takes up a dwelling and lives there"; "Pred. über den 3. Art. vom 5.3.1523," WA 11:53: "Honor is given to the Holy Spirit, since the Spirit is identified as the one who is life-giving, since He acts through whatever is preached so that He may live in hearts"; cf. WA 11:112.11f.; 113.12ff.; "Pfingstpred. vom 24.5.1523," WA 12:572.6–24; "Pred. über Joh. 14:23ff. vom 15.5.1524," WA 15:564.27–37; "Pred. über Apg. 2 vom 31.5.1528," WA 27:150.11ff.; "Predigten über Joh. 6 vom 4.2. u. 25.2.1531," WA 33:146.8–26; 149.32–40; 192.33–42 (AE

news to press on into the center of our heart, He comforts the conscience that is under accusation and in despair as well, and makes it free and happy.[220] If the Spirit inflames our heart with His flames of love, He takes control over all the emotional elements of our being at the same time, streaming through them with His passion, so that we acquire our own passion for obeying God's commandments, willingly giving ourselves over to Him and to the neighbor.[221] When the Spirit takes control over our heart, He comes with His almighty, holy "super-will" as well,[222] which is superior to our impotent and conflicted will that resists; we are drawn into the relationship with Him where we are moved from within to love. These multifaceted aspects are taken up by Luther in a Pentecost sermon (1523) in a way that is typical: The Spirit composes "a fiery flame in our heart and makes it lively, so that it splits up into fiery tongues and an energetic hand; a new person comes forth who detects that he now has a completely different discernment, disposition, and sense than he had beforehand. Everything is now enlivened, there is lively discernment, light, courage, and heart, which burns now and desires to do everything that pleases God."[223]

The way it is formulated in the Small Catechism reads "enlightened with His gifts";[224] it is stated in the reverse in the Large Catechism, where those who are not Christian are portrayed as those who "are enlightened and graced with none of the gifts from the Holy Spirit.[225] The seven gifts of the Spirit are identified on the basis of the

---

23:1–197); song: "Nun bitten wir den heilgen Geist," WA 35:448.1f. (AE 53:263–264); "Credo-Pred., Schmalkalden, 11.2.1537," WA 45:23.10ff.

[220] "Gal.-Komm., 1519," WA 2:536.23ff.; 602.18–23 (AE 27:151–410); WA 11:112.20f.; "Pfingstpred. vom 24.5.1523," WA 12:573.2f.; 574.18f.; 575.29f.; "Vom Abendmahl Christi, 1528," WA 26:505.34ff. (AE 37:151–372); "Gal.-Komm., 1535," WA 40.1:571.12–587.1 (AE 26:1–461).

[221] "Pred. über 1 Tim. 1:8ff. vom 18.3.1525," WA 17.1:125.2: "the heart kindles faith and love"; cf. "Von der Freiheit eines Christenmenschen, 1520," WA 7:36.2–4; 38.6–10; 66.3–28; 69:12–16 (AE 31:327–377); "Post. über Joh. 1:19–23 zum 4. Advent 1521," WA 7:536.39–537.11; "Pfingstpred. vom 24.5.1523," WA 12:570.9–19.

[222] Cf. "Auslegung deutsch des Vaterunsers, 1519," WA 2:101.16–19 (AE 42:15–81).

[223] WA 12:570.12; cf. "Pred. über Apg. 2 u. Joh. 14:23f. vom 27.5.1520," WA 9:462.26–465.10; "Pfingstpred. vom 24.5.1523," WA 11:111.16–22; "Pred. über Eph. 3:14–21 vom 1.10.1525," WA 17.1:438.14–22; "Pred. über Joh. 14:23ff. vom 1.6.1528," WA 27:160.10–161.7; "Pred. über Apg. 1:4ff. vom 15.5.1535," WA 41:244.14ff.; "Credo-Pred., Schmalkalden, 11.2.1537," WA 45:22.13–23.12.

[224] *BSLK*, 512.3f.

[225] *BSLK*, 661.16f.

Vulgate text of Isa. 11:2f.; they were given catechetical status already in the era of the early Church,[226] as passed on in tradition by Peter Lombard,[227] and were used frequently in the written reflections that helped one prepare for confession in the Middle Ages.[228] One is reminded of them in Hrabanus Maurus' hymn "*Veni creator Spiritus*" and in Luther's version as well:[229] "With sevenfold gifts you are / the finger of God's right hand."[230] Luther even articulates each one of them in the "*Dictata super Psalterium*,"[231] but dislodges them, along with a plethora of other aids for confessing sin, by replacing them with the commandments.[232] He seems to make reference to them in the Magnificat, by means of the imagery of the seven-branched candle stand; at this point, he divides the human being up into body, soul, and spirit, patterning that on the design of the temple;[233] he admittedly no longer mentions each one specifically when he discusses this passage.[234] In "*Enarrationes epistularum et evangeliorum, quas postillas vocant*" (1521), he recasts the list by using the Decalogue; [235] most importantly, he purposely proposes a new catalog of the gifts of the Spirit in 1539 in "*Von den Konziliis und Kirchen*."[236] We thus ought not to try to force his reflections on the gifts of the Spirit of God to conform to some pattern based on the

---

[226] "Tractatus de septem vitiis et septem donis Spiritus sancti" (PL 40:1089–92).

[227] Peter Lombard, *Sententiarum* III, dist. 34; Bonaventure, *In Sententiarum* III, dist. 34, p. 1, a. 2, q. 1f.; Thomas Aquinas, *In Sententiarum* III, dist. 34, q. 1, a. 2; idem, *Summa theologiae* I/II, q. 68, a. 4 and 7. Cf. Lottin, *Les classifications des dons du Saint Esprit au 12e et 13e siècle.*

[228] Boeckl, *Die sieben Gaben des Hl. Geistes*; Weidenhiller, *Untersuchungen*, 26ff., 30ff., 34, 44, 51, 79, 110, and often elsewhere.

[229] The original reading: "*Tu septiformis munere / dextrae dei tu digitus*" ["You with seven-formed gifts / your finger at the right hand of God"]; cf., in addition, the other translations by Wackernagel, *Das deutsche Kirchenlied*, 2, nos. 46, 985, 1073, 1372 (esp. those by Th. Müntzer); cf. Schlisske, *Handbuch der Lutherlieder*, 213.

[230] *EKG* 97, st. 4 (= WA 35:446.14 [AE 53:260–262]; *LSB* 498/499).

[231] WA 4:326.19–328.7 (AE 11:1–553).

[232] Cf. "Instructio pro confessione peccatorum, 1518," WA 1:262.23; "Decem praecepta Wittenbergensi praedicata populo, 1516–17," WA 1:516.30.

[233] Cf. pp. 89–91.

[234] WA 7:551.21 (AE 21:304): "His soul is the holy place, with its seven lamps, that is, all manner of reason, discrimination, knowledge, and understanding of visible and bodily things".

[235] WA 7:535.21: "This second circle, therefore, which must be taught, is fear of God, love, peace, goodness, gentleness, humility, patience, forbearance, generosity, and other fruits of the Spirit as taught in the Decalogue."

[236] WA 50:626.15–627.17 (AE 41:3–178).

number seven.[237] Luther creatively recasts them afresh at times, at which point the Decalogue indirectly provides orientation for all aids that help one to confess one's sin.[238] He also interprets the gifts of the Spirit as "*pictura et descriptio regni Christi*"[239] in his interpretation of Isaiah; there he explicates the individual gifts in such a way that he comes up with a description of the cosmos that is affected spiritually in every facet by the life of Christ; the arch starts with an enlivened knowledge of God and pure teaching and goes through times of protection when tempted, reaching to supply provisions for proper life together with fellow human beings and for a holy way to use all things; the fear of God furnishes the framework and holds all the aspects of life together.[240]

In the Small Catechism, Luther singles out only faith for special attention, distinguishing it thereby from the rest of the gifts of the Spirit, which are not discussed specifically. This corresponds to the way he used the catechetical form of presentation when he wrote against Karlstadt and in his Confession of 1528: God deals with us externally through Word and sacrament; internally, He comes "through the Holy Spirit and faith, along with other gifts."[241] Thomas Aquinas had already accorded greater clarity to the murky term of the "grace given graciously (*gratia gratis data*)" insofar as he identifies the charisms as being another way to describe the gifts of grace that are given to each Christian, available to each to assist in working for the salvation of one's fellow human being.[242] Luther distinguishes still more carefully between the *charis* of God, which alone redeems, and the charisms of the Spirit, which are provided for us to empower

---

[237] Girgensohn, *Katechismus-Auslegung*, 1:152: "But Luther restrains himself and does not name specific gifts and does not seek to establish a hard and fast order." This must be mentioned in opposition to the interpretation in Meyer, *Historischer Kommentar,* 342.

[238] See also the enumeration that is set forth in Hardeland, *Katechismusgedanken*, 254f.

[239] WA 25:132.20–133.22 (AE 16:1–349) and WA 31.2:84.12–85.36 (Citation: ibid., 85.26).

[240] Ibid., 85.20–27; a summary is presented in WA 25:133.3–5.

[241] "Wider die himmlischen Propheten, 1525," WA 18:36.13; "Vom Abendmahl Christi, 1528," WA 26:506.5 (AE 37:151–372): "The Holy Spirit . . . gives Himself to us wholly and completely . . . , inwardly through faith and other spiritual gifts."

[242] Thomas Aquinas, *Summa theologiae* I/II, q. 111, a. 4f.; at this point see the commentary by von Balthasar in: "Thomas Aquinas, *Summa theologiae*," in the German Thomas-Ausgabe, 23:268–73 (AE 37:3–150).

the public proclamation of the Gospel.[243] The grace of God, which alone is able to save, is comprehended when the Spirit effects saving faith, hidden from the first in Christ's alien righteousness. At the same time, this proper faith in Christ sets in motion the "*entelechy*" (Tr.: proper human drive) of genuine love of God and the neighbor.[244] Luther thus separates this from the rest of the charisms, which gush forth from the heart that is changed by faith in Christ. Saving faith alone, and the selfless love that springs forth from that faith, go the distance by being active within the framework of eschatological deliverance. The rest of the charisms, including the miraculous faith that can move mountains (1 Cor. 13:2; Matt. 17:20), remain in the realm of the earthly and are subject to various interpretations;[245] wherever the central gift of the Spirit is not at work in every aspect, they fall under God's eschatological judgment.[246]

The reformer thus assigns even the charisms, which are provided among the gifts of the Spirit for the benefit of the community, to the status of being under the temporal rule of God; they are distinctive in that they provide for the public proclamation of the Word of God; the saving work of the Spirit is effected thereby.[247] What is true of all who are outfitted with such gifts is that none who are gifted thus have the power to actually effect eschatological salvation for anyone; salvation grows in each individual solely on the basis of faith in Christ's alien righteousness.[248] The other gifts of grace will enrich us for salvation and not for judgment only after the Spirit uses such gifts to enlighten our heart, providing us with saving faith and with the

---

[243] On this, see Althaus, *Theologie Luthers*, 357–85; Peters, *Glaube und Werk*, 216–21.

[244] "Zirkulardisp. de veste nuptiali vom 15.6.1537," WA 39.1:318.16: "Faith is itself the form and foremost act or perfection of love (ἐντελέχεια, *charitatis*). Love, by contrast, is the work and fruit of faith"; cf. "Gal.-Komm., 1519," WA 2:566.28–567.23 (AE 27:151–410); "Gal.-Komm., 1535," WA 40.2:34–39 (AE 27:1–144), in both instances on Gal. 5:6.

[245] "Promotionsdisp. von Bachofen vom 24.4.1543," WA 39.2:236, Thesis 7: "The gifts of the Spirit cannot be given and be present apart from faith in Christ and love."

[246] "Promotionsdisp. von Schmedenstede vom 7.7.1542," according to ibid., 236, Theses 7–12; ibid., 237, Theses 23–32; WA 39.2.190, Theses 41–46 (AE 34:299–321).

[247] "Promotionsdisp. von Bachofen vom 24.4.1543," WA 39.2:237, Thesis 23: "I should say such faith, as the term is commonly used, is like those movements by which heroic men are excited."

[248] "Promotionsdisp. von Bachofen vom 24.4.1543," WA 39.2:237, Thesis 32: "Faith in Christ is a particular gift to each one in whom He lives" (Rom. 1:17).

love that springs forth thereby. These overarching connections are admittedly barely mentioned in the formulations of the catechisms.[249]

3. Sanctification Based on Justification, Appropriate for the "Proper Ordering" of a Christian Life[250]

That faith is of first order, and is the highest order, can be confirmed by the terminology that is used in the Small Catechism: "sanctified and kept in the true faith."[251] There is more for us than just being called through the external proclamation of the Gospel, being enlightened internally in a proper manner within our heart by means of the correct saving faith, and being recipients of the gifts of the Spirit; from within, in the heart that has been changed by faith, the Holy Spirit saturates our entire being as the "one who makes holy"[252] and the one who renews the heart from the inside outward. The "true faith" terminology differentiates the holiness that is put into effect by the Spirit of Christ from every human effort to effect change within, on the basis of one's own power and strength, and to create itself anew. In the Large Catechism, Luther barely mentions this frontal assault on the works righteousness that is rooted in the late Middle Ages, with its attempt to sanctify the self.[253] At this point, he makes more of the term "sanctification" that came down through tradition, taking it in the sense that would convey what the proper biblical term would convey during the Middle Ages, as one would strive for righteousness; he uses this very concept to combat an antinomianism that seeks freedom from all demands. "For this type of Christ would be worthless and empty, to have died for sinners of the type that do not wish to give up on sinning and to lead a new life after their sins have been forgiven.[254] True faith in Christ authenticates itself precisely by the way it wages the relentless battle against sin, admittedly not by means of one's own power, but solely through a

[249] See *BSLK*, 512.3f. (SC); 661.16ff.; 673.35–39 (LC).

[250] For texts and literature on this, see p. 306.

[251] *BSLK*, 512.4f.

[252] *BSLK*, 654.4 (LC).

[253] Cf. pp. 243–244, n. 219.

[254] "Von den Konziliis und Kirchen, 1539," WA 50:599.21 (AE 41:3–178); "Thesenentwurf über 1 Kor. 13:2, 13, 1535," WA 39.1:77, Thesis 4: "It can be answered by the pious as well: This faith, even if received as the faith that justifies, is not as great as love, for without such [love], faith is nothing."

constant return to Christ's offering, as Luther makes clear when discussing baptism.[255]

The Spirit sanctifies us by means of the daily forgiveness of one's offenses.[256] Crawling back constantly, when returning to our baptism, causes sanctified actions to sprout and grow, and one "improves daily";[257] from within one's own being, one presses on toward the eschatological time when the entire human nature will be made new.[258] Sanctification takes place within the framework of the Decalogue, in the callings and estates that are God-ordained, which flow out of the "general order that results in Christian love."[259] In that sense, the reformer can say: "We are blessed through Christ alone." With reference to the daily authentication of faith by acts of love, he can add: "yet both actions are holy, working through faith such as this and also through the divine estates and orders";[260] one is the work of the Lord Christ, the other is appropriated to the Spirit, for Luther praises the Church as a "Christian, holy people, in whom Christ lives, works, and reigns through *redemptionem*, through grace and the forgiveness of sins, and the Holy Spirit works through *vivificationem* and *sanctificationem*, through sins being swept away daily and through the renewal of life."[261]

Luther discovered how to depict God's way of dealing with the one who is confessing: connect back to one's baptism and then come right up to the act of confessing one's sins by incorporating the works of the Spirit of God, using primarily the perfect tense: "The Holy Spirit has . . . me";[262] he does not identify the entry point into the Christian life as baptism, though that would correspond to the general experience of the common people he is addressing; the call of the Gospel is accentuated, which would more appropriately describe what happens in a mission situation. But the chain of events stretches from the past through the present and on into the future. Luther identifies

[255] See Volume 4.

[256] *BSLK*, 659.7–10 (LC).

[257] *BSLK*, 659.2; 673.44 (LC).

[258] *BSLK*, 659.10–16 (LC).

[259] "Vom Abendmahl Christi, 1528," WA 26:505.11 (AE 37:151–372).

[260] Ibid., 505.18; ibid., 505.16: "But regular actions of this sort do not provide a way to blessedness; instead, the only way that is above all these other ways is namely faith [up]on Jesus Christ; for this is a very different way of being holy and blessed."

[261] "Von den Konziliis und Kirchen, 1539," WA 50:625.23 (AE 41:3–178); cf. passages such as "Ennaratio Jes. 53, 1544," WA 40.3:726.20–31; 727.21–26.

[262] *BSLK*, 512.2 (SC).

the forgiveness of sins, which is constantly in force, as the work of the Spirit that reshapes the present ever anew; the Spirit forgives all sins, daily and richly.[263] One's hope is for a future that will bring with it the unique experience of the resurrection from the dead and the enduring gift of eternal life.[264] This shows how the action of God in the past that provided the power to make one holy now determines and influences the present and reshapes it to be the down payment on the future; in this way, it shows itself giving shape to history.

The chain of verbs: called, enlightened, sanctified, and kept, sound much like the words from the Solid Declaration II:50: "called human beings to eternal salvation, draws them to Himself, converts them, brings them to a new birth, and sanctifies them."[265] Lutheran orthodoxy sought to develop its teaching in the basis of the *Ordo salutis*,[266] and catechetical instruction finally succeeded in imposing that same pattern on how the Small Catechism was taught during the nineteenth century,[267] having developed fully only at the end of the eighteenth century. The central terms they used: *Vocatio—illuminatio—conversio—sanctificatio—unio mystica*.[268]

Such a schematization has been rightly rejected ever since the beginning of the twentieth century;[269] as Tetelbach noted, one admittedly ought not to give up once again on accentuating the dynamic activity of the Spirit of God.[270] Luther emphasizes this for the first time in his Pentecost sermon in 1523,[271] after he had articulated already, in fixed form, central anthropological thoughts in

---

[263] *BSLK*, 512.9 (SC); 658.19–29 (LC).

[264] *BSLK*, 512.10f. (SC); 674.3–6 (LC).

[265] *BSLK*, 891.44ff.: "to call human beings to eternal salvation, to draw them to Himself, to convert them, to give them new life, and to make them holy."

[266] See Elert, *Morphologie*, 1:123–54; Hägglund, *De homine*, 361–92; idem, *Rechtfertigung—Wiedergeburt—Erneuerung in der nachreformatorischen Theologie*; Fahlbusch, "Heilsordnung"; Köberle, "Heilsordnung."

[267] Harnisch, *Entwürfe und Stoffe zu Unterredungen über den KK Luthers*, 2:347–97; Lührs, *Katechismusschule*, T: 2:150–95; T. Harnack, *Erklärung des KK Dr. M. Luthers*, 235; von Zezschwitz, *System der christlich kirchlichen Katechetik*, 2.1:396–405.

[268] Thus in Danow (1741–82) and in Reinhard (1753–1812).

[269] See Meyer, *Berufen, erleuchtet, geheiligt*; cf. idem, *Historischer Kommentar*, 361–63.

[270] Tetelbach, *Güldenes Kleinod*, 1569 (Reu, *Quellen*, 1.1:689.40–690.8).

[271] WA 11:111–14 = WA 12:568–78; some such ideas are found already in "Pred. über Joh. 14:23ff. vom 8.6.1522," WA 10.3:155–60; cf. the collection of evidence in Mülhaupt, *Ev.-Auslegung*, 4:412–40.

the first Invocavit sermon,[272] though he did not always mention the *Spiritus Creator* in this context. As for the "proper ordinances of the Christian life," which grow out of the Gospel and which press one forward to perform deeds of love for the neighbor, one finds him articulating such activity of the Spirit of God within the believer in a terse way in 1525, in "Deuteronomion Mosi cum annotationibus," as well as when he wrote against Karlstadt.[273] Luther does not depict stages within some process of religious purification, nor does he identify steps of mystical progress; instead, he describes how the Spirit of God falls upon a person and how He breaks into the life of a human being. We do not climb upward to God; instead, through the Spirit, God bends down to us.

Thus, unlike Karlstadt's idea that the flesh must be mortified,[274] and unlike some arduous meditation on Jesus or imitation of Christ that finds pleasure in good deeds,[275] the starting point for Luther comes by paying careful attention to the Word of God, with its dialectic of the accusation of the Law and the emancipation effected by the Gospel.[276] The Spirit has bound the way He works to activity that takes place within the external hearing of the Word and yet remains free to offer or withhold the faith.[277] Wherever the Spirit makes salvation accessible to us in the hearing of the Gospel, that is where He works justification; our heart learns about the freedom of God that comes with a comforted conscience; we venture to call upon the holy God as our Father.[278]

The heart that is renewed in faith does not remain a closed entity; the new heart directs our physical human nature outward to confess

---

[272] WA 10.3:1–13 (AE 51:70–75).

[273] "Dtn. cum annotationibus, 1525," WA 14:681.12–682.3 (AE 9:1–311); ibid., 682.2: "This is the summary and the true order of the Christian life, which depends on the Word and begins with it, and it extends to the works of love toward the neighbor"; "Wider die himmlischen Propheten, 1525," WA 18:65.3–66.11 (AE 40:73–223); cf., in addition, ibid., 139.13–26 and "Fastenpost. über Röm. 12, 1525," WA 17.2:5.17–22.

[274] "Dtn. cum annotationibus, 1525," WA 14:682.10 (AE 9:185): "For the Spirit comes to them, not from hearing the Word, which they proudly despise, but from mortification."

[275] Ibid., 682.10f.; "Von den himmlischen Propheten," WA 18:138.10–26.

[276] "Dtn. cum annotationibus, 1525," WA 14:681.14–20 (AE 9:1–311); "Von den himmlischen Propheten," WA 18:65.9–23 (AE 40:73–223).

[277] "Dtn. cum annotationibus, 1525," WA 14:681.22 (AE 9:184): "For the Spirit blows where He wills, not where we will"; see pp. 243–44, n. 219.

[278] "Dtn. cum annotationibus, 1525," WA 14:681.23–27 (AE 9:1–311).

the faith and to serve in love.[279] God's Spirit takes hold of us as His coworkers in His work of redemption.[280] Faith that is not hypocritical shows itself at work in the divinely ordained estates in a fruitful way through love and is tangible and visible in good works.[281]

And yet, at the same time, we experience pushback from what is outside[282] and what is inside; God lays upon us the "beloved, holy cross."[283] As was the case already with the First Article, the Third Article discusses the opposition of satanic forces in a merely cursory fashion[284] and does not unfold the depths of the issue thematically. That issue is finally treated in greater depth in the Lord's Prayer.[285] Despite all the laziness and fear of suffering within our flesh, despite all fear concerning those who are entrusted to our care,[286] and all the furtive glances that we cast toward honors accorded by the world, despite every manner of inner doubt and the agonizing struggles instigated by Satan,[287] the Spirit of God brings us through it all, sanctifies and purifies the person who is obedient to the faith, and thus strengthens that individual with a confident hope that remains steadfast.[288] This dynamic "*verus ordo Christianae vitae* (true way to live the Christian life)"[289] gives structure, as well, to Luther's treatment of the spiritual rule of Christ according to the seven gifts of the Spirit mentioned in his treatment of Isaiah.[290]

---

[279] In "Von den himmlischen Propheten," Luther mentions: 3. "the judgment, the work that is to kill the old man, 4. the work of love toward the neighbor" (WA 18:65.24, 31 [AE 40:73–223]).

[280] Cf. Seils, *Der Gedanke vom Zusammenwirken*, esp. 99–113, 124–30.

[281] "Rhapsodia seu concepta in librum de loco iustificationis . . . , 1530," WA 30.2:659.16: "Then, through itself, faith is made, so that we work, and in this manner faith thickens into works and is made altogether palpable."

[282] "Dtn. cum annotationibus, 1525," WA 14:681.32 (AE 9:184): "This is the source of persecution, the cross, and trouble over the Word in the world."

[283] *BSLK*, 677.21 (LC, Third Petition of the Lord's Prayer).

[284] *BSLK*, 658.24 (LC): "Sins of our flesh"; 660.10f.: "that the world and all misfortune die out."

[285] See Volume 3.

[286] *BSLK*, 677.22–30 (LC, Third Petition of the Lord's Prayer).

[287] *BSLK*, 686.24–41 (LC, Sixth Petition of the Lord's Prayer).

[288] "Dtn. cum annotationibus, 1525," WA 14:681.33 (AE 9:184): "Thus faith is tested and perfected till hope is made perfect, which makes us sure of our salvation."

[289] Ibid., 682.2.

[290] WA 25:133.3 (AE 16:1–349): "The Spirit of wisdom and understanding pertains to holding to the word of faith; the Spirit of counsel and might to the cross; the Spirit of knowledge and fear to the practice of life among the brothers"; cf. "Jes.-Vorl.," WA 31.2:85.20–27.

Luther's ideas appear again when Melanchthon makes use of them not only in the Augsburg Confession but most especially in the Apology, in his explanation of his views on the structural nature of anthropology and psychology.[291] The elements that form links in the chain from the Word proclaimed to works of love are stated here as follows: *Promissio Euangelii—Spiritus sanctus—fides—Spiritus sanctus—nova vita in cordibus (renovatio cordis)—spirituales motus seu affectus—bona opera* as *impletio legis*.[292] The Holy Spirit appears twice. Within the discussion about justification, the proper sequence is as follows: Gospel—*Spiritus sanctus—fides*; faith is the free gift of the Spirit, who has bound Himself to the Gospel. With respect to sanctification, the following sequence is appropriate: *Fides—Spiritus sanctus—nova vita in cordibus*;[293] faith receives the Spirit as that gift of God that creates our hearts anew. "At all times, faith takes hold of grace and the forgiveness of sins, and nothing else. And since the Holy Spirit is given at the same time through faith, the heart is made fit to do good works."[294] With respect to the essential elements, this sequence was articulated by Luther when he sought to position the sacraments within the framework of promise and faith, as well as in his commentaries on the Psalms;[295] he brings the entire discussion together in "*De captivitate Babylonica*": "*Verbum dei omnium primum est, quod sequitur fides, fidem charitas, Charitas deinde facit omne bonum opus, quia . . . est plenitudo legis* (The Word of God comes first of all, then follows faith, faith then moves to love, and love then produces all sorts of good deeds, which . . . is the fulfilling of the Law)."[296] Luther later expanded even more on this and took a more lively approach when identifying the different aspects than did Melanchthon; he is able to depict the communal aspects of our

---

[291] AC XX (*BSLK*, 80.18–21); Ap IV (*BSLK*, 168.53–169.14; 173.9–15; 185.23–35; 187.27–35).

[292] Melanchthon reflected very carefully on this anthropological and psychological linkage in the commentary of Romans of 1532 and in the middle of the Loci; cf. Greschat, *Melanchthon neben Luther*, 110–65. Concerning the earlier history of these reflections in Melanchthon, cf. Maurer, *Der junge Melanchthon*, 2:361–92; 489–96.

[293] Ap IV (*BSLK*, 169.14–20; 185.23–35).

[294] AC XX (*BSLK*, 80.17–21).

[295] Cf. Peters, *Evangelium und Sakrament*, 142ff.

[296] WA 6:514.19 (AE 36:3–126).

Christian existence in majestic color;[297] he even places the Holy Spirit into the mix internally, in one sense; but in another sense he protects the Spirit's personal majesty still more.[298]

Luther's most expansive attempt to identify individual links in the chain, and his liveliest treatment with respect to the Spirit, comes in the first disputation against the Antinomians.[299] He proceeds here by using the same pattern as was used in the Invocavit sermons and in the Prologue to the German Mass, describing the *Spiritus sanctus* first of all as the "*Auctor legis* (author of the Law)," before dealing with the Spirit as He is received on the basis of the Gospel.[300] No one can be attacked in the conscience by the full force of the law if this is not linked to the Spirit as the "*Auctor legis*," who once upon a time etched the stone tablets with His divine finger, and who now writes on the tablet of one's heart.[301] For this reason, it is proper to say: "First off, before all works and things, one hears the Word of God; therein, the Spirit punishes the world because of sin (John 16:8)."[302] Here the Spirit speaks to us as the "*nudus Deus in maiestate* (God is His pure majesty)"[303] and comes against us as "*Deus in sua natura* (God in His nature),"[304] swooping down upon our heart and conscience with His fire of judgment.

If sins are recognized, then one can hear about the grace of God; the Spirit comes in the same message and gives faith, where and to whom He desires."[305] At this point the Spirit gives Himself to us as

---

[297] Maurer, *Der junge Melanchthon*, 2:263: "With respect to the benefits of Christ, Melanchthon never veered from the path set by Anselm, never understanding the internal nature of the community in Christ because of his humanistic rationality. This is where the greatest differentiation can be shown between his Loci and Luther's tractate on freedom. It is here that he refuses to follow the attempt to make the mystery of the incarnation fruitful theologically with respect to the justification of the sinner."

[298] Tetelbach, *Güldenes Kleinod*, (Reu, *Quellen*, 1.1:690.7): "And thus it is that the beginning, middle, and end of our salvation is the work of the Holy Spirit."

[299] WA 39.1:369.19–371.16; 383.10–26; 389.2–391.20; in the theses themselves, by contrast, the reference to the Spirit is merely mentioned, idem, 349, Theses 37f.

[300] "1. Invocavit-Pred. vom 9.3.1522," WA 10.3:2.1–5.5 (AE 51:70–75); "Vorrede zur Dt. Messe, 1526," WA 19:77.13–78.12 (AE 53:51–90).

[301] "1. Antinomerdisp. vom 18.12.1537," WA 39.1:371.1: "The Law does not show sin to be what it is without the Holy Spirit. God the legislator makes this happen."

[302] "Wider die himmlischen Propheten, 1525," WA 18:139.20 (AE 40:73–223).

[303] "1. Antinomerdisp. vom 18.12.1537," WA 39.1:391.3.

[304] Ibid., 391.18.

[305] "Wider die himmlischen Propheten, 1525," WA 18:139.22 (AE 40:73–223).

"*Donum per Christum* (gift through Christ),"[306] wrapped within the sign of forgiveness. The tension between the *Deus absconditus* (hidden God) as the *Deus nudus in maiestate sua* and that of the *Deus revelatus* as the *Deus in carne involutus* (God enfolded in flesh) is applied thus by the reformer to the Spirit as well. The "opposing nature" that is characteristic of Law and Gospel is rooted in the doctrine of the Trinity; this aspect distinguishes Luther's teaching from the entire tradition up to his time.[307] The Spirit as "*Donum*" is our "*Vivificator et Sanctificator*."[308] Luther portrays His workings in the rich linkage of aspects that are put into schematic form by Melanchthon; the chain really ought to be expanded by inserting *Lex—Spiritus sanctus*. Even when one is being confronted by the sting of the Law in one's conscience, whenever it drives us to the Gospel, it is the work of the gracious Spirit of God.[309]

The Reformed catechisms establish the foundation for this linkage that describes the workings of the Spirit here on earth, with respect to what happens in the Church, by basing it on Rom. 8:28–30, with reference to God's eternal "*Praescientia*" as well as "*Praedestinatio*."[310] At this point they follow Augustine,[311] as well as Luther's lectures on Romans,[312] and additionally what Luther writes against Erasmus.[313] Luther, when at work in the catechisms, concentrates his observations consciously on the earthly activity of the Spirit of God and expands this to identify how that activity will affect the end of time, but he does not connect the Spirit back to the first things. He is thus careful to observe the counsel that Staupitz

---

306 "1. Antinomerdisp. vom 18.12.1537," WA 39.1:370.20f.; 391.19.

307 Cf. Peters, *Trinitätslehre*, cols. 568f.

308 "1. Antinomerdisp. vom 18.12.1537," WA 39.1:389.7; 391.19.

309 "2. Antinomerdisp.," WA 39.1:445.11: "But because we say that despair is useful, it is not considered to be a benefit of the Law, but of the Holy Spirit, who makes the Law to be neither a brigand nor a devil, but a teacher . . . ; this is not done by the power of the Law but by the Gospel, and the Holy Spirit is thus interpreting the Law."

310 Calvin, *Genfer Kat.*, quest. 93, 100; *Heidelberger Kat.*, quest. 54.

311 Augustine admittedly deals more with predestination in the *Enchiridion* (25.98–103); but Rom. 8:29ff. is dealt with in passages such as *De correptione et gratia* 9:23 (Augustinus, *Schriften gegen die Semipelagianer*, 196): "Whosoever, therefore, in God's most providential ordering, are foreknown, predestinated, called, justified, glorified—I say now, even although not yet born at all, are already children of God, and absolutely cannot perish" [Nicene and Post-Nicene Fathers, 1st Series, 5:481].

312 WA 56:383.25–388.2 (AE 25:1–524).

313 "De servo arbitrio, 1525," WA 18:683.11–691.39; 705.14–733.21 (AE 33:3–295).

offered to him once concerning confession of sins, which introduces us to his Christocentric thought process: "Begin your course at the wounds of Christ and describe Christianity for yourself from that point; predestination is at work then already."[314] The one who is making confession knows himself to be enveloped and protected all around by the sanctifying activity of the Spirit, which allows a person to find God's fatherly heart in the offering of Christ.

The conclusion to this discussion underscores the relationship of the Spirit to Christ once again. The lively chain of events that comes into existence when the Spirit is at work has a singular result: coming to Christ and remaining in Christ and thus coming to God. The Spirit proclaims the one who was crucified and raised to life, and has no other message; He thus guides us into truth only insofar as He envelops us ever more deeply into the mystery of Christ. Luther is careful here to preserve the tension in the messages about the Paraclete in the Johannine addresses that describe the imminent departure of Jesus;[315] the Holy Spirit does not take us further on, beyond Jesus Christ, but only deeper into a relationship with Him. At this point, the Spirit is like a poor lute-player who knows how to play but one song.[316] This "bringing to the Lord Christ"[317] is admittedly nothing less than the Triune God coming to the human being. According to John 14:23,[318] Luther depicts it as God making His home within us. By means of His sanctifying work, the Spirit prepares us to be the dwelling place for the Son and the Father. We are to become a house of the living God, both in body and soul.[319] God is a carpenter and is at work in this His dwelling place every day,

---

[314] WATR 2:227, no. 1820 (AE 54:123–165); Scheel, *Dokumente zu Luthers Entwicklung*, no. 262; cf. "Gen.-Vorl., 1535–45," WA 43:461.10 (AE 5:1–386): "*Audi filium incarnatum, et sponte se offeret praedestinatio.*"

[315] On this, see Behm, παράκλητος; Bornkamm, *Der Paraklet im Johannes-Evangelium.*

[316] This is according to "Pred. über Joh. 3:16ff. vom 20.5.1532," WA 36:182.8–11; cf. "Pred. über Joh. 15:26ff. vom 8.5.1524," WA 15:555.26–39; "Pred. über Joh. 15:26ff. vom 13.5.1526," WA 20:390.2–6.

[317] *BSLK*, 654.39f., 16f. (LC).

[318] See "Pred. über Joh. 14:23 vom 1.6.1528," WA 27:159–66; "Pred. über Joh. 14:23 vom 17.5.1529," WA 29:359–65; cf. Mülhaupt, *Ev.-Auslegung*, 4:422–25, 430–35.

[319] "Pred. über Joh. 14:23 vom 1.6.1528," WA 27:160.11: "Then the Holy Spirit comes with all gifts and builds the holy mansion, the temple, the house of God. That dwelling is nothing else since, body and soul, the human being is the house of God"; idem, 161.8: "The mansion is not yet finished, but it is built; He is preparing it so that it will be ready for the Last Day."

in order to make it sturdy for the Day of Judgment.[320] But as He accomplishes His eschatological activity, He confiscates our entire physical existence, now already, in order to rule therein by faith and love. The reformer thus teaches what can be given mere mention in the catechisms, that of an *Unio fidei,* though certainly not an *Unio mystica,*[321] not with Christ alone but with the entire Trinity.[322] Whoever remains under the control of this gracious working of the Spirit of God in faith and love, willingly living in oneness with God, is "no longer a mere human being, but a divine being and is to be more honored than sun and moon, heaven and earth and whatever appears before one's eyes; for God Himself is within him and does such things that no human being or creature can do."[323]

THE SAVING ACTION OF THE SPIRIT OF GOD IN THE CHURCH

Following this train of thought, we can start once again from the outside, looking in, by considering the terms "*sancta ecclesia*" and "*communio sanctorum*" and go forward from that point to discuss the workings of the Spirit of God, in order finally to determine the proper positioning of the individual Christian within the Christian Church.

1. THE CHURCH AS THE "HOLY CHRISTIAN CHURCH"[324]

The reformer points out, with respect to Acts 19:39f.: The word '*ecclesia*' is not adapted from the realm of what is religious and cultic, but has its roots in the political arena. In its most basic sense, the term identifies "those who have been called out and summoned to come together by the herald," the "assembly of full citizens who are properly summoned to congregate together";[325] this would mean that the "purest translation"[326] would be simply: general assembly.[327]

---

[320] "Pred. über Joh. 14:23 vom 17.5.1529," WA 29:360.14f.

[321] (From the editor: In the manuscript, A. Peters placed the words *"Communio fide"* above the words "*Unio fidei.*")

[322] Elert, *Morphologie*, 1:154: "The later teaching about the mystical union is . . . to be traced back with good reason to Luther"; on this point, see the more precise discussion in Peters, *Gegenwart Gottes—Wort Gottes*, esp. 211f.

[323] "Pred. über 1 Joh. 4:16 vom 16.6.1532," WA 36:438.21; cf. "Weihnachtspost. über Joh. 1:1–14, 1522," WA 10.1.1:199.19–27 (AE 52:41–88).

[324] *BSLK*, 655.44–656.26 (LC).

[325] Schmidt, ἐκκλησία, 516ff.; "Von den Konziliis und Kirchen, 1539," WA 50:624.24 (AE 41:3–178): "At this point and often elsewhere, Ecclesia or Church

And yet, this political term, which announces the universal and official summons that no one dare ignore, is connected now with God; the Church conceptualizes itself as the "assembly of God in Christ";[328] the Christians are "a special, called people . . . , a Christian, holy people,"[329] "called together"[330] under Christ as head, through the Spirit of God in one faith and thus, the "*ecclesia Christi*" or "*Dei*."[331] The reformer is thus drawn most especially to use the terminology that was used in the paraphrases of the Symbols during the tenth to twelfth centuries[332] and the popular literature from the late Middle Ages that was based thereon,[333] which confessed a "holy Christendom."[334] The "little word church"[335] by itself is a "blind, meaningless word,"[336] because it does not direct our attention to the multitude that is called together, but rather toward church buildings. This word is thus used in Luther's Bible in the Old Testament alone; with the exception of Gen. 49:6, it refers to the building where worship takes place, the sanctuary.[337] "On the Papacy at Rome, against the most well-known Romanists in Leipzig" (1520) shows the reformer battling valiantly against the notion that the "spiritual, inner

---

means nothing other than a gathered people . . . , just as the mayors call their populace to the meeting hall."

[326] Schmidt, ἐκκλησία, 507.9.

[327] *BSLK*, 656.6, 18; 656.24f.: "community or assembly"; cf. "Von dem Papsttum zu Rom, 1520," WA 6:292.37f. (AE 39:49–104); "Eine kurze Form, 1520," WA 7:219.2; "Kat.-Pred. zum 3. Art. vom 10.12.1528," WA 30.1:92.6 (AE 51:162–169); *Nürnberger Kinderpredigten* (Reu, *Quellen*, 1.1:519.22): "a Christian people or assembly or community."

[328] Schmidt, ἐκκλησία, 509.24; 511.37; 534.14f.

[329] "Von den Konziliis und Kirchen, 1539," WA 50:624.27 (AE 41:3–178).

[330] *BSLK*, 657.29 (LC).

[331] "Ad librum Ambrosii Catharini responsio, 1521," WA 7:712.39; 770.8; 713.3; 720.18; 722.18; 743.2; "Assertio omnium articulorum, 1520," WA 7:127.2.

[332] Hahn, *Bibliothek*, §§ 100, 102, 103, 105, and often elsewhere.

[333] Cf. Meyer, *Historischer Kommentar*, 104f.

[334] *BSLK*, 656.26 (LC); "Von den Konziliis und Kirchen, 1539," WA 50:624.34 (AE 41:3–178): "or as one seeks to articulate it, the Holy Christian Church"; cf. passages such as "Ein Sermon von der Bereitung zum Sterben, 1519," WA 2:694.30 (AE 42:95–115); "Von dem Papsttum zu Rom, 1520," WA 6:292.26–297.35 (AE 39:49–104); "Eine kurze Form, 1520," WA 7:219.11; "Pred. zum 3. Art. vom 6.3.1523," WA 11:53.24; "Kat.-Pred. zum 3. Art. vom 10.12.1528," WA 30.1:92.8 (AE 51:162–169); song: "Gott sei gelobet und gebenedeiet," WA 35:452.5 (AE 53:252–254) = *EKG* 163, st. 3 (*LSB* 617).

[335] *BSLK*, 656.7, 17 (LC).

[336] "Von den Konziliis und Kirchen, 1539," WA 50:625.5 (AE 41:3–178).

[337] According to Althaus, *Theologie Luthers*, 249, n. 6.

Christian Church,"[338] which alone is attested in the Scriptures, is to be identified with and judged on the basis of the physical and external buildings, rites, and church ordinances.[339]

Luther's derivation of "*Curia*," as a loanword from Latin[340] seems to be based on what Tertullian wrote in his *Apologeticum*: "When we are gathered together, we are exactly the same as what we are when we are scattered, all of us, one with another, what each is individually. . . . When righteous and good people assemble together, when pious and pure people unite together, that is not deserving of the name of some splinter group, but should be called a senate."[341] Tertullian praises the characteristic of the Church that it is obligated to operate everywhere in the open. The term that Tertullian found important for explaining an actual situation appears to Luther to explain a derivation; etymologically, however, "*curia*" belongs to "*quiris*," full citizen [Tr.: in their civil capacity as Romans].[342] In addition, reference to the Celtic "*kyrk*," which is similar to the Latin "*circus*," in that it defines a space that is enclosed on all sides, is rejected today as well.[343] What is left, which Luther had suggested initially,[344] is the everyday Greek vulgar form κυρικόν, (from the older κυριακόν), which was used in the feminine and might have come into the vocabulary of the Old High German through either an early missionary effort of the Gothic-Arian movement (Gothic: "*kyrikô*")[345] or by way of Marseille—Lyon—Trier.[346] By means of this newly constructed vocabulary word, the Christians give witness that their community; the places where they gather together for worship of God are subject to and belong to the Lord. The reformer wanted to accentuate this foundational concept in his use of the word Christian Church (*Christenheit*), "so that it will be demonstrated that

---

338 WA 6:297.1 (AE 39:49–104).

339 The polemic against a misunderstanding of this type is taken up in the *Nürnberger Kinderpredigten* (Reu, *Quellen*, 1.1:519.23–26) and by Dietenberger, *Katechismus* (Moufang, *Katholische Katechismen*, 26).

340 *BSLK*, 656.22 (LC).

341 Tertullian, *Apologeticus* 39:21.96ff. (CCSL 1:153; cited according to BKV 24:146f.).

342 *BSLK*, 656, n. 7.

343 Cf. Schmidt, ἐκκλησία, 535, n. 92.

344 *BSLK*, 656.21 (LC).

345 Thus Kluge, *Gotische Lehnworte im Althochdeutschen*, 124ff.

346 Thus Frings, *Germania Romana*, 24, 31, 37f., 46, 50, 120, and idem, *Grundlegung einer Geschichte der dt. Sprache*, 20, 59.

the Christian Church as a whole has no other head, on earth either, except Christ, since Christians bear no other name than that of Christ."[347]

2. The Communio *Sanctorum* as a "Holy Community"[348]

Luther considers the phraseology "*communio sanctorum*" that is used in the *Textus receptus* to be a gloss[349] to "*sancta ecclesia*"; only after the time of Rufinus[350] would it have made its way into the text of the Apostles' Creed.[351] With respect to the content, its purpose is to underscore: this holy gathering is a "community, within which are none except completely holy people, . . . a holy community."[352]

As far as interpretations of the Symbol are concerned, this phrase appears for the first time in writings of Niceta of Remesiana (about 400); in the context in which it is mentioned, it designates all who have lived from the creation of the world up to those who will be living at the time when Christ's return ensues, the "*sanctorum omnium congregatio*" of the patriarchs, prophets, apostles, martyrs and righteous ones, as well as the angels, whom we will join someday to acquire an eternal portion.[353]

And yet, the formula "*Communio sanctorum*"[354] has an earlier history in the East that can be clarified only in part. As can be noted in what Jerome writes during his sojourn in the Desert of Chalcis between 374 and 379, in the confession of faith that he had been

---

[347] "Von dem Papsttum zu Rom, 1520," WA 6:295.7 (AE 39:49–104); cf. ibid., 297.36–298.26; "Pred. de sacramento vom 24.3.1529," WA 29:153.2: "Ecclesia Christiana est Christo subdita"; cf. "Ad librum Ambrosii Catharini responsio, 1521," WA 7:709.25–33.

[348] *BSLK*, 657.1–42 (LC).

[349] *BSLK*, 657.4.

[350] See "Resolutio Lutheriana super propositione sua decima tertia de potestate papae, 1519," WA 2:190.20–25; *BSLK*, 656, n. 1; Rufinus, *Expositio symboli* 34; Denzinger, 16.

[351] "Resolutio . . . , 1519," WA 2:190.23ff.; "Pred. zum 3. Art. vom 6.3.1523," WA 11:53.20–23; "Kat.-Pred. zum 3. Art. vom 10.12.1528," WA 30.1:92.9 (AE 51:162–169); cf. Erasmus, *Explanatio Symboli*, col. 1174C; Calvin, *Inst.*, 4:1.3.

[352] *BSLK*, 657.11.

[353] Niceta, *Explanatio symboli* 10 (PL 52:871A–C); ibid.: "Therefore, in this one Church you should believe that the communal relationship will follow after the saints. By decree, this one universal Church was established throughout the entire globe of the earth; this communal relationship you ought to retain firmly."

[354] On this, see Kattenbusch, *Symbol*, 2:927–50; Kelly, *Creeds*, 388–97; Eichenseer, *Apostolicum*, 377–87; Elert, *Abendmahl und Kirchengemeinschaft*, 166–81 (excursus); Schulz, *Communio sanctorum*.

asked to compose,[355] and which is supported in the decrees of the emperors and in decisions of councils,[356] one has a general right to participate communally in the Lord who is given to us under bread and wine. The proclamation in the liturgy: "The Holy One for the Holy Ones!"[357] shapes the character of this spiritual, embryonic cell group. The original meaning must thus have been something like: "Participation in the body and blood of Christ that is present in a most mysterious way . . . in the community of the brothers who believe."[358] When the Eucharist is celebrated, still another point of emphasis involves the further dimension of *koinonia* with the fathers and saints now fallen asleep, even though this may not be stated in a strict formula in so many words.

As this phraseology made its way to the West, it acquired a new meaning because of the veneration of the saints and martyrs. According to a passionate sermon preached by Victricius of Rouen in 396, concerning the relics that were sent to him by Ambrose, such relics were supposedly conveying the concrete presence of those who had died, to whom God had supposedly bound Himself in a most miraculous way.[359] This addition to the Creed works its way into the Symbols in Gaul and in Spain during the fifth century, always in the sequence "*sanctorum communionem*."[360] The personal aspect comes front and center;[361] "*communio sanctorum*" attests to the oneness of those who believe, amongst one another and with those who were righteous throughout the ages, as well as with the angels, but most especially with the martyrs who had been uniquely exalted by God and by the particular communities that were according them honor at any particular time.

---

[355] Jerome, *Epistulae* 92:3 (CSEL 55:150f.); cf. Elert, *Abendmahl und Kirchengemeinschaft*, 12f.

[356] See the analyses in Elert, *Abendmahl und Kirchengemeinschaft*, 171ff.

[357] *Apostolic Constitutions and Canons* 8:13.12; Cyril of Jerusalem, *Catecheses mystagogicae* 5:19; "Testamentum Domini n. J. Chr.," Quasten, *Monum. Eucharistica et Lit. vetustissima*, 5:250.28; Brightman, *Liturgies Eastern and Western*, 1:475, 480, and more elsewhere.

[358] Eichenseer, *Apostolicum*, 386; Elert, *Abendmahl und Kirchengemeinschaft*, 13f., 168, 175ff.

[359] Victricius, *De laude sanctorum* (PL 20:443–58).

[360] Cf. Denzinger, 26–29.

[361] See the examples in Kattenbusch, *Symbol*, 2:941ff.; Elert, *Abendmahl und Kirchengemeinschaft*, 10f., 170ff.

The meanings accorded to both scenarios had been merged together already by Augustine, admittedly without the phrase having taken on a fixed, set meaning;[362] but it was indeed true that Christ's one body encompassed both the "*ecclesia peregrinans*," consisting of pilgrims still on their journey down below, and also the "*ecclesia beata*," made up of the angels and those whose journey was complete, most especially the martyrs; both assemblies were present at the offering of the mass as well as in constant communication with one another by means of petitions.[363]

During the Middle Ages, this viewpoint of the church fathers became more coarse and contractual, devolving into teaching about the treasure of Christ and the saints. The pope, as the one who administered the keys of the kingdom of heaven because the Lord had accorded to him that power, was in charge of giving access to truly repentant sinners, by according to them plenary indulgence. By and large, the paraphrases of the Symbols explained the "*communio sanctorum*" in an individualistic way,[364] though the sacramental aspect admittedly is present here as well.[365] One thinks of the unity of the believers in heaven and on earth, which grows out of participation in the Christian Church's sacred treasures.[366]

---

[362] See the examples in Eichenseer, *Apostolicum*, 377ff.

[363] Augustine, *Enchiridion de fide, spe, et caritate* 15:56; 16:61; on Augustine's understanding of the Church, see Hofmann, *Der Kirchenbegriff des hl. Augustinus*; Ratzinger, *Volk und Haus Gottes in Augustins Lehre von der Kirche*. A corresponding overview is offered in Erasmus, *Explanatio Symboli*, col. 1174Df.: "Some more recent theologians, however, interpret the holy church as a society of earthly soldiers under the leadership of Christ, and the communion of saints as a society of saints triumphant in heaven. Others, again, explain the communion of saints as the church's intercessory prayer, useful to all who belong to the body of the holy church. Still others explain it as the sacraments of the church, which are of no value to anyone except those who attach themselves to the church. Yet another group thinks that the word 'communion' designates the Eucharist . . . because this sacrament signifies and strengthens the very close connection between the mystical body and the head" [Erasmus, 70:336–37].

[364] Hahn, *Bibliothek*, §§ 101–17.

[365] A Norman-French translation constructs the formula: "*la communion des seintes choses*" (Hahn, *Bibliothek*, § 74); Abelard also writes in his *Expos. symb*. (PL 178:629): "We are able to speak of the saints in a neutral sense, that is, as sanctified by both bread and wine in the Sacrament of the Altar." And yet, the understanding that is non-commital is rare.

[366] Concerning the interpretation, cf. Althaus, *Communio sanctorum*, 1:10ff.

In keeping with some paraphrases of the Symbols from the twelfth century,[367] Luther wanted to render "association of saints" (*Gemeinschaft der Heiligen*),[368] which did not sound right in German, as "congregation of saints" (*Gemeinde der Heiligen*),[369] as "communion or assembly (*Gemeine* or *Sammlung*) . . . of those who live in true faith, hope, and love."[370] But this would forfeit the biblical sense of the word "*Koinonia*," since that term refers to "the association formed by those who participate in whatever is appended in the genitive [Tr.: = association *of*]; in its most basic sense, it identifies the participation itself, not a community formed by numerous subjects who are bound together by such participation in the same event. And, in fact, the original meaning is that one is guaranteed the right to participate, so that it is the status that is being communicated; the genitive actually serves as the subject of those (who themselves) are participating or designates the actual participation, which can therefore thus also have a personal dimension."[371] For this reason, κοινωνία, in the specific meaning of the word, cannot be used as another way to say ἐκκλησία, and is thus to be interpreted, with respect to its context, as needless repetition.[372] Luther's translation "a holy community" (*ein heilige Gemeine*)[373] conceals the original meaning. For this reason, the modern ecumenical rendering returns to "communion of saints" (*Gemeinschaft der Heiligen*); one can justify this translation on the basis of the fact that "community" can be understood too much in the sense of a physical assembly.

The biblical sense of the word "communion," with specific permission granted to participate in core activities, as is guaranteed to an individual, or else the right to participate that is obtained by someone else, is not a foreign notion to Luther. He interprets the concept in this way when he states: "I am a part and member of that same communion, with rights to all its benefits, and thus a participant

[367] Hahn, *Bibliothek*, §§ 108, 111: "I believe in the community of all God's saints"; idem, § 110: "I believe in the community of the Holy Christian Church."

[368] *BSLK*, 656.1–4 (LC).

[369] *BSLK*, 657.11.

[370] "Von dem Papsttum zu Rom, 1520," WA 6:293.2 (AE 39:49–104).

[371] Von Soden, *Sacrament und Ethik bei Paulus*, 8, note.

[372] Seesemann, *Der Begriff KOINONIA im NT*, 99: "Nowhere in Paul is κοινωνία used by Paul to refer to a 'community' in the sense of a *societas* –association. The term κοινωνία cannot be used as a parallel term for ἐκκλησία."

[373] *BSLK*, 657.13f.

and fellow member."[374] When he was commenting on 1 Cor. 10:16f., being particularly exercised, as he was, in his battle with the "Enthusiasts," he made it clear that the genitive at this point identifies the benefit that we get to share, which by extension binds us together, one to the other.[375] We walk with Christ "in the communal relationship of sharing all of what is His and He is in a communal relationship with all of our possessions."[376] Particularly in his early sermons on death and on the Lord's Supper,[377] Luther emphasized both the "*admirabile commercium*," the "happy exchange and encounter"[378] between Christ and the believer, as gift and responsibility, grace and calling. Christ and His saints come before God on our behalf and He protects us in all temptations, so that we can act in mercy for those on earth who are "needy" in body or soul. The priesthood of all believers is properly located spiritually at this point. "The foundation of the Church is Christ's priesthood, conceptualized thereby in its essence as the priesthood of Christians, one for the other."[379] It is lived out as one gives of self to the neighbor in both internal and external ways, in proclamation of the Word, petition, and caring actions. A person in the late Middle Ages especially sought the intercessions of the saints on behalf of his own earthly needs and looked for the way that their accomplishments could be transferred over to his account through indulgences. The

---

[374] *BSLK*, 657.33–35; Albrecht, in WA 30.1:189, n. 3: "In the sixteenth century *Gemeinschaft* means normally, as with the Latin *communio*, being bound together, common claim or common participation in something."

[375] "Vom Abendmahl Christi, 1528," WA 26:490.26 (AE 37:151–372): "Community at this point means the common possessions that many partake of and enjoy, as that which is given communally among all of them"; cf. ibid., 490.7–497.22; "Wider die himmlischen Propheten, 1525," WA 18:168.14–24; 199.19–27 (AE 40:73–223).

[376] "Sermon am Gründonnerstag, 2.4.1523," WA 12:486.8.

[377] "Resolutiones disp. de indulgentiarum virtute, 1518," WA 1:593.2–38 (AE 31:77–252); "Gal.-Komm., 1519," WA 2:602.15–605.34 (AE 27:151–410); "Tessaradecas consolatoria . . . , 1520," WA 6:130.24–132.24 (AE 42:117–166); "Von der Freiheit eines Christenmenschen, 1520," WA 7:25.26–26.17 (AE 31:327–377); "De libertate christiana, 1520," WA 7:54.31–55.36 (AE 31:327–377); "Post. über Joh. 1:19–23 zum 4. Advent 1521," WA 7:520.29–33; "Magnificat, 1521," WA 7:597.9–18 (AE 21:295–355); "Pred. über Apg. 1 vom 18.5.1520," WA 9:458.4–26.

[378] "Von der Freiheit eines Christenmenschen, 1520," WA 7:25.34 (AE 31:327–377).

[379] Althaus, *Theologie Luthers*, 270; cf. ibid., 262–78. Concerning the priesthood of all believers, see above all others Niedermeier, *Das allgemeine Priestertum aller Gläubigen und das geistliche Amt*; Sommerlath, *Amt und allgemeines Priestertum*; Storck, *Das allgemeine Priestertum bei Luther*; Brunotte, *Das geistliche Amt bei Luther*; Lieberg, *Amt und Ordination bei Luther und Melanchthon*, 40–103.

reformer showed how it was Christ who sacrificed Himself on our behalf and freed us from concern for ourselves, so that we can act freely toward others in love. He summarized the quintessence of those early sermons in his Short Form of 1520: "I believe that all things are in common in this communion or Christian assembly and every single thing belongs to the other as well, and nothing belongs to anyone alone, so that for me and for every believer all prayers and good works are to come to the aid of the entire communion; we are to stand by one another and must support one another at all times, in life and in death, and thus each one is to carry the other's burden, as Saint Paul (Gal. 6:2) teaches."[380]

These insights are sadly not treated fully in the catechisms. The fact that Luther did not abandon such thinking altogether after the battle for the real presence,[381] but can still articulate such issues after 1524, can be demonstrated in his commentary on the High Priestly Prayer that was formulated at the same time as he was preaching his catechetical sermons.[382] In this context, he depicts the spiritual comfort that comes for each individual from the calming assurance that each one is "brought by the Spirit of God into the body," into the *Communio sanctorum*; Luther is supported by the evangelists in maintaining that the oneness of the Church is rooted in Christ's oneness with the heavenly Father. Whoever dares to lay hands on any individual believer gets entangled in the unbreakable unity that each one shares with Peter, Paul, Mary and Isaiah, with Christ Himself, with all angels and creatures, finally in reality with God the Father Himself,[383] since each Christian is part of the body of the Church, and the Church reposes in Christ and Christ Himself reposes in the Father. "As the Father and the Son are a divine being, Christ is thus also a Christian being with His Christendom."[384]

---

[380] WA 7:219.11; cf. "Sermo de digna praeparatione cordis pro suscipiendo sacramento eucharistiae, 1518," WA 1:333.13–26; "Sermon von dem hochwürdigen Sakrament, 1519," WA 2:745.1–746.5 (AE 35:45–73); "Tessaradecas consolatoria . . . , 1520," WA 6:131.14–29 (AE 42:117–166).

[381] Althaus sees it thus, *Theologie Luthers*, 278.

[382] WA 28:70–200.

[383] "Zu Joh. 17:11ff. vom 26.9.1528," ibid., 150:10ff.

[384] "Zu Joh. 17:20f. vom 17.10.1528," ibid., 187.19; see also "Zu Joh. 17:11ff. vom 26.9.1528," ibid., 182.1–185.1; 147.1–152.14; "Zu Joh. 17:22f. vom 24.10.1528," ibid., 187.1–190.18. Hardeland, *Katechismusgedanken*, 248, already calls attention to these passages; he mentions, in addition, "Pred. über Joh. 20:11ff. vom 21.4.1530," WA 32:80.9–83.15 and "Osterpred. vom 10.4.1531," WA 34.1:293.4–298.4. The

That which is applicable for the individual believer is even more true for Christendom as a whole; it is completely enveloped and hidden within the almighty saving presence of the triune God.[385] It is not the Spirit alone who "remains" with His community until the Last Day.[386] He constantly draws all members together under the one Christ, who is the head,[387] and holds the community close by its Lord.[388] The Church is thus framed by the presence of Christ; the merciful God-Father is Himself close at hand in Christ at the same time. Along with Tertullian and Augustine,[389] Luther praises the Church as the place where the triune God prepares the eschatological dwelling place, where, though hidden, He is enthroned already and reigns in faith and in love.[390] It "is true: Christ desires to have His dwelling where the Father and Holy Spirit are and want to dwell, the entire Trinity [Tr.: *Dreifaltigkeit*] dwells in the true Church; what the true Church does and orders, that is what God does and orders."[391]

---

reformer carries the argument forward in opposition to both the Arians and the Swiss, stating that our essential oneness with God in Christ goes beyond the level of any community of those who are like-minded and who desire to be together (*unitas cordis vel voluntatis*) ("Zu Joh. 17:22f. vom 24.10.1528," WA 28:187.10–25).

385 See further citations in Höhne, *Luthers Anschauung über die Kontinuität der Kirche*, 107–10.

386 *BSLK*, 657.42–44 (LC).

387 *BSLK*, 657.28–30.

388 *BSLK*, 512.7 (SC).

389 Tertullian, *De baptismo* 6:2.11–14 (CCSL 1:282); idem, *De corona* 3:3.15–17 (CCSL 2:1042); Augustine, *Enchiridion de fide, spe, et caritate* 15:56 (CCSL 46:80): "The temple of God, then, that is, of the Supreme Trinity as a whole, is the Holy Church, embracing in its full extent both heaven and earth" [Nicene & Post-Nicene Fathers, 1st Series, 3:256]; see the numerous further examples in Hofmann, *Der Kirchenbegriff des hl. Augustinus*, 133–95.

390 "Dict. super Psalt., 1513–16," WA 3:532.17–26 (AE 11:1–553); "Eine einfältige Weise zu beten, 1535," WA 38:374.33–35 (AE 43:187–211); "Gen.-Vorl., 1535–45," WA 43:597.11–602.5 (AE 5:1–386); "Predigten über Joh. 14 und 15, 1537/38," WA 45:606.26–607.25 (AE 24:1–422); "Pred. über Joh. 14:23–31 vom 24.5.1539," WA 47:772–79 (AE 51:301–312); "Von den Konziliis und Kirchen, 1539," WA 50:625.22–26 (AE 41:3–178).

391 "Pred. über Joh. 14:23–31 vom 24.5.1539," WA 47:773.26 (AE 51:301–312).

3. The One, Holy, Catholic Church, as That Which is Sanctified in Faith through the Gospel and Is the United "Christian Church on Earth" in Love[392]

We need to go deeper still in explicating how Luther renders and interprets the adjectives "holy" and "catholic." We will additionally have to clarify how the tradition came into being and what is meant by it.[393] The New Testament already prepares the way for ἅγια ἐκκλησία being used;[394] it appears specifically in Ignatius of Antioch, in the prescript of the Letter to the Trallians, as well as in the Shepherd of Hermas.[395] The concept is intimated in Ignatius's Letter to the Smyrnians.[396] The predicate καθολική appears there for the first time as well,[397] in which both nuances of meaning are suggested from the outset. The first emphasis was most important for Ignatius, μία μόνη, *una sola*;[398] later on, οἰκουμενική, *universalis*, *universa*, is emphasized too. In the Martyrdom of Polycarp, the community at Smyrna greets the other communities, which are also scattered, as strangers and sojourners, as colonies "τῆς ἁγίας και καθολικῆς ἐκκλησίας (of the holy and catholic Church)";[399] this is the first time that the two adjectives are linked together.

When he writes against second century Gnostic heresies, Irenaeus articulates in detail how God's plan of salvation included one Church that was all-encompassing. One finds reference thereafter to the "*sancta ecclesia*" in the baptismal questions from the Apostolic Tradition, as recorded by Hippolytus;[400] the Papyrus from Deir-Balyzeh speaks of the "*sancta catholica ecclesia*"[401] as the spiritual location for the divine work of salvation and thus as the all-encompassing place of protection for the baptized. The Old Roman Baptismal Symbol shows that "*sancta ecclesia*" is in use already. The

---

392 *BSLK*, 657.25–658.2; 659.44–660.13 (LC).
393 Cf. Kattenbusch, *Symbol*, 2:689–706.
394 In passages such as 1 Cor. 14:33; Eph. 5:27; 1 Pet. 2:5, 9.
395 Herm., *Vis.* 1:1.6; 3:4; cf. *BSLK*, 24.
396 Ign., *Smyrn.* 8:1.
397 Ibid., 8:2.
398 According to Kattenbusch, *Symbol*, 2:922, 926.
399 *Martyrdom of Polycarp, Inscr*. (SC 10:242); cf. Kattenbusch, *Symbol*, 2:923.
400 Botte, *Note sur le symbole baptismal der Saint Hippolyte*, 191.
401 ἐν τῇ ἁγίᾳ καθολικῇ ἐκκλησία (Roberts/Capelle, *An early euchologium*, 32f., 60f.; Kelly, *Creeds*, 88f.; Denzinger, 2.

phraseology "*catholica ecclesia*" appears at first in the East[402] and makes its way to the West toward the end of the fourth century. Niceta of Remesiana uses it;[403] Augustine does not seem to be aware of its use as a fixed element in a confession of faith.[404] It is taken up most especially in the early fifth century in Gaul and Spain[405] and finds its place in the *Textus receptus* through that avenue.

In terms of content, the adjective "*sancta*" points back to the sanctifying work of the Spirit of God in the believers, whereby the Church is extracted from the world that is passing away and God's sanctifying work is positioned in its proper location. It is God . . . who identifies how the Church is distinctive, separates it out, marks it as unique, makes it holy: to the extent that the Holy Spirit takes control over the heart of human beings and establishes His rule, God justifies and sanctifies sinful human beings and in just this way provides the foundation for the communion of saints."[406]

Because of the conflicts waged by the Church-at-large against splinter groups, the added descriptor "*catholica*" came to take on a new meaning, in which context the additional adjective "*apostolica*"[407] was at work as well. The *Ecclesia catholica* is not merely an all-encompassing Christendom that spans the entire inhabited world, in contrast to the sects that were able to plant their feet in only a few neighborhoods of the world. It is concurrently the "completely valid," only true and orthodox Church, because it has preserved the apostolic traditions within the community of bishops, purely and publicly.[408] The "*per totum orbem, per omnem mundum diffusa*," which articulates the extent of the spatial expanse, faded into the background of the tradition as time passed, as is demonstrated in

---

[402] In the *Symbol from Jerusalem* (Denzinger, 41), in Epiphanius (Denzinger, 42, 44) and in some other Symbols (cf. Lietzmann, *Symbolstudien*, 208f.), and finally it is found also in the Nicene Creed (Denzinger, 150; *BSLK*, 26f.).

[403] Niceta, *Explanatio symboli* 10 (PL 52:871A); Denzinger, 19.

[404] On Augustine, see Eichenseer, *Apostolicum*, 392–98.

[405] Cf. Denzinger, 23, 26–29 and Kelly, *Creeds*, 385f.

[406] Küng, *Die Kirche*, 386.

[407] Cf. Lietzmann, *Symbolstudien*, 208ff.

[408] Augustine, *De Genesi ad litteram imperfectus liber* 1 (CSEL 28.1:461.2): "which is called Catholic, because it is everywhere perfect, not at all weak, and because it is spread throughout the whole world" [Augustine, Fathers of the Church, 84:147]; Isidore, *Sententiarum libri tres* 1:16.6 (PL 83:572A/B): "The Church is thus called holy . . . the Church, in fact, is universal since it is extended throughout the whole world and is built up as a community from all nations." Further examples are in Eichenseer, *Apostolicum*, 391, n. 168.

the well-known formulation of Vincent of Lerins: "*Quod ubique, quod semper, quod ab omnibus creditum est; hoc est etenim vere proprieque catholicum* (What has been believed everywhere, always, and by all; this is truly and properly catholic)."[409] Cyril of Jerusalem articulates the extensive and the intensive power of salvation of the one, holy, catholic Church succinctly, in his eighteenth catechetical lecture that is addressed to those about to be baptized: The Church is called catholic because everywhere and unceasingly it teaches everything that the human being needs to know, whether visible or invisible, whether heavenly or earthly, because it leads the entire human race, rulers and subjects, educated and uneducated, to worship God, because it deals with and brings restoration for every manner of sin that is perpetrated by soul and body, and finally because it possesses within itself every manner of virtue, whether such appear in deeds or words or in any sort of gracious gifts."[410]

Luther enters into this tradition, but admittedly follows the custom that had developed in the fifteenth century,[411] which rendered the adjective "*catholica*" as "*christenlich*" or "*christlich.*" But he takes this alteration, which he had inherited from tradition, and turns it into a polemical term as a way to oppose the Church being bound to the papacy: "One can do no better than to translate *Catholica* into German with *christlich,* as has been done elsewhere already. The point: wherever Christians are, throughout the entire world, that is where the pope blusters and wants to have his manor house alone to be identified as the Christian Church."[412] The reformer places his finger thereby on an interesting problematic. The papacy had not, as yet, been mentioned anywhere in the paraphrases of the Creed during the Middle Ages; Peter Lombard's massive effort to gather together all the Sentences accords it only brief mention, under the church orders for the presbyter.[413] Thomas Aquinas constructs the bridge from the Church to the papacy in his commentary on the Apostles'

---

[409] Vincent of Lérins, *Commonitorium* 2:3.5 (*Florilegium Patristicum* 5:11f.).

[410] Cyril of Jerusalem, *Catechesis* 18:23 (PG 33:1044A/B), cited from BKV 41:351ff.

[411] Cf. Meyer, *Historischer Kommentar*, 95; Dibelius, *Das Vaterunser*, 114–19.

[412] "Die drei Symbola, 1538," WA 50:283 (AE 34:197–229), glosses.

[413] Peter Lombard, *Sententiarum* IV, dist. 24.9 (PL 192:904): "And Christ first selected twelve disciples and called them apostles, whose succession the major bishops carry in the Church. Then He designated another seventy-two disciples, whose succession priests carry in the Church. One, however, stood out among the apostles as foremost, Peter, whose vicar and successor is the highest bishop, being called apostolic and pope, certainly father of fathers."

Creed with the aid of the "*fundamentum secundarium*" of the apostles and their teaching, which he permits to coalesce into the person of Peter; the Church of Peter in Rome alone remained protected from all the heresies and was thus pure with respect to the living faith.[414] The papacy is mentioned specifically only in the catechisms from the Counter-Reformation era.[415]

Luther's blunt way of countering with an attack against the "*Ecclesia romana*" is certainly but one of the external symptoms of a deeper adjustment in the view of the nature of Christendom. Without giving up on the notion that the Church spans the globe through space and time, the reformer rejects the Church's selfconscious claim that its character is that of the "*Ecclesia triumphans*." Guided by the Scriptures, especially by the relentless battle of the prophets against the people who had trashed the place that He established for them to dwell in safety, as well as the castigation of the apostles against a self-righteousness that caused some to separate from others, he frames it as follows: The Church remains here on earth under the cross of its Lord, which has been fighting a bitter battle against the "sanctuaries of Cain"[416] that are populated by the hypocrites who lay their own accomplishments before God and claim to save themselves on the basis of their own works. True Christians live "far from one another,"[417] in the Diaspora, not only in the world, but also in the visible Church. "*Abscondita est ecclesia, latent sancti* (the Church is hidden, the saints unseen)."[418] And yet, once again, this paradoxical cruciform nature of the Church is merely hinted at in the catechisms; what stands in the center here is the joyful confession about the "*sancta ecclesia catholica*."

In agreement with the tradition he inherited, the reformer underscores the catholicity of the Church, with respect both to its spatial and temporal dimensions; he admittedly treats this as a constant, which always accompanies the polemic against the papacy and its claims. The "one, holy, communal Christian Church"[419] is

---

[414] Thomas Aquinas, *Expositio in Symbolum Apostolorum*, §§ 985f.

[415] In the Roman Catholic catechisms that are printed in Moufang, *Katholische Katechismen*, the pope (or else Rome) is mentioned in Dietenberger (26), Fabri (425), Wicelius (481) and Canisius (565, 567).

[416] "Weihnachtspost. zu Gal. 4:1–7, 1522," WA 10.1.1:330.21; 331.17; 368.8; 374.3.

[417] "Von weltlicher Oberkeit, 1523," WA 11:251.36 (AE 45:75–129).

[418] "De servo arbitrio, 1525," WA 18:652.23 (AE 33:3–295).

[419] "Eine kurze Form, 1520," WA 7:219.2.

intended to convey "as far as the world stretches."[420] As a community of those who properly worship God in the Holy Spirit, it is not bound to a particular place, but is scattered "throughout the world"; it is not only where the Roman pope claims to rule, but is also among the "Turks, Persians, Mongols."[421] At the same time, the Church permeates all ages as well; even though it came forth on Pentecost in a new format, according to plan, it is not instituted by that event;[422] its origin is in Paradise and it will make its way forward under the power of the Spirit of God to the Last Day.[423] Making use of Paul (1 Cor. 10:1–13) and John (John 8:50–58), as well as Hebrews 11, Luther follows the early church fathers and draws the arch back all the way to the foundation of the world.[424] The Church was founded in Paradise, when God gave Adam the fruits of all the trees in the divine garden, but God charged him not to eat from the tree of knowledge; the Church was reconstituted after the fall by means of the promise of Christ's offering that would take place in the future, which God uttered in what is known as the *Protoevangelium* (Gen. 3:15).[425] From that time on, throughout the entire Old Testament, the "*Christus incarnandus* (Christ becoming incarnate)" plan unfolds. Thus, from the time of Adam, the one holy people of God has been wandering through time and space in various forms on the way toward the promised fulfillment; the Spirit of God is at work therein, carrying out His eschatological mission work through the Gospel.[426] Through

---

[420] Ibid., 219.1; "Dict. super Psalt., 1513–16," WA 3:138.23 (AE 10:1–464): "The Church is scattered throughout all nations": ibid., 350.33: "The Church is scattered among the countries of the earth."

[421] "Vom Abendmahl Christi, 1528," WA 26:506.36, 38 (AE 37:151–372).

[422] Cf. "Pred. über Apg. 2 vom 18.5.1529," WA 29:373.14–374.1; Luther understands the Acts of the Apostles here as the history of the Holy Spirit.

[423] "Weihnachtspred. über Jes. 9:2–7 vom 26.12.1525," WA 19:164.11–17.

[424] See passages such as "Promotionsthesen für Schmedenstede vom 7.7.1542," WA 39.2:187f., Theses 1–20 (AE 34:299–321); "Gen.-Vorl., 1535–45," on Gen. 2:16f., WA 42:79.1–81.14 (AE 1:1–359); "Fastenpost. über 1 Kor. 10, 1525," WA 17.2:129–35; "Festpost. über Mt. 1:1–16, 1527," WA 17.2:468–75. Additional examples are in Höhne, *Luthers Anschauung über die Kontinuität der Kirche*, 20ff.; Bornkamm, *Luther und das Alte Testament*, 176–84.

[425] "Gen.-Vorl., 1535–45," WA 42:141.1–147.41 (AE 1:1–359); "Promotionsthesen für Schmedenstede vom 7.7.1542," WA 39.2:187, Thesis 1 (AE 34:303): "One and the same God has been worshipped from the beginning of the world in different ways through faith in the same Christ."

[426] Concerning the missionary dimension of the Church, see Elert, *Morphologie*, 1, § 28, 336–51; ibid., 338: "The Gospel is always on the rise, always underway, always on the offensive. It is to go to all peoples."

Word and faith He draws human beings into faith daily[427] and thus prepares the human race extensively and intensively[428] for the final consummation. The sanctifying activity of the Spirit that encircles the globe is emphasized by Luther at the conclusion to the Third Article in the Large Catechism.[429] Section I of the Fourth General Assembly of the Ecumenical Conference of 1968 in Uppsala [Tr.: entitled "The Holy Spirit and the Catholicity of the Church"] is more specific still: "Christ's plan is that human beings of all time, all races, all places, and all situations are to be led by the Holy Spirit under the universal fatherhood of God to be an organic and living unity in Christ."[430]

By contrast with the early Church, particularly with respect to Augustine,[431] Luther directs his attention specifically to earthly aspects;[432] Christ for him is admittedly the head and Lord, over the angels as well, which He associates as having interaction with us in the worldly and spiritual realm; but Luther does not buy the notion that human beings were created to replace the host of the fallen angels. In contradistinction to what was taught in the Church of the Middle Ages and to teachings current in the Roman Catholic Church of his day,[433] he did not describe the heavens as populated with the host of those who had been fully justified, as the Church Triumphant already in the present. He reserves the eschatological fulfillment of the Scriptures for the Last Day. The righteous who have fallen asleep rest in the bosom of Abraham until the day when Christ is to return, which is taught as a promise in the Word of God.[434] At the same time, Luther brings the Last Day into the immediacy of the here and now; since time is suspended when death comes, we are drawn right into

---

[427] *BSLK*, 660.6f. (LC).

[428] *BSLK*, 660.5–13.

[429] *BSLK*, 660.3–13; cf. 673.45–674.6 (LC, Second Petition of the Lord's Prayer).

[430] *Bericht aus Uppsala 1968*, 9.

[431] Augustine, *Enchiridion de fide, spe, et caritate* 9:29; 15:56; 16:61f.; idem, *De civitate Dei* 22:1.2; Thomas Aquinas, *Expositio in Symbolum Apostolorum*, § 982: "But this Church has three parts. One is on earth, another is in heaven, another is in purgatory."

[432] *BSLK*, 512.5 (SC): "The entire Christian Church *on earth*"; cf. *BSLK*, 655.3; 657.27; 660.2 (LC).

[433] According to the Union Council at Lyon, 1275 (Denzinger, 856ff.), and Florence, 1439 (Denzinger, 1304ff.), those humans who were freed from needing punishments for sins would be taken up into heaven immediately after death; cf. Schmaus, *Katholische Dogmatik*, 4.2, § 302.

[434] See below, pp. 304–306, and Althaus, *Theologie Luthers*, 343–49.

the Last Day as soon as we die.[435] The "in between" of the so-called "intermediate period" has been left for us by God in darkness; we ought not to seek to expend effort on our part to enlighten ourselves about it. Even if the saints, as the angels, might pray also for us in "heaven," we are to offer no worship services for them, since this is forbidden in the First Commandment; we ought to remember them 'in the Lord,' and ought to yearn to follow them zealously in their faithful obedience,[436] but ought to direct our attention solidly upon the work of God in His Christian Church on earth here below.

Along with tradition, the reformer underscores the unity of the Church in faith and in love. Even though the Christian Church is scattered physically throughout the world, it is still "gathered spiritually in one Gospel and faith," under Christ as head.[437] The Spirit of God has "called [it] together,"[438] and with the manifold gifts at its disposal preserves it in the concord of love that comes from the "correct, only faith."[439] Both aspects resonate in the way this is formulated in the catechisms, as was true already in the early Church formulas; this faith is "uniquely one (*einzig*)"[440] and is concurrently

---

[435] "Pred. über 2 Petr. 3 vom 8.2.1523," WA 14:71.4 (AE 30:147–199): "When we are dead, each one will have his last day"; "Pred. über Mt. 9:18ff. vom 10.11.1532," WA 36:349.8: "As soon as the eyes close, you will be awakened"; "Ennaratio Ps. 90, 1534–35," WA 40.3:525.21 (AE 13:101): "This entire time which exists from the beginning of man's creation will seem to Adam, when he rises from the dead, as though he had slept only one hour."

[436] *BSLK*, 424.10–425.25 (SA); cf. also the texts noted in *BSLK*, 424, n. 3 and AC XXI and Ap XXI.

[437] "Vom Abendmahl Christi, 1528," WA 26:506.39 (AE 37:151–372); "Pred. über Joh. 1:8f. vom 11.8.1537," WA 46:587.8 (AE 22:1–530): "consequently, where the Christian Church is scattered here and there, made up of all manner of peoples in the whole world from beginning to downfall, scattered in the middle of the day and the middle of the night, according to this section they are equal and one, because they confess and hold to CHRISTUM alone for their light and know of and preach nothing but what is about Christ alone, as we, God be praised, do here, and direct all our teaching, writing, preaching"; cf. "Wider das Papsttum zu Rom, 1545," WA 54:284.10–26 (AE 41:257–376). Calvin accentuates the unity of the teaching, *Inst.*, 4:1.9 (Opera Selecta 5:13, 31): "The universal Church . . . nevertheless agrees in one truth of divine doctrine, and is tied together in the bond of one religion."

[438] *BSLK*, 657.29 (LC).

[439] *BSLK*, 657.29–32; 512.7f. (SC).

[440] Thus in the Latin rendering: "*in vera ac unica fide*" (A), or as "*per rectam unicam fidem*" (B).

"unified and in concord."[441] In both the Large Catechism and in the Pentecost hymns, Luther therefore characterizes faith as holding fast to that which cannot lead astray and to the truth that alone can save; he attributes to love the power that can unify sinners,[442] which precludes arrogantly culling out the impure from the pure. The reformer renews the battle fought during the early Church era between the Church-at-large and sectarian splinter groups.[443] He never intended to "establish a Lutheran Church"; he fought against such a move with sarcastic mockery, appalled that one would identify the "children of Christ" by using the "wretched name" of his "poor, stinking sack of maggots."[444] He reproached the papacy for its claim to have the right to rule, calling it "rottenness" of the same sort. The church is never "*ecclesia romana*" and "*papistica*," nor is it *ecclesia lutherana*"; it will always remain "*ecclesia Dei*,"[445] forever "*ecclesia Christi*,"[446] which means "*ecclesia in Spiritu aedificata super Petram Christum* (the Church in the Spirit, built upon Christ the rock)."[447]

---

[441] Albrecht, in WA 30.1:368, n. 3: "*concors, unanima fides*"; cf. Meyer, *Historischer Kommentar*, 369; "Kat.-Pred. zum Symbolum vom 23.5.1528," WA 30.1:10.33: "The Holy Spirit holds the Christian Church in a sense of concord and by faith."

[442] *BSLK*,657.30–34 (LC); *EKG* 163, st. 3 [*LSB* 617]: "*Herr, dein Heilig Geist uns nimmer laß / der uns geb zu halten rechte Maß / daß dein arm Christenheit / leb in Fried und Einigkeit*" (Tr.: roughly: Lord, let your Holy Spirit never leave us / who helps us to stay on the right course / so that your poor Christian Church / may live in peace and unity); cf. *EKG* 98, st. 2, 3 [*LSB* 497]; 99, st. 2, 3 [*LSB* 768]; 142, st. 3; Cf. Althaus, *Martin Luther und die Einheit der Kirche Christi.*

[443] *BSLK*, 657.32 (LC).

[444] "Eine treue Vermahnung, sich zu hüten vor Aufruhr und Empörung, 1522," WA 8:685.9 (AE 45:51–74). "Lutherisch" or else "martianisch" was a mocking name used by the opponents; Luther freely used it here and there; cf. Kinder, *Der ev. Glaube und die Kirche*, 136f., n. 1. Luther's view on the relationship between the person and the faith is formulated briefly in "Von beider Gestalt des Sakraments zu nehmen, 1522," WA 10.2:40.7 (AE 36:231–267): "If you consider it to be true that Luther's teaching is evangelical and the pope's is unevangelical, then you must . . . thus say: Luther is either a simpleton or holy, which means nothing to me, yet his teaching is not his, but is rather Christ's own."

[445] See "Assertio omnium articulorum, 1520," WA 7:127.2; "Ad librum Ambrosii Catharini responsio, 1521," WA 7:720.18; 733.6; 743.2; 751.26.

[446] See passages such as "Ad librum Ambrosii Catharini responsio, 1521," WA 7:712.39; 717.32; 753.29; 762.19; in addition, "Von dem Papsttum zu Rom, 1520," WA 6:300.34: "No one speaks thus: 'I believe in the Holy Spirit, a holy, Roman Church, a community of Romans,' which means it is clear that the Holy Church is not bound to Rome, but is as wide as the world, gathered together spiritually in one faith and not physically"; for still other passages, cf. "Resolutio Lutheriana super

But this proper and true Church has been doing battle since the time of Abel with the satanic church of Cain; "there are two types of churches, from the beginning of the world until its end, which St. Augustine[448] terms the churches of Cain and Abel. And the LORD Christ . . . Himself distinguishes between two churches, one proper and one false (Matt. 7:15).[449] By contrast with Augustine, Luther does not orient the church of Cain along the lines of the *Civitas terrena*, emphasizing its earthly nature, but along the lines of the piety that comes from works, as practiced by the monks, which revolves around the question of salvation.[450] This sharpened the battle and placed the Christian Church more consciously under the cross of its Lord. It does not live on the basis of the majestic, human effort to transcend the self by striving to improve one's sanctified living; it remains a sinful existence, but is under the constant sanctifying activity of the Spirit of God. At its deepest level, its holiness remains a "*sanctitas passiva*"; it does not go its way under its own power, as a "*sanctitas activa*."[451] It is the community of the sanctified and justified believers only as the place of refuge for the sick, for those who are being sanctified and justified constantly. "The Church remains as a dependent sinner before God until the Last Day; it is holy only in Christ its Savior, through grace and the forgiveness of sins."[452] As had been articulated already at the Council of Carthage, which met at the impetus of Augustine in 418,[453] the Christian Church here on earth remains under the petition to the Father: "Forgive us our sins!"[454] The Church is thus

---

propositione sua decima tertia de potestate papae, 1519," WA 2:203.28–208.29; 236.14–21; "Leipziger Disp., 1519," WA 2:279.11–280.9; 405.11–40; 429.25–435.9.

[447] "Ad librum Ambrosii Catharini responsio, 1521," WA 7:709.26.

[448] Augustine, "Ennaratio in Ps. 142:3," (PL 38:1846).

[449] "Wider Hans Worst, 1541," WA 51:477.39 (AE 41:179–256).

[450] On this, Holl, *Die Entstehung von Luthers Kirchenbegriff*, with the corrections in Müller, *Ekklesiologie und Kirchenkritik beim jungen Luther*, esp. 114f.

[451] "Gal.-Komm., 1535," WA 40.1:70.14 (AE 26:25): "Christian holiness is not active but passive"; ibid., WA 40.2:103.28 (AE 27:82): "They are saints, not by active holiness but by passive holiness"; "Predigten über Joh. 14 und 15, 1537–38," WA 45:616.5 (AE 24:1–422): "I am not holy because of myself, but through Christ's blood, so that I am sprinkled, yes, washed in baptism, in the same way through His Gospel, which is spoken over me every day."

[452] "Von der Winkelmesse und Pfaffenweihe, 1533," WA 38:216.5 (AE 38:139–214).

[453] Denzinger, 228ff.

[454] "Thesen zur 3. Antinomerdisp., 1538," WA 39.1:351, Theses 25f.: "But it is fitting for this prayer to be prayed in faith by the whole Church in the presence of the entire world and from whatever holy place there is, even to death. For the whole

holy only in the eschatological sense; there will be a transition from faith to sight in the end; its existence matches that of each individual Christian, "*Simul iusta et peccatrix*,"[455] it is "the holy Church of sinners."[456]

We thereby arrive afresh at the essential conundrum of our life before God; as is true about each individual, Christians in the aggregate do not live because of the charisms accorded to them, but solely by the power of the gracious promise of their creator and redeemer. The Christian Church is and remains "*Factura et creatura verbi* (a product and creation of the Word)";[457] "*tota vita et substantia ecclesiae est in verbo Dei* (the entire life and substance of the Church is in the Word of God)."[458] The Church escapes being hypocritical only where God is at work in His Word, which creates salvation and gives faith in Christ, as a gift; the Church of Jesus Christ exists there alone, since "God's Word cannot exist without God's people; stated from another vantage point, God's people cannot exist without God's Word."[459] The Church is nothing other than the wonder of the power of the Word that comes forth ever anew."[460]

The continuity of Christianity is thus also "established on the basis of the continuity of the Word."[461] The continuity of this apostolic proclamation is not under our control, as our personal resource and guarantee, shall we say, because of some suggested

---

Church is holy and understands itself to have sin and to be repenting at all times"; "Vorl. über Ps. 45, 1532/33," WA 40.2:560.10 (AE 12:263): "The appearance of the church is the appearance of a sinner."

[455] "Osterpred. vom 9.4.1531," WA 34.1:276.6: "No person on earth is as much a sinner as a Christian; he feels sin more than anyone else. No sinner is as great as is the Christian Church. . . . The Christian and the Christian Church are thus the real sinners, because they are truly aware of sins."

[456] Cf. von Balthasar, *Sponsa Verbi*, 203–305; Rahner, *Kirche der Sünder und sündige Kirche*.

[457] "Dict. super Psalt., 1513–16," WA 4:189.22 (AE 11:340): "For the Word of God is the instrument by means of which He produced that making"; "Pred. über 1 Tim. 1:3ff. vom 17.3.1525," WA 17.1:110.13: "The Word establishes the Church; the Church does not regulate the Word."

[458] "Ad librum Ambrosii Catharini responsio, 1521," WA 7:721.12.

[459] "Von den Konziliis und Kirchen, 1539," WA 50:629.34 (AE 41:3–178).

[460] Althaus, *Theologie Luthers*, 251.

[461] Höhne, *Luthers Anschauung über die Kontinuität der Kirche*, 16; "Dict. super Psalt., 1513–16," WA 4:169.30 (AE 11:1–553): "Because the Church is always coming to birth and is always changing in faithful succession, the Church is one thing and another and is still always the same."

unbroken chain of imposition of hands through the bishops;[462] we can and should implore that in, with, and under our careful efforts, its effect would be guaranteed by the Spirit of God. As is true of created things in general, the Church does not exist because of its own efforts; its continuity is grounded in the Gospel, through which the creator will rescue His fallen creatures and bring them into the *eschaton*, when God ultimately stays true to His promise.

As is true of the individual believer, the same holds true analogously for the Church as a whole; the Spirit sets in motion a chain of activities through the verbal proclamation of the Gospel; the power of salvation is effected by the inward workings of the Spirit, who "calls, gathers, enlightens, and sanctifies" us in "the true, only faith"[463] and saves us by bringing us into the *eschaton*. "It is demonstrated here that the Holy Spirit is right there with the Christian Church and makes it holy, namely through Word and sacrament; He thereby works faith inwardly, along with the knowledge of Christ; these are the tools and means through which He sanctifies the Christian Church and purifies it continuously, so that it can be called holy before God as well, in no sense because of what we ourselves do or are, but because the Holy Spirit has been given to us."[464]

This tension between the external and internal workings of the Spirit was articulated in fixed form by Luther when he wrote "On the Papacy at Rome, against the most well-known Romanists in Leipzig" (1520), using the formula that differentiates the "two churches"; in this way, he differentiates between "physical, external Christianity," which is scattered abroad throughout the world-at-large, and the "spiritual, internal Christianity," which is not bound to places, times, and rites, but is gathered instead "harmoniously in one faith."[465] This

---

[462] "Disp. de potestate concilii, 1536," WA 39.1:186.18: "It is easy to congregate together, but they cannot be assembled in the Holy Spirit unless they have based this on the foundation of the apostles, instead of their own thoughts; they go forward by the analogy of faith"; ibid., 191.28: "This is the true definition of the Church, not that which comes after the apostles, but that which confesses Jesus Christ to be the Son of God, that He suffered and was crucified for our sins"; "Promotionsdisp. von J. M. Scotus vom 3.2.1542," WA 39.2:176.5: "Succession is bound up with the Gospel"; idem, 177.2: "Succession should be based on the Gospel." See, in addition, Schlink, *Die apostolische Sukzession*.

[463] *BSLK*, 512.4–6 (SC).

[464] "Pred. über Joh. 14 und 15, 1537–38," WA 45:614.34 (AE 24:1–422).

[465] WA 6:296.38–297.9 (AE 39:49–104); cf. "Antwort auf das Buch Bock Emsers, 1521," WA 7:684.9–33 (AE 39:137–224); "Ad librum Ambrosii Catharini responsio,

distinction can still be misunderstood if used in a spiritualistic sense, just as what might correspondingly happen when speaking about the Church that is hidden by God.[466] But Luther's concern is not about an anthropology in the Platonic mold; his concern is for the strictly eschatological alignment of the Church-at-large, analogous to the individual Christian. The true Christian Church does not have its basis for existence because of some this-worldly agenda; one's citizenship is accorded by the God who remains unseen. Looking strictly outward from its center and being moved to respond [by the Spirit], as an eschatological entity,[467] it presses forward, unrestrained by strictures of the temporal world, and surrenders none of its actual existence to any temporal power, no matter what form that may take. The Christian Church exists solely and exclusively as an entity "that flees and abandons home, space, goods, honor, body, and everything that exists here within the temporal realm, as it proceeds through all of this into eternal life in the same way an individual goes forward through sin, martyrdom, suffering, and death."[468] As is true for the individual believer, whose relationship to the faith is not self-controled, but can be maintained steadfast only by the power of God's Spirit, on the journey through the waters of chaos that come with self-doubt and through the attempt to justify oneself, the same is true for the Church in its eschatological existence in faith; one does not have available and one cannot guarantee on earth that it can be protected from all attacks from the outside and from all temptations from within; as the communion of believers, it survives only because of the saving actions of the triune God. Just as the individual remains a believer because of the eschatological saving work of God and finds

---

1521," WA 7:710.1–13; 719.26ff.; 722.4ff.; "De abroganda missa privata, 1521," WA 8:419.23ff.; "Gal.-Komm., 1535," WA 40.2:105.9ff. (AE 27:1–144); Calvin, *Inst.*, 4:1.7.

466 "Wider Hans Worst, 1541," WA 51:507.31 (AE 41:179–256): "It is a high, deep, hidden thing, the Church, so that no one is able to recognize it or see it, but only in baptism; sacrament and Word one must comprehend and believe"; "Dict. super Psalt., 1513–16," WA 4:81.12 (AE 11:229): "Christ's work and creation, the Church, does not appear to be anything outwardly, but her entire structure is inward in the presence of God, invisible." Cf. Kinder, *Der ev. Glaube und die Kirche*, 93–103; Olsson, *Sichtbarkeit und Verborgenheit der Kirche nach Luther.*

467 This threefold characteristic of our individual personhood, which Joest, *Ontologie*, §§ 8–10, describes with reference to the individual, would apply for Luther to the Christian Church as well.

468 "Antwort auf das Buch Bock Emsers, 1521," WA 7:684.16 (AE 39:137–224).

his true existence in this faith alone, the Church, as well, holds fast to its true place on earth in the confession of the faith; it is, in truth, "the reality of the faith; faith is the Church, in the fullest sense."[469] Luther brings together both aspects, the homelessness with respect to this world, and the eschatological certainty of the Christian, in the words of his song about the "honored maid."

"The mother must be alone,

yet God will still protect her

and be the true Father."[470]

4. The Church as Partner in the Saving Work of God for the Individual

The ultimate impotence of the Church before God corresponds at the same time to the ultimate power that is accorded to it by God. God takes us as sinful human beings and makes us worthy as well, precisely within the dimension of Christ's saving work, so that we become His coworkers without being pressured, and yet we are responsible. The reformers held fast to the foundational statement from the early Church: "Only one who wishes to have the Church as mother gets to have God as father."[471] The reflections offered to this point are to be taken in the strict sense, speaking only of the "*Ecclesia proprie dicta* (the Church properly so called),"[472] which encompasses the whole host of those who are written into the book of life and whom God alone knows; the thoughts that now follow have to be expanded to include the hypocrites who are mixed in within it. Just as

---

[469] Brunstäd, *Theologie der luth. Bekenntnisschriften*, 129. More specifically still, Rahner formulates it, in *Dogmatische Randbemerkungen zur Kirchenfrömmigkeit*, 395: "One does not get shocked when one formulates it to say that the Church exists because it is believed. Naturally, it is and remains, even when an individual or many individuals do not believe. But it would exist no longer if it were no longer believed at all."

[470] WA 35:463.10 (AE 53:292–294).

[471] Cyprian of Carthage, *De catholicae ecclesiae unitate* 6 (CSEL 3.1:214.23): "*habere non potest Deum patrem, qui ecclesiam non habet matrem*"; Augustine, *De symbolo ad catechumenos* 1:1 (PL 40:627): "But ye begin to have him for your Father [God Almighty], when ye have been born by the church as your Mother" [Nicene and Post-Nicene Fathers, 1st Series, 3:369]; Quodvultdeus, *De symbolo* 3:13.1 (CCSL 60:363): "One does not have God as Father, if one is not willing to have the Church as mother."

[472] Ap VII (*BSLK*, 240.31).

the faith can be perceived and detected in good works, true Christianity is manifested in the proclamation of the Word and in acts of love.[473] To the extent that the reformers describe the Church as a "mother, who produces and carries every Christian through the Word of God,"[474] commencing with a description of the empirical Church,[475] on that level weeds are growing resplendently next to the wheat; from that perspective it is possible for the proclamation of the Word to take place without saving faith resulting. And yet, in the catechisms, Luther always speaks of the "*Ecclesia large (late) dicta*"[476] and the "*Ecclesia proprie (stricte) dicta*"[477] as if one and the same. Using a standard that is rooted in loving hope, we are to recognize the empirical Church as the bride of Christ and as the mother of the believers, and as such we are to praise it.[478]

Despite the use of the general term, the Church of God is where the Gospel of Jesus Christ is proclaimed and where the forgiveness of sins is distributed, and nowhere else. Everything connected with it is in service to Office of Reconciliation. Everything in the Church is directed toward the forgiveness of sins[479] and toward comfort for troubled consciences. In a succinct manner, the reformer articulated an insight that became ever deeper, starting with the path set forth by the early Church, which had been given further clarity in the Middle Ages.[480] The forgiveness of sins is the arrow of God by means of which the work of salvation that has its effect throughout the world, as articulated in the Creed, thrusts its way into my personal existence; this is where the "*Articulus stantis et cadentis Ecclesiae* (article on which the Church stands or falls)" has its proper place in the Symbol

---

473 "Promotionsdisp. von J. M. Scotus vom 3.2.1542," WA 39.2:161.8: "The Church is visible because it comes together for confession"; ibid., 161.16: "It is necessary for the church to be wrapped up in flesh . . . it is visible, to be sure, because it confesses sin"; "Gal.-Komm., 1535," WA 40.1:426.11 (AE 26:1–461): "Faith is constantly making alive, justifying, not remaining idle; it is incarnate and is made human."

474 *BSLK*, 655.4f. (LC).

475 Calvin speaks of this specifically, *Inst.*, 4:1.4.

476 Ap VII (*BSLK*, 236.7).

477 Ap VII (*BSLK*, 240.31).

478 "De servo arbitrio, 1525," WA 18:652.1 (AE 33:88): "I call them and believe them both to be the Church of God; but I do so by the rule of love, not the rule of faith"; cf. Calvin, *Inst.*, 4:1.8.

479 *BSLK*, 658.25–29 (LC).

480 Pseudo-augustine, *Sermo* 240:1 (PL 39:2189); Quodvultdeus, *De symbolo* 1:10.1 (CCSL 60:329); Thomas Aquinas, *Expositio in Symbolum Apostolorum*, § 996: "But the forgiveness of sins follows on the basis of these seven sacraments."

of the faith;[481] the forgiveness of sins is at the same time the basic foundational event that all the sacraments serve; the *Remissio peccatorum* (remission of sins) binds together the Second Chief Part with the last two Chief Parts, with Baptism and with Holy Communion, but naturally also with the Office of the Keys. The petition for forgiveness establishes the center of the Lord's Prayer; absolution alone frees us to new obedience of the Commandments, which means that the *Remissio peccatorum* shows itself to be the high point, through which all the chief actions that give witness to the saving actions of God take hold of our own heart; "forgiveness of sins is much more than a couple of words; the entire Kingdom of Christ is founded thereon."[482]

The phrase "*remissio peccatorum*," as recorded in the *Textus receptus*, is translated by the reformer as: (a) forgiveness of sin(s)."[483] In the fifteenth century, the word "*Vergebung*," "forgiveness" (also: "*Vergebnis*") successfully repressed words that had been used in earlier German renderings: "pardon, unburdening, indulgence, dispensation (*Erlaß*, *Antlaß*, *Ablaß*, *Ablassung*)."[484] In this way, Luther accentuates the personal dimension. The modern ecumenical translation carries through by using "forgiveness" instead of the more materialistic term "remission (*Nachlaß*)."

Luther assigns the offices of the Christian Church to this central sacrament of the forgiveness of sins in the Large Catechism as well.[485] He places the "preaching of the Gospel"[486] at this point, at the head of the list, in the Small Catechism; it brings front and center "all manner of messages of comfort"[487] for every catechetical student. According to Luther's Preface to the German Mass of 1525, the children were not merely to immerse themselves in learning the catechism; they were to place biblical "*Loci Communes* (common

---

[481] At this point, see Luther's concept of writing that is implanted "'De loco iustificationis,' 1530," WA 30.2:663.24–664.12.

[482] "Sermon über Mt. 9:1–8: Vom Reich Christi . . . , 2.10.1524," WA 15:703.24.

[483] "Eine kurze Form, 1520," WA 7:218.22; "Betbüchlein," WA 10.2:393.12 (AE 43:3–45); *BSLK*, 511.42 (SC); 556.14 (Preface to the Large Catechism); 653.28f. (LC); cf., in addition, Melanchthon's *Enchiridion* (MGP 20:33.2) and the *Laienbüchlein* (MGP 20:203.37; 204.27).

[484] Cf. Hahn, *Bibliothek*, §§ 93, 95, 101–06, 108, 110, 111, 114–17; Meyer, *Historischer Kommentar*, 95.

[485] *BSLK*, 658.10–42.

[486] *BSLK*, 654.25 (LC).

[487] *BSLK*, 658.13f.

topics)"[488] into their little sack of faith, as well as to have acts of love to place into another sack; each of those sacks would then have two smaller sacks within. The faith sack is divided again, into Law and Gospel: In Adam, we are all lost—in Christ we are rescued. The love sack is divided again, as well, into works and suffering: In Christ, we are to serve everyone and treat them well; additionally, we are "to suffer gladly and to tolerate all sorts of evil."[489] In the Large Catechism Luther mentions only those sayings that bring comfort from the second of the little sacks of faith, which the father confessor could use to assure those who are burdened with agonizing struggles.[490] They fortify the contention that all proper preaching of the Gospel is imbued with the character of absolution, for "Gospel proclamation is itself a form of common absolution; it is a promise, which all members together and each one individually should take very seriously, based on God's command and instruction."[491]

Alongside preaching the Gospel, as the central foundational element, three other elements appear, all instituted by Christ Himself as well, which set in motion how salvation touches each individual person, namely, Baptism, the Lord's Supper, and the Office of the Keys; these signs are drenched through and through with the Word, by means of which the Church of God achieves physical form and power to bring about results in this world. We can pass these by for the moment and recommend the detailed discussions of these last Chief Parts that will be treated in later volumes of this commentary series.

As the Words of Absolution are distributed and received, two aspects are intertwined, the *Coram Deo* and the *Coram hominibus* (in the presence of God and in the presence of other human beings).[492] God bears with us and forgives us, as we are forgiving and bearing with others. Luther explicates this intertwining relationship in both the Fifth Petition of the Lord's Prayer and in his discussion about

---

[488] WA 19:78.18 (AE 53:51–90); cf. ibid., 77.11–78.24; "Festpost. zu Joh. 1:1–14, 1524/27," WA 17.2:319.9: "Such a *Locus communes* or commonly held element of the faith should be placed before the children and plowed in."

[489] "Vorrede zur Dt. Messe, 1526," WA 19:77.23–78.11 (AE 53:51–90).

[490] *BSLK*, 519.30–32 (SC, Confession).

[491] "Brief an den Nürnberger Rat vom 8.10.1533," WABr 6:529.62, no. 2052.

[492] *BSLK*, 658.33–35 (LC).

confession.[493] "Two kinds of confessions" are commanded by God, the direct confession of sins before Him and the apology proffered to the fellow human being who has been harmed.[494] We obtain God's pardon not solely in the word of absolution offered by the father confessor,[495] in the word of encouragement offered by the Christian brother or sister;[496] as the Fifth Petition explains it; it happens additionally when we forgive our neighbor[497] or else seek pardon from someone else.[498] God does not relieve us of the burden of our guilt because of or only as empowered by reconciliatory actions with fellow human beings; and yet, analogously to the way the sacrament takes effect,[499] we are to comprehend God's free and undeserved grace, which occurred before any of our efforts, as the "valid sign" and "seal"[500] that undergirds our own forgiving.

"All the offices of Christianity" serve the function of offering assurance that guilt will be forgiven richly and daily."[501] They are to make available the elements of the Gospel that the Lord Himself instituted, "openly and specially," and through these elements are to open heaven's doorway for sinners who are ready to repent. This would be the place to sketch out the ramifications of Luther's teaching about the *Ministerium verbi divini* (ministry of the divine Word).[502]

The true "spiritual estate," which God Himself "established and instituted with the precious blood and the bitter death of His only Son, our Lord Jesus Christ,"[503] encompasses for Luther the pastorate, as

---

[493] Cf. Volume 3, Fifth Petition of the Lord's Prayer and Volume 5, Exhortation to Confession.
[494] *BSLK*, 727.21–32 (LC, Exhortation to Confession).
[495] *BSLK*, 517.13ff. (SC, Confession).
[496] *BSLK*, 449.12f. (SA).
[497] *BSLK*, 684.31–685.37 (LC, Fifth Petition of the Lord's Prayer.
[498] *BSLK*, 728.17–32 (LC, Exhortation to Confession).
[499] *BSLK*, 685.30–34 (LC, Fifth Petition of the Lord's Prayer).
[500] *BSLK*, 685.5, 18 (idem).
[501] *BSLK*, 658.17 (LC, Third Article).
[502] In addition to the literature mentioned above, p. 264, n. 379, see, additionally, books such as Creutzig, *Amt und Ämter in der lutherischen Kirche*; Söhngen, *Kirchenregiment und geistliche Leitung in der lutherischen Kirche*; Sommerlath, *Das Amt und die Ämter*; Brunner, *Vom Amt des Bischofs*; Liermann, *Luther ordnet seine Kirche*; Goppelt, *Das kirchliche Amt nach den luth. Bekenntnisschr. und nach dem NT*; Lohse, *Das Verständnis des leitenden Amtes*.
[503] "Eine Pred., daß man Kinder zur Schule halten solle, 1530," WA 30.2:527.14 (AE 46:207–258).

well as the school and all people who are installed in offices to assist them.[504] Even the tiniest little cell of the Church is part of the "*Familia*," part of the household of the master,[505] where father and mother carry out their offices as bishop and lady bishop of the household.[506] This most narrow circle: master's house, school, and pastorate, are provided oversight by the office of the superintendent, by colleagues who carry out visitations and establish consistories, and by synods and councils. For the congregations of the Reformation, the theological faculty of the University of Wittenberg, as well as the Wittenberg congregation, took on concurrently the role of the mother congregation. Supportive roles were played by the subordinate officials and by the Christian authorities who provided help and protection for "city hall and castle."[507] By means of an artfully constructed wickerwork of mutual care and oversight that provided direction for its central task, support was given for God's battle against the princes of this world, to bring about the salvation of the human race. "But God had to be both the highest and yet closest authority, who would establish a ring or circle (orbit) against the devil and who would accomplish everything for all estates, in fact for all creatures."[508] This broad ring or circle operates within the framework of the question of salvation, "in the office of preaching or office of bishop . . . which the Son of God Himself set in motion, along with all the apostles, prophets, and patriarchs."[509] Whoever serves in this office is praised by Luther as "an angel of God, a proper bishop before God, a savior of many people, a king and prince in Christ's kingdom and among God's people, a teacher, and a light of the world."[510]

---

[504] Cf. ibid., 528.28: "the pastoral office, teacher, preacher, reader, priest (which one calls chaplain), sexton, schoolmaster, and whatever additionally belongs to such offices and persons"; cf. "Vom Abendmahl Christi, 1528," WA 26:504.30–35 (AE 37:151–372); "Von den Konziliis und Kirchen, 1539," WA 50:641.16–19 (AE 41:3–178).

[505] "Von den Konziliis und Kirchen, 1539," WA 50:652.3 (AE 41:3–178).

[506] See Volume 1, pp. 26–31, 197–99.

[507] "Von den Konziliis und Kirchen, 1539," WA 50:652.4 (AE 41:3–178).

[508] Ibid., 652.7.

[509] "Wider das Papsttum zu Rom, 1545," WA 54:284.38 (AE 41:257–376).

[510] "Eine Pred., daß man Kinder zur Schule halten solle, 1530," WA 30.2:533.21 (AE 46:207–258); cf. ibid., 536.30–35; 542.28–31; 558.28f.; "Post. zu Mt. 11:2ff. zum 3. Advent, 1521," WA 7:511.4–11.

In the Large Catechism, Luther does not actually assign the specific offices and estates to the office of the pastor as such, such as the service of the public proclamation, distribution of the sacraments, pastoral care, and congregational leadership as that which was instituted by the Lord through the apostles; he assigns these to the Spirit of God Himself, who carries out the work of reconciliation throughout the world. The manifold types of service and offices are assigned to Him directly and immediately, because they are rooted in the prophetic and royal office of the priesthood of all believers.[511] They are assigned specifically to the public office of the pastor only secondarily, because whoever serves in such a capacity is given the specific pastoral role on behalf of that community as a whole. From beginning to end, everything is directed toward the Good News, toward the Gospel, "the hand of God who rescues me, a lost and condemned human being, by the power of the cross of Jesus, from the damnation of death, and incorporates me as a member of the body of the one who died and rose, so that I may participate in eternal life with God because of His love."[512]

With the exception of Zwingli, but along with all the other reformers, Luther agrees with the statement made by Cyprian during the early church era: "*Extra ecclesiam nulla salus* (there is no salvation outside the Church)."[513] Whoever separates from the Christian Church separates himself from the truth and thereby from the triune God Himself. Augustine brought the sacramental, communal relationship of love that is established by the Eucharistic sacrificial meal to the fore; each individual receives hereby a way to participate in the stream of grace that affords salvation, which flows

---

[511] Concerning the relationship between the priesthood of all believers and the public office of preaching and shepherding, see most especially Brunotte, *Das geistliche Amt bei Luther*; Lieberg, *Amt und Ordination bei Luther und Melanchthon*, 40–132; Althaus, *Theologie Luthers*, 245–96.

[512] Brunner, *Vom Amt des Bischofs*, 297.

[513] Cyprian of Carthage, *Epistulae* 73:21; cf. idem, *Epistulae* 4:4; 74:7; Irenaeus, *Adversus haereses* 4:53.1 (Harvey, *S. Irenaei Libros quinque adversus Haereses*, 2:261): "But he will judge all who are outside the truth, that is, outside the Church"; Augustine, *De baptismo* 4:17.24 (CSEL 51:250.25): "*Salus extra ecclesiam non est*" ("Salvation does not exist outside the Church"); Rufinus, *Origenis Homilae in librum Josua* 3:5 (GCS 30:307.9): "Outside this house, that is, outside the Church, no one will be saved; if anyone has gone out these doors, he is made party to his own death"; Calvin, *Inst.*, 1:4f.; idem, *Genfer Kat.*, quest. 104f.; *Heidelberger Kat.*, quest. 54; Bullinger, *Zweites Helv. Bekenntnis*, Art. 17.

through the heavenly and earthly Body of Christ, having been provided by the sacrificial offering of its Head. The Middle Ages witnessed the development of a cosmic array of grace, offered through the seven sacraments.[514] From the time of his first lectures on the Psalms, Luther considers grace to come through the *Viva vox Evangelii* (living proclamation of the Gospel) and through the promise of forgiveness,[515] which comes from the all-availing sacrifice of Christ.[516] He considers it a complete contradiction that one could attempt to achieve one's own sanctification by works.[517] The question about the internal nature of the Church is thus revealed; one deals afresh with the spiritual way to distinguish between the true Church of God and the pseudo-church of Satan.

Preaching that is not centered on proclaiming the alien righteousness of Christ affords no deliverance; unless *Solus Christus—sola gratia—sola fide* is proclaimed publicly, even if one were to perform Christian deeds and keep on uttering the word Church with one's mouth, salvation would be absent;[518] God's wrath and condemnation would be all that is there,[519] since neither the Spirit of God nor the true Church can be truly present without that proclamation.[520] For each individual, even though one were to remain within the community of the Church and honor Word and sacrament in an external way, such a person would finally be seeking to become righteous on the basis of his own efforts alone, which means that he has excommunicated himself inwardly and has rejected salvation in Christ.[521]

Luther sharpens Augustine's insights against the Donatists[522] and differentiates between the life and the witness of the Church; as it travels along on its journey, the Church appears to be sinful; but in its

---

[514] Augustine's viewpoint is presented by Hofmann, *Der Kirchenbegriff des hl. Augustinus*, 390–413 (§ 26, Eucharist and Church); concerning the Middle Ages, see the summary in Thomas Aquinas, *Summa theologiae* III, q. 65, a. 1; idem, *Expositio in Symbolum Apostolorum*, §§ 988–98.

[515] *BSLK*, 658.35–37 (LC).

[516] *BSLK*, 655.29–32.

[517] *BSLK*, 658.38–42.

[518] *BSLK*, 655.22–28.

[519] *BSLK*, 661.14.

[520] *BSLK*, 655.23, 28f.

[521] *BSLK*, 658.38–42.

[522] Cf. Hofmann, *Der Kirchenbegriff des hl. Augustinus*, 124–32; von Balthasar, *Sponsa Verbi*, 203–305.

witness to Christ, the true Church manifests itself as separated from all error.[523] And yet, this affirmation of its complete infallibility remains a confession of faith.[524] The individual Christian knows that he must exist in a world that is weighed down with the burden of sin and in the midst of error all around; he experiences his salvation in Christ only in the assurance of faith. In the same way, the Church itself remains weighed down with the burden of sin by necessity and it, as well, is hidden within the presence of God who produces powerful works by true faith in Christ, despite being tempted by false teaching. One thing only remains clear about the Church; the joyous message of Christ's all-sufficient sacrifice brings forgiveness. The Church is charged with telling this news and its own life is wrapped up in that same message.

For this reason the reformer accords great honor to the office, which is charged with proclaiming propitiation, in most superb terminology: "*Extra ecclesiam nulla salus* (outside the Church there is no salvation)," which means: "*Extra praedicationem Evangelii nulla salus* (outside the preaching of the Gospel there is no salvation)." The human being can live before God only in the power of the declaration that one's guilt has been removed; the charge to declare someone to be innocent is entrusted to the Christian Church alone. Luther is more provocative still in the way he articulates this in the Short Form of 1520: "I believe that the forgiveness of sins exists in that selfsame community, and nowhere else; outside of that community nothing can help, no matter how many and great one's good works might be, to accord one the forgiveness of sins. But within such a community nothing can bring harm, no matter how many, how large the sins, and how often one has sinned; this remains the reality wherever and as long as one remains in that same unique community."[525] This and similar comments[526] are doubtless overstated

[523] "Leipziger Disp., 1519," WA 2:429.25: "The authority of the Church is great and infallible, which is guided by the Spirit of Christ; I confess this with my whole heart"; "Ad librum Ambrosii Catharini responsio, 1521," WA 7:713.7: "We confess that the Church does everything rightly"; cf. "Von der Winkelmesse und Pfaffenweihe, 1533," WA 38:216.11–22 (AE 38:139–214); "Wider Hans Worst, 1541," WA 51:516.32–522.17 (AE 41:179–256); cf., in addition, the references gathered together in Kinder, *Der ev. Glaube und die Kirche*, 129, n. 1.

[524] Ad librum Ambrosii Catharini responsio, 1521," WA 7:710.2: "It is necessary that the Church is without sin, invisible and spiritual, perceived by faith alone."

[525] WA 7:219.17.

and are formulated in a way that could be misunderstood; that is because such statements fail to deal specifically with the other side of the issue, the constant battle that Christians wage against sin. And yet, such statements are by no means "stupid contradictions in terms" and "theological misstatements."[527] They accentuate at the deepest level the either-or dichotomy that God, in Christ, has imposed upon all human beings. We all exist under the holy God, with His absolute demand for obedience, which is imposed in the fullest sense in the life and death of Jesus with respect to everything that is involved in the human condition. "God's wrath and displeasure hover above us at all times, for we are unable to accomplish all that God demands of us."[528] That is the condemning judgment of the law. At the same time, however, we all stand under the offer of grace that has no requirement attached; it is offered freely by the same God, through the Word about Christ's cross and resurrection that tells us about what was accomplished on our behalf. This is the word of absolution that comes from the Gospel. Since we cannot respond properly to God, not one time in a thousand, it is foolish and senseless for us to attempt to motivate Him to be gracious to us on the basis of a righteousness that we ourselves construct; all that remains is constant flight to the outstretched arms of Jesus on the cross, which concurrently means to be under the Office of the Keys that the Church administers. The Spirit of God is present in a gracious manner here alone;[529] this topic will be dealt with in detail most especially when confession is discussed.

The song of praise that comes forth, when the Church administers the Office of the Keys for our benefit, renews for us the question about the relationship of the individual Christian to the Church-at-large. Various commentators who discuss their understanding of "just as"[530] in the Small Catechism arrive at different conclusions.[531] Does Luther intend merely to use it to show that the chain of the events of salvation provided by the Spirit of God to the individual forms a

---

[526] Cf. "De capt. Babylonica, 1520," WA 6:529.11–17 (AE 36:3–126); "Rationis Latomianae . . . confutatio, 1521," WA 8:107.6–12; 125.39–126.5 (AE 32:133–260).
[527] This must be stated in opposition to the view of Joest, *Paulus und das lutherische Simul Iustus et Peccator*, 313.
[528] *BSLK*, 661.31–33 (LC).
[529] *BSLK*, 658.30–33.
[530] *BSLK*, 512.5 (SC).
[531] Cf. Meyer, *Historischer Kommentar*, 367; Albrecht, in WA 30.1:368, n. 1.

parallel situation to God's activity in the Church, or does my deliverance find its anchor point in the actions of salvation carried out when the Spirit provides them for the Christian Church? Does the "just as" in the Third Article function in a way similar to the "just as" in the Second Article,[532] which grounds my new existence in Christ's resurrection and lordship? The Small Catechism does not provide proof positive, but does indicate its stance to an extent.[533] The correct faith of each individual is at the same time enfolded within the "harmonious and accepted faith" of the Christian Church as a whole,[534] "in which"[535] the individual can obtain forgiveness, and nowhere else. That is clearly more than a simple set of parallel statements; "in Christ"[536] seems to provide a more specific definition of what it is to be "in the Christian Church." The Church itself becomes the place to which human beings can flee: "*ecclesia* is to be my fortress, my castle, my chamber."[537] But it becomes that only because the Spirit of God brings us, through the Church, to the exalted Lord and preserves each one in a relationship with Him in the true faith.

What is merely intimated in the Small Catechism is dealt with in detail in the Large Catechism. The Church is first described as the protective space and the divinely designated location for the work of salvation as it is given to the individual, the means and organ[538] "through" which the Spirit carries out His office as the one who sanctifies. "The Church is the fruit, place, and organ through which the Holy Spirit works on an individual."[539] But when the Symbol speaks about "Mother Church,"[540] it goes beyond the literal and

---

[532] *BSLK*, 511.36 (SC).

[533] We ought to and have to make use of the Large Catechism in this way to explicate the matter, against Meyer, *Historischer Kommentar*, 367.

[534] Cf. pp. 273–74, notes 440–42.

[535] *BSLK*, 512.8 (SC).

[536] *BSLK*, 512.12.

[537] "Gen.-Vorl., 1535–45," WA 44:713.1; ibid., 43:597.31 (AE 8:245): "For where God dwells, there the Church is, and nowhere else; for the Church is God's house and the gate of heaven, where the entrance to eternal life and the departure from the earthly to the heavenly life are open."

[538] *BSLK*, 654.52.

[539] Kinder, *Der ev. Glaube und die Kirche*, 35.

[540] On the Church as "Mother of the Believers," see "Dict. super Psalt., 1513–16," WA 3:279.21 (AE 10:1–464); "Pred. über Lk. 1:13 vom 24.6.1518," WA 4:630.14; WABr 1:129.47; "Sermo de virtute excommunicatione, 1520," WA 1:641.28; 640.30–34; cf. "Sermon von dem Bann, 1520," WA 6:70.38–71.12 (AE 39:3–22);

specific conceptual framework. The Church itself is not actually characterized as the functioning instrument that brings about salvation; it turns into the personal partner with the Spirit of God. This is clearly expressed when the terminology is used: She is "the mother that brings to life and carries every individual Christian, through the Word of God."[541] The Church is the "*Cooperatrix*," she who is a coworker with the Spirit of God, so that the little word "bear [Tr.: bring to life]" almost permits one to think of a *Concreatrix* and thus simultaneously *Coredemptrix*, of that which is creating within the dimension of eschatological salvation.[542] We must analyze that in much greater detail still. One thing can be said for sure at the outset. The Church—as comparable to someone who is physically a mother in the temporal realm—is the one who is responsible as the co-worker of the *Spiritus Creator* in the spiritual realm, functioning in this role in a very specific sense. She can be distinguished from human beings who know nothing of the hidden, creative activities of God, since the Church is a co-worker of the Spirit of God, having complete insight into the divine will to bring salvation. The Church is the co-worker, unrestrained in its eschatological responsibility in the presence of the eternal judge and redeemer.[543] And yet, as the text of the Large Catechism explains it clearly,[544] the Church is not a co-redeemer in the strict sense of the term. Luther makes this clear by means of a unique change of subject. The Church brings to life and carries every single Christian by means of the Word;[545] it is the Word, however, that reveals and presents the Spirit of God Himself, in that He allows that Word to drive deep into the heart. We come once again upon that

---

WA 2:556.5–10 (AE 27:151–410); "Gal.-Komm., 1519 u. 1535," on Gal. 4:26, WA 40.1:662.1–665.5 (AE 26:1–461); "Weihnachtspost. zu Lk. 2:33–40 u. zu Jes. 60:1–6, 1522," WA 10.1.1:405.12–406.11 (AE 52:102–148); 542.10–12; "Pred. über Joh. 16:20f. vom 7.5.1536," WA 41:577, 3–9; "Pred. über Joh. 3:6f. vom 6.4.1538," WA 47:20.19–23 (AE 22:1–530).

[541] *BSLK*, 655.3–5 (LC).

[542] "Pred. über Joh. 16:20f. vom 7.5.1536," WA 41:577.4: "It is another mother, the Church, who brings one to life, but through death"; but cf., in addition, "Pred. über Mt. 28:10ff. vom 15.3.1525," WA 17.1:99.5: "No one is made a Christian unless he believes in the Word. The Word is therefore mother" (Isa. 49:1).

[543] Cf. Seils, *Der Gedanke vom Zusammenwirken*, 188–91; Steck, *Lehre und Kirche bei Luther*, 73f.

[544] *BSLK*, 655.2–8.

[545] "Pred. über Joh. 3:6f. vom 6.4.1538," WA 47:20.20 (AE 22:1–530): "Christ, who places you in your Christian Church through baptism and the Word of God, into the lap of Christian churches, as does our beloved mother."

mysterious delineation of the boundary between the external and the internal.[546] The Church is responsible in an observable way for proclaiming the Word, but it can get the message only as far as the ear; it has no ability to drive into anyone's heart the saving faith that alone can save; for this reason, the Church is the "co-worker" for salvation, in the full sense, but no one would consider it to be "co-redeemer" as well.

If one uses the analogy of the Church having full power and being impotent concurrently, one can characterize what is true of each individual believer. In the one sense it is true: Each one is to honor the Church and to be under its discipline; one ought to love it with every fiber of one's heart and mind,[547] this poor, miserable and sinful Christian Church, wherever it is located, where people congregate around Word and sacrament, in which the weeds will threaten to choke the wheat until the end of time. At the same time, however, one is not to pull back from the Church because it errs and fails, in order to construct a sinless and error-free utopian community. That is the reason for the summons to maintain concord in love, as well as to do battle against all sectarian separatist groups.[548]

But the other sense is true as well: The individual Christian is a free child of God in faith, under the power of the unfettered Word of

---

[546] Cf. pp. 239–243.

[547] See the first stanza of the hymn "Von der Heiligen Christlichen Kirchen," in which Luther maybe has it sound like a secular love song or a song to Mary (WA 35:462 [AE 53:292–294]): "*Sie ist mir lieb, die werde Magd / und kann ihr nicht vergessen / Lob, Her und Zucht von ihr man sage / sie hat mein Herz besessen. / Ich bin ihr hold / und wenn ich sollt / groß Unglück han / da liegt nicht an. / Sie will mich des ergetzen / mir ihrer Lieb und Treu an mir / die sie zu mir will setzen / und tun all mein Begier*" ["Dear is to me the holy Maid, / I never can forget her; / For glorious things of her are said; / Than life I love her better: / So dear and good, / That if I should / Afflicted be, / It moves not me, / For she my soul will ravish / With constancy and love's pure fire, / And with her bounty lavish / Fulfill my heart's desire"; translated by James F. Lambert, *Luther's Hymns*, Philadelphia: General Council Publication House, 1917, 126]. In "Von den Konziliis und Kirchen, 1539," Luther writes "The condemnation of the council ought not cause me to tremble in fear, but the condemnation of the holy Church would put me to death in an instant by the will of the one who says 'I am with you to the end of the world.' Oh, one cannot bear that Man's condemnation" (WA 50:615.17 [AE 41:3–178]).

[548] *BSLK*, 657.31f. (LC). Kinder, *Der ev. Glaube und die Kirche*, 21: "According to the Bible of the Old and New Testaments there is no personal saving existence of the human being in relation to God without at the same time being placed into the divine and holy community"; cf. Höhne, *Luthers Anschauung über die Kontinuität der Kirche*, 40–72.

God, meant to exist in the immediate presence of one's heavenly Father. "No individual Christian is duty bound under any particular church organization."[549] Obedience with respect to God and with respect to the Church is not one and the same. The authority of the Church is on the same level with parents and other temporal authorities, related to the Fourth Commandment, but that commandment is placed under the First Commandment that reigns supreme over all; "cursed into the depths of hell is every form of obedience to authority, father, mother, even to the Church itself, if that is disobedient to God. . . . I speak here against father, mother, friendship, authority, the Christian Church itself, if such would hinder me from hearing God's Word."[550]

On the basis of the promise given to every Christian to be able to discern the spirits, every single Christian is called, when living within the sphere of "physical, external Christian Church," to continually distinguish the "spiritual, internal Christian Church"[551] from the church of Satan that opposes it. Just as Luther himself had to live out his life painfully under the ban of the Church that hung over his head, each Christian of necessity has to live under the external act of excommunication if that is the way to keep oneself from being excluded from the internal community of the believers.[552] He would have to endure the attacks against his person with humor, but needs to set himself relentlessly against attacks on the pure Gospel, if necessary by himself acting to excommunicate the opponent.[553]

---

549 Althaus, *Theologie Luthers*, 253.

550 "Wochenpred. über Mt. 12:46–50, 1528," WA 28:24.15; "Antwort auf das Buch Heinrichs v. England," WA 10.2:256.29: "Here I stand, here I hold firm, here I am proud and say: God's Word is more than all else to me, divine majesty stands on my side, for which reason I do not care a wit if there are a thousand Augustines against me, a thousand of Henry's Churches, and I am certain that the true Church holds fast with me to the Word of God and lets Henry's Churches hold fast to the words of humans."

551 "Von dem Papsttum zu Rom, 1520," WA 6:298.1 (AE 39:49–104).

552 At this point, cf. Schlink, *Theologie der lutherischen Bekenntnisschriften*, 284–94.

553 "Brief an Spalatin vom 10.7.1520," WABr 2:137.25, no. 310: "Certainly for me, the die has been cast, both the fury and good will of Rome are despised. I do not want to be reconciled to them nor to be partners with them forever; they should condemn and destroy me. And yet, unless warmth is no longer in me, I will publicly condemn and set aside the entire papal law; that is that Lernaean heresy [Tr.: the Lernaean hydra is the fiercest opponent of Hercules], and it will have been set forth publicly and humiliated in the end, which to this point has escaped notice, for I do not wish to inflate the enemies of the Gospel still more."

Despite such afflictions, he is not to paint the external community within the Church with such a broad brush that everyone in that community is considered to be enslaved under Satan's tyranny, just because some Christians have been led astray in their conscience. Children of God who are free have direct access to the Father in the Spirit through the Son, while at the same time placing themselves under the authority of the visible Church community through the faith that relies on the Gospel; this does not happen because of one's own reason or strength, but because the Spirit of God makes one confident internally, within one's heart.

Resurrection of the Body and Eternal Life[554]

The reformer always renders the words of the *Textus receptus*, "*carnis resurrectionem et vitam aeternam,*" as "resurrection of the flesh and an eternal life."[555] Along with the old word "*Urständ*,"[556] the late Middle Ages employed a variety of words, "*Aufstehung* and *Wiederaufstehung*, *Auferstehung* and *Wiederauferstehung*."[557] Luther stays with the ordinary genitive "of the flesh," even though that term would have sent the minds of the members of his congregation right to the butcher shop.[558] The new ecumenical text alters the reading to "resurrection of the dead" and intends thereby to accentuate the resurrection of "all human beings," as well as that of our entire human nature that has fallen under the curse of death. There may be a secret effort to spiritualize the meaning when this alteration is used; Luther would have been happier to be blunt and say "resurrection of the body

---

[554] *BSLK*, 659.1–31 (LC). On Luther's eschatology, see Foerster, *Das Jüngste Gericht bei Luther*; Althaus, *Unsterblichkeit und ewiges Leben bei Luther*; ibid., *Luthers Gedanken über die letzten Dinge*; ibid., *Die letzten Dinge*; Stange, *Luthers Gedanken über die Todesfurcht*; Seeger, *Die eschatologische Grundhaltung in Luthers GK*; Torrance, *Kingdom and Church*; Pflanz, *Geschichte und Eschatologie bei M. Luther*; Schumann, *Luthers Trostgedanken wider den Tod*; Quanbeck, *Luther and Apocalyptic*; Joest, *Ontologie*, 320–53; Asendorf, *Eschatologie bei Luther* (Lit!).

[555] "Eine kurze Form, 1520," WA 7:218.23; "Betbüchlein," WA 10.2:393.13 (AE 43:3–45); *BSLK*, 511.42f. (SC); 556.14–16 (Preface to the Large Catechism); 653.29f. (LC).

[556] As, for example, in Hahn, *Bibliothek*, §§ 93, 95, 101, 103, 108, 114–17.

[557] "Eine kurze Form, 1520," WA 7:218.23; "Betbüchlein," WA 10.2:393.13 (AE 43:3–45); *BSLK*, 511.42f. (SC); 556.14–16 (Preface to the Large Catechism); 653.29f. (LC).

[558] *BSLK*, 659.25–27 (LC).

or the corpse."[559] He adjusts the common rendering "eternal life" to read "an eternal life,"[560] since he is emphasizing at the same time how God "will give [this] to me together with all believers in Christ."[561] The ecumenical text returns to the rendering "eternal life"; at this point one could insert an interpretive phrase that is recorded in a low German congregational Symbol: "[eternal], as God Himself is."[562]

Luther interprets resurrection to life everlasting as that which is completely the result of the saving actions that took place on earth and that took effect through the Spirit of God. Present and future eschatology are not at odds; each depends on the other. The Spirit of God draws us into an eschatological movement already in the here and now, which will be realized fully only on the Last Day. The catechisms support this interpretation as well: "Luther's theology is eschatological through and through, in the strict sense of anticipating the end of time."[563] The present work of the Spirit intertwines with what will happen on the other side, allowing me to be completely obedient to Christ, so that I "might live under Him in His kingdom and serve Him in everlasting righteousness, innocence, and blessedness."[564]

1. The Eschatological Orientation of Justification and Sanctification

Here on earth the Spirit of God allows progress and continual improvement in sanctified living,[565] since He "daily and richly forgives [us] all sins."[566] As Luther will explicate the matter when we study his treatment of baptism, one is to hold firm to the validity of both elements of baptism. The "total aspect" is what describes the battle between the new and the old person; but the "partial aspect" describes constant growth in sanctification as well.[567] The insight that

---

[559] *BSLK*, 659.28f.

[560] Hahn, *Bibliothek*, §§ 114 (115), 116, 117; Meyer, *Historischer Kommentar*, 96; Melanchthon, *Spruchbüchlein* (MGP 20:33.3f.)

[561] *BSLK*, 512.11–13 (SC); cf. 659.6f. (LC) and "Eine kurze Form, 1520," WA 7:220.1f.

[562] Hahn, *Bibliothek*, § 102.

[563] Althaus, *Theologie Luthers*, 339.

[564] *BSLK*, 511.34–36 (SC); cf. 674.27f. (LC, Second Petition of the Lord's Prayer).

[565] *BSLK*, 659.1f., 18f.; 673.44 (LC, Third Article and Second Petition of the Lord's Prayer).

[566] *BSLK*, 512.9f. (SC); 659.9f., 20 (LC).

[567] The terms are used by Joest, *Gesetz und Freiheit*, 55–82.

our sins remain with us ought not to lead us to despair, so that we give up the battle and simply acquiesce to its reality; whoever wants daily forgiveness without constant growth in sanctification has denied Christ and falls under judgment. "A Christian should have the Holy Spirit and lead a new life, or else know that Christ is not his."[568] One has to fight through a Libertinism that either minimizes the problem or is fatalistic. But it is true at the same time as well: We do not battle against sin by our own power alone; it is the work of the Spirit, who by means of Word and faith holds us constantly above the abyss of Pharisaic self-righteousness and above that of bewildering doubt. All self-glorification is excluded hereby. Continual growth in sanctification is not empowered by the strength of an individual who has been renewed by the Spirit; it blooms from within, on the basis of the daily forgiveness that frees us from the guilt that entangles us. We do not take possession of our new life with our own fist, as a guarantee of the eschatological fulfillment; we hide ourselves day after day in the promise of the Spirit of God, a promise that He plans to fulfill in us the work that has been begun.[569]

The double aspect of forgiveness and sanctification reflects the twofold work of Christ. He resolved the question about guilt in that He becalmed God's holy wrath on our behalf and provided open access to the Father's heart; He resolved the question about power in that He tore us free from the tyranny of powers that bring destruction. He uses the canopy of His Spirit to protect us against the constantly surprising attacks from such forces. Luther pointed out in the Second Article that the question about power is seen in its full force only in connection with the question about guilt; the resolution about power is evident only when the guilt issue is resolved.[570] In an analogous sense, the physical human being becomes new according to the Third Article because the conscience is being freed continually; sanctification has its roots in justification, just as the question of power has its roots in the question about guilt, not the other way around. But since the question about power is important in its own right and has its own visibility, alongside the question about guilt, sanctification is an independent theme on its own as well, in addition

[568] "Von den Konziliis und Kirchen, 1539," WA 50:600.11 (AE 41:3–178).
[569] "Gen.-Vorl., 1535–45," WA 44:270.13 (AE 6:36): "All things have been made and are restored through the Word; we are created from the Word, and we must return to the Word."
[570] See pp. 142–163.

to the issue of forgiveness; the Large Catechism goes so far as to treat sanctification as the central topic of the Third Article.

This is reinforced, once again, by the use of markedly eschatological statements that arch back to Luther's understanding of the "*Imago Dei*" from the beginning of time, and how that was lost, as was discussed in the treatment of the First Article.[571] That discussion showed that there were two sides to the *Imago Dei*, the internal relationship of the human being to God, breathing without fear in an immediate awareness of consciousness of God, and the external relationship that each human being has to his or her own physical existence, as well as to other creatures; that effortless lordship was carried out initially over one's own members and in dominion over the world that had been entrusted. In the same way, the eschatological renewal of the Imago *Dei* shows the same two aspects, which Luther admittedly mentions only briefly; life before God "in everlasting righteousness, innocence, and blessedness,"[572] freed from all sin and guilt,[573] as well as the "new, immortal and exalted body,"[574] extracted from the attacks of the evil world, from all misfortune, and from the last enemy, death.[575] Since Luther accentuates the sanctifying work of the Spirit in the Large Catechism, the resurrection comes front and center as well, which he describes purely and simply in the positive sense, as reawakening to life everlasting.

2. The Reawakening of this Physical Body

By contrast, in the Small Catechism, one notes the incongruence between the reawakening, which is to take place for all who have died, over against eternal life, which is promised only to those who are believers in Christ; a slightly unbalanced treatment is offered thereby. The phrase "in which Christian Church"[576] seems to be inclusive, as if to apply to everything else that is said in what follows. But Luther interrupts the sequence by asserting that "on the Last Day [He] will awaken me and all the dead,"[577] but then resumes his train

[571] See pp. 94–104.
[572] *BSLK*, 511.35f. (SC); 659.13; 674.27f. (LC, Third Article and Second Petition of the Lord's Prayer).
[573] *BSLK*, 659.14.
[574] *BSLK*, 659.15f.
[575] *BSLK*, 653.1ff.; 659.14f; 660.10f.; 674.25f. (LC).
[576] *BSLK*, 512.8 (SC).
[577] *BSLK*, 512.10f.

of thought with the phrase "me, with all believers in Christ."[578] The activity of the Spirit of God, when awakening the dead, includes every member of the human race; but Luther does not treat this topic independently. The more strongly dogmatic, confessional tradition deals with the rejection of the condemned and the reception of the redeemed as if the situations are almost the same.[579] But as is true of catechetical tradition in general, Luther concentrates here almost exclusively on the redemption of Christians.[580] Since he does differentiate between "all the dead" and "all believers in Christ," he indirectly deals with the teaching of Origen that all would be brought back once again, as well as the teaching that even the satanic forces would be saved. He articulates his rejection of *Apokatastasis* (restoration) in his Confession of 1528 as well; Melanchthon deals with this in AC XVII and makes reference to the way the Anabaptists deal with the matter.[581]

Luther interprets the formula "resurrection of the flesh,"[582] which had come down through tradition, in the Large Catechism; our thinking ought not to be directed toward the meat that the butcher offers for sale, but rather toward the physical existence of all people, according to their condition, for everyone will die physically.[583]

As for the awakening of the dead and life eternal with God, both subjects were dealt with in graphic form already in Jewish

---

[578] *BSLK*, 512.11f.

[579] See pp. 292–93, notes 553–55.

[580] But *BSLK*, 661.14f. (LC): "because of which they will remain in *everlasting* wrath and damnation."

[581] "Vom Abendmahl Christi, 1528," WA 26:509.16ff. (AE 37:151–372); AC XVII (*BSLK*, 72.10–13); Na 16 (*Nürnberger Vorform d. CA*, *BSLK*, 72.26–31; Schwabach Article 13 (*BSLK*, 72.24–26). On Luther's rejection of *apokatastasis*, cf., in addition, "Röm.-Vorl., 1515–16," on Rom. 8:28, WA 56:385.23–386.12 (AE 25:1–524); "Sendbrief über die Frage, ob auch jemand, ohne Glauben verstorben, selig werden möge, 1522," WA 10.2:322.8–326; "De servo arbitrio, 1525," WA 18:708.5–9 (AE 33:3–295).

[582] *BSLK*, 659.23–29 (LC).

[583] Concerning this misunderstanding, see, in addition, "Daß diese Worte Christi noch fest stehen, 1527," WA 23:243.27f. (AE 37:3–150); "Kat.-Pred. zum 3. Art. vom 10.12.1528," WA 30.1:93.17 (AE 51:162–169); concerning the proper understanding, see "Eine kurze Form, 1520," WA 7:219.27: "all flesh, that is all human beings according to the body or flesh"; "Weihnachtspost. über Joh. 1:1–14, 1522," WA 10.1.1:235.20 (AE 52:41–88): "I believe the resurrection of the flesh, that is, all human beings." Girgensohn, *Katechismus-Auslegung*, 1:162: "Here the expression intends to say that the entire human being, with body, soul, and spirit, is to be called back to life."

apocalyptic[584] and were topics for discussion in the New Testament as well. But the New Testament orients these images with reference to the reawakening of Jesus; He is the "firstborn from the dead" (Col. 1:18; Acts 26:23; Rev. 1:5).

One detects already in Paul how the argumentation is set forth on two different fronts. In opposition to the expectations of Judaism, which concentrated on purely earthly and tangible scenarios, Paul states his thesis that has its basis in Christ's sacrificial offering: Our old, fleshly, human nature will not inherit the Kingdom of God (1 Cor. 15:50). Against the Hellenistic and Gnostic concepts, which speak of the inability of the inner person to die, he comments: God alone was of a mind to rescue us from this world of death. As the Gospel pressed forward, from a setting where the Jewish population predominated, into the Hellenistic realm, the populace cast aspersions, with vitriol, to express their skepticism about the witness to the bodily resurrection (Acts 17:31f.). The first tracts of the apologists were dedicated already to an intensive treatment of these points. Unless one is dealing with a later insertion, the apology of Aristides anticipates the concluding statement of Gregory of Nazianzus, already in 140,[585] when it says of Christians: They await the awakening of the dead and the life of the world to come.[586] Justin sharpens the point still more about 150, in his Dialogue with Trypho, when he speaks of the "resurrection of the flesh";[587] what these witnesses articulated takes on a set form with Tertullian, who expands on what Christ's return involves, to say: "*Venturum iudicare vivos et mortuos per carnis etiam resurrectionem* (will come to judge the living and the dead even through the resurrection of the flesh)."[588] In Egypt, "the stronghold of Gnosticism," it seems that the "*resurrectio carnis*" first appeared in the baptismal questions and thereby made its way into the Creed as well.[589] This phrase is linked to eternal life in

[584] See passages such as Isa. 26:19; Dan. 12:1–3; Enoch 51:4; Ezra 7:29ff.; Syr. Bar. 50.2ff. On this, see Volz, *Die Eschatologie der jüd. Gemeinde im ntl. Zeitalter*; Plöger, *Theokratie und Eschatologie*; Nikolainen, *Der Auferstehungsglaube in der Bibel und in ihrer Umwelt*; Strobel, *Kerygma und Apokalyptik*.

[585] Denzinger, 150; *BSLK*, 27.10–12.

[586] Aristides of Athens, *Apologia* 15: "awaiting the resurrection of the dead and the life of the age to come."

[587] Justin, *Dialogus cum Tryphone* 80:5 (PG 6:664C–668A).

[588] Tertullian, *De virginibus velandis* 1:3.22 (CCSL 2:1209).

[589] Botte, *Note sur le symbole baptismal der Saint Hippolyte*; Eichenseer, *Apostolicum*, 440.

the Jerusalem Symbol.[590] It would have made its way from there through the Balkans and North Italy, as well as through North Africa,[591] to the West, which is how it made its way into the *Textus receptus*.

Throughout the entire history of commentary that discussed how the two aspects are related, one notes how a way was sought between the Scylla of a chiliastic materialism and the Charybdis of a Gnostic spiritualizing. The points that are accentuated in such an effort have gone forth in many different directions. In those places where the awakening of all the dead was linked with judgment, statements such as the following are to be found: "It will happen that all will rise, with their own bodies, which they carry here as their own."[592] The emphasis is placed most clearly on what one can grasp, on what is material, linking the identity of the body that died with the one that will rise. One does not take "body" at this point to refer to the person, insofar as he "has a relationship with himself,"[593] but rather the human being who is related to others, in his ability to communicate within the world.[594] Such a human existence, which is tied with our earthly existence in the world, will be materially reconstructed by God the Creator in the awakening of the dead. Each one will then be able to give an account of his deeds, envisioned as happening within the framework of the final judgment: This, our human body that can communicate, will be placed before our Lord and Judge.

By contrast, if one links the awakening of the dead with eternal life, one must of necessity distinguish this explicitly over against any earthly resuscitation. Chrysostom and Augustine teach that this eschatological awakening from the dead for life everlasting ought not

---

[590] Cyril of Jerusalem, *Catechesis* 18:28 (PG 33:1049B); Denzinger, 41.

[591] See the examples in Denzinger, 22 (21), 15, 19; Kelly, *Creeds*, 174–79.

[592] Denzinger, 801: "*omnes cum suis propriis resurgent corporibus, quae nunc gestant*"; cf. Denzinger, 16, 72, 540, 684. This identity is envisioned already in the Syr. Baruch apocalypse 50:2ff.

[593] Bultmann, *Theologie des Neuen Testaments*, 196.

[594] Bultmann's identification of the body with one's relationship to the self (*Theologie des Neuen Testaments*, § 17), which he shares in common with the tradition of German idealism, is refuted by Käsemann and explicated further: For Paul, physical existence is "the nature of the human being in his need to participate in creaturely things, and in his ability to communicate in the widest sense, namely, in his relationship to a world that is always hidden from him" (Käsemann, *Zur paulinischen Anthropologie*, 43). On the tradition, see, in addition, Boliek, *The Resurrection of the Flesh.*

to be confused with a temporary, short-lived "awakening" that would extend one's life on earth, as the Lord accorded Lazarus; an extension of life of this sort remains within the realm of a hard and fast judgment of death; the other presses ahead proleptically to describe coming before the one who is Lord over death and life. In order to preserve this distinction, the "*resurrectio carnis*" was expanded by the phrase "*vita aeterna*" in the Symbol of the faith.[595]

As the church fathers spun their thoughts in many different directions by orienting their thinking toward the dignity of the resurrection body, they added specificity more or less to how one who arose would appear. Irenaeus already had to deal very specifically with opposition from the Gnostics who played on the word from the apostle, "Flesh and blood cannot inherit the kingdom of God" (1 Cor. 15:50), in their opposition to a resurrection of the flesh: It is true that our flesh cannot participate in divine lordship with what is within one's own self, but such can happen by means of the activity of the Spirit of God.[596] And Augustine depicts the concord between the spirit and the flesh in the one who is exalted in the Enchiridion, on the basis of its anthropological dimensions as well: The breath of life will saturate and bring to life that person's flesh; the individual will not in any way resist that life breath; we will no longer have to endure temptations from either without or within.[597] Augustine's views were passed down to the Middle Ages, being expanded to provide details about how the body of the one who would rise would look, morphing finally into the grotesque.[598]

The reformer stepped without hesitation into this broad stream of tradition; but he emphasizes that in the *Resurrectio carnis* we will confess our faith in the *Creatio ex nihilo*. Being more perceptive than

---

[595] John Chrysostom, *Homiliae in epistulam i ad Corinthios*, 40:2 (PG 61:349); Augustine, *De symbolo ad catechumenos* 9:17 (PL 40:636); cf. idem, *Enchiridion de fide, spe, et caritate* 23:84; Peter Chrysologus, *Sermone* 63–65 ("De Lazaro a mortuis suscitato," PL 52:375–86); further examples are in Eichenseer, *Apostolicum*, 465–68.

[596] Irenaeus, *Adversus haereses* 5:9.4.

[597] Augustine, *Enchiridion de fide, spe, et caritate* 23:91 (CCSL 46:98): "Because so perfect shall be the harmony between flesh and spirit, the spirit keeping alive the subjugated flesh without the need of any nourishment, that . . . so we shall not have ourselves for enemies within" [Nicene and Post-Nicene Fathers, 1st Series, 3:266].

[598] Augustine, *Enchiridion de fide, spe, et caritate* 84–93; idem, *De civitate Dei* 22:12–21; Peter Lombard, *Sententiarum* IV, dist. 44; Thomas Aquinas, *Summa theologiae* III, suppl. q. 79–86; idem, *Expositio in Symbolum Apostolorum*, §§ 1004–09.

the apostle Paul and the apologists, he perceived that there is a limit to what supporting argumentation one can offer while still bound to our earthly existence.[599] He knew of the cardinals who were arrogant in their mockery[600] and of questions posed by farmers who wondered whether some sort of "ruffian"[601] is going to still remain within us, which even the overarching power of death would not be able to snuff out. By contrast, he does not resort to looking for our own life powers, not even to some type of divine cell of life that is planted into our being through Word and sacrament.[602] Our earthly and physical existence is delivered over to destruction, our flesh will be "executed and cut to bits with all the other filth."[603] Luther can sketch this out drastically, in gruesome detail.[604] But it is not just the grave and decomposition that intervenes between death and resurrection; especially prominent is the fire of the holy, judging wrath of God's judgment.[605] It will burn out the last remnants of the dregs of the old man. It is thus the *Spiritus Creator* who alone brings about our resurrection, in a "moment,"[606] when Christ will break in and alter the world.

---

[599] The main passages are "Pred. über 1 Kor. 15, 1532–33," WA 36:478–696 (AE 28:57–213) and "Leichenpred. für Kurfürst Johann vom 18.8.1532," WA 36:237–70 (AE 51:231–255); on this, see Zahrnt, *Luthers Predigt am Grabe.*

[600] Cf. "Vorrede zum Ratschlag eines Ausschusses etlicher Kardinäle, 1538," WA 50:296.21–270.10 (AE 34:231–267); "Pred. über 1 Kor. 15:1ff. vom 11.8.1532," WA 36:478.1–482.2.

[601] "Pred. über 1 Kor. 15:28f. vom 10.11.1532," WA 36:601.29 (AE 28:57–213); "Pred. über 1 Kor. 15:33f. vom 1.12.1532," WA 36:620.29 (AE 28:57–213).

[602] This is how Paracelsus and Böhme see it; cf. Bornkamm, *Äußerer und innerer Mensch bei Luther und den Spiritualisten*, esp. 103f.

[603] *BSLK*, 659.3f. (LC).

[604] See passages such as "Pred. über 1 Kor. 15:12ff. vom 22.9.1532," WA 36:532.13 (AE 28:57–213); "Pred. über 1 Kor. 15:36ff. vom 19.1.1533," WA 36:655.9f.; 654.5–10; 658.1f. (AE 28:57–213).

[605] "Pred. über 1 Kor. 15:44ff. vom 1.2.1533," WA 36:663.6 (AE 28:57–213): "It is to grow foul in the grave, and fire from heaven will go afterwards through all the tombs"; cf., in addition, "Decem praecepta Wittenbergensi praedicata populo, 1516–17," WA 1:515.21–24; "Adventspost. zu Lk. 21:25–33, 1522," WA 10.1.2:116.10–117.16; "Disp. de iustificatione, 1536," WA 39.1:95.18ff. (AE 34:145–196).

[606] *BSLK*, 659.22 (LC).

3. Eternal Life for the Exalted Human Body from the Vantage Point of the Settled Conscience that Will Gaze upon God

Along with the theologians of the early Church and the Middle Ages, the reformer portrays the "new, immortal and exalted body"[607] with the same detailed level of description that he used about the death of the old body.[608] Everything that belongs to this physical life, fallen under the sentence of death, such as eating and drinking, urinating and defecating, bearing and raising children, will all be left behind, but the body and skeletal structure, all reasoning, skin and hair, flesh and blood and all one's limbs will remain, as is true of the Resurrected Lord, though freed from the entire stigma of God's wrath, from disfiguring mutilations, and from earthly burdens that weigh one down, so that each will have a physical body that matches the fully human body that Christ had in adulthood.

This fully formed spiritual flesh will be saturated within by the godly joy that each human being will have, that his life can be complete only when gazing upon God.[609] As even now a Christian does not live life just by daily bread on the earth that is passing away, but by the Word of God, life there will be lived exclusively in adoration of God.[610] At this point, Luther's insights into how humans were created originally in the image of God, and also how that image was lost when Adam fell, take a turn when Christ's obedience of God anticipates the crowning restoration.[611] The reformer does not concentrate the end and goal of God's action to be that one gets a new body; the renewed heart and mind are front and center, freed from every accusation of the Law, released from all doubt and despair,

---

[607] *BSLK*, 659.15f. (LC).

[608] On this, see passages such as "Predigten über 1 Kor. 15:35–55 vom 8.12.1532–14.4.1533," WA 36:632.5–636.6; 648.4–22; 651.1–7; 655.10–658.8; 660.5–661.7; 662.9–18; 670.1–675.5; 679.10–680.10 (AE 28:57–213).

[609] "Pred. über Joh. 17:24–26 vom 31.10.1528," WA 28:196.3–7; "Pred. über 1 Kor. 15:28f. vom 10.11.1532," WA 36:593.12–594.2 (AE 28:57–213).

[610] Ibid., 594.1: "And thus good conscience in the soul, no one will terrify or trick you, make you err and upset you, but you will have a view of everything, because the heart will be full, full"; "Pred. über 1 Kor. 15:44ff. vom 1.2.1533," WA 36:662.11 (AE 28:57–213): "Life springs from the view of God and from the soul"; cf. "Pred. über 1 Petr. 3, 1523," WA 12:366.25–31 (AE 30:1–145); "Pred. über Joh. 6:45–47 vom 11.2.1531," WA 33:164.16–165.3 (AE 23:1–197); "Pred. über Ps. 8 vom 1.11.1537," WA 45:232.11–25 (AE 12:1–136).

[611] See pp. 94–104.

filled with life and blessedness as one gazes in adoration upon God. But this eschatological freedom that saturates the conscience that is at rest within God permeates the entire human being, without resistance; restored thus, a person fulfills God's will in spontaneous joy and with an agility that matches the way angels serve.[612]

And yet, just as the exalted body of the resurrected Lord carried the physical marks where the nails had been driven and the mark where the lance pierced His side, the exalted bodies of those who belong to Him will shine forth with whatever they suffered because of Him. That which the Spirit of God effected in us, through our daily sanctification, will not be snuffed out either, but rather purified through the fire of judgment and will thus shine through all eternity before the throne of God.[613] Just as the Christian Church is united in one faith and one love even though it functions here on earth by means of its manifold charisms and acts of service,[614] there as well, in eternity, the different levels of honor will be manifested in the concord of love in faith, to praise God alone more wondrously still.[615]

The reformer does not fall prey to a spiritualizing nihilism, which is characteristic of most eschatological reflections offered by modern theology; Luther's view is that the creator holds fast to His creatures right through the absolute power of death; this is true not only with respect to our physical life, the work we performed, and the suffering

---

[612] "1. Antinomerdisp. vom 18.12.1537," WA 39.1:365.4: "in the life to come, a most delightful and perfect obedience to the Law will be in them, so that they make bodies from their souls, as angels do now"; "Pred. über Joh. 6:45–47 vom 11.2.1531," WA 33:164.16 (AE 23:1–197): "Flesh and blood is otherwise only a wall between me and Christ; then it will be away as well, and Christ will be for me nothing but righteousness and salvation."

[613] On this, see passages such as "Grund und Ursach aller Artikel, 1521," WA 7:349.19ff. (AE 32:3–99); "De votis monasticis, 1521," WA 8:652.37–40 (AE 44:243–400); "Entwürfe zu De loco iustificationis, 1530," WA 30.2:670.26–30; "Wochenpred. über Mt. 7, 1530," WA 32:538.4–10; 543.1–544.7 (AE 21:1–294); "Pred. über 1 Kor. 15:36ff. vom 19.1.1533," WA 36:653.1–654.2 (AE 28:57–213).

[614] *BSLK*, 657.30–32 (LC).

[615] "Wochenpred. über Mt. 7, 1530," WA 32:544.2 (AE 21: 294): "Yet there will be a difference in clarity and glory, with which we will be decorated and brightened, just as at present in this life there is a difference in gifts, so that one works and suffers more than another; but in that life everything will be manifest, so that all the world will see what each one has done and which ones will thus have greater glory, for which the entire heavenly host will rejoice." Peter Lombard, *Sententiarum* IV, dist. 49.4 (PL 192:959): "Where God is all in all, He will be in unmatched clarity, as well, through joy, so that what individuals will have may be in common for all, because the glory of the head will also be in all through the bond of love."

we endured, but holds true for the non-human creatures as well. Romans 8:18–23[616] reports that the entire creation groans with eager longing for the eternal life that comes from God. All such creatures are to be rescued, as well, from death's destiny, from the tyranny of godless human beings, and from the demonic powers of destruction. "Just as the human being in this life is 'pure material' for God, pressing forward toward what will be his future bodily form, the entire creature, cast now into oblivion, is likewise material for God, to be used to make its future glorified form."[617] The faith thus overshadows not only our own bodily existence, but encompasses all creatures that are part of God's eschatological promise.

The believer thus considers himself to be hidden within Christ's victory even in death; he trusts the promise of God: "My Word remains forever, and you also, in the Word."[618] Luther's utterances are offered in this connection, when he seems to accept the Greek teaching about the immortality of the soul;[619] but he orients himself in that context by referring to the Word of God that alone is powerful. It is concurrently both the curse and the nobility of all human existence that we are summoned before God at the heart of our existence, and we are dealt with by Him on the basis of our conscience. No human can flee from confrontation with God, not even in death.[620] In eternity, human beings who close themselves to God's summons will experience exactly what Christ suffered in the Garden of Gethsemane

---

[616] At this point, see "Pred. über Röm. 8:18ff. vom 20.6.1535," WA 41:301–18, this has been dealt with by Ellwein, *Epistel-Ausl.*, 1:128–49; in addition, see "Pred. über Ps. 8 vom 1.11.1537," WA 45:229–34 (AE 12:1–136).

[617] Althaus, *Theologie Luthers*, 354, according to "Disputatio de homine, 14.1.1536," WA 39.1:177, Theses 35f. (AE 34:139): "35. Therefore man in this life is the simple material of God for the form of his future life. 36. Just as the whole creation which is now subject to vanity [Rom. 8:20] is for God the material for its future glorious form"; cf. Joest, *Ontologie*, 347–51.

[618] "Ausl. von Ps. 147, 1532," WA 31.1:456.8 (AE 14:107–135).

[619] At this point, note the difference of opinion between Stange and Althaus; cf. p. 293, n. 554.

[620] "Gen.-Vorl., 1535–45," WA 43:481.32 (AE 5:76): "Accordingly, where and with whomever God speaks, whether in anger or in grace, that person is surely immortal. The Person of God, who speaks, and the Word point out that we are the kind of creatures with whom God would want to speak eternally and in an immortal manner"; "Pred. über Lk. 16:19–31 vom 22.6.1522," WA 10.3:191.13: "it is to be known that the soul or spirit of the human being has no basis or solid reason that he would be able to continue to live, except the Word of God, until the time when he comes into the bright vision of God on the Last Day."

and upon the cross on Golgotha and what Luther himself experienced in his own person as well:[621] After the Last Judgment, their martyrdom will be primarily a matter of their physical existence; that will be their lot all over again after they are reawakened. First of all, and most importantly, God's holy wrath of judgment will rest upon their heart and conscience.[622] The stigma of the conscience that accuses and confuses will be known to them already in that mysterious time between their death and their judgment. "Such are the doubt-filled thoughts of a person whose conscience knows that he has renounced the Word of God forever and can receive no help for all eternity."[623]

Since the redeemed are to be given a comforted conscience and a happy heart at the time of judgment, which will endure for all eternity and will penetrate their entire, renewed, bodily existence, their intermediate state[624] will be impacted as well. Luther seeks concurrently to understand that intermediate condition on the basis of our earthly existence in the faith. In both life and death we wrap ourselves up in God's promise; it furnishes for us the broad space to live life in the midst of death.[625] "The human being thus overcomes death through the Word of life, if he holds to it firmly and believes and travels with it to death";[626] God's creative Word does not permit our inner being to remain in death; it brings it through God's holy wrath of judgment all the way to life everlasting. Word and faith thus provide the actual "place" where the Christian Church lives, already in the here and now on earth; both protect a believer in death as well,

---

621 "Resolutiones disp. de indulgentiarum virtute, 1518," WA 1:555.26–559.5 (AE 31:77–252); "Op. in Ps., 1518–21," WA 5:590.13–591.11.

622 "Op. in Ps., 1518–21," WA 5:590.13: "The external fire is nothing compared to this internal fire"; "Resolutiones disp. de indulgentiarum virtute, 1518": WA 1:558.14 (AE 31:77–252): "And this internal fire is much more severe than the external."

623 "Pred. über Lk. 16:19–31 vom 22.6.1522," WA 10.3:193.18.

624 Concerning the so-called intermediate state, cf. "Adventspost. zu Lk. 21:25–33, 1522," WA 10.1.2:117.17–118.9; "Pred. über Lk. 16:19–31 vom 22.6.1522," WA 10.3:191.11–198.19; "Fastenpost. zu Joh. 8:46–59, 1525," WA 17.2:234.32–236.35; "Ennaratio Ps. 90, 1534–35," WA 40.2:502.16–503.27; 510.6–512.11 (AE 12:197–410); "Gen.-Vorl., 1535–45," WA 43:357.23–363.27 (AE 4:1–409).

625 "Gen.-Vorl., 1535–45," WA 43:361.12 (AE 4:314): "His Word is surely far greater and far more extensive. Therefore the whereabouts of the souls is the Word of God or the promises in which we fall asleep."

626 "Fastenpost. zu Joh. 8:46–59, 1525," WA 17.2:235.39.

until the full power of the Word of the *Spiritus Creator* summons us to eternal life in the presence of God.

This brings the interpretation of the Third Article to a conclusion; it can be summarized in the following thesis: By means of the "elements" that have been unfolded, through the Church as Holy Christendom, through the multifaceted ways the promise of forgiveness is articulated in all offices and estates, through the bodily awakening from the dead and eternal life before God, the Spirit of God alters us and restores us to the original image of the one who was offered for us and who rose. The Third Article thus remains coupled with the central Second Article that deals with our redemption, as the central point of the Apostles' Creed, furnishing the center of the catechism as a whole.

Texts and Literature Concerning Sanctification that Proceeds from Justification

WA 10.3:1–13: "1. Invocavit-Predigt vom 9.3.1522" (AE 51:70–75)

WA 11:111–14 = WA 12:568–78: "Pfingstpredigt über Joh. 14:23ff. vom 24.5.1523"

WA 14:681.12–682.3: from "Deuteronomion Mosi cum annotationibus, 1525" (AE 9:1–311)

WA 18:65.3–66.11; 139.13–26: from "Wider die himmlischen Propheten, 1525" (AE 40:73–223)

WA 39.1:369.19–371.16; 383.10–26; 389.2–391.20: from "1. Antinomer-Disputation vom 18.12.1537"

Literature

Elert, *Morphologie*, 1:123–54.

Prenter, *Spiritus Creator*, 247–64.

Peters, *Gegenwart Gottes–Wort Gottes*

BIBLIOGRAPHY

Adam, Alfred. "Apostolikum I." *RGG* 1:510–13.

_____. *Lehrbuch der Dogmengeschichte*, Gütersloh, 1965–68.

Albrecht, Otto. *Luthers Katechismen*. Schriften des Vereins für Reformationsgeschichte 33, no. 121/122. Leipzig: Verein für Reformationsgeschichte, 1915.

Alpers, Harm. *Die Versöhnung durch Christus*. Göttingen, 1964.

Althaus, Paul. *Communio sanctorum*, 1. Munich, 1929.

_____. *Die letzten Dinge*. 9th ed. Gütersloh, 1964.

_____. "Luthers Gedanken über die letzten Dinge." *Luther-Jahrbuch* 23 (1941): 9–34.

_____. "Martin Luther und die Einheit der Kirche Christi." *Luther* 37 (1966): 1–9.

_____. "Niedergefahren zur Hölle." *Zeitschrift für Systematische Theologie* 19 (1942): 365–84.

_____. *Paulus und Luther über den Menschen. Ein Vergleich*. 4th ed. Gütersloh, 1963.

_____. "Der Schöpfungsgedanke bei Luther." *Sitzungsberichte der bayerischen Akademie der Wissenschaften. Philosophisch-philologische und historische Klasse* (1959)/ H. 7:3–18.

_____. *Die Theologie Martin Luthers*. Gütersloh: Gütersloher, 1962.

_____. *Unsterblichkeit und ewiges Leben bei Luther*. Gütersloh, 1930.

Asendorf, Ulrich. *Eschatologie bei Luther*. Göttingen, 1967.

_____. *Gekreuzigt und Auferstanden. Luthers Herausforderung an die moderne Christologie*. Arbeiten zur Geschichte und Theologie des Luthertums 25. Berlin, Hamburg, 1971.

Asheim, Ivar. *Glaube und Erziehung bei Luther*. Heidelberg: Quelle & Meyer, 1961.

Audet, Jean-Paul. "L'annonce à Marie." *Revue Biblique* 63 (1956): 346–74.

Augustinus Aurelius. *Enchiridion de fide, spe et caritate*. Edited by J. Barbel, Düsseldorf, 1960. (Test. 1).

Augustinus. *Schriften gegen die Semipelagianer*. Edited by S. Kopp and A. Zumkeller. Würzburg, 1955.

Aulen, Gustaf. "Die drei Typen der christlichen Versöhnungslehre." *Zeitschrift für Systematische Thelogie* 8 (1931): 510–38.

_____. *Den kristna försoningstanken*. Lund, 1930.

Von Balthasar, Hans Urs. *Sponsa verbi*. Einsiedeln, 1960.

Barth, Hans Martin. *Der Teufel und Jesus Christus in der Theologie Martin Luthers*. Göttingen, 1967.

Barth, Karl. *Credo. Die Hauptprobleme der Dogmatik dargestelt im Anschluß an das Apostolische Glaubensbekenntnis*. 3d ed. Munich, 1935.

_____. *Dogmatik im Grundriß*. Zurich, 1947.

_____. *Die Kirchliche Dogmatik*. Zurich, 1932ff.

Baumgärtel, Friedrich. "Καρδία." *TWNT* 3:609–11.

_____. "Πνεῦμα, etc." *TWNT* 6:357–66.

Beck, Anton (editor). *Kirchliche Studien und Quellen*. Amberg, 1903.

Behm, Johannes. "Καρδία." *TWNT* 3:611–16.

_____. "Παράκλητος." *TWNT* 5:798–812.

Beisser, Friedrich. *Claritas scripturae bei M. Luther*. Göttingen, 1966.

Bericht aus Uppsala 1968. *Offizieller Bericht über die vierte Vollversammlung des Ökumenischen Rates der Kirchen Uppsala 1968*. Edited by N. Goodall. Geneva, 1968.

Bericht der vierten Weltkonferenz für Glauben und Kirchenverfassung Montreal 1963. Edited by P. C. Rodger and L. Vischer, Geneva, 1963.

Bieder, Werner. "Πνεῦμα, etc." *TWNT* 6:367–73.

_____. *Die Vorstellung von der Höllenfahrt Jesu Christi*. Zurich, 1949.

Billing, Einar. *Försoningen*. Uppsala, 1921.

Bloch, Ernst. *Tübinger Einleitung in die Philosophie*. Vol. 1. Frankfurt/Main, 1970.

Boeckl, Karl. *Die sieben Gaben des Heiligen Geistes in ihrer Bedeutung für die Mystik nach der Theologie des 13. und 14. Jahrhunderts*. Freiburg im Breisgau, 1931.

Bohlin, Torsten. *Den korsfästa Skaparen*. Stockholm, 1952.

Bohne, Gerhard. ". . . nicht aus eigener Vernunft noch Kraft . . ." "Pädagogische Randbemerkungen zu Luthers Erklärung des dritten Artikels." Pages 123–32 in *Ich glaube eine heilige Kirche*. Festschrift for H. Asmussen. Edited by W. Bauer. Hamburg, 1963.

Boliek, Lynn Elvin. *The Resurrection of the Flesh*. Amsterdam, 1962.

Bornhäuser, Karl. *Der Ursinn des Kleinen Katechismus D. M. Luthers*. Gütersloh, 1933.

Bornkamm, Günther. "Der Paraklet im Johannes-Evangelium." Pages 68–89 in vol. 1 of *Geschichte und Glaube. Gesammelte Aufsätze*, 3. Munich, 1968.

_____. "Zur Interpretation des Johannes-Evangelium. Eine Auseinandersetzung mit Ernst Käsemanns Schrift 'Jesu letzter Wille nach Johannes 17'." Pages 104–21 in vol. 1 of *Geschichte und Glaube. Gesammelte Aufsätze*, 3. Munich, 1968.

Bornkamm, Heinrich. "Außerer und innerer Mensch bei Luther und den Spiritualisten." Pages 85–109 in *Imago Dei*, Festschrift for G. Krüger. Edited by H. Bornkamm. Gießen, 1932.

_____. *Luther und das Alte Testament*. Göttingen, 1948.

_____. *Das Wort Gottes bei Luther*. Munich, 1933. Pages 147–86 in *Luther. Gestalt und Wirkungen*. Gütersloh, 1975.

Bornkamm, Karin. *Luthers Auslegung des Galaterbriefes von 1519 und 1531*. Ein Vergleich. Berlin, 1963.

_____. "Das Verständnis christlicher Unterweisung in den Katechismen von Erasmus und Luther." *Zeitschrift für Theologie und Kirche* 65 (1968): 204–30.

Botte, Bernhard. "Note sur le symbole baptismal de Saint Hippolyte." Pages 189–200 in *Mélanges J. de Ghellinck*. Gemblous, 1951.

Brightman, Frank E., ed. *Liturgies Eastern and Western* 1. Oxford, 1967. (1st ed., 1896).

Bring, Ragnar. *Dualismen hos Luther*. Lund, 1929.

Brunner, Emil. *Dogmatik.* 3 vols. Zurich, 1946–60.

Brunner, Peter. "Der Ersterschaffene als Gottes Ebenbild." Pages 85–95 in *Pro ecclesia*, 1. Berlin, 1962.

_____. "Vom Amt des Bischofs." Pages 235–309 in *Pro ecclesia*, 1. Berlin, 1962.

_____. "Zur Lehre vom Gottesdienst der im Namen Jesu versammelten Gemeinde." Pages 83–364 in *Leiturgia*, 1. Edited by K. F. Müller and W. Blankenburg. Kassel, 1954.

Brunner-Traut, Emma. "Die Geburtsgeschichte der Evangelien im Lichte ägyptischer Forschungen. *Zeitschrift für Religions- und Geistesgeschichte* 12 (1960): 97–111.

Brunotte, Wilhelm. *Das geistliche Amt bei Luther*. Berlin, 1959.

Buchrucker, Armin Ernst. "Nullus Diabolus—Nullus Redemptor. Die Bedeutung des Teufels für die Theologie Martin Luthers." *Lutherischer Rundblick* 16 (1968): 150–60.

Buchwald, Georg. "Luther über die Welt als 'Mitwirkerin Gottes'." *Luther* 23 (1941): 49–73.

Bultmann, Rudolf. "Πιστεύω, C–D." *TWNT* 6:197–230.

_____. *Das Evangelium des Johannes*. Vol. 2 of Kritisch-exegetischer Kommentar über das Neue Testament. 10th ed. Göttingen, 1941.

_____. *Theologie des Neuen Testaments*. Tübingen, 1958.

Burba, Klaus. *Die Christologie in Luthers Liedern*. Gütersloh, 1956.

Burn, A. E. *Niceta of Remesiana*. Cambridge, 1905.

Calvin, Johannes. *Unterricht in der christlichen Religion* (based on the last edition, as translated and edited by O. Weber). 4th ed. Neukirchen: Neukirchener, 1986.

_____. *Opera selecta*. Edited by P. Barth and W. Niesel. Munich, 1926–36.

Von Campenhausen, Hans. *Die Jungfrauengeburt in der Theologie der alten Kirche.* Sitzungsberichte der Heidelberger Akademie der Wissenschaften. Philosophisch-historische Klasse, 1962/63.

Caspari, C. P., ed. *Alte und neue Quellen zur Geschichte des Taufsymbols und der Glaubelsregeln*. Reprint. Brussels, 1964.

_____. *Ungedruckte, unbeachtete und wenig beachtete Quellen zur Geschichte des Taufsymbols und der Glaubensregel*. 3 vols. Place of publication not stated, 1866–75. Reprint. Brussels, 1964.

Christus und die Kirche. Bericht der Theologischen Kommission über Christus und die Kirche an die vierte Weltkonferenz für Glaube und Kirchenverfassung Montreal 1963. Faith and Order Papers, no. 38. Zurich: Ökumenischen Rat der Kirchen, 1963.

Congar, Yves. "Kirche und Welt." Pages 102–26 in *Weltverständnis im Glauben*. Edited by J. B. Metz. Mainz, 1965.

_____. "Regards et réflexions sur la christologie de Luther." Pages 457–86 in vol. 3 of *Das Konzil von Chalkedon. Geschichte und Gegenwart*. Würzburg, 1962.

Constitutio dogmatica de Ecclesia. LTK. Supplementary Volume 1: 156–347.

Crehan, Joseph Hugh. *Early Christian Baptism and the Creed*. London, 1950.

Creutzig, Hans-Emil. *Amt und Ämter in der lutherischen Kirche*. Leipzig, 1938.

Cullmann, Oscar. *Die Christologie des Neuen Testaments*. 2d ed. Tübingen, 1958.

_____. *Die ersten christlichen Glaubensbekenntnisse*. Zollikon, Zurich, 1943.

Deissler, Alfons. "Gottes Selbstoffenbarung im Alten Testament." Pages 226–71 in *Mysterium Salutis. Grundriß heilsgeschichtlicher Dogmatik,* vol. 2. Edited by J. Feiner and M. Löhrer. Einsiedeln, Zurich, Cologne, 1967.

Delling, Gerhard. "Παρθένος." *TWNT* 5:824–35.

Dibelius, Martin. "Jungfrauensohn und Krippenkind." Pages 1–78 in vol. 1 of *Botschaft und Geschichte*. Gesammelte Aufsätze. Edited by G. Bornkamm. Tübingen, 1953.

Dibelius, Otto. *Das Vaterunser*. Gießen, 1903.

Von Dobschütz, Ernst. *Das Apostolicum in biblisch-theologischer Beleuchtung*. Gießen, 1932.

Doerne, Martin. "Praktischer Schöpfungsglaube nach Luther." *Luther* 25 (1954): 24–40.

Dölger, Franz Joseph. *Ichthys,* 1. Münster, 1928.

Dörries, Hermann. *Das Bekenntnis in der Geschichte der Kirche.* Göttingen, 1946.

_____. *De Spiritu sancto. Der Beitrag des Basilius zum Abschluß des trinitarischen Dogmas*. Göttingen, 1956.

Denzinger, Henricus, and Adolphus Schönmetzer, eds. *Enchiridion Symbolorum*. 36th ed. Freiburg in Breisgau, 1976.

Duchrow, Ulrich. *Christenheit und Weltverantwortung*. Stuttgart, 1970.

Düfel, Hans. *Luthers Stellung zur Marienverehrung*. Göttingen, 1968.

Ebeling, Gerhard. "Gewißheit und Zweifel." *Zeitschrift für Theologie und Kirche* 64 (1967): 282–324.

_____. Luther. *Einführung in sein Denken*. Tübingen, 1964.

_____. *Das Wesen des christlichen Glaubens*. Tübingen, 1959.

Eichenseer, Caelestis. *Das Symbolum Apostolicum beim hl. Augustinus*. St. Ottilien, 1960.

Elert, Werner. *Abendmahl und Kirchengemeinschaft in der alten Kirche hauptsächlich des Ostens*. Berlin, 1954.

_____. *Morphologie des Luthertums*. 2 vols. Reprint. Munich, 1958.

Ellwein, Eduard. "Die Christusverkündigung in Luthers Auslegung des Johannesevangeliums." *Kerygma und Dogma* 6 (1960): 31–68.

_____. *D. M. Luthers Epistel-Auslegung*, 1. Göttingen, 1963.

_____. Summus Evangelista: *Die Botschaft des Johannesevangeliums in der Auslegung Luthers*. Munich, 1960.

Erasmus. "Explanatio Symboli, quod dicitur apostolorum." *Opera Omnia*, 5:1134–96. Leiden, 1704.

Fahlbusch, Erwin. "Heilsordnung." In 2d ed. of *Evangelisches Kirchenlexikon,* 2:91–94. Göttingen, 1956–61.

Foerster, Sabine. *Das Jüngste Gericht bei Luther*. Philosophische Dissertation Frankfurt, 1922.

Foerster, Werner. "Κύριος." *TWNT* 3:1038–56; 1081–98.

_____. *Herr ist Jesus*. Gütersloh, 1924.

Foerster, Karl. "Idiomenkommunikation." *LTK* 5:607–09.

Frank, Franz Heinrich Reinhold. *Die Theologie der Concordienformel historisch-dogmatisch entwickelt und beleuchtet*. Erlangen, 1858–65.

Frings, Theodor. *Grundlegung einer Geschichte der deutschen Sprache*. 2d ed. Halle, 1950.

Frings, Theodor/Müller, Gertraud. "Germania Romana" in *Teuthonista. Zeitschrift für deutsche Dialektforschung und Sprachgeschichte*. Beiheft 4, 1932.

Funk, Franz Xaver and K. Bihlmeyer, eds. *Die Apostolischen Väter*. 3d ed. Tübingen, 1924.

Funk, Franz Xaverm, ed. *Didascalia et Constitutiones Apostolorum*. 2 vols. Paderborn, 1905.

Geffcken, Johannes. *Der Bildercatechismus des fünfzehnten Jahrhunderts und die catechetischen Hauptstücke in dieser Zeit bis auf Luther*, 1. Leipzig, 1855.

Gennrich, Paul Wilhelm. *Die Christologie Luthers im Abendmahlsstreit 1524–29*. Göttingen, 1929.

Gerdes, Hajo. "Zu Luthers Lehre vom Wirken des Geistes." *Luther-Jahrbuch* 25 (1958): 42–60.

Gewiess, Josef. "Die Marienfrage Lk. 1:34." *Biblische Zeitschrift* 5 (1961): 221–54.

De Ghellinck, Joseph. *Patristique in moyenage*. Gembloux, 1949.

Gillhoff, Johannes. *Zur Sprache und Geschichte des Kleinen Katechismus*. Leipzig, 1909.

Girgensohn, Herbert. *Katechismus-Auslegung*, 1. Witten, 1956.

Goeters, J. F. Gerhard. "Christologie und Rechtfertigung nach dem Heidelberger Katechismus." Pages 31–47 in *Das Kreuz Jesu Christi als Grund des Heils*. 2d ed. Edited by E. Bizer, et al. Gütersloh, 1968.

Goppelt, Leonard. "Das kirchliche Amt nach den lutherischen Bekenntnisschriften und nach dem Neuen Testament." *Lutherische Rundschau* 14 (1964): 517–36.

Grass, Hans. *Die Abendmahlslehre bei Luther und Calvin*. 2d ed. Gütersloh, 1954.

Greschat, Martin. *Melanchthon neben Luther*. Witten, 1965.

Grillmeier, Alois. “Der Gottessohn im Totenreich.” *Zeitschrift für Theologie und Kirche* 71 (1949): 1–53.

Grillmeier, Aloys and Heinrich Bacht, eds. *Das Konzil von Chalkedon. Geschichte und Gegenwart*. 3 vols. 2d ed. Würzburg, 1951–54, 1962.

Grillmeier, Aloys. “Die theologische und sprachliche Vorbereitung der christologischen Formel von Chalkedon.” Pages 5–202 in vol. 1 of *Das Konzil von Chalkedon. Geschichte und Gegenwart*. Würzburg, 1962.

Haenchen, Ernst. *Die Apostelgeschichte*. Vol. 3 of Kritisch-exegetischer Kommentar über das Neue Testament. 12 ed. Göttingen, 1959.

Hägglund, Bengt. “Die Bedeutung der ‘regula fidei’ als Grundlage theologischer Aussagen.” *Studia theologica*. Lund, et al., 12 (1958): 1–44.

_____. *De Homine*. Lund, 1959.

_____. “Rechtfertigung—Wiedergeburt—Erneuerung in der nachreformatorischen Theologie.” *Kerygma und Dogma* 5 (1959): 318–37.

Hahn, August, ed. *Bibliothek der Symbole und Glaubensregeln der Apostolisch-katholischen Kirche*. 3d ed. Breslau, 1897.

Hahn, Ferdinand. *Christologische Hoheitstitel*. Göttingen, 1963.

Hardeland, August. *Luthers Katechismusgedanken in ihrer Entwicklung bis zum Jahre 1529*. Gütersloh, 1913.

Von Harnack, Adolf. *Lehrbuch der Dogmengeschichte*. 3 vols. 4th ed. Tübingen, 1909/10.

_____. “Zur Abhandlung von Holl: Auslegung des zweiten Artikels des sog. apostolischen Glaubensbekenntnisses.” Pages 112–16 in *Sitzungsberichte der preußischen Akademie der Wissenschaften. Philosophisch-historische Klasse*, 1919.

Harnack, Theodosius, *Katechetik und Erklärung des Kleinen Katechismus Dr. Martin Luthers*. Erlangen, 1882.

_____. *Luthers Theologie mit besonderer Beziehung auf seine Versöhnungs- und Erlösungslehre*. Erlangen, 1862–86. Reprint, Amsterdam, 1969.

Harnisch, Wilhelm. *Entwürfe und Stoffe zu Unterredungen über Luthers kleinen Katechismus*, 2. Halle, 1827.

Harvey, W. Wigan (editor). *Sancti Irenaei Libros quinque adversus Haereses*, Two volumes. Cambridge, 1857. Reprint Ridgewood, New Jersey, 1965.

Heidegger, Martin. *Was ist Metaphysik? Einführung in die Metaphysik*. Tübingen, 1958.

Heim, Karl. *Jesus der Weltvollender*. Tübingen, 1937.

Heintze, Gerhard. "Luthers Pfingstpredigten." *Luther-Jahrbuch* 36 (1967): 117–40.

Hendry, George S. *The Gospel of the Incarnation*. Philadelphia, 1958.

Hermann, Ingo. *Kurios und Pneuma. Studien zur Christologie der paulinischen Hauptbriefe*. Munich, 1961.

Hermann, Rudolf. "Zu Luthers Lehre von Sünde und Rechtfertigung (1952)." Pages 391–427 in *Gesammelte Studien zur Theologie Luthers und zur Reformation*. Göttingen, 1960.

Herrmann, Wilhelm. *Der Verkehr des Christen mit Gott, im Anschluß an Luther dargestellt*. 7th ed. Stuttgart, Berlin, 1921.

Hirsch, Emanuel. *Hilfsbuch zum Studien der Dogmatik*. 4th ed. Berlin, 1964.

_____. *Lutherstudien*, 1. Gütersloh, 1954.

Hoffmann, Georg. *Die altlutherische Orthodoxie vor 250 Jahren im Kampfe wider das Apostolikum*. Breslau, 1912.

_____. "Apostolikum II." *RGG* 1:513–16.

_____. "Der Kleine Katechismus als Abriß der Theologie Martin Luthers. *Luther* 30 (1959): 49–63.

_____. *Die Lehre von der fides implicita und die Reformation*, 2. Leipzig, 1906.

Hofmann, Fritz. *Der Kirchenbegriff des heiligen Augustinus*. Munich, 1933.

Höhne, Wolfgang. *Luthers Anschauung über die Kontinuität der Kirche*. Berlin, Hamburg, 1963.

Holl, Karl. "Die Entstehung von Luthers Kirchenbegriff." Pages 288–325 in vol. 1 of *Gesammelte Aufsätze zur Kirchengeschichte*. 2d/3d eds. Tübingen: Mohr, 1923.

_____. "Was verstand Luther unter Religion?" Pages 1–110 in vol. 1 of *Gesammelte Aufsätze zur Kirchengeschichte*. 2d/3d eds. Tübingen: Mohr, 1923.

_____. "Zur Auslegung des zweiten Artikels des sogenannten apostolischen Glaubensbekenntnisses." Pages 2–11 in *Sitzungsberichte der preußischen Akademie der Wissenschaften. Philosophisch-historische Klasse*, 1919.

Huhn, Josef. *Das Geheimnis der Jungfrau-Mutter Maria nach dem Kirchenvater Ambrosius*. Würzburg, 1924.

_____. "Das Mariengeheimnis beim Kirchenvater Ambrosius." *Münchener theologische Zeitschrift* 2 (1951): 130–46.

Iserloh, Erwin. "Sacramentum und Exemplum. Ein augustinisches Thema lutherischer Theologie." Pages 247–64 in vol. 1 of *Reformata Reformanda*. Festschrift for H. Jedin. Edited by E. Iserloh and K. Repgen. Münster, 1965.

Iwand, Hans Joachim. "Sed originale per hominem unum." *Evangelische Theologie* 6 (1946): 26–43.

_____. *Rechtfertigungslehre und Christusglaube*. Munich, 1930.

_____. "Wider den Mißbrauch des 'pro me' als methodisches Prinzip in der Theologie." *Evangelische Theologie* 14 (1954): 120–25.

Jacobs, Paul (editor). *Reformierte Bekenntnisschriften und Kirchenordnungen in deutscher Übersetzung*. Marburg, 1950.

Jansen, Reiner. *Studien zu Luthers Trinitätslehre*. Basler Studien zur historischen und systematischen Theologie, 26. Bern, Frankfurt, 1976.

Jeremias, Joachim. "κλείς." *TWNT* 3:743–53.

Jetter, Werner. *Die Taufe beim jungen Luther*. Tübingen, 1954.

Joest, Wilfried. Gesetz und Freiheit. *Das Problem des Tertius usus legis bei Luther und die neutestamentliche Parainese*. 3d ed. Göttingen, 1961.

_____. *Ontologie der Person bei Luther*. Göttingen, 1967.

_____. "Paulus und das lutherische Simul Iustus et Peccator." *Kerygma und Dogma*, 1 (1955): 269–320.

Josefson, Ruben. "Christus und die hl. Schrift." Pages 57–63 in *Lutherforschung heute*. Edited by V. Vajta. Berlin, 1958.

Kadai, Heino O. "Luther's Theology of the Cross." Pages 230–67 in *Accents in Luther's Theology*. Edited by H. O. Kadai. St. Louis, London: Concordia, 1967.

Kantzenbach, Friedrich Wilhelm. "Christusgemeinschaft und Rechtfertigung. Luthers Gedanke vom fröhlichen Wechsel." *Luther* 35 (1964): 34–45.

Käsemann, Ernst. "Geist und Geistesgaben in NT." *RGG* 2:1272–79.

_____. "Aufbau und Anliegen des johanneischen Prologs." Pages 155–80 in vol. 2 of *Exegetische Versuche und Besinnungen*. Göttingen, 1964.

_____. "Die Heilsbedeutung des Todes Jesu bei Paulus." Pages 61–107 in *Paulinische Perspektiven*. Tübingen, 1969. (= *Zur Bedeutung des Todes Jesu*. Edited by H. Conzelmann, et al. 2nd ed. Gütersloh, 1967).

_____. "Erwägungen zum Stichwort 'Versöhnungslehre' im Neuen Testament." Pages 47–59 in *Zeit und Geschichte*. Festschrift for R. Bultmann. Edited by E. Dinkler. Tübingen, 1964.

_____. *Jesu letzter Wille nach Johannes 17*. Tübingen, 1966.

_____. "Zur paulinischen Anthropologie." Pages 9–60 in *Paulinische Perspektiven*. Tübingen, 1969.

Kattenbusch, Ferdinand. *Das Apostolische Symbol*. 2 vols. Reprint Hildesheim, 1962.

_____. *Luthers Stellung zu den ökumenischen Symbolen*. Gießen, 1883.

Kelly, John Norman Davidson. "Apostolisches Glaubensbekenntnis." *LTK* 1:760–62.

_____. *Early Christian Creeds*. 3d ed. London, New York, 1963.

Kierkegaard, Sören. *Der Begriff Angst*. Edited by W. Diederichs, Leipzig, 1958.

Kinder, Ernst. "Christus als Hohepriester nach Luther und den lutherischen Bekenntnisschriften." Pages 99–120 in *Dank an P. Althaus*. Edited by W. Künneth and W. Joest. Gütersloh, 1958.

_____. *Der evangelische Glaube und die Kirche*. Berlin, 1958.

_____. "Der Gebrauch des Begriffs 'ökumenisch' im alten Luthertum. Zugleich ein Beitrag zur Frage der Rezeption der altkirchlichen Symbole durch die lutherische Reformation." *Kerygma und Dogma* 1 (1955): 180–207.

_____. *Die Erbsünde nach der Lehre der ev.-luth. Bekenntnisschriften*. Stuttgart, 1959.

_____. "Die soteriologische Motive der altkirchlichen Glaubensbekenntnisse." *Lutherische Rundschau* 11 (1961): 20–27.

Kirsten, Hans. *Die Taufabsage. Eine Untersuchung zu Gestalt und Geschichte der Taufe nach den altkirchlichen Taufliturgien*. Berlin, 1960.

Kittel, Gerhard. "εἰκών." *TWNT* 2:380–86; 391–96.

Kleinknecht, Hermann Martin. "εἰκών." *TWNT* 2:386–87.

_____. "Πνεῦμα, etc." *TWNT* 6:330–57.

Kluge, Friedrich. "Gotische Lehnworte im Althochdeutschen." *Beiträge zur Geschichte der deutschen Sprache und Literatur* 35 (1909): 124–60.

Knolle, Theodor. "Hebräische Heilsnamen in Luthers Liedern." *Luther-Jahrbuch* 22 (1940): 46–82.

Köberle, Adolf. "Heilsordnung." *RGG* 3:189–90.

Köhler, Walther. *Luther und die Kirchengeschichte nach seinen Schriften*. Erlangen, 1900.

Kolde, Dietrich. *Der Christenspiegel des Dietrich Kolde von Münster*. Franziskanischer Forschung, Part 9. Edited by C. Drees. Werl (Westphalia), 1954.

Koopmans, Jan. *Das altkirchliche Dogma in der Reformation*. Munich, 1955.

Krauss, Alfred. "Das Mittlerwerk nach dem Schema des munus triplex." *Jahrbücher für deutsche Theologie* 17 (1872): 595–655.

Kretschmar, Georg. "Himmelfahrt und Pfingsten." *Zeitschrift für Kirchengeschichte* 66 (1954/55): 209–53.

_____. *Studien zur frühchristlichen Trinitätstheologie*. Tübingen, 1956.

Krusche, Werner. *Das Wirken des Heiligen Geistes nach Calvin*. Göttingen, 1957.

Kuhn, Karl Georg. "μαραναθά." *TWNT* 4:470–75.

Kühn, Ulrich. *Via caritas. Theologie des Gesetzes bei Thomas von Aquin*. Göttingen, 1965.

Küng, Hans. *Die Kirche*. Freiburg in Breisgau, Basel, Vienna, 1967.

Landgraf, Artur M. *Dogmengeschichte der Frühskolastik*. Regensburg, 1952–56.

Lessing, Gotthold Ephraim. "Über den Beweis des Geistes und der Kraft." Pages 79–89 in vol. 7 of *Lessings Werke*. Edited by G. Witkowski. Leipzig, no year provided.

Lieberg, Hellmut. *Amt und Ordination bei Luther und Melanchthon*. Göttingen, 1962.

Lienhard, Marc. "Les cantiques de Luther et leur témoignage christologieque." *Positions luthériennes* 20 (1972): 234–49.

_____. *Luther, Témoin de Jésus-Christ. Les étapes et les themes de la Christologie du Réformateur*. Paris, 1973. *Martin Luthers Christologie*. Göttingen, 1979.

Liermann, Hans. "Luther ordnet seine Kirche." *Luther-Jahrbuch* 31 (1964): 29–46.

Lietzmann, Hans. "Die Anfänge des Glaubensbekenntnisses." Pages 163–181 in *Kleine Schriften* 3. Texte und Untersuchungen zur Geschichte der altchristlichen Literatur, 74. 1962.

_____. "Die Urform des apostolischen Glaubensbekenntnisses." Pages 269–274 in *Sitzungsberichte der preußischen Akademie der Wissenschaften. Philosophisch-historische Klasse*, 1919. Pages 182–88 in *Kleine Schriften* 3. Texte und Untersuchungen zur Geschichte der altchristlichen Literatur, 74. 1962.

_____. Symbolstudien 1–14. Pages 189–281 in *Kleine Schriften* 3. Texte und Untersuchungen zur Geschichte der altchristlichen Literatur, 74. 1962.

_____, ed. *Symbole der alten Kirche.* (Kleine Texte für [theologische und philologische] Vorlesungen und Übungen, 17/18). 4th ed. Bonn, 1935.

Lindroth, Hjalmar. "Descendit ad inferna." *Svensk teologisk kvartalskrift* 8 (1932): 121–40.

_____. Försoningen. *En dogmhistorisk och systematisk undersökning.* Uppsala, 1935.

Ljunggren, Gustaf. *Synd och skuld i Luthers teologi*. Stockholm, 1928.

Von Loewenich, Walther. *Die Eigenart in Luthers Auslegung des Johannes-Prologs*. Sitzungsberichte der bayerischen Akademie der Wissenschaften—Philosophisch-philologisch und historische Klasse. 1960. H. 8.

_____. *Luther als Ausleger der Synoptiker*. Munich, 1954.

_____. "Luthers Auslegung der Pfingstgeschichte." In *Vierhundertfünfzig Jahre Luther Reformation*. Festschrift for F. Lau. Göttingen, 1967.

Löfgren, David. *Die Theologie der Schöpfung bei Luther*. Göttingen, 1960.

Lohse, Bernhard. *Ratio und Fides. Eine Untersuchung über die ratio in der Theologie Luthers*. Göttingen, 1958.

_____, ed. *Der Durchbruch der reformatorischen Erkenntnis bei Luther*. Darmstadt, 1968.

_____. "Das Verständnis des leitenden Amtes in lutherischen Kirchen in Deutschland von 1517–1918." Pages 55–74 in *Kirchenpräsident oder Bischof?* Edited by I. Asheim and V. R. Gold. Göttingen, 1968.

_____. "Christologie in Ablaßstreit." *Luther-Jahrbuch* 27 (1960): 51–63.

Loofs, Friedrich. *Leitfaden zum Studien der Dogmengeschichte*. 5th ed. Halle, 1953.

_____. "Der articulus stantis et cadentis ecclesiae." *Theologische Studien und Kritiken* 90 (1917): 323–420.

Lottin, Paul. "Les classifications des dons du Saint Esprit au 12e et 13e siècle." *Revue d'ascétique et de mystique* 11 (1930): 269–85.

Ludolphy, Ingetraut. "Luther über Astrologie." *Luther* 33 (1962): 65–76.

_____. "Luthers Naturverständnis." *Luther* 35 (1964): 69–80.

Lührs, Albert. *Katechismusschule für Lehrer in Kirche, Schule und Haus über Dr. M. Luthers kleinen Katechismus mit Erklärung*. Hannover, 1863/65.

Mahlmann, Theodor. *Das neue Dogma der lutherischen Christologie. Probleme und Geschichte seiner Bedeutung*. Gütersloh, 1969.

Martensen, Hans L. "Ubiquitätslehre." *LTK* 10:442–43.

Martin von Amberg. *Der Gewissensspiegel*. Edited by St. N. Werbow. Berlin, 1958.

Maurer, Wilhelm. "Die Anfänge von Luthers Theologie. Eine Anfrage an die lutherische Kirche." *Theologische Literaturzeitung*, 77:1–12. 1952. Reprinted in *Kirche und Geschichte. Gesammelte Aufsätze*, 1. Pages 22–37 in *Luther und das evangelische Bekenntnis*. Göttingen, 1970.

_____. "Die Einheit der Theologie Luthers." *Theologische Literaturzeitung* 75:245–52. 1950. Reprinted in *Kirche und Geschichte. Gesammelte Aufsätze*, 1. Pages 11–21 in *Luther und das evangelische Bekenntnis*. Göttingen, 1970.

_____. *Historischer Kommentar zur Confessio Augustana*. 2 vols. Gütersloh, 1976, 1978.

_____. *Der junge Melanchthon zwischen Humanismus und Reformation*. Vol. 2, *Der Theologe*. Göttingen, 1969.

_____. "Studien über Melanchthons Anteil an der Entstehung der Confessio Augustana." *Archiv für Reformationsgeschichte* 51 (1960): 159–207.

_____. *Von der Freiheit eines Christenmenschen*. Göttingen, 1949.

_____. "Zur Entstehung und Textgeschichte der Schwabacher Artikel." Pages 134–51 in *Theologie in Geschichte und Kunst*. Festschrift for W. Elliger. Edited by S. Herrmann and O. Söhngen. Witten, 1968.

Melanchthons Werke (Studienausgabe). Gütersloh, 1951–75.

Metzger, Günther. *Gelebter Glaube. Die Formierung reformatorischen Denkens in Luthers erster Psalmenvorlesung*. Göttingen, 1964.

Metzke, Erwin. *Sakrament und Metaphysik*. Stuttgart, 1948.

Meyer, Hans Bernhard. *Luther und die Messe*. Paderborn, 1965.

Meyer, Johannes. *Luther und das Apostolikum*. Berlin, 1918.

_____. "Berufen, erleuchtet, geheiligt." *Neue kirchliche Zeitschrift* 27 (1916): 343–65.

_____. "Die Doppelgestalt des ersten Artikels bei Luther." *Neue kirchliche Zeitschrift* 28 (1917): 530–55.

_____. *Historischer Kommentar zu Luthers Kleinem Katechismus*. Gütersloh, 1929.

_____. "'In Gott' und 'an Gott' glauben als Verdeutschung des Credere in deum bei Luther." *Theologische Studien und Kritiken* 92 (1919): 262–78.

_____. "Luthers Ringen um ein Gesamtverständnis des dritten Artikels." *Neue kirchliche Zeitschrift* 30 (1920): 359–76.

Modalsli, Ole. *Das Gericht nach den Werken*. Göttingen, 1963.

Mohrmann, Christine. *Etudes sur le latin des chrétiens*. Rome, 1958.

Morin, Germanus, ed. *S. Augustini Sermones post Maurinos reperti*. Rome, 1930.

Moufang, Christoph, ed. *Katholische Katechismen des sechszehnten Jahrhunderts in deutscher Sprache*. Mainz, 1881. Reprint, Hildesheim, 1964.

Mühlen, Heribert. "Das Christusereignis als Tat des Heiligen Geistes." Pages 513–46 in *Mysterium Salutis.* Vol. 3 of *Grundriß heilsgeschichtlicher Dogmatik*. Edited by J. Feiner and M. Löhrer. Einsiedeln, Zurich, Cologne, 1967.

Mühlenberg, Ekkehard. *Apollinaris von Laodicea*. Göttingen, 1969.

Mühlhaupt, Erwinm, ed. *D. M. Luthers Evangelien-Auslegung*. 2d ed. Göttingen, 1954.

_____. *D. M. Luthers Psalmen-Auslegung*. Göttingen, 1959–65.

Müller, E. F. Karl. "Jesu Christi dreifaches Amt." *Realencyclopädie für protestantische Theologie und Kirche*, 3d ed. 8:733–41.

Müller, Gerhard. "Ekklesiologie und Kirchenkritik beim jungen Luther." *Neue Zeitschrift für systematische Theologie* 7 (1965): 100–28.

_____. "Luthers Christusverständnis." Pages 41–57 in *Jesus Christus. Das Christusverständnis im Wandel der Zeiten*. Marburger theologische Studien, 1. Marburg, 1963.

Niedermeier, Gerhard. "Das allgemeine Priestertum aller Gläubigen und das geistliche Amt." *Zeitschrift für systematische Theologie* 7 (1930): 337–62.

Niesel, Wilhelm. *Die Theologie Calvins*. 2d ed. Munich, 1957.

Nikolainen, Aimo T. *Der Auferstehungsglaube in der Bibel und in ihrer Umwelt*. 2 vols. Helsinki, 1944–46.

Nillson, Kjell Ove. *Simul. Das Miteinander von Göttlichem und Menschlichem in Luthers Theologie*. Göttingen, 1966.

Oestergaard-Nielsen, Harald. *Scriptura sacra et viva vox.* Munich, 1957.

Olsson, Herbert. "Sichtbarkeit und Verborgenheit der Kirche nach Luther." Pages 336–60 in *Ein Buch von der Kirche.* Edited by A. Nygren. Göttingen, 1950.

Otto, Rudolf. *Die Anschauung vom heiligen Geiste bei Luther*. Göttingen, 1898.

Pannenberg, Wolfgang. *Grundzüge der Christologie*. Gütersloh, 1964.

_____. "Die Aufnahme des philosophischen Gottesbegriffes als dogmatisches Problem der frühchristlichen Theologie." *Zeitschrift für Kirchengeschichte* 70 (1959): 1–45.

Pedersen, E. Thestrup. "Schöpfung und Geschichte bei Luther." *Studia Theologica.* Lund, et al., 3 (1950): 5–33.

Persson, Per Erik. *Representatio Christi*. Göttingen, 1966.

Pesch, Otto Hermann. *Die Theologie der Rechtfertigung bei M. Luther und Thomas von Aquin*. Mainz, 1967.

Peters, Albrecht. "Evangelium und Sakrament nach den Bekenntnissen der lutherischen Reformation." Pages 125–76 in *Oecumenica*. Gütersloh, 1970.

_____. "Gegenwart Gottes—Wort Gottes." Pages 210–22 in *Zur Aufbauung des Leibes Christi*. Festschrift for P. Brunner. Edited by E. Schlink and A. Peters. Kassel, 1965.

_____. *Glaube und Werk. Luthers Rechtfertigungslehre im Lichte der Heiligen Schrift*. 2d ed. Berlin, 1967.

_____. "'Ich glaube an Gott!' Was heißt das?" *Kerygma und Dogma* 15 (1969): 259–79.

_____. "Luthers Christuszeugnis als Zusammenfassung der Christusbotschaft der Kirche." *Kerygma und Dogma* 13 (1967): 1–26, 73–98.

_____. *Realpresenz*. 2d ed. Berlin, 1966.

_____. "Reformatorische Rechtfertigungsbotschaft zwischen tridentinischer Rechtfertigungslehre und gegenwärtigem evangelischem Verständnis der Rechtfertigung." *Luther-Jahrbuch* 31 (1964): 77–128.

_____. "Die Trinitätslehre in der reformatorischen Christenheit." *Theologische Literaturzeitung*, 94:651–70 (1969).

Pflanz, Hans-Henning. *Geschichte und Eschatologie bei M. Luther*. Stuttgart, 1939.

Pittinger, W. Norman. *The Word Incarnate*. New York, 1959.

Plöger, Otto. *Theokratie und Eschatologie*. Neukirchen: Neukirchener, 1959.

Poschmann, Bernhard. *Buße und letzte Ölung*. Handbuch der Dogmengeschichte 4, 3. Freiburg in Breisgau, 1959.

_____. *Paenitentia secunda*. Bonn, 1940.

Prenter, Regin. "Luthers Lehre von der Heiligung." Pages 64–74 in *Luther-Forschung heute*. Edited by V. Vajta. Berlin, 1958.

_____. *Schöpfung und Erlösung. Dogmatik*. Göttingen, 1958ff.

_____. *Spiritus Creator*. Munich, 1954.

Procksch, Otto. *Theologie des Alten Testaments*. Gütersloh, 1950.

Quanbeck, Warren A. "Luther and Apocalyptic." Pages 119–28 in *Luther und Melanchthon*. Edited by V. Vajta. Göttingen, 1961.

Von Rad, Gerhard. "εἰκών." *TWNT* 2:378–80, 387–90.

_____. *Das erste Buch Mose*. Das alte Testament Deutsch, 2. 2d ed. Göttingen, 1958.

_____. *Theologie des Alten Testaments*. 2d ed. Munich, 1958.

Rahner, Karl. "Chalkedon—Ende oder Anfang?" Pages 3–49 in vol. 1 of *Das Konzil von Chalkedon. Geschichte und Gegenwart*. Würzburg, 1962. Pages 169–222 in *Schriften zur Theologie*, 1. 3d ed. Einsiedeln, 1958.

_____. "Dogmatische Randbemerkungen zur Kirchenfrömmigkeit." Pages 379–410 in *Schriften zur Theologie*, 5. Einsiedeln, 1962.

_____. "Der dreifaltige Gott als transzendenter Urgrund der Heilsgeschichte." Pages 317–404 in *Mysterium Salutis. Grundriß heilsgeschichtlicher Dogmatik*. Edited by J. Feiner and M. Löhrer, 2. Einsiedeln, Zurich, Cologne, 1967.

_____. "Kirche der Sünder und Sündige Kirche nach den Dekreten des Zweiten Vatikanischen Konzils." Pages 301–45 in *Schriften zur Theologie*, 6. 3d ed. Einsiedeln, 1962.

_____. "Theos im Neuen Testament." Pages 91–167 in *Schriften zur Theologie*, 1. 3d ed. Einsiedeln, 1958.

Ratzinger, Joseph. "Himmelfahrt Christi." *LTK* 5:360–62.

_____. *Volk und Haus Gottes in Augustins Lehre von der Kirche*. Munich, 1954.

Von Raumer, Rudolf. *Einwirkung des Christentums auf die altdeutsche Sprache*. Stuttgart, 1845.

Reicke, Bo. *The Disobedient Spirits and Christian Baptism*. Copenhagen, 1946.

Reischle, Max. "Die katechetische Behandlung des dritten Artikels von Luthers Kleinem Katechismus." *Zeitschrift für Theologie und Kirche* 6 (1896): 1–46, 111–66.

Reu, Johann Michael, ed. *Quellen zur Geschichte des kirchlichen Unterrichts in der evangelischen Kirche Deutschlands zwischen 1530 und 1600*. Gütersloh, 1904ff.

Rheinfelder, Hans. *Kultsprache und Profansprache in den romanischen Ländern*. Geneva, Florence, 1933.

Ritschl, Albrecht. *Die christliche Lehre von der Rechtfertigung und Versöhnung*. 4th ed. Bonn, 1909.

_____. *Fides implicita*. Bonn, 1890.

_____. *Unterricht in der christlichen Religion*. 6th ed. Bonn, 1903.

Ritschl, Otto. *Dogmengeschichte des Protestantismus*, 1. Leipzig, 1908.

Riviere, Jean. *Le dogme de la Rédemption chez St. Augustin*. Paris, 1933.

Roberts, Colin H. and Bernard Capelle. *An early euchologium. The Der-Balizeh Papyrus, enlarged and reedited*. Bibliothèque du muséon 23. Louvain, 1949.

Rost, Gerhard. "Luthers Schöpfungsglaube und Geschichtstheologie." *Lutherischer Rundblick* 6 (1958): 2–14.

Scheel, Otto, ed. *Dokumente zu Luthers Entwicklung*. 2d ed. Tübingen, 1929.

Scheffczyk, Leo. "Lehramtliche Formulierungen und Dogmengeschichte der Trinität." Pages 146–220 in *Mysterium Salutis. Grundriß heilsgeschichtlicher Dogmatik*. Edited by J. Feiner and M. Löhrer, 2. Einsiedeln, Zurich, Cologne, 1967.

_____. *Schöpfung und Vorsehung*. Handbuch der Dogmengeschichte 2, fascicle 2a. Freiburg im Breisgau, 1963.

Schempp, Paul. *Luthers Stellung zur heiligen Schrift*. Munich, 1929.

Schindler, Alfred. *Wort und Analogie in Augustins Trinitätslehre*. Tübingen, 1965.

Schlier, Heinrich. *Der Brief an die Epheser. Ein Kommentar*. Düsseldorf, 1957.

Schlink, Edmund. "Die apostolische Sukzession." Pages 160–95 in *Der kommende Christus und die kirchliche Tradition*. Göttingen, 1961.

_____. *Theologie der lutherischen Bekenntnisschriften*. Munich, 1948.

Schlisske, Otto. *Handbuch der Lutherlieder*. Göttingen, 1948.

Schmaus, Michael. "Ämter Christi." *LTK* 1:457–59.

_____. *Katholische Dogmatik*, 4.1. 5th ed. Munich, 1957. 5. 2nd ed. Munich, 1961.

_____. "Die Spannung von Metaphysik und Heilsgeschichte in der Trinitätslehre Augustins." Pages 503–18 in *Studia patristica* 6. Berlin, 1962. (= Texte und Untersuchungen zur Geschichte der altchristlichen Literatur, 81).

Schmid, Joseph. *Das Evangelium nach Matthäus*. 3d ed. Regensburg, 1956.

Schmidt, Karl Ludwig. "ἐκκλησία." *TWNT* 3:502–39.

Schmidt, Kurt Dietrich. "Luthers Lehre vom Heiligen Geist." Pages 145–64 in *Schrift und Bekenntnis. Zeugnisse lutherischer Theologie*. Festschrift for S. Schöffel. Edited by V. Hentrich and Th. Knolle. Hamburg, Berlin, 1950.

Schmidt, Martin Anton. "Heiliger Geist, dogmengeschichtlich." *RGG* 2:1279–83.

Schott, Erdmann. *Fleisch und Geist nach Luthers Lehre*. Leipzig, 1928.

Schulte, Elzear. *Die Entwicklung der Lehre vom menschlichen Wissen Christi bis zum Beginn der Scholastik*. Paderborn, 1914.

Schulz, Frieder. "Communio sanctorum." *Kerygma und Dogma* 12 (1966): 154–79.

Schumann, Friedrich Karl. "Imago Dei." Pages 167–80 in *Imago Dei*. Festschrift for G. Krüger, edited by H. Bornkamm. Gießen, 1932.

_____. "Luthers Trostgedanken wider den Tod." Pages 115–26 in *Wort und Gestalt*. Gesammelte Aufsätzen. Witten, 1956.

Schwarz, Reinhard. *Fides, spes und caritas beim jungen Luther*. Berlin, 1962.

_____. "Gott ist Mensch. Zur Lehre von der Person Christi bei den Ockhamisten und bei Luther." *Zeitschrift für Theologie und Kirche* 63 (1966): 289–351.

Schwärzweller, Klaus. "Delectari assertionibus. Zur Struktur von Luthers Pneumatologie." *Luther-Jahrbuch* 38 (1971): 26–58.

_____. *Theologia crucis*. Munich, 1970.

Schweizer, Eduard. "πνεῦμα." *TWNT* 6:387–453.

Seeberg, Erich. *Christus Wirklichkeit und Urbild*. Vol. 2 of *Luthers Theologie*. Göttingen, 1937.

Seeberg, Reinhold. *Lehrbuch der Dogmengeschichte*. Leipzig, 1908–20.

Seeger, Ulrich. "Die eschatologische Grundhaltung in Luthers Großem Katechismus." *Evangelische Theologie* 2 (1935): 67–95.

Seesemann, Heinrich. *Der Begriff KOINONIA im NT*. Beihefte zur Zeitschrift für die neutestamentliche Wissenschaft, 14. Gießen, 1933.

Seils, Martin. *Der Gedanke vom Zusammenwirken Gottes und des Menschen in Luthers Theologie*. Gütersloh, 1962.

Siggins, Jan Dudley Kingston. *Martin Luther's Doctrine of Christ*. Yale Publications in Religion, 14. New Haven, London, 1970.

Sjöberg, Erik. "πνεῦμα, etc." *TWNT* 6:373–87.

Skydsgaard, Kristen E. "Das apostolische Glaubensbekenntnis als Lehrnorm und als Gotteswort." Pages 41–60 in *Zur Auferbauung des Leibes Christi*. Festschrift for P. Brunner. Edited by E. Schlink and A. Peters. Kassel, 1965.

Von Soden, Hans. "Sakrament und Ethik bei Paulus." Pages 1–40 in vol. 1 of *Marburger Theologische Studien*, H. 1. 1931.

Söhngen. Gottlieb. *Die Einheit in der Theologie*. Munich, 1952.

Söhngen, Oskar. "Kirchenregiment und geistliche Leitung in der lutherischen Kirche." Pages 257–75 in *In Deo omnia unum*. Festschrift for F. Heiler. Edited by C. M. Schroeder. Munich, 1942.

Sommerlath, Ernst. "Das Amt und die Ämter." Pages 292–307 in *Viva vox Evangelii*. Edited by Luth. Kirchenamt. Hannover, Munich, 1951.

_____. "Amt und allgemeines Priestertum." Pages 40–89 in *Schriften des theologischen Konvents augsburgischen Bekenntnisses,* 5. 1953.

_____. *Der Sinn des Abendmahls nach Luthers Gedanken über das Abendmahl 1527/29*. Leipzig, 1930.

Stalder, Kurt. *Das Werk des Geistes in der Heiligung bei Paulus*. Zurich, 1962.

Stallmann, Martin. "Der zweite Artikel als katechetisches Problem." Pages 28–38 in *Die biblische Geschichte im Unterricht*. Göttingen, 1963.

Stange, Carl. *Luthers Gedanken über die Todesfurcht*. Berlin, 1932.

Steck, Karl Gerhard. *Lehre und Kirche bei Luther*. Munich, 1963.

_____. *Undogmatisches Christentum?* Theologische Existenz heute, 48. Munich, 1955.

Stomps, Magda A. H. *Die Anthropologie M. Luthers*. Frankfurt/Main, 1935.

Storck, Hans. *Das allgemeine Priestertum bei Luther*. Theologische Existenz heute, 37. Munich, 1953.

Strobel, August. *Kerygma und Apokalyptik*. Göttingen, 1967.

Stuhlmacher, Peter. *Vom Verstehen des Neuen Testaments. Eine Hermeneutik*. Grundrisse zum Neuen Testament, 6. Göttingen, 1979.

_____. "Zur Paulinischen Christologie." *Zeitschrift für Theologie und Kirche* 74 (1977): 449–63.

Tappolet, Walter. *Das Marienlob der Reformatoren*. Tübingen, 1962.

Teilhard de Chardin, Pierre. *Die Zukunft des Menschen*. Olten, 1963.

Ternus, Joseph. "Das Seelen- und Bewußtseinsleben Jesu." Pages 81–237 of vol. 3 in *Das Konzil von Chalkedon. Geschichte und Gegenwart*. Würzburg, 1962.

Theologia Deutsch, edited by Gottlob Siedel. Gotha, 1929.

Thieme, Karl. *Die Augsburgische Konfession und Luthers Katechismen auf theologische Gegenwartswerte untersucht*. Gießen, 1930.

_____. "Tritheismus 1529 und 1929." *Theologische Blätter* 8 (1929): 172–78.

_____. "Zur Trinitätsfrage." *Zeitschrift für Theologie und Kirche* 8 (1927): 251–68.

Thomas von Aquin. "De articulis fidei et ecclesiae sacramentis." Pages 141–51 in vol. 1 of *Opuscula Theologica*. Edited by R. A. Verardo. Turin, Rome, 1954.

_____. "Expositio in Symbolum Apostolorum." Pages 193–217 in vol. 2 of *Opuscula Theologica*. Edited by R. M. Spiazzi. Turin, Rome, 1954.

_____. *Summa Theologiae*. Edited by P. Caramello. Turin, Rome, 1952–56.

_____. *Die deutsche Thomas-Ausgabe, Summa Theologica*. Vol. 23. Edited by the Albertus Magnus Akademie Walberberg. Heidelberg, Munich, Graz, Vienna, Salzburg, 1954.

Thomasius, Gottfried. *Christi Person und Werk*. 3d ed. Erlangen, 1886–88.

Tiililä, Osmo. *Das Strafleiden Christi*. Helsinki, 1941.

Tillich, Paul. *Systematische Theologie*. Stuttgart, 1954–66.

Torrance, Thomas F. *Kingdom and Church*. London, 1956.

Trillhaas, Wolfgang. *Das Apostolische Glaubensbekenntnis. Geschichte, Texte, Auslegung*. Witten, 1953.

Turner, H. E. W. *The Patristic Doctrine of Redemption*. London, 1952.

Ullmann, Wolfgang. "Das filioque als Problem ökumenischer Theologie." *Kerygma und Dogma* 16 (1970): 58–76.

Vogelsang, Erich. *Der angefochtene Christus bei Luther*. Berlin, Leipzig, 1932.

_____. *Die Anfänge von Luthers Christologie nach der ersten Psalmenvorlesung*. Berlin, 1929.

_____. "Weltbild und Kreuzestheologie in den Höllenfahrts-streitigkeiten der Reformationszeit." *Archiv für Reformationsgeschichte* 38 (1941): 90–132.

_____. "Luthers Torgauer Predigt von Jesu Christo vom Jahre 1532." *Luther-Jahrbuch* 13 (1931): 114–30.

Volz, Paul. *Die Eschatologie der jüdischen Gemeinde im neutestamentlichen Zeitalter*. 2d ed. Tübingen, Leipzig, 1934.

Vorländer, Dorothea. *Deus incarnates. Die Zweinaturenchristologie Luthers bis 1521*. Untersuchungen zur Kirchengeschichte, 9. Witten, 1974.

Wackernagel, Philipp, ed. *Das deutsche Kirchenlied von der älteste Zeit bis zu Anfang des 17. Jahrhunderts*. 5 vols. Leipzig, 1864–77.

Watson, Philip. "Luther und die Heiligung." Pages 75–84 in *Luther-Forschung heute*. Edited by V. Vajta. Berlin, 1958.

Weber, Otto. *Grundlagen der Dogmatik*. Neukirchen: Neukirchener, 1955.

Weidenhiller, Egino. *Untersuchungen zur deutschsprachigen katechetischen Literatur des späten Mittelalters*. Munich, 1965.

Weiser, Artur. "πιστεύω, B." *TWNT* 6:182–97.

Werkbuch Gottesdienst. Wuppertal, 1967.

Westermann, Claus. *Genesis*. Biblischer Kommentar I/1. Neukirchen: Neukirchener, 1974.

_____. *Der Segen in der Bibel und im Handeln der Kirche*. Munich, 1968.

Wiegand, Friedrich. *Das apostolische Symbol im Mittelalter*. Gießen, 1904.

_____. *Symbol und Katechumenat.* Part 1. *Die Stellung des apostolischen Symbolums im kirchlichen Leben des Mittelalters*. Leipzig, 1899.

Wildberger, Hans. "Glauben im Alten Testament." *Zeitschrift für Theologie und Kirche* 65 (1968): 129–59.

Wingren, Gustaf. *Evangelium und Kirche*. Göttingen, 1963.

_____. *Luthers Lehre vom Beruf.* Munich, 1952.

_____. *Schöpfung und Gesetz*. Göttingen, 1960.

Wobberman, Georg. "Die Frage nach Gott in Luthers Großem Katechismus." Pages 418–35 in *Festgabe für J. Kaftan*. Tübingen, 1920.

_____. "Luthers trinitarischer Monotheismus." *Zeitschrift für Theologie und Kirche* 9 (1928): 237–52.

Wolf, Ernst. "Asterisci und Obelisci zum Thema: Luther und Athanasius." *Evangelische Theologie* 18 (1958): 481–90.

_____. "Die Christusverknüpfung bei Luther." Pages 30–80 in vol. 1 of *Peregrinatio*. Munich, 1954.

Zahrnt, Heinz. "Luthers Predigt am Grabe." *Luther* 29 (1958): 106–14.

Zellinger, J. "Der Geköderte Leviathan im Hortus deliciarum des Herrad von Landsperg." *Historisches Jahrbuch* 45 (1925): 161–77.

Von Zezschwitz, C. A. Gerhard. *System der christlich kirchlichen Katechetik*. 2d ed. Leipzig, 1872.